A Perilous Calling

The Hazards of Psychotherapy Practice

A Perilous Calling

The Hazards of Psychotherapy Practice

Michael B. Sussman, Editor

A WILEY-INTERSCIENCE PUBLICATION

JOHN WILEY & SONS, INC.

New York • Chichester • Brisbane • Toronto • Singapore

This text is printed on acid-free paper.

This publication is designed to provide accurate and authoritative information in regard to the subject matter covered. It is sold with the understanding that the publisher is not engaged in rendering professional services. If legal, accounting, medical, psychological, or any other expert assistance is required, the services of a competent professional person should be sought.

Library of Congress Cataloging-in-Publication Data:

A perilous calling : the hazards of psychotherapy practice / edited by
Michael B. Sussman.
p. cm.
Includes bibliographical references and index.
ISBN 0-471-05657-X
1. Psychotherapists—Job stress. 2. Psychotherapists—Mental
health. I. Sussman, Michael B.
RC451.4.P79P47 1995
616.89'023—dc20 94-34135
CIP

Printed in the United States of America.

10 9 8 7 6 5 4 3 2 1

For Marcella

If a little knowledge is dangerous, where is
the man who has so much as to be out of danger?

Thomas Henry Huxley
On Elemental Instruction
in Physiology, 1877

About the Contributors

Gina Arons, PsyD, is a clinical psychologist in private practice in Watertown, Massachusetts.

Marc Berger, PsyD, is a clinical psychologist in private practice in Acton and Marlboro, Massachusetts.

Nancy A. Bridges, LICSW, BCD, is a clinical supervisor in the Department of Psychiatry, Cambridge Hospital, and Lecturer on Psychiatry, Harvard Medical School. She is also Associate Clinical Professor, Smith College School for Social Work.

Gloria Garfunkel, PhD, is Mental Health Coordinator at Peabody Medical Associates, a staff-model HMO of Blue Cross/Blue Shield of Massachusetts. She received her PhD in Psychology and Social Relations from Harvard University in 1984.

William N. Grosch, MD, is Associate Professor of Clinical Psychiatry and Director of the Psychiatry Outpatient Clinic at Albany Medical College. He is also Director of Pastoral Services for the Capitol District Psychiatric Center in Albany, New York, and a Fellow of the American Psychiatric Association.

Peter Gumpert, PhD, is a clinical and organizational psychologist with a private practice in Boston. He currently serves as a faculty member and senior clinical supervisor at the Boston Institute for Psychotherapy. He is President and Principal Consultant in the Boston organizational consulting firm of GLS, Inc., and serves on the steering committee of the Consortium for Psychotherapy.

Eric A. Harris, EdD, JD, served for 10 years as the Director of Professional Affairs of the Massachusetts Psychological Association. He is a lawyer and psychologist in private practice in Lexington, Massachusetts, legal counsel to Choate Health Systems, Inc., and a special consultant on managed care to the APA Practice Directorate.

David A. Jobes, PhD, is in private practice in Washington, DC. He is Associate Professor of Psychology at The Catholic University of America, and Assistant Director of the National Center for the Study and Prevention of Suicide at the Washington School of Psychiatry.

Judith V. Jordan, PhD, is Director of the Women's Studies Program and Director of Training in Psychology at McLean Hospital. She is also Assistant Professor of Psychology, Department of Psychiatry, Harvard Medical School.

R. Tracy MacNab, PhD, is in private practice in Newton Centre, Massachusetts, and is a staff psychologist at The Marino Center for Progressive Health. He is a consulting psychologist at Saint Elizabeth Medical Center, the Faulkner Center for Reproductive Medicine, and the Addiction Treatment Center of New England.

Susan Scholfield MacNab, MSW, PhD, is both a social worker and a psychologist in private practice in Newton Centre, Massachusetts. She is a senior clinical supervisor at the Boston Institute for Psychotherapy and a cofounder of the Consortium for Psychotherapy.

John T. Maltsberger, MD, is on faculty, Boston Psychoanalytic Society & Institute. He is a Lecturer on Psychiatry, Harvard Medical School, and Associate Psychiatrist, McLean Hospital.

Michael F. Myers, MD, is Director of the Marital Discord Clinic, Department of Psychiatry, St. Paul's Hospital in Vancouver. He is Clinical Professor in the Department of Psychiatry, University of British Columbia.

K. Tracy Munn, PhD, is in private practice in Somerville, Massachusetts, and is Staff Psychologist at the University Counseling Services, Boston College.

Donald L. Nathanson, MD, is Executive Director of The Silvan S. Tomkins Institute. He is Clinical Professor of Psychiatry and Human Behavior at Jefferson Medical College, and Senior Attending Psychiatrist at the Institute of Pennsylvania Hospital.

David C. Olsen, PhD, is Executive Director of the Samaritan Counseling Center in Schenectady, New York, and Adjunct Professor of Family Therapy at the State University of New York at Oneonta.

Judith Ruskay Rabinor, PhD, is Director of the American Eating Disorders Center of Long Island. She is a faculty member and supervisor at the Center for the Study of Anorexia and Bulimia in New York City and has a private practice in Lido Beach, New York.

Michael J. Salamon, PhD, is Executive Director of the Adult Developmental Center in Woodmere, New York.

Constance Seligman, MSW, ACSW, is a senior clinician at St. Clares Riverside Community Mental Health Center in Denville, New Jersey, and adjunct faculty member, Columbia University.

Michael Shernoff, MSW, ACSW, is currently in private practice in Manhattan and adjunct faculty member at Hunter College Graduate School of Social Work. He founded and until 1993 was codirector of Chelsea Psychotherapy Associates. Formerly a board member of the National Lesbian/Gay Health Foundation, he was also on the National Association of Social Workers Committee on Lesbian and Gay Issues from 1986 through 1989.

Norman F. Shub, LISW, BCD, is Clinical Director of the Gestalt Institute of Central Ohio, and President of Gestalt Associates.

Ronald D. Siegel, PsyD, is a clinical psychologist in private practice in Hingham and Watertown, Massachusetts. He is a Clinical Instructor in Psychology at Harvard Medical School, and Chief Psychologist at Cambridge Youth Guidance Center.

Edward W. L. Smith, PhD, is Professor of Psychology and Coordinator of Clinical Training at Georgia Southern University. Since 1971, he has traveled widely, offering professional training in psychotherapy throughout the United States and abroad. He is a past Chair of the Training Committee of the American Academy of Psychotherapists and a Fellow of both the Georgia Psychological Association and the American Psychological Association.

Martha Stark, MD, is a psychiatrist/psychoanalyst in private practice in Newton Centre, Massachusetts. She is on faculty at the Boston Psychoanalytic Institute and at the Massachusetts Institute for Psychoanalysis, where she is also a supervising analyst.

Michele Steinberg, PhD, is a clinical psychologist and Project Coordinator at the Adult Developmental Center in Rockville Centre, New York.

Michael B. Sussman, PsyD, is a clinical psychologist in private practice in Boston. He is a Clinical Instructor in Psychology at Harvard University and Clinical Supervisor at the Codman Square Health Center in Dorchester.

Edward Tick, PhD, is engaged in the private practice of psychotherapy in Albany, New York. He is a past editor of *Voices,* the journal of the American Academy of Psychotherapists.

Bryan Wittine, PhD, is a psychologist in private practice in Oakland and San Rafael, California. He is Founding Director of the graduate program in transpersonal psychology at John F. Kennedy University in Orinda, California, and an analytic candidate at the C. G. Jung Institute of San Francisco.

Foreword

One of the most dramatic shifts in psychotherapeutic practice in the last decade is the increased recognition of the importance of the therapist's contribution to the therapeutic process. When formal psychotherapy was first discovered about a century ago, its founder, Sigmund Freud, advised therapists to model themselves after the surgeon "who puts aside all of his feelings, even his human sympathy, and concentrates his mental forces on the single aim of performing the operation as skillfully as possible." Freud never abandoned the paradigm of the abstinent, anonymous surgeon, and in contrast to his comprehensive and meticulous discussions of transference, he wrote very little on the subject of countertransference.

Freud's original idea that countertransference denotes unconscious interference with the therapist's ability to understand patients has been re-examined. Current usage includes all of the practitioner's emotional reactions in the treatment situation. Eschewing the medical model of the healthy and wise physician ministering to the sick and naive patient, most modern clinicians now view the therapeutic process as consisting of two vulnerable human beings who are constantly affecting and influencing each other. Although the participants have different roles, they are equal partners with many mutual interests. They are both "more human than otherwise," as Harry Stack Sullivan was fond of saying.

One of the leading pioneers in helping mental health professionals better appreciate the role of the therapist's contribution to the therapeutic situation, particularly the influence of countertransference, is Dr. Michael Sussman. In *A Curious Calling* (1992), he exposes several unconscious motivations existing in all of us that determine our choice of work as mental health professionals. Sussman brilliantly, lucidly, and comprehensively demonstrates how and why we become "wounded healers." He also convincingly documents how countertransference reactions influence our therapeutic interventions more than any other variable.

In *A Perilous Calling,* Michael Sussman has taken us several miles further on the road to therapeutic enlightenment. In this book we learn more about why we choose psychotherapy as a career. At work are rescue fantasies, erotic and murderous wishes, defenses against anxiety and other vulnerabilities, superego mandates, and much more. We learn from *A Perilous Calling* that therapists, like patients, have many infantile wishes that they are trying to resolve in the therapeutic situation and, also like their therapeutic counterparts, need to protect themselves in a variety of neurotic ways.

Dr. Sussman's colleagues in *A Perilous Calling* emerge as very humane individuals who show much maturity and courage. To expose vulnerabilities, to share countertransference reactions freely, to acknowledge therapeutic blunders, are most admirable traits. The contributors to this volume serve as role models for all of us as they analyze their subjective responses and show the impact of these responses on the therapeutic process.

One of the many lessons that I learned from this wonderful volume is that when I feel or act omnipotently in the therapeutic situation, I am trying to silence my impotent and vulnerable feelings. I also realized that when I am overtalkative and overactive, I am uncomfortable with my passivity.

Every reader will find himself or herself in *A Perilous Calling* because conducting psychotherapy always arouses danger for all of us. What Sussman and his colleagues do for us is to reassure us that making errors, acting out certain countertransference problems, ignoring messages of patients is par for the therapeutic course. They seem to agree with Freud who was fond of saying,"What we can't reach by flying, we have to reach by limping. It is no sin to limp."

Another feature of *A Perilous Calling* which I very much appreciate is that all therapists have to cope with different countertransference issues at different times, depending on many variables, such as the patient's productions, the therapist's stage of life, current level of training, unresolved conflicts, and current stresses. Humbly, we learn to accept that no therapist in working with patients is exempt from experiencing childish fantasies toward them, assuming defensive postures with them, or making therapeutic interventions that emanate more from the therapist's own anxiety, disturbing memories, or superego injunctions, than exclusively from the patient's productions.

The final lesson we learn from *A Perilous Calling* is that to do therapy well we have to strive to become more loving and less hateful human beings, accepting that our patients have strengths that we may not have, and that we have limitations that they may not have.

Dr. Michael Sussman and his impressive array of contributors to *A Perilous Calling* will assist thousands of clinicians in carrying out their therapeutic missions with a keener appreciation of the humanity underlying their attempts to help their fellow human beings.

HERBERT S. STREAN, DSW

Distinguished Professor Emeritus, Rutgers University
Director Emeritus, New York Center for Psychoanalytic Training

Acknowledgments

I would like to thank all the clinicians who have contributed to this volume, for they are a rare breed. In the face of powerful taboos against self-disclosure, they have chosen to write openly about some of the most difficult and private aspects of practicing psychotherapy. In the process, many have taken the sorts of risks that we typically expect of our patients but rarely ask of ourselves. I salute their courage and their commitment to the goal of humanizing the professional climate in which we work.

I am indebted to Marilyn Weller, a Boston-based freelance editor whose expertise has been invaluable. In addition to providing superb editing and consultation, she sustained my morale when the going (and the drafts) got rough. She has been a joy to work with, and if this book is my baby, Marilyn is surely its godmother.

It is a privilege and a pleasure to be associated with John Wiley & Sons. I am especially grateful to Herb Reich, Senior Editor in Psychology, for recognizing the volume's potential at an early stage in its development. His enthusiasm has made my job easier; his suggestions have made this a better book. I would also like to thank Maggie Kennedy and Nancy Marcus Land for their excellent work in overseeing the book's production.

I received additional assistance from Phyllis Benjamin on the editing of my own chapter, and helpful comments from Marcella Bohn, Martha Stark, Stuart Copans, Stephen Farina, and Janet Fritz.

I wish to express my appreciation to Sanford Gifford of the Boston Psychoanalytic Institute for allowing me to make use of the library facilities, and to Ann Menashi, the Institute's splendid librarian.

I am beholden to Marcella Bohn, true friend and mentor, for her support and guidance. I am also grateful for the encouragement I have received from Connie Seligman, Gerry Kaiser, Lynn West, Martha Stark, and my parents, Maurice and Raquel Sussman.

Finally, thanks to the publishers who granted permission to include in this book material first printed in the following publications: *American Journal of Orthopsychiatry* (Chapter 15), *Suicide and Life Threatening Behavior* (Chapter 19), *Massachusetts Psychologist* (Chapter 21), W & W Norton Comlpany, Inc. (Chapter 23).

MICHAEL B. SUSSMAN, PSYD

Contents

PART FIVE: PROFESSIONAL, ETHICAL, AND LEGAL ISSUES

PART SIX: THE THERAPIST'S RENEWAL

Introduction

There is a growing sense of pessimism and discouragement among psychotherapists in the United States. We are in the midst of a radical shift in the way psychotherapy is practiced, and the direction of change does not appear to be advantageous either to therapists or their clients. At a time when psychotherapeutic treatment has become more sophisticated, more widely applicable, and more socially acceptable than ever before, it is increasingly difficult for most Americans to obtain or afford. Third parties, whose concerns are primarily financial, now dictate who deserves treatment and how it is to be conducted. In a culture that craves the quick fix, advances in biological treatments threaten to turn psychotherapy into an upper-class indulgence. As the demands and frustrations of practice escalate and the rewards and satisfactions diminish, clinicians are struggling to avoid becoming bitter or cynical about their work.

In assembling this volume on the hazards of psychotherapy practice, I have witnessed an interesting phenomenon. When told the book's title, nonpractitioners almost invariably respond—"hazards to the *therapist?*"—apparently taken aback by either the novelty or the peculiarity of the topic. Indeed, the hazardous aspects of the profession are typically concealed, even within the field.

Although it is rare that the problem is openly acknowledged, ample evidence indicates that the practice of psychotherapy poses significant dangers to clinicians. Recent reviews of the relevant literature point to a high incidence of mental illness (especially depression), drug and alcohol abuse, sexual acting-out, and suicide among therapists (Guy, 1987; Kilburg, Nathan, & Thoreson, 1986; Sussman, 1992). Stress, job dissatisfaction, workaholism, and burnout have become issues of major concern to professional caregivers (Cherniss, 1980; Farber, 1985; Farber & Heifetz, 1982; Freudenberger, 1974; Freudenberger & Robbins, 1979; Prochaska & Norcross, 1983; Wood, Klein, Cross, Lammers, & Elliot, 1985). Several studies suggest that the physical, psychic, and social isolation frequently associated with clinical work can exact a heavy toll on the emotional adjustment of practitioners (Bermak, 1977; Deutsch, 1984; Hellman, Morrison, & Abramowitz, 1986; Tryon, 1983). In addition, working as a psychotherapist can have a negative impact on marriage (Bermack, 1977; Cray & Cray, 1977; Farber, 1985), parent-child relationships (Cray & Cray, 1977; Guy, 1987; Henry, Sims, & Spray, 1973; Maeder, 1989), and on friendships and social life (Burton, 1975; Freudenberger & Robbins, 1979; Guy, 1987).

The strains of maintaining continual proximity to emotional pain and suffering are inherent in clinical work, but perhaps are nowhere as evident as in the treatment of trauma victims. Clinicians who work with this population may undergo vicarious traumatization (McCann & Pearlman, 1990) in which exposure to clients' traumatic experiences results in enduring psychological consequences for the therapist. Traumatic imagery may be incorporated into the practitioner's memory system, returning as flashbacks, nightmares, or intrusive thoughts. Faced with repeated stories of cruelty and perversion, therapists may develop a bleak view of human nature, become fearful and less trusting of others, and experience a sense of separateness and alienation from family, friends, or coworkers.

Even when these disturbing issues are recognized, they are typically addressed in a rather detached and academic fashion. With the exception of a handful of admirable renegades (Burton, 1970; Chessick, 1978; Edelwich, 1980; Freudenberger & Robbins, 1979; Goldberg, 1986; Greben, 1975; Greenson, 1966; Groesbeck & Taylor, 1977; Searles, 1966; Strean, 1988; Wheelis, 1959), psychotherapists have been reluctant to write candidly and subjectively about the perilous aspects of their calling. The present volume represents an attempt to overcome the professional taboos that have obstructed frank discussion of this important topic.

* * *

People do not become astronauts or firefighters without some appreciation of the dangers that they will face. But such an informed decision is rare in the case of psychotherapists. Prospective clinicians typically understand that their *clients* will face various risks and that some may not survive. Most people who become therapists appear to be largely unprepared, however, for the many perils that they themselves will encounter along the way.

What can account for this lack of awareness? Perhaps the perilous aspects of clinical work, unlike some other professions, are not readily apparent. Except when dealing with violent patients, clinicians rarely face immediate threats to their safety. Most of the occupational hazards are cumulative, only surfacing over extended periods of practice.

One would expect that novice therapists would be forewarned of potential dangers by their teachers and supervisors. One might further imagine that training programs and employers of therapists would focus on the issue of prevention. Such an enlightened concern, however, has been sorely lacking in our field. Although this neglect may appear to some as a conspiracy of silence, it is unlikely that it stems from malicious intent. Rather, it derives from a complex combination of professional, personal, and historical factors.

First, due to the fundamental inequality of roles inherent in the therapeutic contract, clinicians' concerns with their own welfare are unlikely to be addressed with patients. Except for providing financial compensation, patients cannot be held responsible for meeting their therapists' needs. While they must abstain from inflicting physical harm, patients are given wide latitude in how they may interact with treaters. Thus, practitioners must be prepared to contend with a good deal of emotional strain if they wish to offer their patients an opportunity for self-exploration and expression. As with parent and child, the therapist's feelings and needs will typically take a backseat to those of the patient.

Although the therapeutic relationship is often an intimate one, that intimacy is typically unidirectional; therapists are generally trained to avoid disclosing their own feelings and personal reactions. When disturbed by their patients' words or behaviors, clinicians are therefore unlikely to address their discomfort or pain. Such constraints protect patients and preserve therapeutic neutrality, but they make it more difficult for therapists to take care of themselves within the clinical interaction.

A second factor that has impeded open discussion of this topic is the taboo regarding self-disclosure between professionals. The large majority of mental health professionals either work in relative isolation or are employed in settings in which they may not feel safe enough to reveal personal matters. Thus, any discussion of one's own emotions, foibles, mistakes, or vulnerabilities may be deemed too threatening. Indeed, in a paper entitled "The Vulnerable Therapist: On Being Ill or Injured," Grunebaum (1993) notes that he was unable to locate a single case report by a therapist who experienced a psychiatric illness. The issue of occupational hazards can hardly be addressed effectively when therapists do not feel free to share their fears and concerns with colleagues or administrators.

Turning to the intrapsychic realm, certain personality characteristics may predispose therapists to overlook the perils of their profession. In a previous volume entitled *A Curious Calling: Unconscious Motivations for*

Practicing Psychotherapy (Sussman, 1992), I examined the psychological makeup of psychotherapists, as well as the hidden aims that practitioners may bring to the role. A review of the literature on therapists, as well as my own interviews with clinicians, revealed certain personality trends that may contribute to an abiding wish to practice psychotherapy. It may be that some of these characteristics also contribute to a tendency to neglect or downplay the hazards entailed in clinical work.

Many therapists, for example, grew up playing the role of caretaker, go-between, parentified child, or burden-bearer within their families of origin. Having learned at an early age to attune themselves to others, therapists often have great difficulty attending to their own emotional needs. Problems in dealing with aggression and assertiveness are also common, as are masochistic trends, potentially compromising therapists' ability or inclination to protect themselves from harm.

Some practitioners may be so overzealous in their need to rescue clients that they throw caution to the wind. Many of these clinicians harbor strong unconscious guilt for real or imagined damage inflicted on loved ones as a child, and they are willing to make great personal sacrifices in order to atone and make reparation. Still others may have entered the field in a counterphobic attempt to allay fears of mental illness and are rigidly defended against acknowledging any threats to their psychological equilibrium. This list is far from comprehensive, but it should hint at the abundance of personal reasons for minimizing one's awareness of occupational hazards.

Even in view of some promising shifts in the current atmosphere, it remains difficult to introduce a volume on the hazards of psychotherapy practice without feeling a need to justify the undertaking. Devoting so much attention to the person of the therapist could appear frivolous or indulgent. Isn't it our patients, after all, with whom we should be concerned?

Indeed, throughout the history of psychotherapy, the personhood of the practitioner has been all but ignored. Successive generations of therapists have received and, in turn, passed along a professional culture that often leaves little room for the clinician's humanity. Only in recent years have we begun to witness widespread recognition of the ways in which this narrow conception of the therapeutic role can be detrimental to practitioners as well as clients.

Ironically, the constriction that characterizes the way in which many therapists are trained to practice is a legacy of the Freudian revolution in the treatment of mental disorders. Regardless of how his theories are assessed, Freud's willingness to expose his most private self to scientific scrutiny must be viewed as nothing short of remarkable. The candid manner in which he discussed his own thoughts, fantasies, dreams, and pathological tendencies remains unparalleled in the psychoanalytic literature that he spawned.

What has happened? Why have we backed off from Freud's courageous example, withdrawing into timid guardedness and shame?

Freud himself must bear part of the responsibility for this retreat. His intolerance of dissension among his followers did little to foster collegial openness. And although Freud introduced the concept of countertransference, he downplayed its significance, viewing it largely as an impediment to the therapeutic process. But it is Freud's concept of analytic neutrality that has probably had the most constricting effect on practitioners of psychotherapy.

For Freud, the analytic setting was to provide the optimal laboratory for studying human psychological functioning. The analyst was to function as a blank screen on which projections of the patient's transference were analyzed. The concept of analytic neutrality emerged from this one-person model, as a means of preserving the "pure culture" of the patient's psyche, free from any interference or "contamination" by the personality of the analyst. Any loss of objectivity on the part of the clinician—be it strong emotions, internal conflict, spontaneous responses, or expressions of personal taste or opinion—was seen as countertransferentially based errors, indicative of incomplete analysis on the part of the practitioner.

We are all familiar with the caricature of the Freudian analyst: Silent and impassive, he maintains strict anonymity and reserve at all times.[1] How naive, we may now exclaim, to have thought that they could screen themselves out of the interaction, thereby permitting an unadulterated picture of the patient to emerge. Such a stance, however, was a reasonable place from which to start studying the workings of the human psyche. Only by first isolating the individual was it possible to begin exploring intrapsychic processes. It would have been difficult, for example, to have arrived at the concept of projective identification—an interactional phenomenon—without a prior understanding of the intrapsychic mechanism of projection. Ultimately, it is important to note, a two-person model of psychotherapy does not supplant the earlier model, but supplements and enriches it.

Freud's metaphor of the analyst as mirror or blank screen (both of which are inanimate objects) has had exceptional staying power.

[1] Schur (1972) points out that Freud had been rather talkative as an analyst until his later years, after oral surgeries for cancer of the jaw made talking painful for him.

Although initially it may have provided a useful guideline for clinicians who were just learning to acknowledge and appreciate intrapsychic phenomena, this analogy ultimately had an insidious effect on the practice of psychotherapy. As Jaffe (1986) writes:

> The professional myths that the healer has no needs, that these needs detract from the provision of adequate service if acknowledged, that feelings are not relevant, and that we can simply turn off our responses to human pain are untenable and contribute to the distress that helping professionals experience in their work and lives. (p. 198)

The misguided attempt to act as blank observers or reflectors of clients turned therapists into "shrinks," literally shrinking their humanity. It not only limited what clinicians could express to their patients but also circumscribed what was acceptable to *experience* in the clinical setting and what could be shared with colleagues. Such constraints made it virtually impossible to address many of the hazards explored in this volume.

Fortunately, the rise of the two-person model of psychotherapy has rendered obsolete the notion of a blank screen. We have conceded the inevitable subjectivity of the therapist and have begun to acknowledge that both participants are influenced by powerful unconscious forces. Moreover, we have recognized that the therapeutic process is a joint creation, involving an interweaving of transferences and countertransferences, of intrapsychic and interpersonal elements. Finally, a more useful—and far less restrictive—conception of neutrality has emerged. As formulated by Greenberg, "neutrality embodies the goal of establishing an optimal tension between the patient's tendency to see the analyst as an old object and his capacity to experience him as a new one" (1986, p. 97). From this object-relational perspective, any attempt to remain neutral in the classical sense of the term reflects resistance in the therapist to experiencing countertransference and to genuine involvement with the patient (Bollas, 1987).

Shifting from the theoretical to the practical, concerns with professional advancement and financial success can also discourage clinicians from addressing the issue of occupational hazards more directly. Therapists are often expected to be paragons of mental health and stability, although many people are drawn to the profession precisely because they have had emotional difficulties of their own. Practitioners may be hesitant to discuss their strains and struggles as therapists when they worry that such disclosures could threaten their livelihood. This fear of exhibiting distress or vulnerability, so at odds with what our work is all about, is implanted early in professional training and reinforced at every turn. As described by Ben-Avi (1977):

> The graduate [of an analytic institute] is an example of what analysis can do. He becomes an object, a result of analytic work, and assumes the burden of being a living demonstration of analysis. It therefore becomes necessary for him to engage in a series of charades: first with his teachers, then with his colleagues and patients. After all, the qualities that are required for graduation will also bring referrals. This is tolerable, if undesirable. The real burden is maintaining this illusion within oneself. What is fostered is a greater concern with how one looks than with who one is. (pp. 175–176)

There can be little doubt that this state of alienation from self and others contributes to such important problems as burnout, addiction, boundary violations, and suicide among practitioners.

Finally, it appears that both patients and practitioners harbor compelling needs to preserve the image of the invulnerable therapist. For patients, this often stems from childhood wishes for an omnipotent parent who can provide the illusion of total safety and withstand the frightening force of the child's anger and destructiveness. By identifying with the enormous power they have attributed to their parents, children seek to recover their lost sense of infantile omnipotence. For patients in psychotherapy to eventually dispense with the idealized image of the invulnerable therapist, they face the difficult developmental tasks of confronting limitations, accepting a restricted range of control, and mourning the loss of cherished illusions.

Therapists may also have a stake in maintaining this illusion of invulnerability, thus colluding with patients' idealizations. For many of us, assuming the role of psychotherapist represents, in part, an attempt to distance ourselves from personal vulnerabilities with which we are uncomfortable. By playing the part of the invulnerable therapist we can seemingly rid ourselves of all our messy emotions, needs, fears, wishes, and irrationalities, relegating such distasteful "stuff" to our patients. Thus, a pernicious double standard develops whereby we try to help our patients acknowledge and accept that which we shamefully repudiate in ourselves.

Indeed, any serious inquiry into the hazards of the profession sets us face to face with the issue of shame. Over the past decade, we have witnessed a burgeoning interest in the affect of shame, which has emerged as a key aspect of human psychology. Correspondingly, there has been a greater emphasis on dealing with issues of shame in the treatment of many forms of emotional disorder. Given this upsurge of interest, it is surprising that so little attention has been paid to the vicissitudes of shame in the psychotherapist. A notable exception is Horner's (1993) paper on occupational hazards, in which she points to the persistence of unrealistic and unrealizable professional ideals as a major factor contributing to burnout. Horner notes that feelings of shame, stemming from being unable to live up to unrealistic standards, lead to a reluctance to discuss treatment failures and to the maintenance of defenses against repeated vulnerability.

In sum, myriad factors have contributed to our profession's neglect of the hazards of psychotherapy practice. Because of significant shifts in clinical theory and technique, however, the time is ripe for a more thorough investigation of these dangers and how they can be prevented or minimized.

* * *

In this volume, I have invited an array of experienced practitioners—psychologists, social workers, psychiatrists, and psychoanalysts—to describe the obstacles and perils that they have encountered in clinical practice. My aim has been to provide a forum for frank discussion of topics and concerns that have gone largely unaddressed in the literature and in professional settings. Comprehensive in scope, the volume provides an in-depth examination of the emotional, intrapsychic, interpersonal, practical, and ethical difficulties facing clinicians. Although certain topics lent themselves to a more scholarly approach, the majority of the chapters are quite personal, subjective, and intimate accounts of the inner experiences and struggles of psychotherapists.

The book is divided into six parts. Part One addresses the therapist's personal development. My own chapter explores the process of disillusionment that can take place when therapists' covert aims and wishes fail to be satisfied in clinical practice. Ed Tick, who had been an antiwar protestor and pacifist, recounts the painful transformation in attitudes and self-image that he has undergone in 15 years of treating Vietnam veterans. Susan Scholfield MacNab describes the continuous interplay between her roles as therapist and mother. Michele Steinberg and Michael Salamon address some of the ways in which therapists' attitudes toward aging and death can be influenced by working with an elderly population. Finally, Connie Seligman discusses how being a patient in interminable treatment can hinder the therapist's personal and professional development.

Part Two focuses on therapists' own illnesses and emotional disturbances. Norman Shub explores an issue that has been entirely overlooked in the literature: What sorts of difficulties are faced by therapists who have characterologic problems of their own? Edward Smith discusses what he has termed "psychotherapist's disease," in which clinicians begin to view all of life in terms of pathology. Judy Rabinor addresses the ways in which female clinicians' own feelings of bodily shame can obstruct or inform their work with eating-disordered clients. Tracy Munn, who suffers from multiple sclerosis, offers a moving account of what it is like to practice psychotherapy when the therapist is seriously ill.

Part Three explores the emotional impact of clinical work on the psychotherapist. Tracy MacNab discusses the feelings of shame and vulnerability that can be elicited in the group therapist. This same theme is addressed by Gina Arons and Ron Siegel, who have developed an innovative tool for locating therapists' areas of discomfort by exploring their responses to real and imagined extratherapeutic encounters with patients. Michael Shernoff, who has treated AIDS patients for more than a decade, tells how he has coped with the devastation that the disease has wrecked on both his professional and personal lives. Lastly, Gloria Garfunkel describes how her work with suicidal clients is affected by her having grown up as a child of Holocaust survivors.

Part Four examines specific clinical dilemmas that can pose hazards to practitioners. Michael Myers addresses some of the problems he has encountered as a psychiatrist treating other physicians and their family members, and Nancy Bridges discusses various countertransference dilemmas encountered in working with therapists. Martha Stark describes the difficulties entailed in treating patients who make use of a defense she terms "relentless entitlement." David Jobes and Terry Maltsberger address what many regard as the ultimate peril for the psychotherapist: dealing with suicidal patients.

Part Five surveys some of the professional, ethical, and legal hazards facing practitioners. Donald Nathanson, well known for his work on shame, describes how trainees can be subjected to shame and humiliation by their supervisors. Terry Maltsberger, a prominent suicidologist who was asked to review the records of Margaret Bean-Bayog's controversial treatment of Paul Lozano, argues that a competent psychiatrist's career was unjustifiably destroyed by the media and the Board of Registration in Medicine. Peter Gumpert and Susan Scholfield MacNab address the dangers and dilemmas presented by the shift to the managed-care model, while Eric Harris provides recommendations for risk management in a managed-care environment. Finally, Judy Jordan describes the evolution of the relational model that she developed with her colleagues at the Stone Center and discusses the difficulties faced by therapists who venture away from traditional approaches to clinical theory and practice.

Part Six addresses issues of prevention and self-care. Here the focus is on measures that therapists can take to maintain and foster their own health. William Grosch and David Olsen offer a prescription for burnout that goes beyond the simplistic formulas that are typically put forth. Bryan Wittine explores the power of spiritual practice in preserving and renewing the well-being of therapists. In the last chapter, Marc Berger offers guidance from senior psychotherapists on sustaining the professional self.

* * *

This volume is intended primarily for psychotherapists and counselors. Clinical instructors and supervisors may find the book particularly useful for training purposes. Much of the material could also be germane to other health professionals, as well as to members of the clergy. Finally, it may be of interest to therapy clients who wish to broaden their understanding of the treatment process.

I believe that clinicians at every level of experience can benefit from reading and thinking about the hazards of the profession. Individuals who are considering entering the field may find that the book helps them to make an informed decision. Trainees can benefit from being exposed to issues that are of vital importance, yet are typically neglected in training. Practicing therapists will find some of their deepest concerns and conflicts mirrored and validated, perhaps for the first time. Readers in general will learn how to take better care of themselves in their work and personal lives, and will discover ways to transform the many perils of practice into opportunities for growth and mastery.

REFERENCES

Ben-Avi, A. (1977). On becoming an analyst. In K. A. Frank (Ed.), *The human dimension in psychoanalytic practice*. New York: Grune & Stratton.

Bermak, G. E. (1977). Do psychiatrists have special emotional problems? *American Journal of Psychoanalysis, 37,* 141–146.

Bollas, C. (1987). *The shadow of the object: Psychoanalysis of the unthought known.* New York: Columbia University Press.

Burton, A. (1970). The adoration of the patient and its disillusionment. *American Journal of Psychoanalysis, 29,* 194–204.

Burton, A. (1975). Therapist satisfaction. *American Journal of Psychoanalysis, 35,* 115–122.

Cherniss, C. (1980). *Professional burnout in human service organizations.* New York: Praeger.

Chessick, R. D. (1978). The sad soul of the psychiatrist. *Bulletin of the Menninger Clinic, 42,* 1–9.

Cray, C., & Cray, M. (1977). Stresses and rewards within the psychiatrist's family. *American Journal of Psychoanalysis, 37,* 337–341.

Deutsch, C. J. (1984). Self-reported sources of stress among psychotherapists. *Professional Psychology: Research & Practice, 15,* 833–845.

Edelwich, J. (1980). *Burn-out: Stages of disillusionment in the helping professions.* New York: Human Sciences Press.

Farber, B. A. (1985). Clinical psychologists' perceptions of psychotherapeutic work. *Clinical Psychologist, 38,* 10–13.

Farber, B. A., & Heifetz, L. J. (1982). The process and dimensions of burnout in psychotherapists. *Professional Psychology, 3,* 293–301.

Freudenberger, H. J. (1974). Staff burnout. *Journal of Social Issues, 30,* 159–165.

Freudenberger, H. J., & Robbins, A. (1979). The hazards of being a psychoanalyst. *Psychoanalytic Review, 66,* 275–296.

Goldberg, C. (1986). *On being a psychotherapist: The journey of the healer.* New York: Gardner Press.

Greben, S. E. (1975). Some difficulties and satisfactions inherent in the practice of psychoanalysis. *International Journal of Psychoanalysis, 56,* 427–433.

Greenberg, J. R. (1986). Theoretical models and the analyst's neutrality. *Contemporary Psychoanalysis, 22,* 87–106.

Greenson, R. R. (1966). That "impossible" profession. *Journal of the American Psychoanalytic Association, 14,* 9–27.

Groesbeck, C. J., & Taylor, B. (1977). The psychiatrist as wounded physician. *American Journal of Psychoanalysis, 37,* 131–139.

Grunebaum, H. (1993). The vulnerable therapist: On being ill or injured. In H. S. Schwartz & A. L. Silver (Eds.), *Illness in the analyst* (pp. 21–49). Madison, CT: International Universities Press.

Guy, J. D. (1987). *The personal life of the psychotherapist.* New York: Wiley.

Hellman, I. D., Morrison, T. L., & Abramowitz, S. I. (1986). The stresses of psychotherapeutic work: A replication and extension. *Journal of Clinical Psychology, 42,* 197–204.

Henry, W. E., Sims, J. H., & Spray, S. L. (1973). *Public and private lives of psychotherapists.* San Francisco: Jossey-Bass.

Horner, A. J. (1993). Occupational hazards and characterological vulnerability: The problem of "burnout." *American Journal of Psychoanalysis, 53,* 137–142.

Jaffe, D. T. (1986). The inner strains of healing work: Therapy and self-renewal for health professionals. In C. D. Scott & J. Hawk (Eds.), *Heal thyself: The health of health care professionals* (pp. 194–205). New York: Brunner/Mazel.

Kilburg, R. R., Nathan, E. N., & Thoreson, R. W. (Eds.). (1986). *Professionals in distress: Issues, syndromes, and solutions in psychology.* Washington, DC: American Psychological Association.

Maeder, T. (1989). *Children of psychiatrists and other psychotherapists.* New York: Harper & Row.

McCann, L., & Pearlman, L. (1990). Vicarious traumatization: A framework for understanding the psychological effects of working with victims. *Journal of Traumatic Stress, 3,* 131–149.

Prochaska, J. O., & Norcross, J. C. (1983). Contemporary psychotherapists: A national survey of characteristics, practices, orientations, and attitudes. *Psychotherapy: Theory, Research, & Practice, 20,* 161–173.

Schur, M. (1972). *Freud: Living and dying.* New York: International Universities Press.

Searles, H. F. (1966). Feelings of guilt in the psychoanalyst. *Psychiatry, 29,* 319–323.

Strean, H. S. (1988). *Behind the couch: Revelations of a psychoanalyst* (as told to Lucy Freeman). New York: Wiley.

Sussman, M. B. (1992). *A curious calling: Unconscious motivations for practicing psychotherapy.* Northvale, NJ: Jason Aronson.

Tryon, G. S. (1983). The pleasures and displeasures of full-time private practice. *Clinical Psychologist, 36,* 45–48.

Wheelis, A. (1959). The vocational hazards of psychoanalysis. *International Journal of Psychoanalysis, 37,* 171–184.

Wood, B., Klein, S., Cross, H. J., Lammers, C. J., & Elliot, J. K. (1985). Impaired practitioners: Psychologists' opinions about prevalence, and proposals for intervention. *Professional Psychology: Research & Practice, 16,* 843–850.

PART ONE

The Therapist's Personal Development

CHAPTER 1

Intimations of Mortality

MICHAEL B. SUSSMAN, PsyD

My childhood dream was to become an astronomer, although I later decided that I disliked the hours. Actually, working at night may originally have been part of the appeal: All alone in the stillness of the observatory, silently contemplating the cosmos while others slept; a solitary explorer probing the outermost reaches of the visible Universe, far removed from the mundane inanities of everyday human existence. It was an image that contained mystery, discovery, and grandeur.

This early, romanticized vision of a career was resurrected at age 13, when I stumbled on *The Interpretation of Dreams.* True, Freud peered into the inner world rather than out toward the distant heavens. That was fine with me, for I was entering adolescence and found myself suddenly entranced by all things psychological. Moreover, both of my parents were biologists, so I was eager to distance myself from the natural sciences. But apart from my fascination with the subject of inquiry, in Freud's writing I recaptured my fantasy of a sublime, transcendent vocation that would satisfy both my dreams of greatness and my wish to possess a secret knowledge of things unseen.

We ask children: "What do you want to be when you grow up?" Notice that the emphasis is not on doing, but on being. Sure, the child who wants to join the police force dreams of high-speed car chases and gunfights with crooks. But more important is the image of *being* a police officer—wearing a badge and uniform, carrying a weapon, embodying authority, courage, and power.

Similarly, when I first aspired to become a therapist, it was only partly out of a wish to help people in distress. I did not simply wish to practice psychotherapy, I wanted to *be* a therapist. I remember, at the age of 19, sitting in the waiting room of a suite of offices, watching as a succession of therapists greeted their patients. Like myself, the other patients appeared to me to be anxious, depleted, needy, and in pain. In contrast, the clinicians struck me as calm, composed, full, and self-contained. I knew then that *I* wanted to be the *therapist,* by God! In my mind, that meant being whole, integrated, at peace, free of dependency needs, and always radiating goodness and well-being.

I only wish it had turned out that way. Clinical practice can be richly rewarding. Yet, I have learned that some of the deepest yearnings that drew me to the profession have not been—and can never be—fulfilled by the practice of psychotherapy. This realization, slow in dawning, has been disheartening, but I have come to view such disillusionment as a necessary part of professional development, which can bring greater maturity and authenticity to my clinical work.

I completed my graduate training six years ago and have been engaged in some form of clinical practice for nearly 11 years in all. This chapter describes some of the underlying aims that contributed to my desire to become a psychotherapist, as well as how they have been fulfilled or frustrated by clinical work. If these motivations sound naive or irrational, that is because they evolved largely outside of conscious awareness, often from childhood sources and were based on an outsider's view of the profession.

I do not mean to imply that I was drawn to this vocation purely from "selfish," ulterior motives. Like most practitioners, I seek to understand and to help those who suffer. Such compassionate, altruistic concern is a crucial element of the desire to practice psychotherapy. Along with these conscious intentions, however, I have become aware of an array of wishes and motivations that were previously held unconscious. As I have argued in a previous volume (Sussman, 1992), we neglect these hidden wellsprings of our therapeutic urges at great peril to our patients. Familiarity with our covert agendas can lessen the likelihood of harming or exploiting the people who have placed themselves in our care. In addition, such self-awareness can enable us to bypass—or at least minimize—some of the hazards that we face as practitioners.

A final caveat: Although I am presenting a composite picture of my covert aims as a therapist, the actual constellation is far from static. Each of these motives has had its own line of development. Some of them took shape long before I could even pronounce the word "psychotherapist"; others emerged only after I entered my own treatment. Some persist in various guises; others died an early death. To better explore the process of disillusionment, I present the yearnings in their early, raw form, rather than their later, more refined and sublimated, manifestations.

I wished for magical powers . . .

They have never appeared. Despite doctoral degree, fellowship, licensure, and publication of a book, wizardry forever eludes me. Some patients get better, others do not. Improvements are rarely as rapid or as dramatic as I once imagined they would be, and they cannot be attributed to treatment with any certainty. I am a competent clinician, at times even inspired. But those childhood wishes to be all-knowing, all-seeing, and all-powerful, which I hoped to hold on to by becoming a therapist, have taken a beating. That, of course, is what we call growing up.

I hoped to be admired and idolized . . .

On some level, I expected the role of psychotherapist to provide me with love and adulation on a grand scale. Like an entertainer who craves applause and acclaim, I believed that my patients' devotion would bolster my sense of self-worth.

As it's turned out, my work as a therapist definitely affects how I feel about myself. When I'm feeling vulnerable, I find that my sense of self-worth is uncomfortably dependent on how my patients are responding to treatment, and on how they seem to be feeling about me. Since both of these factors are in constant flux, they do not provide any firm foundation for self-evaluation.

Like many therapists, I thrive on feeling helpful and needed. It is gratifying to be the object of idealized transferences in which I am perceived as wise, powerful, benevolent, and special in the eyes of my patients. But however satisfying this idealization may feel, it does little to fortify my core sense of goodness. In part, my awareness of the transferential aspects of such responses keeps me from taking personal credit for eliciting them.[1] Ultimately, the yearning for self-acceptance cannot be fulfilled in any permanent way by receiving adulation from patients—or from anyone else for that matter. Until this elementary lesson is truly appreciated, the therapist—like the performer who hungers for one more standing ovation—may strive for acclaim that proves forever ephemeral in its impact.

I hoped to make up for the damage I believed I had inflicted on my family as a child . . .

This doesn't work. Guilt feelings endure, apparently unaffected by current attempts at atonement and reparation. When my rescuing and

[1] As Freud (1915/1958) so aptly put it, "[The analyst] must recognize that the patient's falling in love is induced by the analytic situation and is not to be ascribed to the charms of his person, that he has no reason whatever therefore to be proud of such a 'conquest,' as it would be called outside analysis" (pp. 160–161).

healing is successful, my sense of relief soon recedes, exposing the same old pool of guilt, undiminished by my good deeds. Why else do I approach the next patient with the same compelling need to help? And when my attempts fail, and patients remain the same or get worse, my early crimes are compounded and the guilt pool inches upward. If one had to devise a way of ensuring that practitioners remain in such an exacting profession, it would be difficult to come up with a more ingenious or effective formula.

Perhaps the greatest sense of failure in regard to rescuing and reparation occurs in reaction to a patient's suicide. Early in my clinical training, I wondered how I might respond to this and imagined that I would probably stop practicing altogether. During my third year of graduate school, a middle-aged patient of mine jumped to her death from the window of her 20th-floor apartment, shortly after transferring to a new therapist. I carry the emotional repercussions of that suicide to this day, and I still wonder whether I might have prevented it. Far from inducing me to leave the field, however, her death only intensified my dedication to the calling.

I hoped to transcend my own aggression and destructiveness . . .

Because I am uncomfortable with anger, hostility, and aggression, I try to deny or evade these aspects of my nature by striving to accept and nurture my patients. This defensive strategy has only been partly successful. Promoting healing in others has, to some extent, allowed for what Winnicott described as a "building up of a self-strength which makes possible a toleration of the destructiveness that belongs to that person's nature" (1986, p. 88). What I failed to anticipate, however, was all of the aggression and hostility generated within the treatment process itself.

Patients develop negative feelings toward therapy and the therapist for a variety of reasons. Such reactions may serve as a means of resisting change, as a way of avoiding closeness, or as a familiar way of establishing closeness (e.g., via battling or abusing). Negative feelings may also arise in response to the many limits and frustrations inherent in the treatment process, in response to actual or perceived errors and failings on the part of the therapist, or as part of transference/countertransference enactments in the therapeutic relationship. No matter how meek or appeasing the therapist might act, it is impossible to escape negativity and aggression on the part of patients. Indeed, a passive, docile bearing may itself provoke fury in certain clients.

Not only do we become the target of anger and aggression, we are often likely to experience such emotions and impulses ourselves. Missed appointments, unpaid bills, lack of progress, suicide threats and attempts, and interrupted weekends can test our benevolence. We may be faced with patients who talk too much or too little, who complain and whine, who ignore or dismiss what we say, who expose our own areas of vulnerability, who cannot allow themselves to receive and then resent their emptiness. We must also deal with parents who undermine their children's treatment, as well as spouses who abuse and terrorize patients and refuse to become involved in therapy. Each of these situations, and countless others, can elicit anything from mild irritation to seething rage in the clinician.

In short, the therapeutic setting does not provide a refuge from so-called negative emotions. Nor should it. Many character-disordered individuals have particular difficulties dealing with the anger they experience and elicit in relationships. Maladaptive ways of handling anger and aggression often play a central role in depression, panic attacks, and eating disorders. Nearly every psychotherapy patient can be expected to reenact hurtful scenarios from the past, in which either patient or therapist is cast in the role of the aggressor. But although I realize that this is all "grist for the mill," actually confronting such feelings remains uncomfortable.

I do my best to be kind, understanding, and helpful to my patients. While these conscious aims emanate from positive, adaptive trends in my personality, they may also serve to conceal the darker side of my nature. By shying away from the aggression that is inevitably generated within the therapeutic process, one may gradually accumulate unexpressed hostility on an unconscious level. I have observed an increase in my own sadistically tinged fantasies since I began clinical practice.[2] I have also become aware, during difficult sessions, of fleeting aggressive images, such as an impulse to yell or to shatter a window. These phenomena may represent the shadow side of my professional attitudes and aspirations. Whereas I am consciously intent on providing acceptance and compassion, my unconscious hostility presses for release. Alternatively, it remains repressed and leaves me feeling depressed.

Ultimately, it is impossible in either personal or professional relationships to be purely good, loving, helpful, and selfless. Any retreat from anger and aggression eventually leads to a return of the repressed (or suppressed). Refusing to acknowledge and accept one's shadow side poses dangers for both participants in the therapeutic process.

I hoped to escape my own problems by focusing on those of other people . . .

[2] Other clinicians who work with traumatized patients have shared similar observations, leading me to wonder whether being exposed on a consistent basis to stories of abuse may be a contributing factor.

This was perhaps the most misguided notion of all. In theory, it seemed simple enough: By dedicating myself to helping others with their problems and by immersing myself in their psychological worlds, I would be relieved from an unrelenting preoccupation with my own issues. How naive this plan now appears!

The good news is that I have been able to put my introspective orientation to constructive use as a therapist. The bad news—in terms of this defensive maneuver—is that clinical work demands continuous monitoring of one's internal processes, and it constantly stirs up one's own emotions, anxieties, memories, vulnerabilities, and both internal and interpersonal conflicts. Far from freeing myself from an inward focus, practicing psychotherapy has only deepened it.

Working as a therapist also makes it necessary to return periodically (or, in some cases, permanently) to personal treatment. In essence, one becomes a psychotherapy patient for life. At the same time, it can become increasingly difficult for the therapist to assume the role of patient. I am much more comfortable sitting in the therapist's seat, and I struggle with the loss of control entailed in being a patient. My knowledge of psychological matters can get in the way of honest, unadorned self-exploration. My familiarity with clinical technique can make it harder to trust the therapist without engaging in a lot of second-guessing and backseat driving. Knowing how frequently confidentiality is compromised has also added to my reluctance to be fully open with a therapist/colleague.

I hoped to internalize my own therapist better by doing what he did . . .

I encountered great difficulty in ending my first therapy experience, returning repeatedly to a therapist from whom I could not separate. In retrospect, part of my desire to practice psychotherapy stemmed from an inability to let go of him. Identifying with his positive qualities has certainly benefited my personal and professional development. But my clinical training led me to question and, ultimately, to reject much of what he did as my therapist. Ironically, by following in his footsteps, I eventually achieved greater separation from him.

I hoped to achieve a deep level of intimacy within a safe context . . .

This wish has fared quite well compared with many of the others, but with notable drawbacks. Through my work as a therapist, I have established intimate contact with an astounding variety of people of all ages, ethnic backgrounds, and socioeconomic levels. Within the safety of a professional relationship with explicit limits and boundaries, I have experienced a level of closeness and engagement rarely achievable in ordinary social relations.

The limits of this sort of intimacy, however, are all too apparent. Although I feel that I am fully engaged during sessions, the fact remains that the intimacy is largely unidirectional. Many of my thoughts and emotions cannot be shared, and the client knows next to nothing about my own history or outside life. This one-sidedness can be quite frustrating, especially when I have lacked sufficient intimacy in my personal life.

At such times, I also run the risk of becoming excessively intimate with a client. If we treat enough clients over the years, the chances are good that we will eventually be matched with someone with whom the "chemistry" is intense. This attraction is not always immediately apparent but may build over the course of treatment. How much of the developing infatuation is countertransferential versus "real" can be difficult to sort out. In only one instance have I found myself in love with a client. The pain involved in acknowledging the need to end the therapy and in letting go of the possibility of continued contact is an experience I do not wish to repeat.

Another troublesome aspect of the intimacy generated in therapeutic relationships is the sheer weight of the emotional demands placed on the therapist. In addition to the realistic demands that are part of helping people in distress, therapists must grapple with all sorts of transferential wishes and expectations that belong to the realms of parent/child, lover/beloved, victim/abuser, wrongdoer/judge, and so on. In attempting to meet or to deal otherwise with these varied demands and expectations, it can be difficult to maintain any emotional reserves for one's private life.

Prone to overidentifying with clients, I tend to experience much of their emotional pain and internal struggles as if they were my own. The permeability of my ego boundaries may facilitate empathic contact, but it also leaves me vulnerable to emotional overload. Especially when working with more disturbed individuals, hearing and digesting their stories of past and present abuse can be highly disturbing and can eventually lead to what Chessick (1978) has described as "sadness of the soul," in which clients' depression and despair are transferred to the therapist.

I hoped to meet my own dependency needs vicariously by attending to those of my patients . . .

Buie (1982–1983) declares that therapists look to their patients to provide a holding environment that sustains them and brings relief from a painful sense of aloneness. When the holding environment offered to a patient is accepted, it serves to hold the therapist as well.

I have found that when I'm well matched with a patient, the therapeutic relationship can fulfill dependency needs on both our parts. Problems emerge, however, when a patient rejects the holding environment or is so demanding and entitled that I am unwilling or unable to provide it. Cancellations, no-shows, and premature endings, moreover, have the potential to trigger painful feelings of loss or abandonment. In addition, practicing psychotherapy appears to have reinforced my tendencies to overlook and suppress my own emotional needs. This has led me, at times, to neglect my social life, leaving me prone—ironically—to needing my patients too much.

I believed that I might become free of limitations . . .

By becoming a therapist, I thought that I could somehow transcend the frustrations and limitations I have struggled with throughout my life. I have always despised confines and constraints, whether they pertained to emotional awareness, intellectual inquiry, interpersonal communication, or creative expression. As a therapist, I hoped to break through barriers in my patients and in myself—barriers to knowledge and emotional truth, to intimacy and self-expression. I longed to free my clients and myself from some of the restrictions imposed by the processes of socialization, adaptation, and conformity. And I dreamed of escaping the tyranny of causality, in which we are prisoners of the past.

These aims have been satisfied—within limits! I have vicariously enjoyed seeing clients surmount limitations and constraints of their own. In the role of clinician, I too can temporarily rise above some of the limits I experience in the rest of my life. But other limits emerge, and I often resist accepting them: limits to my knowledge and skill, limits to my influence on patients, limits to my emotional reserves, limits to my potential for personal growth. Even more difficult to accept are the ever-escalating external constraints imposed by insurance companies, regulatory agencies, and government policies. It will be an increasing challenge to the profession as a whole to balance the legitimate need for oversight and accountability with the seemingly arbitrary limitations and restrictions that are being foisted on us.

Mortality is our ultimate limitation, and I am convinced that a part of me has hoped somehow to elude it by practicing psychotherapy. The godlike qualities we associate with the role of psychotherapist brings with them the implicit promise of immortality. In addition, our notions of rescuing and remaking people nourish the fantasy of living on through our clients. Several studies (Cohen, 1983; Fieldsteel, 1989; Van Raalte, 1984) have noted an unwillingness on the part of therapists to acknowledge to clients their own mortality, even in the face of terminal illness. I must admit that I still harbor hopes for immortality. But given my track record on fulfilling covert wishes as a therapist, I'm not holding my breath (which could, after all, put the matter to rest).

* * *

The reader may conclude that after a relatively brief period of time in practice, I have become jaded, even cynical. Indeed, many of the illusions I held on entering the profession have been lost or modified by experience. In addition, my study of therapists' motivations and covert aims (Sussman, 1992) may well have hastened and deepened my disenchantment.

But disillusionment does not have to bring despair, nor must disenchantment bring unemployment. Without doubt, facing one's delusions and self-deceptions can be humbling; I am no longer the sorcerer or the sage, the oracle or the shaman, the martyr or the savior. Yet it seems to me that such a process of disillusionment is all but inevitable and that it represents a crucial, if painful, transition in the personal evolution of the psychotherapist.

The term "disillusionment" can have negative connotations, but only to the extent that we are invested in maintaining our illusions. The process of disillusionment precedes and prepares the way for a more accurate perception and a fuller acceptance of reality. Why should such a prospect be avoided?

The psychotherapeutic enterprise may itself be envisioned as a process of guided disillusionment. We attempt to provide a supportive setting in which our clients can face and relinquish their illusions and misconceptions. Over time, they let go of their need to see themselves as either all-good or all-bad, as excessively dependent or entirely independent, as always in control or as utterly helpless. As treatment proceeds, clients may be willing to surrender the illusion that they can ever win the parental love and approval for which they longed as children, and may give up the conviction that they can manage to change or manipulate the people around them so as to fulfill their unmet childhood needs. Clients may also relinquish expectations such as that life be fair, that emotions make logical sense, that everyone like and approve of them, or that the therapist provide a magical cure.

But how can we, as therapists, effectively facilitate this maturational process if we are intent on maintaining our own illusions?

As we know, the process of confronting difficult truths can be painful, and it generates resistance in our own psychotherapy as much as it does in that of our patients. For some of us, entering the profession may have served, in part, to preserve our illusions. Many of the unpleasant realities we have faced as psychotherapy patients can be effectively avoided or repudiated by identifying with, and eventually becoming, the idealized figure of the all-knowing, all-loving, all-powerful, perfected therapist. It is amusing at first blush, but disturbing in its implications, to conclude that becoming a therapist can represent a form of acting-out within one's own therapy.

Whether or not we have worked through these issues for ourselves within a therapeutic setting, it is unrealistic to expect any therapist to enter the field completely free of illusions. A mature sense of disillusionment, which is necessary for our full professional development, can only come within the context of accumulated clinical experience.

* * *

What, then, lies on the far side of disillusionment? Once our therapeutic zeal has been tempered, and our need to cure is less compelling, what is left?

What first appears is a sense of emptiness. As with any loss, the renunciation of some of our deepest hopes and wishes does not take place without a period of mourning.

As we emerge from the realm of disillusionment and loss, a new landscape gradually takes shape. While our fantasies have not been fulfilled, the reality of the work turns out to have its strong points.

The many joys and challenges of practicing psychotherapy, which are easily overlooked when we are faced with disappointments, can now be better appreciated. Whatever the difficulties entailed, we encounter a unique opportunity to assist in relieving human suffering. As therapists, we have occasion to connect with people who had given up on trusting anyone, and we can provide the balm of compassion and understanding to those who have sustained emotional wounds. We help people rediscover parts of themselves they lost along the way, and we nurture growth in those who are stagnating. We find real pleasure in witnessing the emergence of a strengthened sense of self, or the renewal of hope in those who had forsaken the future.

We may also begin to appreciate the ways in which practicing psychotherapy facilitates our own growth. The work allows us to emphasize and to reinforce what is best in ourselves, while providing repeated opportunities to face and accept our dark sides. Through a process of desensitization, we learn to better tolerate aggression and to come to terms with our fears. Weathering the process of professional disillusionment enhances self-acceptance, bringing a degree of maturity that our personal treatment may have failed to produce. It can also bring a greater capacity for authentic hope, which—as Searles (1977) points out—"emerges through the facing of feelings of disappointment, discouragement, and despair" (p. 483).

Whatever the benefits to the practitioner, the fundamental goal of our work is to help our clients, and it is my impression that the process of disillusionment ultimately makes us better clinicians. When the fog clears, we find ourselves appropriately suspicious of our altruism as practitioners and more realistic in our expectations of the psychotherapy process. Facing our limitations can make us more humane and accessible as therapists, and less likely to set ourselves apart from those who sit across from us. Finally, by embracing these intimations of mortality, we offer a model of courageous acceptance to our clients, for whom therapy—and life—must one day end.

REFERENCES

Buie, D. H. (1982–1983). The abandoned therapist. *International Journal of Psychoanalytic Psychotherapy, 9,* 227–231.

Chessick, R. D. (1978). The sad soul of the psychiatrist. *Bulletin of the Menninger Clinic, 42,* 1–9.

Cohen, J. (1983). Psychotherapists preparing for death: Denial and action. *American Journal of Psychotherapy, 37,* 222–226.

Fieldsteel, N. D. (1989). Analyst's expressed attitudes toward dealing with death and illness. *Contemporary Psychoanalysis, 25,* 427–432.

Freud, S. (1958). Observations on transference love. *Standard Edition,* 12:159–171. (Original work published 1915.)

McWilliams, N. (1987). The grandiose self and the interminable analysis. *Current Issues in Psychoanalytic Practice, 4,* 93–107.

Searles, H. (1977). The development of mature hope in the patient-therapist relationship. In K. A. Frank (Ed.), *The human dimension in psychoanalytic practice* (pp. 9–27). New York: Grune and Stratton.

Sussman, M. B. (1992). *A curious calling: Unconscious motivations for practicing psychotherapy.* Northvale, NJ: Jason Aronson.

Van Raalte, P. (1984). *The impact of death of the psychoanalyst on the patient.* Unpublished doctoral dissertation, New Brunswick, NJ: Rutgers University.

Winnicott, D. W. (1986). *Home is where we start from.* New York: Norton.

CHAPTER 2

Therapist in the Combat Zone

EDWARD TICK, PhD

"O for a Muse of fire, that would ascend / the brightest heaven of invention . . . ," Shakespeare implored to open *Henry V,* his historical drama of war and kingship. The bard was striving to bring a kingdom, an epoch, and its apocalypse and restoration, into the space of a small wooden theater. Could we but join him in unleashing the full powers of our imaginations:

> Then should the warlike Harry, like himself,
> Assume the port of Mars; and at his heels,
> leashed in like hounds, should famine, sword and fire
> Crouch for employment. . . .

I, too, have often prayed for a Muse of Fire to express the conflagrations of agony and courage, terror, rage, and brotherhood that I have seen and shared as psychotherapist for Vietnam veterans. I, too, have trembled before the march of destruction that famine, sword, and fire have made through the psyches of my clients, our nation, and humankind. I, too, feel small and unworthy to adequately express and explore so great a subject as war and its devastation. And, mysteriously, I have felt blessed beyond telling in the presence of those flowers that sometimes bloom even in the deepest pits of hell.

I have been a psychotherapist in general private practice since 1975. In 1979, a year before Post-traumatic Stress Disorder (PTSD) was established as a diagnostic category and included in DSM-III, I began treating Vietnam combat and noncombat veterans. Over the years, such treatment has become not only one of my clinical specialties but, more profoundly, an obsession with which I labored greatly until I was able to master its negative motivations and impact and transform it into a life-affirming calling (Tick, 1986).

This calling appears all the more unusual because, during the Vietnam War, I was college deferred and an active antiwar protestor, had no friends or relatives fighting in Vietnam, became a vegetarian, considered myself a pacifist, was preparing my conscientious objector plea to avoid military service, and was considering leaving the country if drafted. All my experiences during adolescence and the early adult years, on the surface, appeared to mitigate against my becoming a specialist in treating the psychological wounds of war. But war and its aftermath can make bedfellows and brothers of men who otherwise would never have met, loved, or struggled together with the deepest wounds of heart and soul.

Elsewhere, I have chronicled the full story of my therapy work with Vietnam veterans and other war-wounded, and my transformation from antiwar college student to postwar homefront medic and healer (Tick, 1989, 1992). Herein I wish to explore, from an experiential and intrapsychic perspective, some of the dangers and hazards to the psychotherapist of work with war veterans and others suffering Post-traumatic Stress Disorder.

Psychotherapy with clients suffering PTSD is arduous work and has striking similarities to its generative traumas. It is full of dangers, surprises, and inevitable losses and sorrow, and it demands that the therapist discover and utilize what is best in him- or herself. It necessitates that the therapist look at aspects of the self and the human condition that we would rather leave unexamined and that the public's conscious awareness, for the most part, denies. It inevitably creates in the mind's eye of the therapist a similar landscape of pain, horror, and hell as the one burned into the client's. Such a landscape is most difficult to survey without turning away in revulsion and fear. Unlike Shakespeare's play of war, it does not disappear with the final curtain, but goes on and on over the years of intensive psychotherapy with the war survivor, becoming more ingrained in and vivid to the therapist as therapy proceeds and deepens.

Such therapy requires that the therapist examine denied aspects of the self—aggression, fear, rage, revulsion, past personal experiences—and own them in a self-disclosing manner far beyond the usual demands of the therapeutic process. Ultimately, it requires and engenders changes in the therapist's character structure that are, perhaps, best expressed in psycho- or mythopoetic terms as the loss of innocence, initiation into the underworld, and transformation from novice or initiate into warrior and king. Such transformation is hard-won and, as many contemporary writers on masculine psychology such as Robert Bly, Robert Moore, Michael Meade, and others argue, is necessary for the achievement of mature adulthood. But many are the dangers and pitfalls, and many the temptations to turn away from such a process of willingly exposing oneself to horrific trauma.

JUNGLE DREAMS

Recently, I was asked to consult with a men's counselor facilitating a group for inmates who were guilty of homicide or other felonies and were incarcerated at Shawangunk Correctional Facility in New York State. After over a year of highly successful work in establishing a first-of-its-kind Men's Prison Council (Clines, 1993), the counselor began having nightmares in which he relived some of the inmates' crimes as well as a recent prison uprising in which guards were stabbed. In his most terrifying nightmare, he saw himself as the victim of brutal violence such as he had heard about from these men but never encountered in actual experience. I recognized that he was undergoing an initiation into the ways of the psychic underworld.

The prison counselor's situation closely paralleled my own work with war veterans. In both instances, a middle-class white Jewish male counselor, who had never previously experienced personal violence or severe brutality, became involved with men from different, less privileged, socioeconomic backgrounds who had been immersed in physical and emotional violence during critical periods of their lives and who had perpetrated it themselves.

I began having dreams of my Vietnam veteran clients' battles, beginning with my third vet client, Ron. He was a reconnaissance patrol squad leader, the first survivor of fierce jungle combat with whom I worked. His stories—of hiding behind fallen comrades in firefights, of finding his lieutenant decapitated, of hiding in a cave while captured friends screamed for his help while being tortured in the jungle nearby—exposed me to levels of horror and brutality I had never encountered or even imagined (Tick, 1985).

At first, like the prison counselor, I dreamed Ron's battles. As we continued in therapy, the sheer brutality of the imagery assaulted my ordinary defenses in a way that I thought must be similar, but far less immediate and severe, than Ron's experiences in combat. Our ordinary defenses can protect us from the ordinary assaults of civilized living, but they are meager and inadequate, and can provide only limited, brief relief when we are relentlessly bombarded by brutality, such as war veterans experienced, or brutal imagery, such as therapists of veterans experience. The field of military psychiatry has studied this problem. Military psychiatry categorically affirms that exposing anyone, even the most healthy and stable human being, to more than a few days of unrelenting combat will inevitably lead to traumatic collapse and inability to function (Gabriel, 1987).

My second stage of dreamlife occurred when I began to see myself in Ron's and other vets' battles. At this stage, my dreams were fairly close replications of what my patients had described in therapy, but I became a character in the dream. I was, intrapsychically, making these dramas my own. I was, imaginatively though not consciously, going through what my clients had experienced. I felt fear, anger, confusion. I lost much sleep. Daily life, current events, the entire world—these were beginning to seem more warlike than ever before. This gave me a strong taste of the degree to which veteran clients unconsciously perceive contemporary life through the lens of their war experiences.

A third stage of dreamlife occurred when, after several years of work with numerous combat veterans, I had the following significant dream:

> I am at the bottom of a barren, steep hill. I am alone and in fatigues. I am unarmed. I am hiding behind a small log, just a little higher and longer than my own body. Hordes of enemy soldiers are charging down the hill right toward me. They are screaming. Their rifles are blazing. They want me dead. I am trapped behind the log while bullets smash into it and chew it away. I cannot run. I cannot fight back. Soon, inevitably, I will be overrun and either taken prisoner or killed.

I awoke from this dream in sheer terror such as I had never felt before. I had seen myself in mortal danger unarmed and alone. I felt what it was like to be threatened by death, but could not see myself armed and killing. While I had crossed over into the terrain of danger and brutality where my vets lived, I still remained the pacifist and protestor, the innocent. After years of vet work, my personality resisted the total transformation necessitated by life in a war zone. I clung to my old values and hovered in a limbo before the horrible and necessary choice that every combat soldier must ultimately make—the decision to kill or be killed. At this stage of my evolution as therapist, I resisted the necessity of ever having to make such a choice, thus denying my own aggression and survival instinct. I was left with terror and the shocking, uncomfortable realization that, unable to make such a choice in a situation that demanded it, I myself would be killed.

On the symbolic level, the dream indicated how I felt specializing in the work with a neglected and dishonored population—the U.S. veterans of Vietnam. I felt "unarmed and alone, as I tried to walk this jungle path on American soil where the Vietnam War still raged long after the Vietnam War had ended" (Tick, 1992, p. 179).

For a long time, I perched on the edge of my denied aggression. By this time, I had integrated horror enough so that I could relate to vets with much greater calm and equilibrium, with much less of my own pain or revulsion present. I had learned to stand before images of brutality and horror with vets and not flinch. I had learned to listen to tales of napalmed children, burned villages, and massacred families without judgment. I was learning the rules of life during warfare: The order of civilization is reversed, destruction rather than creation, death rather than life, insanity rather than sanity, are the norms. I had learned not to flee from this invisible line of horror, to stand there while my vet clients approached it a second time through therapy, and to help them see what they had seen, this time with their hearts.

But I held on fiercely to my pacifism, as if it were a last line of defense that could protect me in the inner jungles. Then I had this dream:

> I am being pursued down a steep hill by enemy soldiers who, armed with AK-47s, are firing wildly at my retreating form. I am in fatigues and armed with my own M-16. I flee amid bullets kicking up dirt around my feet. I run breathlessly until I come to a school building. I bolt into the building, up the stairs, through all the rooms, desperate to find a safe hiding place. The enemy soldiers follow me into the school and begin a room-to-room search, poking their AKs around desks, under tables, in closets. There are so many of them, I fear I am doomed.
>
> Finally, I run into a bathroom, then into a toilet stall. I stand on the toilet seat so that my feet will not be visible from below. I ready and clutch my rifle and wait with bated breath. I hear my enemies coming closer, getting louder. My breath is caught in my throat. My heart is pounding. I am sweating like a faucet. Then the soldiers crash into the bathroom, screaming for me, poking their guns under the stall and pointing them at my door, slamming against the stall to try and get me out.
>
> I am in abject terror. My heart hurts more than ever in my life. I poke my gun under the stall and scream, "No! No!" over and over. They keep pushing, shooting, banging. I scream "No!" again and pull my trigger. I pull and pull and shoot, wildly, desperately, trying to kill my enemies not out of anger or hatred or vengeance, but just to save my own life.

In that dream, after years of struggle and denial, I finally saw myself choosing to kill another human being rather than passively letting myself be killed. At that moment, I overcame a passive response to life-threatening violence conditioned in me in part by my Jewish heritage, especially as a child of the generation of the Holocaust. I also achieved a breakthrough in my understanding of the motivations that drove most men to kill during warfare. Previously, I had worked with vets on their killing rages, their desire for vengeance, the blind, dehumanizing hatred that awakened in people who saw their own best friends blown to shreds or riddled with bullets or skewered with bungee sticks. With this dream, however, I realized that hatred and rage were not necessarily core human motivations, but rather reactions conditioned by the war environment. More basic, more healthy, and more important for vet clients to recover was the fundamental human response to the horrible conundrum soldiers had to face: In a situation of kill or be killed, many, perhaps most of us, feeling the terror of our own imminent death, would kill. I finally recovered such a basic, previously disowned, survival instinct in myself. For the first time in my life, I saw and felt that I would choose to kill rather than be killed.

Significantly, after this recovery, I experienced several important and surprising personal changes. First, my nightmares ceased. At about the same time, I gave up vegetarianism, became generally more assertive and self-valuing, made subtle but important shifts in my value system and, ironically, became less temperamental. It was as if the recovery of my survival instinct and concomitant overcoming of my inhibition against any and all killing allowed a final integration of previously disowned, externalized, and projected male warrior energy that accompanied the experience of horror.

Combat vets confirmed my insight. "You don't kill because you want to hurt somebody," one Marine combat veteran told me. "Only sick people do that. It isn't a killing rage really. It's just a rage to save your own life. You're trying to stop the other guy from killing you while at the same moment he's trying to stop you from killing him. In the bush, you don't kill from rage. You kill from fear." This insight is echoed by Richard Gabriel (1987), who stated that only sociopathic personalities can endure the stress of modern warfare unaltered.

From the time of this dream, I used this new awareness in my therapy work with vets. I worked to help them recover their true feelings at the moment they first killed. With much struggle, many were able to open their hearts to the overwhelming degree of sheer terror for their lives that they had felt. Prior to reexperiencing the terror, psychically numbed vets tend to think of themselves as cold-blooded killers, dangerous, enraged, sinful. But when they recover their original terror, they realize that they were, in fact, just utterly terrified young men trying desperately to save their own lives in the only way available to them. With that realization, guilt and self-condemnation lift away and their own rehumanization process proceeds. It was only possible for me to guide them home through such a transformation after I had intrapsychically experienced this warriorlike transformation away from civilization and into primitivity myself.

REFLECTIONS ON THE INTRAPSYCHIC DIMENSIONS OF WORK WITH VETERANS

This history of my dreamlife spanning approximately the first six years of my work with combat veterans demonstrates an initiation process I had to undergo in order to do healing work for vets as well as to mature aspects of my own personality. It can be summed up, as in Joseph Campbell's (1949) psychomythical analysis, as initiation.

Campbell explains that the psychomythic hero's journey is a cyclical process of three stages. The first stage is the departure from the ordinary shared world and the descent into a world that has its own unfamiliar rules and dimensions. People who leave the daily life of our civilization for a combat zone certainly experience this departure. Military training attempts to provide them with the martial skills necessary to perform and survive. But they remain woefully, inadequately prepared, psychologically or spiritually, for what they will encounter in the other world. Further, if they are too young for the encounter, still developmentally immature, they will not even have a fully developed personality structure with which to resist trauma or into which to integrate it. Then the trauma itself becomes, simultaneously, developmental experience and a rupture of the established self and world orders. This was the case with the vast majority of men in Vietnam combat, whose average age was 19, compared with the average age of World War II combatants, which was 26.

The therapist, too, in the hours spent with such clients, experiences a departure from the ordinary world and a descent into a psychic space with its own rules, demands, and dangers. The first stages of my dreamlife represented this departure and showed the rupturing of my unconscious order and its saturation with previously unknown or distanced violent imagery.

Initiation is the second stage of the hero's journey. During the initiatory stage, we must survive a succession of difficult, challenging, and often life-threatening ordeals. We must master the ways of the underworld, the alternate reality in which we are now traveling, and allow what we experience there to destroy our old conceptions of life. We must find the strength and skills within ourselves and the help from without and beyond ourselves to survive the intolerable, horrible, and the threatening. We must be broken and broadened.

Such initiation ought to be a rite of passage. There is a great emphasis in American popular culture, promoted by movies, television, books, and legend, on viewing the experience of warfare per se as a rite of passage transforming boys into men. In the modern combat zone, however, no rite of passage actually occurs. It remains incomplete because there are no elders, no initiators present, who can guide and ceremonialize the personality transformations of the soldier. The incomplete initiation, the failed rite of passage, the seeker stuck in the underworld and needing to be guided to light and maturity, is very often what the therapist encounters when a veteran presents him- or herself for therapy. A great deal of what we call Post-traumatic Stress Disorder may best be understood as development arrested through its encounter with terror and horror.

Initiation cannot occur when the guide or elder has not been initiated. Thus, in the therapist too, initiation must occur. Therapy with combat veterans cannot occur under the guidance of a therapist who has not learned the ways, not necessarily of the literal combat zone, but certainly of the psychic combat zone. My first dream of being attacked represented my immersion in the psychic underworld of combat while still resisting its demands, still clinging to my final defense—the denial that I, too, had an inner killer.

My denial prevented my learning an essential lesson of the underworld—that killing rage is really, except perhaps in sociopathic personalities, the rage to live and the terror of violent death; all of us have planted in our minds and cells such a rage to live that we very well may, if confronted with the ultimate choice, kill rather than be killed. This is not more than the application in extremis of Spinoza's dictum that every creature seeks to persist in its own being. We each want to live. Almost all of us are capable of killing to preserve our own lives. Truly realizing this in a personal way, we become one with those who have killed and can help them regain their humanity. My final dream, in which I saw myself as killing to live, represented a dark epiphany, a necessary transformation through dream experience and thus into my awareness, of the denied killer in myself.

The final stage of the hero's journey is the return to the shared world with wisdom gained and the intent to give that wisdom, in some form, to the culture.

In all traditional and classical societies, returned warriors served many important psychosocial functions. They were keepers of dark wisdom for their cultures, witnesses to war's horrors from personal experience who protected and discouraged, rather than encouraged, its outbreak again. During wartime, they turned outward to meet threats from other people, but during peacetime they turned inward to protect against and keep under control the outbreak of violent and aggressive behaviors between their own people.

As a society, we have not initiated and thus transformed our veterans into warriors. Belated praise and parades notwithstanding, we have not truly welcomed them home and not helped them heal. Perhaps most destructive and telling of all, we have no class of citizen-warriors within which returned warriors can serve or function. Our veterans are alone with the memories of and traumas from their combat experiences as well as with the skills gained and courage demonstrated.

As a therapist for combat veterans, I am in the strange and uncomfortable position of trying to help bring men home to a country that has no class or clan or society in which they can serve and belong. The mythopoetic cycle, as outlined by Campbell, is meant to transform us from uninitiated, innocent, and naive young people into mature, competent, wise elders who are the heroes of our own intrapsychic adventures and who, simultaneously, have invaluable service and wisdom to offer our cultures. In a tragic sense, it is impossible to complete such a psychological mythopoetic journey in a culture that denies the initiates' experiences and fails to provide pilgrims with an audience, a set of rituals, or a social class to which they can return.

Thus, the final stage of psychotherapy with war veterans must often be the empowering of both therapist and client to find meaningful ways of carrying traumatizing memories and experiences as well as creating experiences to foster the return stage of the hero's journey and the societal homing that veterans have been denied.

TAKING A PLACE IN HISTORY

There are inherent psychohistorical dimensions in conducting therapy for Vietnam veterans in which both therapist and client participate. Though I participated in the antiwar movement during the 1960s, I was left with a sense of rage, mistrust, and impotence regarding my ability to significantly affect the course of national history. But by conducting therapy with veterans, I have been able to transcend these feelings and gain the sense that I have successfully taken my small place in history. Though I could not stop a war, I could, finally and truly, help "bring the boys back home."

By conducting therapy with Vietnam veterans, I discovered the parts of myself that were wounded by the times we all lived through as well as the parts of myself that were inadequately developed. Thus, through struggling in consciousness with every issue and dream that arose for me during the conduct of therapy, I was able to heal the personal wounds that occurred as a result of my own coming of age during the 1960s. Further, I was able to complete some of the psychological maturation that did not occur because of my own lack of certain transformational experiences and the absence of elders to guide it. Finally, I was able to contribute to healing the rift that had opened in the Vietnam generation between those who fought the war and those who protested it. I attained a deeply satisfying brotherhood with men from whom I had previously been alienated and estranged.

I am left with the conviction that therapy is inevitably a psychohistorical enterprise. As therapists, we treat those suffering from our collective social wounds. By agreeing to treat them and experiencing secondary trauma from exposure to their memories, we, too, are wounded and we, too, must heal. On however small a scale, we are participating in the diseases and the healing not only of our clients but of ourselves and our culture. Psychotherapy is too young a profession, and our social problems too vast, for us yet to determine whether it can actually change the direction of history. But inevitably, as therapists, we take our places in history, standing with those most affected for better or worse and discovering, in the process, how we too are survivors of that same history.

In introducing *Henry V,* Shakespeare apologized for his unworthiness at attempting to accomplish so great a task as portraying the full scope of war and kingship in so tiny a space:

> . . . But pardon gentles all
> The flat unraised spirits that have dared
> On this unworthy scaffold to bring forth
> So great an object . . .

It is, as the bard said, truly impossible to reduce so large and terrible a story as the Vietnam War and its effect on our generation and nation into so small a space as a book chapter or the therapy hour. But each of our minds is much more than the stage on which the great dramas of history and culture are reenacted. By practicing psychotherapy in the combat zone, I have in my own way been to war and back and have found my way of participating in the greatest and most monstrous adventure of my generation.

REFERENCES

Campbell, J. (1949). *The hero with a thousand faces.* New York: Meridian.

Clines, F. (1993, February 23). Men's movement challenges prison machismo. *New York Times,* Bl & 6.

Gabriel, R. (1987). *No more heroes: Madness and psychiatry in war.* New York: Hill and Wang.

Shakespeare, W. (1978). *Henry V.* In A. L. Rowse (Ed.), *The Annotated Shakespeare* (Vol. II). New York: Potter.

Tick, E. (1985). Vietnam grief: Psychotherapeutic and psychohistorical implications. *The Psychotherapy Patient, 2*(1), 101–116.

Tick, E. (1986). The face of horror. *The Psychotherapy Patient, 3*(2), 101–120.

Tick, E. (1989). *Sacred mountain: Encounters with the Vietnam beast, Volume one: 1979–1984.* Santa Fe, NM: Moon Bear Press.

Tick, E. (1992). *Sacred mountain: My odyssey in healing the wounds of war.* Unpublished manuscript.

CHAPTER 3

Listening to Your Patients, Yelling at Your Kids: The Interface between Psychotherapy and Motherhood

SUSAN SCHOLFIELD MACNAB, MSW, PhD

I am a mother and a psychotherapist. As a psychodynamically trained therapist, listening is central to my clinical work; as a mother, listening is also important. But the enormously complicated and powerful feelings that I, like all mothers, have toward my children sometimes affect my capacity to respond as empathically or gracefully as I would like.

There is a continuous interplay between my role as a mother and as a psychotherapist. Becoming a mother altered my way of thinking about my patients' lives, and my clinical experience has lead to wishes to be a near-perfect mother. Although the challenges of family life have included some difficulties with influences from my professional life, my understanding of developmental and psychological issues have also been personally helpful. I have found many compelling, painful, rewarding, and often unavoidable opportunities to explore the interface between motherhood and psychotherapy (MacNab, 1989). What I am learning and struggling with as a mother isn't necessarily left outside the office door. And, the poignant narratives of my patients, often replete with complaints of inadequate or hurtful parenting, can haunt me hours later as I deal with some family conflict.

The mingling of experiences from different aspects of my life has resembled the therapeutic process itself with its shifting between present, past, and future experiences of wishes and fears. A colleague recently told me about a group process experience with mental health professionals. She complained about the leader, "She seemed to think we wanted to talk about our disappointment in our parents, but we [the women in the group] wanted to talk about our feelings about being bad mothers to our own children." We shared a laugh and began talking about the shame and guilt that accompany some aspects of mothering, and which may be highlighted in surprising ways in the interface between our own family life and our lives as psychotherapists.

When I was a younger therapist and before becoming a mother, I listened to patients' memories of their disappointments and occasionally identified with their negative assessments of their mothers' capabilities. Intellectually, I had a more encompassing understanding of psychic distress than simply to blame mothers for children's unhappiness, but emotionally it was easy to join the patient in his or her blaming of parents. During certain phases of my own analysis, the imperfections of mothers were in high relief. Fathers were not immune to my critical attitudes, but mothers' deficiencies were often experienced as the most painful. Aren't mothers supposed to be the last refuge for their children? We often are, but as I learned firsthand later on, our efforts to protect and nurture our children cannot always succeed. We struggle with the same wishes and fears that are sources of so much human suffering.

When I began clinical work, I had a more linear and simplistic understanding of human development, partially because of some inadequacies in the then current analytic theories, particularly in the area of female development. Also, the clinical approach perpetuated by a largely male medical establishment encouraged more distant, impersonal, "blank screen" techniques. The implication was that the doctors had all the answers. In addition, I was only beginning to develop an appreciation of the many ways patients change their understanding of past and present events during intensive psychotherapies.

Over time, I learned that a person's narrative evolves through therapy's prism and/or other significant life events. My experiences as a patient and as a clinician and my own adult development increased my awareness of the complexity of human relationships. In spite of my maturity as a clinician, however, I was not prepared for the emotional impact of motherhood on my clinical work, and vice versa. Motherhood brought me increased discomfort with certain of the memories and associations I was hearing from my patients. I recognized similarities at times to what I was saying to and hearing from my own children—a lack of parental empathy! Was I too involved with telling my children what to do instead of listening to them? Would my children be blaming me for their difficulties?

In my own analysis, I struggled with concerns over what seemed missing or problematic in my childhood. I believed that these hard-won insights would help me be a better mother and that, as mental health professionals, my husband and I had an inside track on parenting. I hoped we would be able to supply the "empathy" that seemed less available to the more impoverished lives of our parents' generation.

This naive arrogance reflected my enthusiasm for psychological theories and techniques that better fit my experiences as a patient and a therapist, particularly recent writings from an object relations or self-psychological approach and attention to gender issues. Family systems training helped me to understand the complexities of intergenerational transmission of fears and conflicts. Increased knowledge of the developmental stages of individuals and of families provided a way to understand the patients I was seeing. My patients and I together came to see the vulnerabilities of preceding generations. Symptomatic behaviors eased.

When I became a new mother, with all the attendant joy and anxiety, I wanted to believe that my years of psychotherapy and training would protect me and my child from almost all the pain I had heard from my patients or had experienced in my own family. In spite of the anxieties and exhaustion, I remember the first year of my first baby's life as being a time of happiness and gratitude for our healthy child.

In my professional role, I did not reveal much information about my pregnancy or baby; rather I inquired about my patients' experiences of the obvious changes in my life. What I heard were the wishes and fears aroused by my pregnancy, my upcoming maternity leave, and new motherhood. I felt a heightened sensitivity to the women longing for children or accepting childlessness. What I think I failed to hear was the hope from my patients who were mothers and fathers that now I would know how difficult parenthood could be. In retrospect, I did not want to know about the emotional tasks ahead during this early time of joy and the intense involvement with the physical needs of my baby. What I did know was that I had lost a certain carefree quality now that there was such a precious responsibility in my life. However, I still didn't realize how emotionally draining parenting can be. I ignored my patients' comments about the early years being the easiest.

Now that I have mothered two infants, I am better able to hear the varieties of experiences that new mothers (and fathers) have and to offer more credence to the topsy-turvy world created by the arrival of a new baby. A psychodynamic stance notwithstanding, new mothers may often need real support. A few carefully chosen comments or questions about the anxiety, changing of priorities, exhaustion, and overwhelming love that a baby evokes can be helpful and implicitly convey understanding of the patient's experience. For example, with a patient who recently returned to full-time work after two months of maternity leave, I inquired about how her lack of sleep and still changing body were contributing to her feelings of being an inadequate wife and mother. Interestingly, her sense of competency rapidly improved as she recognized how much she was doing without sufficient rest or help. The meanings of my support for her were then explored from a transferential and historical perspective.

These, in retrospect, are the easier issues in psychotherapy and motherhood. The need for support, the exhaustion, and the enormous love and concern for a new baby seem understandable and are an inevitable part of motherhood that can be examined both personally and in psychotherapy. I often provide patients with support and understanding not available elsewhere. I have become more comfortable with this well-considered offering of support to patients around parenting issues. I also remember the meaningful experience of receiving support from my analyst at a time when one of my young children was having a problem. She both acknowledged having similar feelings when one of her children struggled and offered a practical suggestion.

The interface between psychotherapy and motherhood became more complex and painful as I discovered that I was not necessarily going to be a better mother than all the mothers I heard about from my patients. It was difficult to mourn the fantasy of perfect mothering (Chodorow, 1978). It was hard to feel guilt, shame, or sadness when I yelled at one of my children or was neglecting their needs in real or imagined ways. This pain can be exaggerated or denied when it resembles feelings and behaviors that my patients recall as damaging. This includes dealing with such issues as how much control and structure to provide, how much empathy, how much frustration, and how much gratification.

In addition, the physiological differences among children may be obscured by an overreliance on psychological theories to explain everything about children's needs and behaviors. With the birth of our second child, who was a more difficult baby and child, I was brought face to face with the power of physiological differences. I experienced firsthand the frustration of trying to sort out the psychological and biological vulnerabilities of young children. This has, in turn, informed my clinical work. For example, a patient in his late 20s who was only recently diagnosed with attention deficit disorder describes his mother as often being disappointed and angry with him. I now have clues to his mother's frustrated and confused responses about this seemingly bright boy who was underachieving. I understand more about the self-recriminations, confusion, and regrets mothers feel, often accompanied by poignant wishes to undo what has been done.

I wanted to be a perfect mother, knowing how to let my children separate, being empathic to all their feelings, and promoting all their special qualities. I was close to accepting being a "good enough" therapist; I realized that my clinical skills could be useful but not magic to most patients. But only a "good enough" mother? Never! I really did not want my children to suffer the hurt and frustration that dominated the lives of my patients.

Some of my unrealistic expectations originated, not in personal family experiences, but from distortions that grew during my two decades of psychotherapy practice, and several years of my own psychotherapy and psychoanalysis. Psychodynamic theories focus intensely on the pernicious influences of mothers and fathers, or their emotional and physical absences. The therapist encourages the patient to explore the roots of painful feelings and their early childhood origins. Destructive patterns are often traced to the frightening, angry, unfeeling, or humiliating ways that patients experienced their parents. We may have moved away from mother blaming—but not far enough. Although the end result of a "successful" therapy may be an understanding of the ways parents did the best they could, often there remains a belief: "If my parents had only . . . , I would not have had to go through so much suffering and so much therapy."

Therapists do recognize that some patients show an amazing resilience to very difficult childhoods, whereas other fairly disturbed patients seem not to have suffered so horribly in their early lives. But we keep looking for the reasons for our patients' pain and carry this over to our present family life. For example, there could be numerous psychoanalytic explanations for my daughter's unique expression of separation anxiety (i.e., running in the opposite direction when I arrived to pick her up at nursery school). I became so lost in discerning the reasons that I missed the central point: "It is time to go!" I sometimes seemed to view achieving an empathic understanding of my child as essential to parenting. It was as if I should be able to figure everything out and make the world easier for my children than it can ever be.

I was upset when my husband suggested that our children would have neurotic qualities like ours. It pained me too much to think that the years of my personal struggles, like those of my patients, could be repeated in any form in my beloved children. So for a few more years, I denied that my children had their own vulnerabilities. I needed to keep them far away from the suffering and the lost opportunities that I and my patients experienced.

I continued to be unwilling to be just a "good enough" parent. This was particularly unacceptable because my patients' stories suggested that what one might assume was "good enough" was nowhere near it. They complained that their talents were not fully developed, and their familial relationships were often permeated with conflict, blame, and guilt. Many of my adult patients seemed to have many regrets and little peace. I wanted to spare my children such struggles and this stunted potential. All of this made it very hard not to be overinvested in having an intensely empathic understanding of my children that, I thought, would keep them happy.

Empathy was certainly a powerful means of change in my clinical work. Kohut's theory, as exemplified in "The two analyses of Mr. Z," was a significant influence on my clinical practice (Kohut, 1978), as was self-psychology with its emphasis on an empathic understanding to promote a fuller inquiry into patients' experiences of narcissistic injuries. I found these ideas to be of immense help in my own work, and I certainly imagined that attention to empathy would be crucial in mothering. And, as much as I can assess these things, it has often been a helpful and loving approach to my children. Who wouldn't want to be a more empathic parent than those encountered in one's own exploration of some of the difficulties of childhood? It is loving to try to provide a better life for your children. So that was one way I understood my role as a mother.

In retrospect, I see that there are several difficulties in bringing such clinical experiences into family life. For example, it becomes hard to remember that I am not in clinical encounters with the broadest range of people. People come into my office in considerable pain and confusion that does not necessarily reflect society as a whole. I spend very defined time with them, and when they feel better, I say good-bye. This intimate and consistent exposure to suffering can be ameliorated in many ways, such as involvements with people and activities very separate from psychology. Nevertheless, the strain of listening to the pain of my patients, which I frequently attribute to the deficiencies of their families, takes its toll on my ability to have a more relaxed approach to my children's struggles. I have overempathized with their frustrations, as if without my acute attention to their troubles, they would collapse. This, in turn, sometimes leads to an escalating frustration between the child and myself. I'm listening too much, trying too hard, and turning my "therapeutic" approaches upside down, all of which may result in my being angry with a child who continues to resist my best efforts to lead him or her into a more perfect childhood.

Mothering (good enough or not), with its overwhelming love, uncertainties, and frustrations, does interact with my clinical work in ways that I believe can be ultimately helpful. The professional challenge is how to tolerate and integrate aspects of my parenting experiences and yet remain sufficiently neutral to these conflicts in my patients so that I can see the similarities and differences between their experiences and mine with equanimity. Along the way, however, there are humbling and confusing encounters. Sometimes, I am less respectful of the wishes and fears of my own children than those of my patients. Another issue concerns power and control as I struggle to set limits with my children, without the benefit of the clarity of the therapeutic agreement. These issues are often reminders of how my clinical wisdom can be far removed from my home life. For example, the clarity of the therapeutic agreement, with its consequences of payment for time, helps me contain the acting-out of my patients better than the sometimes erratically administered consequences for my children when they are late for school.

Being a participant and an observer in therapeutic change, while mysterious in its own ways, gives me opportunities to feel more competent, more compassionate and more knowledgeable than in everyday family life. Going to the office (besides being a relief at times from the confusing demands of family life) is an opportunity to relearn how useful consistent listening can be. Family life seems to move at a more unpredictable pace than therapeutic work. Learning to respect the resistances, fears, and differences in my children is a greater challenge than understanding and responding to these issues in clinical work. It is both useful and humbling to see how difficult and complex the balancing of needs within a family can be.

Parent blaming has diminished since I have come to know how easy it is to feel too overwhelmed to handle a child's demands. For example, a 38-year-old mother of three came to my office asking for an evaluation and treatment for one of her daughters, almost the same age as my youngest child. Her child's symptoms were partially attributable to a serious physical trauma early in life. This woman's marriage and family life were very different from mine, but her daughter's accident evoked for me easily aroused fears about my own children's safety. This was no doubt communicated through my questions. They indicated my concern in her available support (marital, extended family, and friends), and her evaluation of her daughter's subsequent medical care. I asked about issues ranging from the family's functioning to her own inner experiences of these events. It seemed useful to me, as well as inevitable, that I should communicate my understanding of how tiring mothering could be and my concern that she was doing so much parenting alone. My own internal self-inquiry (how would I feel about this injury to my child; is this clarifying or confusing my understanding of her responses?) blended with my previous clinical knowledge to inform my questions and responses to her.

I hoped to discover with her what her understanding was of the choices and events in her life and her family's life.

This patient would usually enter my office with a rushed, self-conscious smile. It was difficult to make eye contact with her, although once she began to fill me in on the latest changes or lack of changes in her child's life, she became more relaxed. I usually listened for quite a while and then attended to what seemed to be her major concerns. The primary focus of our work together was on the specifics of her fears and her efforts to bring change to herself, her traumatized child, and her family. My understanding as a mother of the need for hope, and the feeling of drowning in the negatives of a difficult family situation were central in establishing a working alliance and an empathic lens for our work.

Has my clinical work been enhanced by the experiences of motherhood? Yes, it has. Despite the fears and denial that I continue to find in myself, I believe that mothering and other aspects of family and community life are now the cutting edge of my personal growth thus adding to my clinical skills. I also believe that my clinical work brings important knowledge to my family life; that is, the inevitability of suffering and the immense healing capacities of compassion for myself and my family.

REFERENCES

Chodorow, N. (1978). *The reproduction of mothering.* Berkeley: University of California Press.

Kohut, H., & Wolfe, E. (1978). The disorders of the self and their treatment: An outline. In P. R. Ornstein (Ed.), *The search for the self: Selected writings of Heinz Kohut: 1978–1981* (Vol. 3, pp. 359–386). Madison, CT: International Universities Press.

MacNab, S. (1989). Countertransference in psychodynamic family therapy with children. In J. Zilbach (Ed.), *Children in family therapy: Treatment and training.* New York: Haworth Press.

CHAPTER 4

Geropsychology: How the Venerable Leave Us Vulnerable

MICHELE STEINBERG, PhD and MICHAEL J. SALAMON, PhD

When she walks into your waiting room, dressed to the nines, a little too proud and defiant, you can feel her anxiety. She is trailed by at least one, sometimes two children who, under other circumstances, are doctors, lawyers, and captains of industry. Today these mature responsible adults seem defeated; they plead with her to be open-minded and to consider options. It is 45 minutes before your scheduled appointment and you listen to the muffled echoes of exasperation through the wall.

On particularly difficult days, you wish you were in the waiting room. Their "mom" is your mom, or your grandmother. Her problems and the children's problems uncomfortably mirror your own, and you are often asked to advise a family on how to deal with conflicts that you yourself have been at a loss to deal with in your own family.

As she enters your office, her resistance is quite clear in her suspicious glance and tone. She is resistant because you are a "head doctor," and she knows she is not crazy. Her children have convinced her to give you a shot, and to placate them, she will. And, that is just what she expects to receive from you, a shot, a quick "cure" for her troubles, both emotional and physical. She answers your initial questions guardedly and then blurts out, "What could such a young doctor possibly understand about an old woman's problems?" and later, "I'm going to have to pay you for just talking?"

We are geropsychologists. The preceding vignette hints at some of the difficulties we face in our day to day interactions with the oldest patient population. With our patients, we glance into a mirror that resembles our future, or perhaps our parents' present situation. We are forced to examine some of life's most challenging issues—disability, death, and spirituality. Our ability to work through uncomfortable countertransference reactions is tested, and since this is a relatively new field, we often lack a supportive forum where we can share our concerns. Here we will explore some of the many challenges we have encountered during our geropsychological practice.

MOTIVATIONS FOR WORKING WITH THE ELDERLY

What motivates a therapist to work with aging patients? For some, current practice has simply been the result of circumstance. In the late 1970s and early 1980s, employment opportunities in the field expanded rapidly as funding became available to perform research and provide clinical intervention with this rapidly growing segment of the population. Many therapists during this time simply jumped on the bandwagon. Our own reasons, however, are likely more typical of practicing geropsychologists. Even in the earliest stages of our education, we were steered by a special interest in the emotional well-being of older people. For both of us, special bonds were formed with older members of our family during our earliest development. Perhaps the most telling aspect of our backgrounds is that we both had grandparents actively involved in child rearing.

Relationships with grandparents and the choice of later work are highlighted by Michael's personal experience. His first professional position as a psychologist was in the nursing home where his grandmother had lived several years earlier. The pull to accept the job outweighed the impulse to avoid unresolved issues. He felt an intense desire to be in the home, and the experience did allow him the opportunity to work through intrapsychic conflict. In Michele's case, her grandmother lived with her while growing up. Her grandmother was very active socially, and Michele's home was often filled with elders engaging in a wide range of activities. These friends helped her develop an ease in interacting with older persons and an interest in their lives.

We are both aware that a motivating factor in work with older clients is the often unconscious desire to serve as a rescuer to a group of individuals who are largely underserved. Although things have improved slightly for practitioners interested in the field, with universities now offering courses on gerontology and geropsychology, there was virtually no information and limited interest in working with this population when we began our careers. In fact, there was widespread pessimism dating back to Freud (1906/1956) about the ability of older persons to respond to psychotherapy. Michele recalls making the decision to work with older adults specifically because very few other clinicians were. She was energized by the idea of pioneering work with this population, seeing it as an opportunity actively to alleviate some of the suffering she had witnessed.

The university where Michael obtained his graduate degree primarily emphasized work with children and their families. The program's director, however, recognized geropsychology as an up-and-coming subspecialty and encouraged him to pursue research and training in this area. Likewise, Michele's advisors, while for the most part lacking experience with an older population, were supportive of her efforts to self-educate.

Among our fellow graduate students, we were both alone in our interest in aging. Although at times this proved isolating when clinical issues about aging arose, we were placed in the role of resident expert. This provided us with significant reinforcement and helped to bolster our desire to work with the aged. Employment opportunities were available when our careers were beginning, specifically because there was a shortage of interested and experienced geropsychologists. It was, at the time, easy to develop relationships with organizations providing services to the aged. For example, after offering free lectures on mental health to senior citizen centers, we rapidly received referrals for a variety of psychological services.

The reasons for choosing a subspecialty are varied and multidetermined. Our informal discussions with colleagues and supervisees, however, lead us to believe that grandparent influence, coupled with a drive toward pioneering, is a powerful motivator toward choosing to work in the field of aging.

COUNTERTRANSFERENCE ISSUES

It has been well documented that therapists approach the therapeutic situation with their own conscious and unconscious conflicts. The most successful therapists have an in-depth understanding of their personal issues and are sensitive to how these might interface with patient dynamics.

As with younger patients, therapists' countertransference reactions to older patients run the gamut; but some responses are unique to this population. In supervising other therapists and monitoring our own reactions, we have found countertransference reactions to be of two types. The first type represents responses to the very real characteristics of the aged patient. The patient may stimulate the therapist's conflicts about relationships with parental figures and cause a reenactment of parent/child or grandparent/grandchild conflicts. The patients' age, too, may stimulate fear about the therapist's own or a parent's aging. The very choice to work with this population may indeed, as Sobel (1980) notes, involve a counterphobic wish to master the fear of aging.

The second type of countertransference reaction has to do with the modifications in technique that accompany work with the older population. For example, work with the sensory impaired often requires the therapist to get physically close to the patient, which for a variety of reasons can be quite uncomfortable. A patient's emotional or physical disability often requires that therapists become involved in concrete services that would typically be avoided with a younger population. This may evoke a feeling in the therapist of being needed excessively, highlighting the therapist's own issues with dependency. These countertransference issues will be discussed in detail in the following sections.

Reenactment of Grandparent/Grandchild Conflicts

Working with an older patient, easily evokes memories and feelings about the therapist's own relationship with grandparents. The pull to slip into the role of adored grandchild may be tempting. The desire to intervene on behalf of a beloved grandparent can be compelling, particularly if one felt powerless to do so as a child. The therapist may experience frustration when a patient resists this role and is neither lovable nor adoring; the unconscious echoes "Grandmother would never be quite so demanding, or ungrateful, or aggressive . . ."

To preserve the image of the patient as benevolent grandparent, the therapist may avoid appropriate interpretation. Both of us have, at times, found it difficult to confront an older patient on a salient issue for fear of evoking an angry or rejecting response. While we may acknowledge a particular patient's dependency as manipulative, we may still have difficulty confronting her for fear of losing the role of all loving, all giving therapist/granddaughter. There is at the same time an unconscious desire on the part of the therapist to maintain a grandmotherly image of the patient by ignoring or even denying the manipulation: "Let's not upset grandmother."

The grandparent/grandchild conflict often manifests for the therapist as a rescue fantasy. Children, when confronted with ill grandparents, express feelings of being overwhelmed and powerless. Such children want to prevent grandparents from having to face hospitalization (or nursing home placement) or want to help them remember things they are no longer remembering. Rescue fantasies of these kind do not necessarily end in childhood but may lay dormant until reevoked during therapeutic contact with an ill older person. For those of us with histories of watching a grandparent deteriorate, psychotherapy can stimulate the desire to undo a terminal situation. We have, at times, become too emotionally involved with a patient or overidentified with their plight, coloring interpretations and interventions. Overidentification can easily result in a fostering of unnecessary dependency and can lead to crossing boundaries, which is no longer therapeutic. As powerful therapists, by "saving" the patient, we unconsciously save our grandmothers and grandfathers.

Stimulation of Fears about Aging

Working with an older population often leads to fantasies of what our own parents might be like at our patient's age. Particularly, frail older patients may make us anxious for our parents' future. Likewise, robust patients may stimulate a wishful-thinking image of our parents' future. We have both found that we view different patients at different ages as examples of what our own parents might be like as they get older. When first meeting a new patient, it is not uncommon for the therapist to think, "This is what my dad might look like 10 years from now." Michele's recent contact with a disabled older woman who physically resembled her deceased mother evoked a strange sense of relief that her mother would avoid many of the plights of aging. Michele, at times, notices that particular patients with characteristics similar to her mother evoke a desire to ease them through this transition of aging in a way in which she will not be able to do for her own mother. Working with older women allows her to make reparations in the area of loss and giving.

A drawback in working with older persons is our deep understanding of the perils of aging in our society. We are acutely aware of the changes in social status, economics, and physical health that accompany aging. This knowledge heightens our desire to control, or at least delay, our own aging process. We both admit to fantasies of mitigating these changes. And, while we have not yet found the fountain of youth, we actively project a strong and vibrant image of ourself into the future and aspire to do things differently than our clients. We frequently view ourselves 20, 30, and even 40 years down the road and imagine what we might look like and be at that time. Michael imagines a guitar in the office—for him a symbol of his youth—while Michele visualizes herself as strong and active with her hair in a long gray braid.

This response to aging also has an impact in our present. We are both very aware of our defensive reactions toward ageist comments. We share a hypervigilance to negative stereotypes and are often upset by the media's insensitivity to aging. At cocktail parties, we are polite to the individual who refers to older people in derogatory terms, but we have, in general, very little tolerance for professionals, especially our colleagues, who perpetuate stereotypes and spread misinformation about the appropriateness of therapeutic training and intervention with the older population.

Adjusting to Patients with Sensory Loss

There are certain givens about therapy that therapists learn early in their training. It is understood, for example, that therapists sit at a reasonable distance from their patients while conducting psychotherapy. And, for the most part, regardless of orientation, touching patients is considered inappropriate. These rules certainly serve an important purpose, as they create a safe environment that allows the patient the freedom to express innermost concerns without worry of uncomfortable levels of intimacy. At the same time, these rules help the therapist maintain an appropriate emotional distance.

The practice of geropsychology requires the therapist to abandon many aspects of treatment that are taken for granted with other populations. Patients often present with sensory impairments that stretch the therapist's ability to remain flexible. Michele vividly remembers her inner struggle as she moved her seat closer and closer to her first hard-of-hearing patient. She was forced to acknowledge that the struggle was not only about how appropriate the action was from a clinical point of view but about exactly how emotionally close she wanted to get to her patients and, by extension, to people in general.

The necessity of modifying techniques to suit the individual patient is perhaps the greatest challenge for the therapist working with the elderly. Training often emphasizes the efficacy of a particular orientation, and there is often little emphasis on creativity and flexibility within its confines. Having to abandon mainstream techniques can cause the therapist quite a bit of anxiety and worry. We both struggled with the issue of whether or not to touch patients. Often, it is not only appropriate to touch older patients, but treatment could not take place otherwise. For example, in ongoing therapy with a blind 96-year-old woman with severe Parkinson's disease, Michele had to hold the patient's hands during sessions to control her violent shaking. In other cases, especially with blind physically disabled patients, touching their shoulder or arm to provide reassurance is important. Therapists working with the very old need to learn to trust their instincts in these situations and this can be quite frightening, particularly for a beginning therapist trying to "go by the book."

Reactions to Exaggerated Dependency Needs

The final countertransference reaction we will discuss involves reactions to the increased dependency needs of older patients. Because many older adults presenting in treatment have suffered multiple losses and/or physical illness, they often exhibit exaggerated dependency needs. They may look for the therapist to fill the role of recently lost supportive friends and family, and may request assistance in managing daily activities.

At times, it is appropriate to indulge rather than interpret these needs so that crucial ego functioning can be reestablished and a patient's anxiety can be lessened. This can be quite uncomfortable, particularly for a psychodynamic therapist who may feel that supportive techniques are less "real" than insightful interventions. Serving a supportive function can arouse anxiety in the therapist, especially one who harbors unexpressed dependency needs. As Sobel (1980) indicated, underlying this anxiety regarding meeting the real needs of the patient is often the primitive but universal fear that to indulge another is to deplete oneself. Therapists with this unconscious dynamic often feel drained and depleted when working with this population.

What is interesting to note is that although these patients may evoke feelings about being excessively needy, they frequently view consistent appointments as unnecessary and will cancel without hesitation should the session coincide with a "real doctor's" appointment or inclement weather. This inconsistency can anger the therapist who unconsciously yearns for appreciation and acknowledgment of increased efforts. It is also possible for therapists to overindulge a patient's dependency needs because this stimulates their own infantile wish to control and/or dominate the patient/parent. In either case, the therapist is forced to confront powerful feelings both from the past and the present that affect the treatment process.

DEATH AND MORTALITY

In our society, there is an ingrained connection between aging, deterioration, and dying. This connection is debilitating and fosters unnecessary morbid expectations for what has the potential to be an exciting and vibrant time of life. Growing old is not synonymous with dying. There is something to be said for the cliche "growing old gracefully"—to see the later part of life as a fluid dance, perhaps slower, but nonetheless filled with both deliberate creation and spontaneous growth.

Because of the ingrained association between aging and disease and/or death, older patients often present with concerns about mortality. Patients may seek therapy because they or a relative are terminally ill, or because recognition of aging has evoked fears related to death and dying. Some patients are afraid of death itself; more are afraid of the possible circumstances surrounding death. This being the case, it is imperative that therapists come to terms with their own mortality so they may create a safe environment for expression of fears and concerns.

In supervising other therapists, both of us have witnessed their anxiety about the subject of death interfering with appropriate exploration of the topic. This manifests most frequently in what the therapist does not say or avoids asking. Sometimes a therapist may unknowingly shift a conversation to a less threatening topic or ignore subtle cues from the patient that express an unspoken concern about dying. This general discomfort with death may indeed play a role in the well-documented reluctance on the part of most therapists to work with older patients (Garfinkle, 1975; Kastenbaum, 1963). In Poggi and Berland's (1985) summary of reasons therapists avoid contact with older patients, they cite the fear of patients dying during treatment as a contributing factor. The death of a patient may be experienced by the therapist as a painful narcissistic blow, or it may stimulate the therapist's own fears of aging and death.

Certainly, it is difficult when a patient dies during the treatment process, and therapists working with an older population are more likely to experience this than those working with a younger population. Reactions to a death will vary based on the therapist's relationship with the patient, the length and intensity of treatment, and the therapist's own issues relative to loss. Lardaro (1989), in her survey of 22 patients who had died during therapy, found that guilt was a common reaction among therapists. We have noticed that after a patient dies, therapists often scrutinize the course of treatment and wonder whether they were inadequate as a therapist, or even contributed in some way to the death. In cases where a patient died before resolving key issues, therapists may imagine that had they been a bit more insightful or empathic, the patient could have died with a greater sense of closure. Therapists may also become guilt ridden over whether their focus on particular problems or their timing of interpretations during sessions were too painful for the patient and therefore contributed in some measure to the death. This reaction seems more common in therapists who have unresolved issues related to aggression, while the former reaction appears to be more common in therapists who have pronounced rescue fantasies.

For both patient and therapist, developing a healthy relationship with actual death and death-related issues, in a death-phobic society, is not easy. As previously discussed, the therapists' personal experience with death will influence their understanding and level of comfort when dealing with death-related material in the therapeutic setting. Michele was confronted with death early in her career, and this had a profound effect on the way she relates to her older patients. While she was a second-year graduate student in her early 20s, her mother became terminally ill. She took a leave of absence to be with her during her illness and death. The experience, while extremely painful, was also pivotal to the course of her life. She and her mother prepared for their loss together and both grew stronger and more appreciative of life. She began to recognize the creative potential for growth and change during the death process and, as a result, now views death as a transition that can transform both the dying person and those around the dying person.

The necessity of being able to focus on positive aspects of death, and being willing to explore death-related issues when working with this population, cannot be overstated. A healthy relationship with death is crucial to living the remainder of life with meaning and purpose. As geropsychologists, it is imperative that we become strong role models for fearful elders.

On a final note, it is worth mentioning that patients exploring feelings and fantasies about death and dying often begin examining religious and spiritual beliefs and ideals as well. This in itself is often a most difficult topic for therapists to explore. There has been, for the most part, a conspiracy of silence surrounding the topic of examining religious and spiritual issues in therapy, and few clinical forums teach therapists to establish an open and genuine dialogue about spiritual issues (Cohen, 1992). There is often an air of suspicion and condescension about psychological practice that includes a spiritual focus. Because of this, geropsychologists must chart new ground in therapy, as well as explore their personal beliefs, in an effort to understand their clients.

CONCLUSION

We have shared some of the challenges and obstacles we have faced as geropsychologists. These include feelings that arise as a result of our patients' advanced age and the modifications in technique this requires, as well as the recognition of our own and others' mortality. This is unlike working with any other age group. At times, we are frightened by the exploration of uncharted ground and our intimate knowledge of how difficult it is to grow old in the United States.

Although the challenges are numerous, there are many sources of gratification for the geropsychologist. The richness of the learning experience and the potential for easing a patient through this final known frontier provide us with more than the usual amount of satisfaction. Geropsychology also offers an arena for mastery of the social and personal traumas of aging and allows us to give more than the usual vent to our desire to heal and nurture. The sense of accomplishment we feel when older people leave treatment claiming to feel better than they have throughout their entire lives is tremendous. We have also made our own transition to the final stage of life that much easier.

REFERENCES

Cohen, P. (1992). A chronicle of the psychotherapy and the spirit program. *Seeds of Unfolding, 9*(3), 4–8.

Freud, S. (1956). On psychotherapy. In J. Riviere (Ed. and Trans.), *Collected papers* (Vol. I, pp. 246–263). London: Hogarth Press. (Original work published 1906)

Garfinkle, R. (1975). The reluctant therapist in 1975. *The Gerontologist, 5*(2), 136–137.

Kastenbaum, R. (1963). The reluctant therapist. *Geriatrics, 18,* 296–301.

Lardaro, T. A. (1989). Till death do us part: Reactions of therapists to the deaths of elderly patients in psychotherapy. *The Gerontologist, 8,* 173–176.

Poggi, R. G., & Berland, D. I. (1985). The therapist's reactions to the elderly. *The Gerontologist, 25*(5), 508–513.

Sobel, E. (1980). Countertransference issues with the later life patient. *Contemporary Psychoanalysis, 16*(2), 211–222.

CHAPTER 5

The Therapist as Patient in Interminable Treatment: A Parallel Process

CONSTANCE SELIGMAN, MSW, ACSW

Psychotherapists are particularly vulnerable to becoming interminable patients of other psychotherapists. Armed with the rationale of professional growth and suffering from the occupational hazard of giving to the point of depletion, we find reason after reason to avoid the wrenching process of separation and individuation that marks the successful completion of treatment. As long as we avoid loss, we bypass a significant developmental experience for ourselves: In avoiding loss we also avoid growth. As we postpone our own painful separation process, we both permit and encourage our patients to do the same. We perpetuate a fantasy of a magical perfect cure that lies at the end of a rainbow called "enough therapy."

However valuable and useful, even necessary, treatment is, a major hazard for the therapist who is also in psychotherapy is believing that all problems might be solved in treatment *if one continues for long enough.* Any problems not yet solved are tabled to address at some more opportune time. This is clearly a prescription for interminable treatment. The blissful hope instilled by this kind of thinking comes at great cost.

For our patients, individuation and independence are sacrificed because they cannot separate from the therapist until the magical "perfect cure" is effected. They develop unrealistic, inflated expectations of themselves, of us as their therapists, and of everyone in their surround.

Practitioners meanwhile burden themselves with superhuman expectations, cheat themselves out of successes, and feel compelled to return to their own therapy to restore the psychic balance that these mind-sets disturb. The template of unrealistic transference expectations can be inflicted on the therapist's personal relationships, causing collisions that add further grist to the proverbial mill.

Therapists are strongly encouraged to be patients, not only so they can cultivate empathy for the patient's position, but also in the belief that this experience allows them to sort out their own personal issues lest they become confused with those of the patient. However, the circumstance of therapist-as-patient produces it own set of issues and problems. The following comments address those issues and my experience with them.

Therapists who are themselves in endless therapy and come to believe in its necessity rationalize, ignore, or, at best, fail to examine how seductive therapy can be. Because therapy can be a mutually rewarding experience for patient and therapist (Sussman, 1992), there is a temptation to sustain it past the point of therapeutic value. McWilliams (1987) describes this predicament elegantly: "An analysis is too long when the amount of learning that is happening in the therapeutic relationship is outweighed by the amount of infantilization occurring" (p. 94).

Being in therapy can be gratifying—it certainly was for me—and the profession provides many rationales for that gratification. My favorite rationale for staying in therapy was to view treatment as a means of keeping my unconscious open to communications from that of my patient; this made my own therapy a requirement of practice. But although I used my work as my rationale for staying in treatment, the real reason was that I liked being in therapy.

While I was in therapy I enjoyed the attention my therapist provided me, which I didn't get from my own distracted parents. I became addicted to this attention, and to keep it, I remained in the role of the dependent one, needing validation and almost by definition feeling insufficient. I pathologized myself to remain in treatment. Negative feelings became symptoms to be overcome. Wellness, once a goal, eluded me while I confused it with a utopia of freedom from all negative feelings or distasteful situations. My dependency needs were gratified rather than processed, for my therapist shared in my illusions.

To counterbalance this dependency, I became a therapist. In this way, I internalized my therapist. (If all proceeds as it should, internalization should allow one to separate from the therapist. But if one has internalized a symbiotic therapist, it is impossible to proceed to the next stage.) Now I have become a source of gratification for my own patients. But while using my patients to satisfy my own needs to be important, I was depriving them of a developmental experience. While forestalling the inevitable moment of separation, I colluded with a kind of denial of reality.

I did not grieve the deficiency of attention in my own past because I did not feel it; I had appended my therapist as a constant source of the missing goods. This meant that I did not complete the painful work of separation for myself.

I therefore stopped expecting my patients to do the work of separation and grieving while I participated in the omnipotent fantasy that I could be the parent they never had. So I kept trying, and failing. And then, I would find myself back in my own therapy because I had become so depleted in this effort.

The fantasy of a magical cure affects therapists in three ways. In our own lives, we become burdened with unrealistic expectations of what we can achieve and what we must accept. Our work with patients suffers because we pass on to them the same expectations. Ultimately, living in a fantasy contaminates all our relationships.

When I had unrealistic expectations of my own treatment, I expected unrealistic levels of cure from my patients' treatment. As this eluded me, my feelings of failure returned me to my own treatment to help me cope. McWilliams (1987) describes "the possibility of a collusion between the analyst's omnipotent strivings and the patient's infantile wishes for either a perfect parent or an ultimately perfect self" (p. 96). I've come to believe that a cure cannot be effected while the therapist is the longed-for source of "the goods." Healing can come only by living through the pain of saying good-bye in an atmosphere of compassion and understanding.

I had had 20 years of personal therapy when I became involved with an accelerated model of psychodynamic therapy. (Those 20 years were not wasted; I learned to do everything except leave.) Prompted partly by my husband (who referred to me as a "therapy addict") and partly by the demands of this model, I began to face the necessity of ending treatment. The anxiety of loss was with me from the first day of this treatment and became a significant focus of it, along with the self-sabotaging defenses I employed to avoid it. What healed me? Facing the loss, not only of my therapist, but of the string of fantasies that I came to believe would signify my complete and total cure.

As I've faced the termination of my own therapy, I've been struggling with the question of how to work from my unconscious without the benefit of being in personal psychotherapy. Interestingly, some colleagues questioned the idea that therapy should ever end. The notion of endless therapy has disturbing implications for me. Besides liberating me from that hazard, separation has provided its own benefits. Terminating has allowed me to feel a kind of grief that I never felt while my therapist provided the good-enough mothering that I had lacked growing up. And with that grief came a kind of exuberance that I like to imagine is similar to the individuation process when rapprochement proceeds in a good-enough way.

Since I have been out of therapy, some surprising things have happened. I still feel afraid of loss, but I know now that I will be able to *survive* loss. This has helped me to face and appreciate reality. My therapist is not the mother or father I never had. I never had nor will I ever have the parent I never had. Therapy should help us to understand what was missing, but it cannot reverse the loss of what we missed. Good therapy can help us to overcome those deficits that arise from faulty parenting. Just as paying for therapy helps us realize that we have to purchase what we did not receive from our parents, termination helps us to realize in a final and painful way what we will never receive. This confrontation with reality taught me that no matter how hard I tried I could not remake the past and I had better learn to adapt myself to it.

When I see my patients struggling with this, I remember how hard I fought this fact for years. For most of my life, my ideal of a husband was a man who could hold me when I cried. I married a man who is honest, who loves me, and brings out the best in me, but who would generally prefer to be in the next room when I cry. How hard I used to insist he be different! How bitter those struggles when he could not. I think the fantasy of being totally understood and accepted (as I felt myself to be by my therapist) in some way prolonged the illusion that one could indeed have it all, and it fed my omnipotence that I could make it happen.

The knowledge that we must ultimately let go forces us to learn how to survive discomfort and how to comfort ourselves. As this happens, we come to have different expectations for what clients can achieve. Together with them, we can tolerate their disappointments. We can be with them, but for the most part we cannot undo their pain. As we become grounded in reality, we become more effective as therapists. The paradox is that we can be of more help as we realize how little we can do.

REFERENCES

McWilliams, N. (1987). The grandiose self and the interminable analysis. *Current Issues in Psychoanalytic Practice, 4,* 93–107.

Sussman, M. B. (1992). *A curious calling: Unconscious motivations for practicing psychotherapy.* Northvale, NJ: Jason Aronson.

PART TWO

The Therapist's Own Ailments

CHAPTER 6

The Journey of the Characterologic Therapist

NORMAN F. SHUB, LISW, BCD

INTRODUCTION TO THE CHARACTER CONCERNS OF THE THERAPIST

Sarah came to me because of my reputation for doing depth therapy, looking for someone she could "trust and feel safe with." After several good sessions, Sarah eagerly accepted my suggestion that she read a brief paper I had written. I told her that I would give it to her at the next session, but I forgot, and when she asked me about it, I froze and lied to her, saying that I had already mailed it. At the following session, Sarah again asked about the paper. I said it must have been lost in the mail, but I would get it for her as soon as possible, which I never did. Later, Sarah once again confronted me, saying that, although the therapy was helpful, she was hurt because she had never received the paper. I told myself that Sarah was making a big deal out of nothing, but she soon withdrew from therapy. My rigid character was the issue.

Character—or characterologic or personality—disorders have long been labeled hard to diagnose and treat and highly resistant to change (Millon, 1981). From the early psychiatric literature (English & Finch, 1956) until today, many clinicians and researchers remain profoundly pessimistic about the prognosis for changing rigid characters, and thus many therapists avoid working with characterologically disordered clients. Even Millon, the harbinger of new times for characterologic individuals, notes, "Personality patterns are deeply embedded and pervasive, and are likely to persist, essentially unmodified, over long periods of time—usually a lifetime" (1981, p. 10).

This chapter explores my struggle as a therapist in dealing with my own character problems as they affect my life and my treatment of clients. I know that struggle well. None of my work with my first four therapists—all wonderful individuals—helped me to focus on my character problems. My therapy focused on early childhood experiences and the impact of my upbringing on the way I felt about myself. I was not aware of how my rigid character narrowed my options for responding to the environment and made me continually interact in the same formulaic manner, thus causing myself and those around me great distress and pain. I was only aware that I continued to do self-destructive things that caused trouble. How can someone struggle to change something he or she is unaware of? Without belaboring the point, I was aware of the things I was doing, but I was not aware of my overall character problem. If a client such as myself is not clear about what the issue really is and if the therapist does not help the client focus on the character as the main problem, then it is impossible to ultimately develop healthier contact with the environment. This was a serious problem for me, and it remains a serious problem for other characterologic therapists as well.

Largely unexplored in the literature are such questions as: What happens to therapists with character disorders? What happens to therapists whose primary personal issues are lodged in their rigid manner of interacting with the environment? Obvious and blatant characterologic symptoms can elicit a negative response from professionals, clients, and the community. Various character structures embody different core traits. Sociopathic, histrionic, narcissistic, and other more obvious character structures are going to elicit more obviously negative judgments. Softer character structures, such as passive-aggressive, dependent, avoidant, and infantile, while not creating the more obvious external problems, cause the same kind of difficulties in the therapeutic relationship. The stigma attached to characterologic individuals (Fiske & Maddi, 1961) that labels them as hurtful, insensitive, self-centered and selfish has caused some therapists to utterly reject the notion that a characterologic person could even consider entering the psychotherapy profession.

Although little has been written about the characterologic therapist, my clinical and workshop experience has introduced me to many individuals besides myself who struggle with these issues:

- Some have only a vague notion that something is wrong; they cannot quite determine what it is.
- Some are aware of their specific self-destructive or difficult behaviors but do not have a clear sense of how to struggle with these behaviors.

- Some suffer but have not been able to find therapists with treatment models that would really help them.
- Still others have successfully identified their character problem, have become aware of the issues, and have worked incredibly hard to change.

The amount of effort required to really change character is enormous. Encountering these individuals is always a joy, as well as a relief. As I have traveled the United States, many therapists have pulled me aside to confide their own characterologic concerns. I possess no hard data to support my hypothesis, but I am convinced that the problem is significant and that, were it more openly and publicly discussed, more individuals would come forward.

In dealing with my own issues and also in treating other therapists with character problems, I have recognized how my process of character change has impacted my life, my work, my reputation, my ability to function in the community and my interactions with family, colleagues, and clients. In this discussion, I will address a number of specific concerns:

1. I hope to raise the consciousness of therapists with character problems and to make them more aware of the overall problem of character structure, its inflexibility, and the potential damage to themselves and clients caused by lack of treatment.
2. I hope to raise the sensitivity level in the mental health profession to therapists with character problems who are struggling to change.
3. I hope to be clear and forthright about the potential damage done to paying clients when the therapist's character interferes with the treatment process.
4. I hope to begin to negate the stigmatizing of all individuals, not just therapists, who struggle with character concerns and to create a more optimistic sense of what is possible in terms of character change.

Because all therapists bring their own issues to the workplace, personal psychotherapy is an essential part of every therapist's training and preparation. Characterologic individuals, however, often experience difficulty obtaining personal psychotherapy because the mental health profession in general tends to not diagnose purely characterologic concerns. Therapists also tend to avoid taking on characterologic therapists as clients because they may be apprehensive about being affected by them or about being able to foster change. Many therapists I have encountered in my training tend to avoid treating characterologic individuals in general because of countertransferential responses. Therapists treating a rigid or nonidentified character problem can experience frustration, anger, and other emotional responses, all of which can engender a feeling of incompetence. Also, many therapists, because they lack understanding or a clear model, feel unable to help affect change in a character structure. Not having an effective or adequate treatment model or adequate training in character work leaves many therapists without the tools and methodology to affect change in these difficult clients. Further, because of the countertransferential feelings and the perceived inflexibility of the characterologic client, many therapists retain the simplistic notion that somehow they may be tainted by associating with too many such people. This notion may sound preposterous, but individuals in workshops and elsewhere have often reported this opinion to me. Klein (1971) and other researchers have also validated the existence of this phenomenon in the mental health profession.

As a training therapist, workshop leader, and consultant, I am amazed by the ferociously negative attitudes toward characterologic individuals expressed in professional settings. I often hear statements like the following:

"In our agency, we don't treat personality disorders."

"I don't take that kind of patient."

"If you put down an Axis II diagnosis, our company won't reimburse."

"What's the point of seeing them? They don't change anyway."

"I don't have the energy."

"I don't like doing this kind of work."

"I don't know how to work with them. They take forever, and they never seem to get better."

"I don't see many characterologic disorders in my practice."

"I'm confused about how to diagnose these types of people anyway."

When faced with such attitudes, we can easily understand why therapists with characterologic concerns find it difficult to locate therapists who are competent to treat them.

THE WORD "CHARACTER"

I prefer the word "character" to the word "personality"—which can be misunderstood (Millon, 1981)—because character calls to mind specific and vivid traits and ways of relating to the world. Character is the stylistic way individuals interact with their environment (Shub, 1992). Character disorder implies rigid traits that limit an individual's options for coping with various situations in the world. In my lexicon, a characterologic problem implies a sameness, an inflexible way in which individuals interact across all aspects of their existence—with partners, families, children, church, work, and professional associates. These rigid character traits are evident to the others who participate in all areas of a person's life.

Professionals report that "traditional" treatment seldom helps clients with narcissistic, histrionic, schizoidal and other entrenched character problems. I believe that, on their own, it is nearly impossible for such people to change their deeply embedded style of relating to the world until they understand their character's impact, are confronted with the need to change, and develop the tools to make that change. Like many of these individuals, I wanted to make these changes. I just did not know how.

MY CHARACTER

My family of origin was extremely dysfunctional and did not reinforce such positive character traits in me as honesty, responsibility, and sensitivity or the abilities to follow through or to invest in others. From the age of three, I retain powerful memories of my father's mistrust of the world. In delicatessens, he would order me to go behind the counter and check that the scale weighing our purchases registered the same number on the back and front. He believed that gas station meters were fixed. Confronted with his mistakes, he denied responsibility, evaded the question, or lied. I have hundreds of memories of observing his inflexible, characterologic way of relating to stressful situations in the outside world and of being expected to emulate this characterologic way of being.

In further clarifying my character development, I see three major influences. The first was that my parents viewed the world as dangerous, suspicious, and fraught with potential harm. The second was that important character traits not only were not reinforced but they were not modeled—an important interactive process in developing a flexible character—so that I could experience the many different ways of responding to situations in life. For example, in stressful situations, my father always lied. I never heard him admit he was wrong, tell the truth, or say he wanted to talk about something; nor did I ever see him take partial responsibility or demonstrate remorse. I saw the same rigid behaviors day after day rather than a continuum of behaviors representing each trait. The third factor was that no attempt was made to encourage me to explore the range of possible responses to a character trait. When I lied about being wrong, I never experienced a consequence. I got away with it. So, as a way of coping, I learned to rely on this narrow point on the continuum of responsibility.

My childhood experience of the points on the honesty/dishonesty continuum was limited. I did not learn to explore any other responses when confronted with my irresponsible acts. Slowly, my character and world view rigidified so that I did not trust others. I was not willing to be vulnerable, honest, open with my feelings, and therefore, establishing positive relationships became extremely difficult. My range of responses to life situations became narrower and narrower. Beginning in adolescence, I evidenced great anger toward the external world and became unwilling to participate according to life's rules.

My mother, a schizophrenic, underwent multiple psychiatric hospitalizations as I grew up. I was constantly exposed to psychiatrists, psychologists, social workers, and other professionals who, my all-knowing dad told me, "didn't know shit." I felt forced to rely on and trust these professionals while my father was telling me, "Don't listen to *them.*"

In an attempt to resolve this confusion and show *them* up, I became interested in the mental health profession. My mother was not improving—was sinking deeper and deeper into her problems—and it seemed that nobody knew how to help. I needed to know why and decided I wanted to become a mental health professional myself so I could learn about problems like my mother's. Also, my father's constant criticism of the profession piqued my interest in it. If he disliked something, I liked it.

My behavior and attitudes, however, conflicted with my goal of being a therapist. Through my late adolescence and into young adulthood, my rigid character became manifest. Increasingly, I dealt with professional, personal, and social situations by lying, exaggerating, being insensitive and selfish, and generally evidencing an inability to respond to anyone emotionally. I did not understand what caring about another human being meant. I began to experience ongoing depression and anxiety over the isolation my behavior caused. I realized that I needed help and began to look for a therapeutic experience that would allow me to deal with the emotional cost of my rigid characterologic behavior. I was extremely unclear about character structure and acutely unaware of the diagnostic picture. I knew, however, that I was doing things that were self-destructive. Again, on some level, I knew that I performed insensitive and irresponsible actions. I thought that if I figured out why, I could stop.

My first therapy experience, at 18, was classically analytic. It brought insight, a great deal of pain and some relief, but it did not focus on my ability to function characterologically more effectively and less rigidly in the external world. I could not successfully engage in conventional insight-oriented or relationship therapy because, with my rigid behavior patterns, I needed to address my character issues before dealing with deeper questions of self. After years of therapy, I continued to lie, manipulate, be irresponsible and generally act in a rigidly characterologic style with my therapist and the other important people in my life.

I tried other therapists with different orientations, but therapy always led to examining my early childhood experiences. I believe that these models simply reinforced my lack of responsibility and supported my belief that the world had cheated me. No one confronted my character. No one helped me begin to understand that dishonesty, manipulation, arrogance, temper tantrums, and irresponsibility undermined the therapy experience and made progress virtually impossible. I needed help to understand this fact, which I could not see by myself. So I remained stuck.

Although early therapy produced little impact on my character, I remained eager to become a therapist, partly in hope of helping myself but also to assist others. As I realized that I was repeatedly doing things that upset clients, three facts became clear to me:

1. I suffered from a serious character problem that was not going to go away through understanding.
2. I was horrified to discover how I was hurting people I was supposed to be helping.
3. I saw that will alone—promising myself to be different—would not change this problem.

How could I continue to accept payment from people I was hurting? How could I continue to recognize myself as a psychotherapist when, in some situations, I was causing further damage?

I was finally motivated to begin examining my own character structure because of the concerned confrontations of my peers and clients and because of other undeniable and mounting factors: my lack of progress in therapy; the exposure of my self in the external world; increasing friend, client, and colleague awareness of my problems; and my behavior's impact on my marriage and family. Slowly, it dawned on me that I had a seriously rigid style of relating to the external world. I felt that being directly and actively involved in my own progress was important. Both the gentle confrontations of concerned friends and clients and the angry confrontations of disappointed and hurt friends and clients caused enough pain and discomfort to force me to look for a therapist with a tough reputation who at least would not let me off the hook. I found a highly respected and reputedly tough therapist who shared my concerns about my unsuccessful therapy and my inability to change. He did not confront the rigidity in my character structure in an organized, methodologically clear way, but he did bring the underlying issues to the fore and helped me struggle with them. He kept me in pain. He helped me focus on what I was doing to others. He stayed with me. Only then was I able to begin the journey to develop more flexibility.

I must note here that my abiding character problems obviously negatively affected my ongoing collegial relationships and my community reputation. Although many respected me as talented and bright, my rigidity and resultant behaviors constantly dragged me down and made my hopelessness increase. The problem seemed never ending. Before becoming aware of my rigid character, I was oblivious to much of the pain I was causing in others. After I recognized and worked to change my character, I realized that I had not lacked good will or a genuine concern for others. But, in my rigid approach to stressful situations, I manifested the destructive and insensitive behaviors that other people found unacceptable and that eventually led them to judge me harshly. A variety of mental health professionals even suggested that someone with my characterologic problems "didn't belong in the profession" and hinted that I should find something more suitable to my nature. To a lesser degree, such judgments remain alive for me today. One of my administrative staff recently told a professional colleague how much I had changed and how hard I was working. My colleague responded, "He'll never change; he can't change—all his therapy won't make a difference!" Knowing that such opinions still exist after I have worked so many years on these issues is disheartening.

Continuous negative, hurtful but true comments about my character and my pain over hurting peers and loved ones, coupled with my difficulty finding a therapist willing and able to help me with my concerns, contributed to a basic dilemma: If my character is manifest to the outside world, or even if it is not, should I try to deal with the issues involved and simultaneously remain in the mental health profession, knowing that the profession might provide little support? And how can I justify staying in a profession where I may hurt some of the individuals who pay me to help them? I will return to these questions.

STRUGGLING WITH CHARACTEROLOGIC CONCERNS

Characterologic therapists are continually confronted with a set of what sometimes seem to be insolvable dilemmas:

- When I was not aware of my character, I knew that sometimes I did hurtful, selfish, and dishonest things, but the extent to which I hurt others was not clear.
- Once I became aware of my character and saw how much I had hurt others, my pain increased as my awareness grew, and my desire to change became intense.
- Simultaneously, I realized that the struggle to change is a long-term one and that I was going to continue to hurt others along the way.
- I wanted to help others and be a therapist and did not want to give up the profession, but I felt judged and unsupported and not encouraged to struggle.
- I had to change for my own, my clients', and my family's sake. At the same time, I was in intense pain, was ashamed for my previous behavior, was trying to figure out what to do, and was generally confused about the state of my professional life.

When therapists come to think of themselves as unacceptable and when others regard them as such, their ability to maintain emotional stability while overcoming their character problems is compromised. The characterologic therapist may hesitate to take therapeutic risks and may live in constant fear of peer judgment. Obviously, being judged is not helpful, for we are already in pain and are ashamed of hurting others. Acknowledging that people with character concerns are good and worthwhile people who can change makes the struggle possible.

PHASES OF THE INNER STRUGGLE TO CHANGE CHARACTER

The Unaware Phase

At the onset of their professional careers, characterologic therapists struggle with many difficult issues and often find themselves in crises involving many of their personal and therapeutic relationships. Constantly reminded of their shortcomings and failings, they will never really escape—and they should not—the awareness that they behave in ways that both they and others find unacceptable. They sometimes experience great difficulty determining how to change these behaviors, and, when confronted with the fact that their behavior is not changing, they experience fear, pain, discouragement, and humiliation.

If such therapists seek treatment, the therapy seldom focuses on their character issues, which may remain largely unaddressed. Often they continue to hurt others with little awareness of their impact. Although they may develop pseudo self-esteem, feel better, and gain some insight and understanding, they repeatedly get themselves in trouble as they hit the wall of their rigid character. They know, if only subconsciously, that they are causing discomfort and pain. I call this the "unaware phase," and I must stress here the confusion caused by living and working in this unaware state. I remember my bewilderment when, after working continuously on my parental issues and doing what I thought were all the right things therapeutically, I still felt like a failure in my career and my family relationships. I knew somewhere inside that I was hurting people, but the knowledge was buried deep, and I was not particularly aware of the impact of my behavior on others.

The Semiaware Phase

Many of the characterologic therapists that I have treated reported that the constant repetition of characterologic rigid behaviors gets them into trouble. As they continually repeat these behaviors, their pain and desperation increase, and they become frustrated with the process of trying to clarify and solve problems. As they begin to realize that traditional therapeutic interventions have not been effective, they enter the semiaware phase. Many therapists at this point forsake therapy for acceptance of themselves as the way they are or continue throughout their life running up against their rigid character because they feel that therapy is not effective with them.

When I was semiaware, I found myself in a major double bind. I was becoming acutely aware of my character issues, but I continued to behave in ways that hurt others. Unlike in the unaware phase, which is distinguished by the therapist's fear and lack of awareness, the application of "will" often dominates the semiaware phase. The therapist does not understand that will alone cannot change character. I, for example, constantly swore to "never do it again!" I would recognize a lie, would survive the confrontation, would sometimes admit responsibility, and then would make a deal with myself never to repeat such behavior. I believed that if I willed myself to stop being characterologic, I magically would stop.

Not only would I promise myself that I would change, but, more dangerously, when I was repeatedly confronted during this phase, I would—deceiving myself that a greater application of will would help—promise others that it would never happen again. From the deepest part of my heart, I wanted it never to happen again. Of course, such self-destructive behavior was disastrous, because my rigid character remained untreated. I inevitably lied about having lied, thus reinforcing the negative understanding of Norman in the world and raising my own level of desperation about ever being able to resolve these problems. However, I did learn in the semiaware phase to "never say never."

The most important outcome of the semiaware phase is the commitment to try and become different: less rigid. My awareness of the impact of my behavior on self and others was clear. My commitment to be different was born from that awareness. The "how" still was unclear. I decided that characterologic people were not bad people; they just did not know how to change.

The Aware Phase

If characterologic therapists receive competent help and support or somehow begin to directly confront their character, they enter the most difficult phase. As the pain of knowing who I was intensified and my character picture became more clear to me, the process of opening up and loosening up and possibly transcending my rigid character became a fact. For characterologic therapists, awareness brings the real pain of knowing who they are and what they have done. As the character picture becomes clearer and the intensification of understanding and feelings about the impact of that behavior on others becomes more powerful, the process of opening up the rigid character has begun. The negative confrontations by others, the knowledge that I was hurting people I cared about, and the caring confrontations of an insightful therapist ultimately helped me become aware and feel committed to change.

When I began to own my own character and to struggle to make it more flexible, the process created changes in all areas of my life. Once I began to work on my character successfully, my world began to change for me. Those closest to my heart were thrilled. Everyone else treated this new effort with renewed suspicion because I had promised to be different so many times. Although this response was disheartening, the relief created by my growing character flexibility offset the disappointment.

I began to develop the options for dealing with stressful situations that I had never learned in childhood. I was excited because I began to see a way out of my dilemma. My progressive experimentation with various character traits engendered a sense of relief I had never felt before. This relief was intensely personal—not shared by others—because I was working in an almost completely skeptical environment. The characterologic therapist in the aware phase must persevere despite the almost-constant (and understandable) skepticism. By writing this chapter, I hope that I can provide some measure of comfort and insight to those enduring this phase. I also hope that it will encourage those who can provide support to do so while it honors their skepticism.

A WORKING THERAPIST WITH CHARACTEROLOGIC PROBLEMS

Working as a therapist with characterologic concerns often presents major professional difficulties. Depending on the nature of the character structure and on the most rigid traits, characterologic therapists can alienate and confuse clients and can create situations that make therapy difficult if not impossible. I wish it were not so, but therapists, like everyone, bring their own issues to a therapy session. Being characterologic makes trying to confront these issues especially difficult. But the alternative to working while attempting to change one's character is self-exile.

Many professionals argue that a characterologic person has no business practicing therapy, and I admit that answering them in a way that does not sound defensive is difficult. But, as human beings, we are all flawed, and where, exactly, do we draw the line as to which flaws disqualify us from attempting to help our flawed brothers and sisters? Characterologic therapists can understand and have a special compassion for problematic behavior and what it is like to repeat the same acts over and over again although, in their hearts, they burn to be different. Characterologic therapists often display a special touch with characterologic clients. The old saw about having been there is not the only thing that makes the characterologic therapist special. In addition, characterologic therapists may more easily develop the ability to identify the client's precise character picture. The ability to discover how a client deals with the world and to draw the character picture so that the client can see it is a special gift. The relief of knowing that the therapist knows encourages the client to stay in treatment.

The characterologic therapist may be especially adroit at defining character structures, precisely drawing character pictures, intensifying them, and confronting clients in a boundary-sensitive way that they can know, see, and feel and that gives them hope they can change. Doing so is a special skill that mental health professionals need when dealing with characterologic individuals. Many therapists have told me that working with characterologic clients has made them more sensitive to and patient with their own character processes, more open to receiving support themselves and more understanding of the difficulties of opening up their own rigid character structures. The gift works both ways. As a characterologic therapist, I have hurt and been hurt, but in reviewing the issue as clearly as I can, I have concluded that characterologic therapists can bring a special skill to the therapy process. At the same time, characterologic therapists also labor under a special burden to struggle with their character issues to make sure that they mitigate as much as possible the impact of those issues on the psychotherapy process. Their responsibility to address these problems is absolute.

The Unaware Therapist

Therapists unaware of their character problems may do harm in therapeutic encounters. Dishonesty, lack of sensitivity, an inability to invest, and similar rigid core traits may interfere with client progress. The mental health profession, as a collective, must become more aware of characterologic rigidity. We must help individuals who struggle with these concerns by confronting them directly and then by supporting their efforts to overcome these concerns.

Helping therapists to become aware that they must seek treatment for their character problems as they realize that their limitations are interfering with their effectiveness with clients is a professional dilemma for all of us. Therapists themselves are ultimately responsible for deciding if and when their characterologic structures are so rigid that they cannot provide effective psychotherapy. However, the truth is that, although therapists are accountable, if they do not or cannot honor that accountability, others must step up and take responsibility. As characterologic therapists, we must constantly monitor and decide if and when our characterologic structures are so hurtful that we cannot provide effective psychotherapy, and if we cannot make that determination, we must be encouraged to remove ourselves from the field of that specific therapeutic relationship. As our profession comes to understand and address the characterologic issue, characterologically disordered therapists can more openly focus on their concerns. Doing so may limit their period of despair and isolation and may shorten the time in which they may hurt clients. As a result, talented therapists with character concerns will be able to maximize their psychotherapeutic potential.

Colleague, Client, and Family Confrontation

I cannot overemphasize the importance of colleagues and significant others lovingly confronting the unaware therapist about hurtful character traits. My own experience, while extremely painful, made profoundly clear how much the people in my life helped me by showing me how my character had directly affected them. They supported me in looking honestly at myself.

During my semiaware and aware phases, my family, colleagues, and clients struggled with me in an ongoing way. I vividly remember one trainee coming to me trembling and saying, "Norman, I love your teaching, but why don't you follow through? I am so scared to tell you this, but your lack of follow-through is ruining this postgraduate institute's training experience for me. You don't need to do this. You're a wonderful trainer, and it doesn't have to be this way. If you could just follow through on what you're doing, I could feel safer and experience the training and the quality of training for what it really is." Such supportive confrontations are extremely difficult for everyone, but they create an environment that fosters significant growth. My student's confrontation highlighted for me in a loving way the importance of continuing to struggle with my character and how I was still hurting people.

Therapists' character problems are sometimes evident only in their most intimate relationships. Characterologic therapists may effectively work with many clients without their rigid character structures interfering in the treatment. However, in the more intimate, long-term, deeper therapeutic relationships with those clients who come to know their therapists well, the character issues inevitably surface. Many therapists are fortunate that their skills, general abilities, and other supportive character traits allow them to maintain healthy therapeutic relationships with most clients to a point.

Focusing on Character Concerns

Once therapists become aware of their characterologic issues, they must expend concentrated effort addressing them. This therapeutic work is excruciatingly painful, and the intense struggle is not confined to their therapy sessions. During my own struggle, I constantly focused on my character structure and my core traits in my supervision and in meetings with my staff, colleagues, and others. I became more deeply attuned to my ongoing process by enlisting feedback, confronting the same issues of honesty, responsibility, sensitivity, exaggerating, and lack of follow-through over and over again, and directly facing my relapses. My rigidity in terms of these traits was constantly examined, looked at, confronted, dealt with and explored in all the arenas I have previously discussed. This process was painful and difficult, but the continuous dialogue allowed me to understand my stuckness and to have grounds for experimenting with being different, for understanding the impact of my behavior on others, and for exploring many new options for relating.

I committed myself to the struggle only after a long period of denial. In the semiaware phase, I knew I had problems, but I was not effectively helping myself in an organized way. Once my character was out in the open—meaning that I had owned it and was able to discuss it—I made tremendous strides with clients, colleagues, friends, and my spouse and family. I also needed to expend extra effort monitoring my characterological impact on my therapeutic processes with clients and on my relationships with colleagues and others in my life. I increased my supervision and engaged in many open dialogues with friends that helped me understand the impact of my character on the external world. Supervision, like personal therapy, became a special experience for me. Although I believe that all clinicians need a competent supervisor, someone who intimately knows them and their work, in this situation it becomes an absolute necessity. My supervisor created a safe environment in which I could explore the impact of my character concerns on my work. The supervision was a feedback loop, an additional resource for understanding the impact of my behavior and intensifying my commitment to dealing more effectively with my external environment. This work enhanced my endeavors to open up my character and sensitized people around me to my struggle.

Self-Imposed Openness in the World

The question of openness about our characterologic issues is difficult for all of us who face these problems. The fear of stigmatization, of being branded and blamed, is high. I am not saying that character problems did not cause great pain to others. I could act dishonestly and irresponsibly, and I deserved the feelings that those traits engendered. What was missing was understanding, insight into the difficulty of the struggle I faced, and support for my attempts to help myself. I experienced isolation for many years. My character structures often invoked shame in me, and I was frightened at the thought of openly discussing my character concerns in the professional community, especially with a client or colleague who was not sensitive to the difficulties involved in my struggle to change. However, I knew that only through openness, through sharing honestly what I was going through and taking responsibility for my issues, could I really begin the process of change. Only by putting my issues out on the table could my friends, my colleagues, my clients, and I be honest with each other if I suffered a relapse.

For me, this openness involved great risk. I already felt that I had poisoned my environment, and I was scared to death of the possible further stigmatization and negative feedback from clients and colleagues. I already felt stigmatized, and I was afraid that openness would add fuel to an already-burning fire. Some of these concerns were well founded, considering my previous painful attempts to discuss my character with unsupportive colleagues. On the whole, however, being open about these struggles saved my emotional life.

The Impact of the Therapist's Characterologic Concerns on the Client

I have discussed the impact of characterologic issues on a therapist's work and life. However, inextricably bound in this equation is the effect on clients. The dynamic that occurs when a therapist's characterologic problems emerge in the therapeutic process is synergistic. Clients are continuously affected by the therapist's personal issues. Characterologic issues can potentially do serious damage in the psychotherapy process. Engendering trust in a deep, ongoing, long-term therapeutic relationship when the therapist experiences difficulty being honest is obviously a struggle. Fostering a sense of safety when the therapist does not always follow through with promises is difficult, as is creating a sense of security if the therapist cannot invest emotionally at the depth required for clients to experience emotional safety.

I must note that a therapist's hidden characterologic issues usually become profoundly visible, and therapists ultimately are forced to deal with clients on these issues. If the mental health profession were more aware and supportive of therapists' struggles with their characterologic issues, the problems caused for the therapists themselves and for their clients could be more easily remedied. If, in postgraduate training, these concerns as well as models for treating characterologic individuals were more fully addressed, helping characterologic therapists and helping therapists help characterologic clients would be more effective.

Client Selection

Therapists struggling with characterologic concerns must exercise caution in selecting clients during all the phases of their work. They must constantly monitor their character structure to make sure that they are not relapsing or that their rigidity is not interfering with their ongoing work. Deep, ongoing, and abiding relationships tend to make the character of the therapist more visible. Constantly monitoring the character, confronting issues of supervision, being open to colleague confrontation and peer support allow the process of client selection to be clearer and cleaner. This fact does not necessarily mean that therapists should avoid work of this magnitude; however, they must be aware that they risk hurting clients in such relationships. Therapists also must recognize the stress factors that evoke their own negative character traits. I, for example, experienced difficulty with individuals I deemed weak, like my mother. That statement may seem simplistic, but some clients tended to evoke my lack of sensitivity and empathy far more than others. Once I became aware of my biases, I avoided indecisive and timid clients until my character became more flexible and I could empathize and respond appropriately to their therapeutic needs.

The Importance of Dealing Openly with Characterologic Setbacks

I cannot overemphasize the critical importance of characterologic therapists taking responsibility for their overall characters. The therapist's setbacks, large or small, that emerge during therapy must be addressed immediately and honestly. Clients always deserve open communication. If setbacks are not addressed, clients become confused about their own processes. They blame themselves or feel betrayed, an unacceptable situation to the ethical psychotherapist. Constant awareness of the possibility of hurtful character traits reemerging is essential. Openness is necessary in the ongoing therapeutic relationship, of which intensive supervision and collegial support are crucial components. Characterologic therapists must be honest and open with their supervisors while discussing their mistakes, setbacks, and issues and, in general, their own therapeutic progress and its effect on the therapy they provide.

Intellectual Honesty

One of the most difficult and challenging aspects of the personal and professional work of characterologic therapists is the necessity for being intellectually honest with themselves about their own issues. Once my character was out in the open and my character picture was clear to me, admitting setbacks and flare-ups and their detrimental effects on others was extremely difficult. As the layers of characterologic issues were uncovered, I had to continually and constantly reconfront myself on deeper, more subtle levels. Intellectual honesty is imperative. Although continually confronting these humiliating truths about ourselves is unremittingly painful, intellectually honest therapists will stay with the process until the deepest level of characterologic impact has been unearthed, understood, and worked through. This process is lengthy, but the gains for therapists, clients, and those surrounding us compensate for the constant vigilance needed to confront painful and difficult issues. Journaling helps greatly in this process.

My experience—and the reported experience of many other characterologic therapists—is that maintaining an ongoing log or journal about our character struggles on a day-to-day or week-to-week basis helps us understand our behavior and increases our ability to open up our rigid characters. Journaling thus serves as an invaluable tool for increasing self-awareness. For a supervisor, a journal can provide additional information about a characterologic therapist's problems and can supply deep, rich insights into the reality of the therapist's struggle.

Constant Support and Awareness

Finally, finding a psychotherapeutic environment in which to work that safely supports character changes is crucial. By this I mean an environment in which colleagues such as the ones I currently have are willing to participate in this difficult, rigorous, grueling, long-term, and complicated process. For their own sake, for other therapists' sake, and for the client's sake as well, characterologic therapists must seek out a workplace in which they feel safe enough to identify their character traits and to closely address them throughout the semiaware and aware phases. Even in the safest work environments, I meet clients and professionals whom I have hurt in the past. The ongoing pain engendered by these people, who need to process past hurts to make themselves safe, is terribly difficult. Such experiences are often bittersweet because these people feel that I have changed enough for them to give me another chance, yet engaging them again frequently requires that I relive past incidents and once again face my insensitivity. Having colleagues who understand, who support, and who are open to my honesty without judgment allows me to process these difficult experiences and to continue to grow and move forward.

This healing process will continue for many years, depending on the nature of the character issues and the length of time the therapist has lived in the community before dealing with the characterologic behaviors. Even so, some individuals will never be willing to work through these past hurts and to forgive. Living with that knowledge is difficult for me. The process of working through characterologic issues may indeed induce too much self-blame. However, the characterologic therapist must be aware of the self-blame problem. For me, this issue was difficult to work out, and it continues to require my attention.

Integrating character change into the intimate systems in which the therapist lives is also critical. For example, therapists who had not previously interacted with their children may suddenly wish to become more actively involved in their lives by talking to them, opening up to them, and going to their games and recitals—a change that can be frightening for the children. Depression, fear, anxiety, and other symptoms can emerge in the family as a result of character change. Characterologic therapists must be aware of possible risk factors and must be prepared to deal openly with them, in both personal life and work, as they emerge.

HOPE FOR THE FUTURE

Many people who have the potential to become talented therapists decide that their characterologic issues make participating in the mental health profession unsuitable for them. But I believe that, with help, they can work through their problems to become effective and sensitive therapists. I hope that with this writing I can begin a process of sensitization to the problems of characterologic therapists and their impact on clients. If we can move forward together to create a safe and supportive atmosphere for characterologic therapists, we can help them heal and grow so that they can contribute their unique talents and strengths to our profession.

REFERENCES

English, O. S., & Finch, S. M. (1956). *Introduction to psychiatry.* New York: Norton.

Fiske, D. W., & Maddi, S. R. (Eds.). (1961). *Functions of varied experience.* Homewood, IL: Dorsey Press.

Klein, D. F. (1986). Approaches to measuring efficacy of drug treatments of personality disorders: An analysis and program. In *Principles and Problems in Establishing the Efficacy of Psychotropic Agents* (Public Health Service Publication No. 2138, pp. 187–204). Washington, DC: U.S. Department of Health, Education and Welfare.

Millon, T. (1981). *Disorders of personality, DSM III: Axis II.* New York: Wiley.

Shub, N. (1992). Gestalt therapy over time: Integrating difficulty and diagnosis. In Edwin C. Nevis (Ed.), *Gestalt therapy: Perspectives and applications.* New York: Gardner Press.

CHAPTER 7

On the Pathologization of Life: Psychotherapist's Disease

EDWARD W. L. SMITH, PhD

When I was in the fourth grade, I transferred from a city school to one in a small town. There I found my new classmates memorizing, under the strict hand of a retired missionary, a short poem, aphorism, or ditty for each letter of the alphabet. Approaching the end of the alphabet, late in the school year, we came to the letter "V" and recited in unison:

> Vice is a monster of so frightful mien
> As to be hated needs but to be seen;
> Yet seen too oft, familiar with her face,
> We first endure, then pity, then embrace.[1]

The meaning, or more precisely, the levels of meaning of this morality poem have continued to unfold for me up to the present. So, as I ponder the question of the hazards of doing psychotherapy, I come back to this quatrain with appreciation. I now apply it to the act of viewing life through a filter of psychopathology.

To paraphrase the poem and put it into prose form, psychopathology, when first clearly seen, is recognized as something wrong. But, with continued exposure, the psychotherapist may move through stages of accepting and tolerating psychopathology, to feeling sorry for it, to even enjoying its presence. It may come to be embraced, taken to one's bosom.

At first, "craziness" is looked on as strange, alien. Depending on how extreme in its nature and how florid in its manifestation, it is seen as something negative. I refer here not to the benign "madness" of the free-spirited or the creatively eccentric, but the craziness of early meaning. In

[1] Only recently, I learned this was taken from Alexander Pope's *An Essay on Man II.*

its archaic meaning, to "craze" was to break, shatter, to weaken and destroy, as in health. When such dementia is seen, it alarms and strongly bids the therapist to take careful notice.

With further exposure, the alarm may be quieted. No longer demanding careful notice, craziness may be accepted as the therapist grows more comfortable in its presence. For most things, continued observational exposure leads to desensitization.

Following such comfort may come a certain pity. Not to be confused with pity for a person so afflicted, this is a pity with mercy toward the pathological phenomenon itself. It is an entering into a ruthful relationship with the craziness, a relationship of compassion for the manifest phenomena themselves. Crazy actions are accepted with mercy.

With continued and deepened familiarity, the therapist may come to enjoy the presence of craziness. Having lost by now its "frightful mien," no longer having an appearance that brings alarm and no longer even a call for sympathy, craziness may be embraced.

One of the possible dangers in this change of view of psychopathology is the loss of the recognition of the seriousness and awfulness of it. I am reminded of a passage in Nietzsche's *Twilight of the Idols* in which he warns of the danger of a "morality of sympathy," or a "morality of pity." The danger is the loss of recognition of the extremes. In his words, "The strength to withstand tension, the width of the tensions between extremes, becomes even smaller today; finally, the extremes themselves become blurred to the point of similarity" (Nietzsche, 1982, p. 540). Without venturing into his line of reasoning or the evidence that he offered, let us hold his conclusion in mind. Sympathy or pity may reduce the perceived distance between extremes. In the case of psychopathology, the pity for it that may follow from a certain degree of familiarity may lead the therapist to see it as being closer to psychic health than is wise or useful.

In my comment, published with the chapter written by Robert J. Willis titled "The Many Faces of the Hesitant Patient," I presented what I termed the first axiom of interpersonal medical dynamics. "Physicians are less afraid of treating their patients than patients are of receiving treatment" (Smith, 1984, pp. 48–49). When stated, this axiom seems so obvious that it can be dismissed and its importance trivialized. The core of the axiom, however, involves exactly the phenomenon that I have been discussing. Using surgery as an example in my comment, I pointed out how the surgeon, exposed over and over to a procedure may come to regard it lightly, compared with the gravity that the patient attaches to the surgical intervention. So, here it is, the thing once regarded as of frightful mien comes to be readily embraced, if not minimized or trivialized.

In my comment, I suggested that psychotherapy is an analogous procedure: ". . . psychotherapists are less afraid of doing psychotherapy than patients are of receiving it. . . . Those of us who belong to the psychotherapy subculture are often so ensconced in it that we fail to appreciate how threatening it can be to the outsider" (Smith, 1984, p. 49).

As therapists become familiar with psychopathology, it may assume a prominent place in their thinking. As is well recognized, perception is an active process in which the person organizes and interprets sensory data according to certain internal structures, at least some of which are learned. So, when concepts of psychopathology have been learned, they can become an internal structure for organizing and interpreting the person's experience of sensory data. Psychopathology can then become a filter through which the world is viewed.

The problem arises when the template of psychopathology is misused or overused. My theory of how this comes about is as follows. If psychopathology is well and truly understood in the larger context of life, then there is no problem. But such understanding requires considerable mental work. It requires that the therapist see and hear clearly and then ruminate over the material as much as necessary to digest it mentally. It has to be chewed on, so to speak, until it is in an assimilable form and can become part of the person. If it is swallowed whole or only partially chewed, it will remain undigested. Such undigested material is introjected and gives rise to mental indigestion. The most dramatic symptom of mental indigestion is vomiting of the undigested material. Not being assimilated as part of the person's self, it is thrown up, projected outward. (I acknowledge Perls, 1992, for explicating these dynamics of introjection and projection.) Introjected material remains too prominent, not being assimilated into the system as a whole. In other words, it remains outside the larger context.

Our understanding may be furthered by a closer examination of projection. In his model, Bellak (1950) delineated five levels of projection. Progressing from a relatively "purely cognitive" level of consensually defined perception, the second level is that of "externalization" of the person's frame of reference. That is, the individual employs a perceptual template which is not wholly consensual in that particular context. Third is "sensitization" or the influencing of perception through a heightened sensitivity to a particular existing stimulus. In this case, projection occurs in the sense that the person's heightened sensitivity will lead to perceiving the sensitivity-relevant stimulus in greater magnitude than is justified by the stimulus itself. "Simple projection," or the disowning and attributing of a person's feeling or impulse to someone else is the fourth level. Most pathological is the fifth level in which the person's feeling or impulse is reversed through the mechanism of reaction formation and the resultant feeling or impulse is disowned and attributed to another person.

Introjected material concerning psychopathology can be projected at either of two levels. The therapist can pathologize first by externalizing a template of psychopathology, rigidly using such filter when it is not useful or is even irrelevant. As such, this is a variation of *la vie en merd.* Second, the therapist can pathologize by being so sensitive to signs of psychopathology that he or she magnifies the slightest hint into the dominant feature. This is the error of overinterpretation.

In summary, then, pathologization of life takes place when the template of psychopathology is introjected rather than integrated into a larger conceptual-perceptual context and is then projected either as a rigid interpretive filter or as a hypersensitivity that results in overinterpreting the data. In either case, psychopathology may be seen where it does not exist or may be seen in exaggerated form where it does.

I believe this "psychotherapist's disease" is fostered if the practitioner—in the course of extended and extensive exposure to psychopathology—relies more and more heavily on this familiar and comfortable framework rather than developing a larger, integrated framework. Equipped with the vocabulary and the concepts, the psychotherapist has a template for filtering information and a sensitization to the symptoms of psychopathology. If, however, he or she has not assimilated the essence-in-context, this material becomes a rigidly applied diagnostic framework evoked by minimal hints of resemblance to psychopathology.

What I am labeling psychotherapist's disease has been recognized elsewhere. I remember references from graduate school to Walter Klopfer's warning of a "maladjustment bias" and to Timothy Leary's calling attention to the "pathology error." In my first course in abnormal psychology, I heard of a close kin, "medical student's disease." Medical student's disease is the frequently found experience of the callow medical student's diagnosing in herself or himself each new disease studied. In the case of medical student's disease, the act is one of self-pathologizing, whereas with psychotherapist's disease, the act of pathologizing is other-directed.

Perhaps an anecdote would be useful at this point. A couple of years ago, I chanced upon an old acquaintance at the Summer Workshop of the American Academy of Psychotherapists. We exchanged greetings and briefly caught up on how we and our families had been. Then she asked me which workshops or events I had attended or planned to attend at the conference. I told her that the main thing I wanted to do was take part in a Native American sweat-lodge ceremony.[2] Her response, offered quickly, was, "You're really getting addicted to those!" I was shocked by what she said and by the quickness of her ejaculation. The fact was that this would be only my second sweat lodge. My first had been 24 months earlier. She knew I had attended the previous one. Yet she interpreted my behavior in the framework of pathology, specifically as an addiction.

Maladjustment bias can be recognized whenever either natural or adaptive behavior is labeled or conceptualized in pathological terms. Thus sadness (as in grieving a loss) becomes "depression" and attention to detail (as in accurate measurement or record keeping) becomes "obsessive-compulsive." The energetic, extroverted child who has been confined and isolated becomes "hyperactive," and the introverted child becomes "avoidant" or "schizoid." A ravenous hunger becomes "bulimia" and any loss of appetite "anorexia nervosa." Lack of gullibility (as in skepticism about public statements made by politicians in the post-Watergate era) becomes "paranoia." Energetic exuberance becomes "manic," and any variation in mood is "bipolar disorder" or "cyclothymic disorder." Excitement becomes "anxiety" and discomfort becomes "phobic." Every pain becomes "psychogenic" or evidence of "somatization disorder." (If the individual is concerned about the pain, "hypochondriasis" is suspected, and if he or she is not concerned, it is either "denial" or "la belle indifference.") Difficulty with a new living or working situation becomes "adjustment disorder," and many variations of personality style become "personality disorders."

Sometimes the maladjustment bias can be recognized by the grossness of the label; that is, the label fails to respect degrees and to differentiate the common and ordinary from the problematic. Examples of such labels are "codependent," "survivor," "addiction," and "abuse." In such instances, the aiding of a spouse who is sick or otherwise in need of support is labeled "codependent" behavior. A person who has a history of any distress becomes a "survivor." Anything that someone does with regularity, be it something of negative, positive, or neutral impact on the person's life is labeled an "addiction." And, finally, any act of impoliteness, rudeness, or harshness comes to be called "abuse." With such overinclusiveness, the utility of the terms is lost. They become meaningless when they are applied so generally that they fail to differentiate between "garden variety" behavior and experience and that which truly constitutes a problem of

[2] The Academy, being committed to the ongoing development of the person of the psychotherapist, offers experiential events at the cutting edge of personal growth, particularly at the Summer Workshop.

psychopathology. Worse, they become misleading. They imply particular dynamics and areas of difficulty where such may not exist. But the problem may be created iatrogenically as result of the imprecise labeling. If diagnosed by an expert as codependent, a survivor, addicted, or abused, surely there is ample "evidence" in all our histories to support such a claim and lead us, if we are willing, into a false understanding of ourselves. The reader can probably recognize examples of such pathology errors manifested.

A final word about such labels is that there is a considerable degree of cultural relativity in the valid application of these. A culture's mores may play a role in what constitutes codependency, addiction, abuse, or being a survivor. Taking the behavior out of its cultural context and judging it by the criteria of a different cultural context could lead to gross and damaging misunderstanding. This recognition, quite recent in psychology's attention to issues of ethnic diversity, has been a primary topic in anthropology for decades. For example, the norm for wine consumption differs between the United States and, say, France or Italy. What is a normal quantity and pattern of wine drinking in those European countries might quickly be taken as evidence for "addictive behavior" from the perspective of an ethnocentric psychotherapist using the U.S. norm as the absolute norm. That psychotherapist might very well diagnose the recent emigrant from France or Italy as abusing alcohol when that person is acting well within her or his cultural norm.

An excellent reminder of the maladjustment bias is offered by an old psychoanalytic joke. It goes as follows, "If you arrive at the meeting early, you are anxious. If you arrive on time, then you are compulsive. But, if you arrive late, you are passive-aggressive." I may add, with tongue in cheek, that if you argue with the preceding assessment, you are surely being "defensive" and "resistant."

As may be apparent from the previous examples, the pathology error has a trivializing effect. When the differentiation between pathology and nonpathology is lost, the words and concepts become vapid. The problem is further understood by the application of some of Goldstein's work (Smith, 1976). Goldstein viewed behavior along a concrete-abstract dimension. Concrete behavior is a direct, automatic reaction to the situation that a person perceives. Thus, it is rigid. In contrast, abstract behavior is flexible. It involves the person's thinking about what is perceived—what does it mean, what are its conceptual properties, what is its relation to other conceptual patterns—and acting on his or her conclusions. The failure to abstract and classify—what Goldstein termed a loss of categorical thinking—limits the individual's orientation and action. The implication of Goldstein's idea has been explicated by Perls (Smith, 1976) in his emphasis on the importance of care in speaking. He pointed out the great importance of using words that express the precise meaning the speaker wants to convey. To avoid "frigidity of the palate," he encouraged the learning of the value of each word, to appreciate the power hidden in the "logos." We could see the pathology error as a case of frigidity of the palate, limiting orientation and action through rigid, concrete thinking. The implications for the "patient," thus pathologized, are obvious.

An explicit attempt to avoid the maladjustment bias has been the articulation of the "Third Force," humanistic psychology. Created in part out of the dissatisfaction with the pathological models of psychoanalysis and the mechanistic, atomistic bias of behaviorism, humanistic psychology has sought to affirm an additional dimension of psychology (Krippner, 1991). Noting the extensive vocabulary and syntax of pathology that the psychoanalytic movement created, humanistic psychology has focused more on the development of language and concepts to describe and facilitate the understanding of creativity, self-actualization, intentionality, natural experience, and spirituality. It offers a growth model rather than a model of pathology.

Being fluent in the Third Force as well as in the other two, is a way of maintaining a broad perspective. It is a way to keep the context large and not succumb so easily to the limitations of an overly prominent or rigid template of psychopathology. Having several conceptual filters and the flexibility to shift among them is an antidote for the introjection and subsequent projection of the filter of psychopathology.

Nietzsche's apothegm can be a warning to the psychotherapist:

> And if thou gaze long into an abyss,
> the abyss will also gaze into thee.
>
> *(Nietzsche, no copyright date, p. 87)*

REFERENCES

Bellak, L. (1950). On the problems of the concept of projection. In L. Abt & L. Bellak (Eds.), *Projective psychology.* New York: Knopf.

Krippner, S. (1991). Foreword. In C. Aanstoos (Ed.), *Studies in humanistic psychology.* Carrollton, GA: West Georgia College.

Nietzsche, F. (No copyright date). *Beyond good and evil.* New York: Carlton House.

Nietzsche, F. (1982). *Twilight of the idols.* In W. Kaufmann (Ed.), *The portable Nietzsche.* New York: Penguin.

Perls, F. (1992). *Ego, hunger and aggression.* Highland, NY: Gestalt Journal Press.

Smith, E. (1976). The roots of Gestalt therapy. In E. Smith (Ed.), *The growing edge of Gestalt therapy.* New York: Brunner/Mazel (Citadel edition, 1977).

Smith, E. (1984). Comment on "The many faces of the hesitant patient" by Robert J. Willis. In J. Travers (Ed.), *Psychotherapy and the uncommitted patient.* New York: Haworth.

CHAPTER 8

Overcoming Body Shame: My Client, Myself

JUDITH RUSKAY RABINOR, PhD

> I used to love my work, but lately I am overwhelmed. The other night I had the most horrifying dream: I dreamt about my bulimia group, but instead of being the therapist, I was a member! Ruth, one of the thinnest members of the group was sneering at me because my thighs were so fat! I woke up sweating. When I saw her in the group the next day, I felt enormous, even though I know I only weigh 105. Since then, I've been seriously questioning myself: How I can possibly be a good therapist if this is how I really feel about my body. I just don't know what is happening to me.
>
> *JoAnn, age 43, a psychotherapist*

Anorexia, bulimia, and body image problems have increased to epidemic proportions in the past two decades. In a culture that silences women's voices and devalues the female body, these disorders strike women 10 times more frequently than men, reflecting profound issues of female identity and the struggle women have nurturing themselves and developing a sense of agency, autonomy, and power. The "relentless pursuit of thinness" (Bruch, 1973) has become a cultural obsession gripping the majority of the female population, not simply anorexic and bulimic women who represent the extreme end of a very long continuum.

In the past decades, clinicians have been challenged to develop a deeper understanding of how the female body has become a life-threatening battleground where intrapsychic, interpersonal, and sociocultural struggles are fought with a new arsenal of weapons: bingeing, purging, and starving. Once thought to be simply a passing fad, it is clear that the cultural mandate to diet and be thin tyrannizes most women; the failure to achieve a "good enough" body lowers women's self-esteem. It is estimated that on any given day 80% of American women are strongly dissatisfied with their bodies (Rodin, 1992; Wolff, 1991). There is little indication as to how much of that 80% are women therapists treating women with disordered eating and body image problems.

For the female therapist, therapy with eating-disordered clients may stimulate feelings of shame on at least three levels: first, from feeling dissatisfied with her own body; second, from feeling like an imposter in her professional role, and third, from early preverbal experiences where intrapsychic struggles were played out in a body devalued because of her gender. On both conscious and unconscious levels shameful feelings may be evoked and reawakened in clinical practice.

My own experience as a psychotherapist and as a supervisor of clinicians treating disordered eating and body image problems has familiarized me with the widespread nature of these layers of shame. Repeatedly, therapists acknowledge resonating to their clients' pain with their own pain, as did JoAnn, whose words opened this chapter. Over the past 15 years, as I have listened to many therapists bravely "confess" to feeling ashamed about their bodies, I have wondered how best to support them in this struggle. For, while I have learned that silencing these feelings only compounds feelings of shame, speaking about them often offers little solace—for our guidelines stress that to heal, we must be healed. "How can I help her (my client) accept her body if I have not really come to grips with mine?" is a lament I have heard repeatedly in my office.

In reading the literature about eating disorders and body image, I am struck by how infrequently female therapists (who are almost the exclusive and certainly are the most prevalent treaters of this population) acknowledge that their clients' suffering is much like their own. Clinical literature rarely mentions that these therapists often dread gaining weight, are vigilant about their own diet and exercise regimes, and suffer from feeling dissatisfied, if not disgusted, with their own bodies. In both colleagial and supervisory relationships with women therapists, despair and shame are repeatedly expressed about *not* having resolved body-image issues. Therapists fear that to be effective, such a resolution must occur. It is my belief, however, that such a resolution is not totally possible, for body dissatisfaction—for women—is normative and how therapists deal with their own negative feelings is generally dismissed. On this topic, clinical literature is silent.

I have several thoughts about this silence. First, in today's cultural climate, which sets forth unachievable standards of slimness, the very awareness of body imperfection evokes deep feelings of humiliation and shame, particularly in women, and understandably in female therapists treating women. When therapists who work specifically with body image disturbances look inward at their own issues, which are inevitably exacerbated in the treatment setting, they may face their own sense of disappointment and failure at not meeting these unachievable standards. Therapists may question their capacity to help others recover from that which remains personally problematic. Unarticulated negative feelings about personal appearance may deepen a therapist's sense of professional competence. The role of healer may feel fraudulent.

In addition to the cultural press to attain an unattainable body, deep emotional issues may be stimulated for therapists who work with body image issues. One premise of psychodynamic psychotherapy is that the earliest sense of self is rooted in the body in preverbal experiences of loss and trauma, love, attachment, abandonment, and betrayal. For both men and women, the sense of self in both the intrapsychic and interpersonal arenas is inextricably intertwined with one's physical body. Yet, from birth, the body is experienced differently by the sexes. This difference is particularly relevant to the mental health of therapists treating women with disordered eating.

In a recent discussion of female development, Boden, Hunt, and Kassoff (1987) identify "bodily shame" as perhaps the most profound level of distress experienced by women (p. 13). From birth, little girls are given the paradoxical message that their interpersonal worth is measured by their physical attractiveness, but that the female body is inherently shameful. As female therapists help eating-disordered clients get in touch with early trauma and losses stored and expressed in their bodies, the therapist's own issues in these areas will likely be exacerbated.

My experience has taught me that when dealing with body shame, the conventional approach to the use of countertransference is not only limited but often interferes with helping clients heal. As women, both therapist and client have been exposed to the societal emphasis on slimness. Because of the shared culture, female therapists will inevitably identify—although perhaps, to a lesser degree—with their client's body dissatisfaction. As such, the impact of society on the therapist as well as the client can be an important factor to be explored. While the therapy relationship always contains resonances of past relationships, a new relationship develops between client and therapist. Feminist theory (Eichenbaum & Orbach, 1983) highlights this new relationship, in which the therapist serves as a role model of a woman who is willing to stand up for what she believes, to speak the unspeakable. This new relationship is often neglected as an important source of healing.

Voicing what has gone unsaid is at the heart of psychotherapy with disordered eating and body image issues. As a therapist, I aim to help my clients find words for what has gone unspoken. Working in this way has caused me to look at myself, my silences. It has also raised several intriguing questions: What happens to the therapeutic process when therapist and client both suffer with similar issues? Can the therapist's voice be healing? Can the therapist's silence be harmful? What happens when the therapist reveals that she suffers—although perhaps to a lesser extent—along with the client? I am convinced that the way in which the therapist experiences her own body and expresses this experience has a profound impact on the course of treatment.

THERAPIST AS WOMAN

After a long and festive Thanksgiving dinner, several out-of-town relatives asked to see a video I was editing about the development and treatment of body image issues and eating disorders in women. Pleased and somewhat flattered, I consented. The tape contained several excerpts from news programs, talk shows, and workshops I had conducted over the past few years. After the company had left, I realized I'd felt ill at ease, somewhat depressed. Had I bored them? I wondered. Did they really want to see the tape? Had I been a show-off? I commented on these thoughts to a friend. Eventually, talked out, we dropped it; but I still felt uneasy.

Later, he came back to me and said, "Did you notice? On the tape, you were discussing how women are judged by their appearance—that women develop anorexia and bulimia to feel powerful and potent; that women become obsessed with dieting, losing weight, and achieving the perfect body, because on the inside, they feel inadequate and empty. You were talking about helping disconnected clients develop an inner identity based on their genuine needs and appetites rather than focus on their appearance . . . but no one paid a lot of attention to what you were talking about . . . instead, everyone kept commenting on how *you looked* on the TV tape."

And suddenly, the whole scene flashed before me: my three aunts, my mother, and several assorted relatives, gathered in my den, all watching the tape.

Comments focused first on my hair:

The length: Longer versus shorter.

Next: Permed versus unpermed.

Then, the color: More or less red?
Is it better brown with only red highlights?
What would Judy look like with blond hair? asked Aunt Jean.

Questions about my clothes:

Was that a blouse or a scarf?
Where did you get that pink jacket?
And who wears pink, anymore, anyway?
How come you didn't wear a black suit? my mother asked me. Black is so much more in!

And finally, my weight:

Judy dear, I think you look heavier now than on TV.
No she doesn't—she looks thinner now!
That's because TV makes everyone look heavier. Thank God, you're not as heavy as you look on that tape! You're much thinner now!

Sickened, I realized my friend was right. I had assumed that the tape would generate an interest in my work; but what had provoked the most attention was what I looked like. The focus had shifted from a presentation of my ideas to a presentation of my appearance, from my insides to my outsides, from my mind to my body. And the shift had occurred so quickly that I was unaware of it.

My lack of awareness startled me. My pride in my work had been swept aside, and instead, I felt as if someone had caught me with my slip showing. And as I thought about it, I realized that what had occurred in that moment had transpired so often in my life that it had once again subtly slipped by me. Slowly, I realized that the very process I see and identify on a daily basis in my office as undermining the development of an authentic and genuine sense of self occurred to me in my own life. And its occurrence was so ego-syntonic that I barely noted it.

The incident reminded me of how easily my feelings of power could be eroded, feelings of insecurity and shame stimulated, and how easily I had lost my voice. On the brink of achieving recognition and power, the women in the room bonded over what women have connected over throughout time—appearance. It reminded me of my connection to my anorexic and bulimic clients, for I, too, am impacted by the same cultural values that impact them—that looks count.

I became aware that what really disturbed me was the recognition that my body had distracted, defeated, and betrayed me. I had felt diminished, trivialized, and inadequate: first, about my hair, and eventually, about my body; and over time, feelings of malaise and depression swept through me. I had lost my center; I had been silenced.

As I mulled over this incident, slowly, the faces of my clients appeared before me:

> First, Audrey, who at 22 "forgot" to tell our bulimia group she had gotten her law school rating and was in the top 10% of her class. Next, Geneen, who didn't want her husband to know that with her new promotion and raise, she would be earning double his salary. Finally, as Randi put it, she didn't know why, but it felt better to be the skinniest girl in the class than the smartest. Often she didn't raise her hand even when she knew the answers. This had finally begun to irritate her. "Being smart makes me feel scared," she'd said, "but not speaking up when I know the answer is ridiculous!" Did I understand? she wondered. I bet she had good reasons to remain silent. That night she dreamt that she graduated cum laude and no one came to her graduation.

WOMAN AS BODY: FEMALE POWERLESSNESS

It is the thesis of feminist writing that women's psychological development within a patriarchal culture is "inherently traumatic" (Brown & Gilligan, 1991). The trauma is gender linked and universal, beginning at adolescence, when girls learn to silence their hungers, appetites, and desires; when girls learn, through our culture, that their value, power, and identity lie in being attractive (which, by today's standards, means being thin).

As a professional specializing in eating disorders, I witness the destructive consequences of a culture that is "beauty bound" and body focused. This body focus that drains, limits, and has derailed my clients is, unfortunately, not limited to them. As a woman, I know firsthand a great deal about how sociocultural phenomena are translated into psychological problems and how they become profoundly intertwined with one's psychological development. I, too, experience a unique sense of power if I think I look good; and on the other hand, I experience a sense of defeat, anxiety, or shame if I feel my looks or appearance displease me—or, if I think I displease others. Feeling I look good enhances my sense of effectiveness, mastery, agency, and my overall well-being.

In my clinical work, as I listen to daily reports of starving, bingeing, exercising, looking "good enough" or "too fat," I deal with the underlying issues of effectiveness, mastery, and agency as my clients starve, vomit, take laxatives, and excessively scrutinize the flab on their thighs and stomachs in an attempt to empower themselves through dieting. Ironically, they disempower themselves, as their relentless dieting exhausts and drains them, reinforcing a sense of inadequacy. In my work, I try to sensitize my clients to the reality of the cultural overvaluation of appearance and slimness that everyone is at times subject to. At the same time, I try to help them realize that while appearance does matter, genuine and long-lasting empowerment comes from how you feel on the inside; that nourishment comes from relatedness and relationship, and that developing connections to one's own inner life and connections to others is a lifetime journey.

I have spent most of my adult life on this journey, discovering a new model of womanhood, and my own journey has taught me a great deal about the journey of my clients. For the very issues I struggle with—empowering myself, speaking up, finding my voice, and reclaiming my body—are the same ones they struggle with because these issues underlie the development of disordered eating.

THE NAKED THERAPIST

It was my first session with Anna, a 29-year-old recovered bulimic. In discussing her previous therapist, I inquired as to why she had left treatment. She shook her head puzzled. I inquired further; in jogging her memory, she recounted the following incident:

> I'm not sure why, but suddenly I remember the time I walked into the locker room of my gym, and who did I see? My therapist! At first she didn't see me, but I saw her. She was changing, taking off her exercise clothes and was totally naked, pulling on her underpants. What amazed me most was her stomach! It looked like she was tucking a small, saggy balloon into her skimpy bikini underwear! Then, I noticed her thighs, bulging out around the legs of her underpants, just like my mother's! I couldn't get over that she was wearing bikinis! I wondered if I would wear bikini underpants if my body looked like hers! For that matter, I wondered if I would even go to a gym if I looked like her! Suddenly our eyes met, for only a moment. She nodded at me, and quickly turned away. Feeling like a voyeur, I quickly left the locker room.

The following session, the therapist had asked Anna how she had felt about their serendipitous meeting. Anna shrugged it off, and the two moved on to another topic. It was never mentioned again.

Anna's story fascinated me. She herself was returning to therapy because recently she had become a therapist. Working with women with eating disorders was affecting her, she said. She noted that she had again become concerned with issues about her body. Her thighs looked enormous. Her weight was a constant preoccupation. Her story continued:

> I remember being surprised that she didn't push me to think about how I really felt seeing her naked, at my gym. Because her usual style was to get me to talk about uncomfortable things. I think I was relieved that she dropped it. But now that *I'm* a therapist, I'm realizing that it wasn't seeing her naked that was so uncomfortable for me. What made it uncomfortable was that we didn't talk about *either* of our feelings about it. I kept waiting for her to bring it up. But she didn't, and I just kept waiting.

Neither Anna nor her therapist mentioned the incident again. Anna never returned to the gym. Eventually she left treatment.

Anna stopped talking, and I found myself immersed in the vivid image of the half-naked, middle-aged, overweight therapist in the locker room, shamefully avoiding Anna's eyes. In those fleeting seconds of silence, I imagined the therapist's engaging in a self-contemptuous inner dialogue, a familiar dialogue that had caused her to disconnect from her client. I was saddened, thinking about the disconnection that had occurred in that locker room. I became aware that I was identifying with the therapist, not Anna. My body shame had, in turn, disconnected me from my client.

"Perhaps," I began tentatively, aiming to reconnect, "she didn't say much because that was her style."

Anna shook her head, disagreeing.

"I'll go out on a limb," I said. "Perhaps she was overwhelmed that you saw her naked."

Anna smiled. I gained courage.

"It's hard to do this work when you don't feel good about your body," I said, "but it's hard to feel good about your body in a culture that presents us with images of models with bodies we will never have."

Anna smiled again, and we were able to reconnect and move on.

THERAPIST IN A GREEN BIKINI

My experience with Anna whetted my curiosity. I began conducting workshops to explore how therapists dealt with their own feelings about their bodies and body shame. As part of the workshop, I developed a guided imagery exercise in which the following situation was presented to therapists:

> Imagine it is the first day after your summer vacation. Jane, bulimic for 7 years enters your office, sits down, and opens the session with: Was that you I saw at Jones Beach this summer? You wait. She persists. July Fourth Weekend . . . was that you on the beach? You pause, trying to remember exactly where you spent the first weekend in July. "Was that you wearing a green bikini?" Take a moment to go into your body; what kinds of thoughts, feelings, and responses does her question generate in you? How do you understand her question? How do you think you might respond?

Responses from psychotherapists indicated that profound feelings of anxiety, awkwardness, discomfort, and competition were evoked:

> I'm wondering if my client thinks I'm fat. My stomach feels big and my thighs feel like they're bulging. I feel self-conscious about my cellulite. "Did you have any feelings about seeing me there?" I ask, hoping to quiet my own feelings.
>
> I felt anxiety . . . In the bikini, I felt vulnerable and exposed, I hated the possibility of being judged. I felt comfortable in the bikini, but what would she think of me?
>
> I wanted to say it wasn't me in the bikini. I wouldn't wear a bikini, wouldn't feel OK enough about my body to expose it so fully.
>
> I would *never* wear a green bikini. Or any bikini! In thinking about wearing one, I felt embarrassed, anxious, ugly, assaulted. What would my patient think?

Most therapists expressed relief to hear their colleagues also suffered from body image dissatisfaction. The ubiquitous nature of body shame was repeatedly revealed. And most therapists were eager to express a host of uncomfortable feelings: feeling fat and ashamed of feeling fat; feelings of fraudulence in the role of healer/helper/therapist; feeling their silence was unauthentic in sessions. "Talking about this with you people helps me accept myself," clinicians repeatedly told me. I began to wonder: If it helped therapists to have their own feelings validated and normalized, wouldn't clients also benefit from the same kind of validation? Wouldn't clients benefit from a more open discussion?

BODY SHAME AND SELF-DISCLOSURE

Therapists are under enormous pressure from the culture at large and the profession in particular to be expert, to provide answers, and to help patients move out of pain and difficulty into a more adaptive place. The profession does not encourage therapists to acknowledge shameful feelings with clients, yet in the process of silencing our own feelings, we inevitably disconnect from our clients. Often this results in the client's responding with withdrawal, isolation, and further disconnections. In my experience, an important way of healing clients' despair has been through my identification with their feelings by sharing my own reactions to their pain. More recently, I have learned that healing occurs by selectively sharing my own experiences as well. My experience, however, contradicts my training, where I was taught to self-disclose cautiously, and only under certain situations, only if my own issues were resolved. Yet in my experience, resolving our body image issues is not easy.

I am a person whose emotions are not easily masked. If I feel annoyed, displeased, despairing, or ashamed, it generally shows. When I sit with clients, their stories impact me. Their stories trigger my stories. This, I believe, is how it should be. When I push away my feelings, or inhibit their expression, I become disconnected both from myself and from the person I am communicating with. Such a disconnection does not facilitate growth in either participant.

When my own stories emerge in a session, I try to think through their meaning, their relevance, their usefulness either to me or my client. When I reveal myself, I attempt to depathologize and help my clients see their own stories in the current cultural context. I hope to serve as a role model of a woman struggling to stay in touch with my own genuine needs, laboring against dysfunctional beliefs that I—and all women—cannot help but absorb through a kind of cultural osmosis. I hope to serve as a role model of a woman struggling to be comfortable with my discomfort, which is exactly what we ask of our clients when they risk changing.

Yet what we are asked to do as therapists is extremely complex. If we are open to our patients' pain, their pain draws us into our unconscious pain. Yet what are we to do when our pain is evoked in a session where the goal is the client's healing? Are we to speak? or to be silent? And if we speak, what are we to say?

Clients need to experience their therapist as a person who is not afraid to be real and to speak the truth, even if the truth is messy, imperfect, and unfinished. If healing is rooted in truth telling, the therapist's truth—

when it has something of genuine importance that can help a client—can be an exciting and healing part of the relationship.

As I have worked in this field, my role has changed. Often I feel like a teacher, friend, or mentor, all wrapped into my therapist self. And although these images do not always feel correct, I am able to acknowledge that it is from this stance that I feel I work best.

In my work, I have come to reject a model of therapy where the therapist is the expert and the patient is troubled, sick, and disturbed. I attempt to be authentic, real, and to evolve a mutual relationship. At times, this feels both impossible and illogical since the focus is on the client's problems, not mine, and I am being paid to be a helper, which inherently imbalances the relationship. Yet, in the face of this imbalance, I find myself struggling, with few guidelines, to achieve this goal.

REFERENCES

Boden, R., Hunt, P., & Kassoff, B. (1987). *Shame and the psychology of women.* Paper presented at the annual meeting of the Association of Women in Psychology, Denver, Colorado.

Brown, L., & Gilligan, C. (1992). *At the crossroads,* (p. 216). Cambridge, MA: Harvard University Press.

Bruch, H. (1973). *Eating disorders: Obesity, anorexia nervosa and the person within.* New York: Basic Books, Inc.

Eichenbaum, L., & Orbach, S. (1983). *Understanding women: A feminist psychoanalytic approach.* New York.

Freedman, R. (1988). *Bodylove.* New York: Harper & Row.

Kasin, E. (1986). Roots and branches. *Contemporary Psychoanalysis, 22,* 451–458.

Rabinor, J. (1993). The bodyself of the therapist. *Full lives.* Carlsbad, CA: Guerze Press.

Rodin, J. (1992, January/February). Body mania: Insights of body image. *Psychology Today, 25*(1), 565–67.

Wolff, N. (1991). *The beauty myth.* New York: Morrow.

CHAPTER 9

Making Room for Illness in the Practice of Psychotherapy

K. TRACY MUNN, PhD

I became ill with multiple sclerosis early in my career, at a time when I was coming of age as a therapist. I was discovering my capacity to help others change and growing confident of the abilities I had internalized. Now, after two years, I am less new to my illness—also less new to my profession—and where once these two aspects of my life seemed only to intersect briefly, they have become entwined, each bearing influences and implications for the other that will continue to change and develop as time passes.

I write here of my early encounters with an illness that is both capricious and ominous in its unpredictability. These encounters were characterized by fear and turmoil, as MS can gradually rob a person of physical and even mental functioning. Questions and dilemmas arose from my work during this time in which I struggled to maintain my professional balance while in a state of continuing personal disorientation. Many of these questions pertained to practicalities; many pertained to my own reactions to illness and how they influenced my work. In all, however, the primary dilemma illness posed to me as a therapist was where to place it as a realistic presence in the therapeutic relationship. Where could it go in the life of a therapy? And what would and should be the bounds of its influence?

I had been taught conservatively to keep to myself, as therapist, the goings-on in my life. I also was sway to our social context, in which stigma and fear are attached to illness. There seems to be little place in our society for the ill or for illness to be included as a normal part of the whole of human existence. Rather, these things are treated as aberrations, to be removed or kept hidden. The same attitude colored my ideas about psychotherapy and, especially, my role as healer in that contract.

Initially, I was afraid my illness threatened the sanctity of the therapeutic endeavor, and I believed it was crucial to keep it and its effects out as best I could.

My aim here is to describe what is not often spoken or recognized. I hope that what I write will foster a finer appreciation for both the experience of illness and that of being a therapist. Both call for the deepest of encounters with our own and others' humanity, if we but allow it. My experience of illness has touched my sensibilities as a therapist irrevocably and, I know, for the better.

FEAR OF THE UNKNOWN

When the signs of MS first appeared in my life, they were hardly remarkable—a few peculiar sensations in my legs and an odd but subtle, electric-like shock when I turned my head. For the most part, these were sensory symptoms, familiar enough but incongruous, out of place—tingling, pins and needles, numbness, tightness, all with no apparent rhyme or reason. They created in me worry and a feeling of estrangement from my familiar bodily self. Although eventually the illness began to affect my mobility and coordination more obviously, my MS has been largely invisible to the observer. For a very long time, its effects were not even verifiable in medical tests and examination. Ultimately, the illness resulted in instances of partial blindness, incontinence, and paralysis of one or another limb. Fortunately, such extreme degrees of awfulness come and go.

Multiple sclerosis is a disease of the central nervous system caused by an autoimmune system dysfunction. It is neither fatal nor contagious, nor heritable. The immune system besets the brain and spinal cord, mistaking the body for an alien, and leaving behind scars that impede neural functioning. These cause sensory and motoric disturbances that are erratic and that vary widely over time and among individuals. There are losses of sensation and bodily control, in the form of numbness, leadenness, spasticity, and a kind of paralysis of normal reflexes. And there are intruding sensations that are bizarre and that lend an illusory quality to one's subjective experience. The left side of my body may feel as if it is plunged in ice water; my hands as if they are being abraded on gravel as I touch soft objects; and my torso as if it is girdled in a metal corset. I lose my balance with a sensation that a tide is pulling sand out from under my feet; I cannot distinguish my keys from my gloves when I reach into a pocket; and walking a short distance creates a cacophony of twinges and aftershocks that reverberate through my joints and spine.

The nameable reality, my diagnosis, did not emerge until the clamor of physical symptoms increased and became outwardly observable. During the nine months until that time, absent of medical proof of my complaints, my doctors were bemused and subtly indicated I was being oversensitive to my body's quirks. I, in turn, took a virtual flight into the psychoanalytic, concocting one interpretation after another, each more clever than the last, in the hope of eradicating my symptomatology by resolving some pertinent inner conflict. It was to no avail, of course, and once the situation was called for what it was, the psychological meanings I had construed glared in their absurdity. Changing the definition of my experience—simply by arriving at a medical, rather than psychological, diagnosis—recast the entire structure of beliefs, feelings, and images I had shaped to give form to the terrifying unknowns of what was happening to me.

The early period of my illness, with its ambiguity and unreality, brought home to me what it is to be naive and dependent. Most profound was my difficulty holding on to my sense of what was real, when this was being discredited and denied by what seemed to be trustworthy sources. The doubt cast on my perceptions rendered me even more at odds with myself than did the symptoms: Could I no longer trust my capacity to perceive, judge, and test the reality of my experience? I was disempowered by my ignorance, and easily influenced. I wondered, is this how double-bind communications create schizophrenics? Which signal, which "reality," should I choose to believe? And how did I know when I was being paranoid or not?

These feelings sensitized me in a new way to the experience of my patients, and what authority my words and actions must carry for them. It also made more distinct for me, as a therapist, differentiations between psychic reality and phenomenal reality. I was more at home with the former. Psychological dynamics and the unconscious were familiar ground to me, and I believed so firmly in their determinism in life, that I had at times underestimated the force of external, or nonpsychological, realities in the lives of my patients—just as I did with myself. Encountering the full ramifications of my misinterpreted personal experience attuned me in a far more sensitive way to the impact on an individual of things external to the self.

My early patienthood also profoundly affected my understanding of the states of helplessness and vulnerability wreaked by unknowable and uncontrollable life events. It fundamentally changed the depth at which I could relate to the similar experiences of my patients, especially those who had been traumatized and those who had many losses to grieve.

Even in general terms, my patients, in their own way, all were braving the ambiguity of the unknown and the vulnerability of entrusting themselves to dependency on a more knowledgeable other.

My illness affected what my profession was to me in other ways. It shattered, for some time, the artfulness and play that I normally found in my work. At times, I hated the unconscious for its frivolity. What did fantasy, especially wishes, have to do with anything? It became a decadent, almost loathsome indulgence, to dwell in the curious, creative land of dreams, play, and metaphor. What had once captivated me intellectually about psychoanalytic work became something I transiently scorned. I began to see all my patients in terms of their emotional well-being and survival, and I became overly determined to make headway with each toward his or her own consolidation.

I was asked once whether my experience of illness led me to lose faith in the process of psychotherapy and its capacity to heal and cure. This has not happened; I continue to believe in the power of my therapist tools, and the power of people to change. Instead, I have gained a grudging respect for the power of illness, whether it be psychological or physical. Illness may persist; there will be limits to what I, as doctor, can do for my patients; and the notion of cure can be only an ideal. My ideas of psychotherapy, which may have been naively idealistic and vaguely grandiose, were demystified, not jaded.

REMAINING HIDDEN: SELF-DISCLOSURE AND PERSONAL VULNERABILITY

Being sick makes one vulnerable. My body and the so-called conflict-free spheres of my ego each were drained by illness, leaving me with fewer resources to weather challenges and demands of any sort. When my MS flare-ups were particularly debilitating physically, when they were traumatizing to my sense of self, or worrisome prognostically, I increasingly needed to devote my resources to mending myself. The less I could do so, the more raw I was in encounters with others, including my patients. My defenses felt so thin and permeable, at times, that I did not feel a very reliable vessel for holding and processing the emotional, unconscious, and transferential contents my patients brought me. I sat uneasily in my role then; and the more so when I felt the added demand of keeping up appearances, so that all would seem normal.

I held a deep identification with the psychoanalytic method, which derived in part from a wish to be a seer and truth-teller, one who could uncover and speak what is hidden or unknown. I have long been fascinated by the unconscious and by the mind's ineluctable drive to communicate and to obscure at once what it uneasily contains. It is an ironic personal fact that I now live with an illness that barely shows itself to the observer, even when besetting me internally with a sensory clamor. As a therapist, the invisibility of my illness and the contrast between how things *are* and how, on the other hand, they *seem,* has made it much more difficult for me to admit to myself, within my role, and to my patients, that I am sick.

I frequently worked with some degree of impairment and continued working through several flare-ups during which I chose not to disclose my illness to my patients. I longed to have them know everything, but forbade myself the telling. At the same time, early on, I could not have them know, for it would have bared me more than I could tolerate. It was necessary then to pretend all was as usual. I finally found neither solution to be tenable—clinically or personally. Disguising myself was inauthentic and frankly draining; revealing all, on the other hand, was too exposing personally and would have been too great an intrusion on my patients.

In the end, it became clear that disclosing my illness was the only thing to do. I resisted this, however, for a very long time. I cautioned myself to ensure that it would be for the sake of individual patients, and not primarily for myself. I feared that by advancing myself and something of my life on the therapeutic scene, I would jeopardize the development of a treatment. I had believed in a natural course that would prevail as long as I kept out of the way of each patient—as if I were not an active participant in how treatment emerged and was formed in the first place; as if we were not two human beings doing our best to engage in helping one. I finally recognized that the process of psychotherapy was mutual and organic regardless of the unusual set of circumstances my life brought to it. My illness simply crystallized this fact.

I had additional concerns. I was afraid of skewing the transference by becoming to my patients a figure with needs, ailments, and deficits. I also was concerned about burdening them with the knowledge of my illness. How would this particular information limit what they could experience toward me? Or what I could experience toward them? In trying to forestall disclosure, hoping the illness would abate with just a little more time, I masked myself more thoroughly than usual with my patients. The detachment this called for was disorienting, almost depersonalizing for me internally. To be sure, self-containment was wise and necessary at times, but how acutely estranging it was to shield myself more broadly in encounters where normally both I and the patient would have felt the flow of an emotional resonance in the space of the contact. I came to feel that this, if anything, was unnatural, and that to continue to hide my illness—with whatever effects it wreaked on my psychic viability to do so—would certainly be a poison to my treatment relationships.

I finally began to tell patients of my illness about a year into it, when I had started missing sessions and relying on a cane to walk. Disclosure did not come easily for me; but neither did it yield the levels of disruption I had feared. I probably could have done it much sooner, without ill effect. My patients' reactions varied widely, as would be expected. What I told each also varied, depending on the climate of the relationship, the treatment, and what each seemed to want or need to know. I was met with deep human responsiveness from most: concern, sadness for me, wishes to help and to assure that I had caring others around me. I was moved in many instances, touched by a kind of love from my patients that spoke to what I meant to them beyond mere transference. I had had no idea of this aspect of the relationship, and it made me wonder how much I unwittingly guarded myself from feeling what could be a fuller personal experience of relatedness with my patients.

Not surprisingly, the material that surfaced immediately after my disclosures was preponderantly about loss and abandonment by nurturing figures. Knowing of my illness legitimately raised fears of depending on me. Later reactions differed in ways that highlighted distinct individual dynamics. One patient, for instance, experienced a head injury that caused temporary neurological symptoms similar to some of my own. As she recovered, she accurately observed my condition declining. She spoke to the guilt she felt about this, and, as in her childhood amidst four competitive sisters, her feeling of needing to keep private how she was doing better than I, as if I would be injured and threatened by it.

For two other patients, the disclosure of my illness seemed to mark a profound turning point in treatment that made accessible material I otherwise had not been able to reach with them. I was so concerned about hampering the treatments, I had not even considered that disclosure might help the work. For one of these patients, my disclosure specifically fostered a deepening of trust and identification. She felt that I, like her, had suffered and struggled to find meaning in a life in which bad things happened. Gradually, this woman, who allowed almost no one to be close to her, began to talk of longings for intimacy and companionship, and began to internalize images of my strength. It became possible for her to take me in as a new and positive introject, when her early internal objects had only been malevolent and abandoning.

While I felt relieved in some basic way to have the presence of my illness known to my patients, I felt protective of myself and my vulnerability. I did not realize I conveyed this until one patient described how she felt I had withdrawn after having shared information about my illness with her. She had a mental image, in which I was a turtle that had drawn inward to hide in its shell, with but an antenna reaching out into the world. What a piquant statement her image made of the struggle I indeed felt: to incubate myself, for the sake of my own preservation, while trying mightily to keep meeting my patients' needs to be seen and heard with sensitivity and understanding.

A DISRUPTED THERAPEUTIC POSITION

Seeing my competence as a therapist persist during the times I was ill was a salve to my esteem and affirmed my being in the world. I needed to know that some effective part of me remained alive, well, and still in the mainstream of life. The long-term treatments I conducted, in particular, were islands of familiar territory to me and provided a steadying reassurance when my health declined. The beast of MS is uncertainty: uncertainty about how long an exacerbation will last, what it will affect, when there will be another, and above all, how much will be permanently lost. When I was new to the illness, I was not so willing to succumb to it and usually erred on the side of stretching my resources to their limits. I was terrified of it getting me, as if to let go of too much would mean the beginning of a slippery slide that I would never be able to halt. With the bite of determination, I held onto every bit of my professional life that I could.

The pockets of competence I witnessed in my work allowed me to preserve a feeling of continuity with my past and with a future I hoped could continue its original trajectory. Over time, when things worsened, with more frequent flare-ups and increasing deficits, it became physically impossible to live on the rewards of determination, and I had to begin relinquishing the professional aims I held close. My energy became so limited that I no longer had the stamina to continue at the pace I had when healthy. The present became all-consuming, and the state of my professional life dimmed in importance in the face of life with a body that was demanding extraordinary amounts of care and accommodation.

The extra effort the illness required of me to keep working was tempered by the growth I saw in my patients and what that meant to me. I saw changes in my patients: They were getting better, developing greater capacities for living fully. This was enormously gratifying. Paradoxically, it was difficult for me to feel I really had played a part in it. During the long period of time when I was on uncertain clinical ground with respect to disclosure, I felt less than ever an agent of each therapy and its positive outcomes. It was all the more moving to be reminded by what in me knew better, that I was hardly an insignificant partner in these treatments. I, in fact, could do something very effective, even while struggling terribly with my own troubles. It became a bitter truth that I could do for my patients what no one could do for me with my illness: My kind of healing was more than palliative, and it would probably persist.

My work was often at its most sensitive and intuitively inspired during the times I was most bared to myself emotionally during episodes of illness. The skin of my ego was so thin then, that I was empathically closer than ever to my patients' affect. There were breakthroughs I made in recognizing my patients' inner dilemmas—insights that might have remained obscure to me had it not been for the otherwise very disorganizing internal disruption I sustained. I worried, however, about the ethics of working in this condition. Just how impeded was I—not only by my struggles and symptoms, but also by the potent medications I required, with all their serious side effects? My conscience was vigilant to these questions regarding my fitness for work, as it was as well to the finer and myriad ways my illness might be affecting the very nature of this work. Did my illness seep into the therapeutic process in ways that were not so truly to the benefit of my patients? I was not always thinking as clearly or fluidly as in the past; nor was I as fully engaged. When functioning and capacity occur on a continuum, as they do in the work of conducting psychotherapy, it is not always so easy to determine just when one is incapable and should stop.

I judged throughout that I was a "good enough" therapist, but I felt I was not as good as I had been, so the question of competence seemed always in front of me, and always needing reassessment. To make matters more complicated, the more closely I examined my work, the more likely I was to find distorting influences—just as would any good therapist. On one notable occasion, I reasoned my way to a decision to forestall disclosing my illness to a particular female patient. Her mother's chronic and painful illness, years earlier, had made my patient the object of serious neglect and outright cruelty as a child. With deceptive rationale, I feared some hobbling of the transference, a crippling of the treatment, if she knew of this real-life aspect of my relationship with her, that I was physically ill. It occurred to me, fortunately, that I could devise the same formulation for nearly all my patients. Perhaps I was only making excuses to avoid the reality of my illness. Indeed, most of my patients had mothers who, if not afflicted with a medical illness, had clearly suffered some sort of psychological sickness that hurt their children.

It was some time before I recognized further what personally motivated me in such a strong wish to protect my patient from reexperiencing the pains of a relationship with a sick mother. I felt, as her therapist, that I was one—a sick mother—and I could not stand the implications about this that arose from my own background. Ill mothers figured large in my family legacy, across multiple generations. In each instance, the lives of these women were cloaked in a context of denial of the illness, ambiguity regarding its severity, and serious neglect of their children's needs for nurturance. A real psychological nerve had been touched. Recognizing it provided me a kind of relief and clarity in regard to approaching my patients, but the lengths to which I had had to go to wade my way to the truth, indicated just how murky my awareness could be. This was unsettling.

I questioned myself in layer upon layer of the relationships with my patients and what I was creating with them. My personal analysis provided me with familiarity with my unconscious and its derivatives, so that I had means for rooting out the evidence and play of motives that might interfere with my work. I took it for granted that such motives existed. The challenge was to catch their manifestations before they were played out too far. I was aware one day of an unusual hardness in me toward a patient whose emotions I knew could cause in her a debilitating passivity. These emotions had paralyzed her in the past, such that she had remained defenseless while suffering gross sexual abuse. On this particular day, I felt a nearly savage impulse to be cold and violating toward her. She stood like a magnet, inviting a sadistic countertransference by her behavior alone. And, as I saw later, I was all the more vulnerable to participating in it, out of my rage at being victimized myself by the paralyzing, incapacitating disease I have. I hated feeling like a victim, and had I not recognized the power of the countertransferential pull, I would have turned this outward, toward this patient who presented herself as weak and victimized.

I suspected many of my patients knew I was sick before I told them. Not one of those I did finally tell, however, had let the awareness become conscious. One woman recalled vague and fleeting worries that I was sick, and we reconstructed how she had protected herself from being fully aware of what she perceived. She had passed nearby me on the street one day when I was first using a cane but was blind to both me and the cane. This highly attuned woman effectually had a negative hallucination. As we explored this, it became clear she was protecting me, as much as herself, in not bearing witness to my illness. She accurately sensed that I did not want my illness acknowledged, but in addition she had a specific fear that she would harm me by noticing and expressing concern. Over the ensuing months, the reaction formation implicit in this surfaced repeatedly. She once brought me roses after I was sick and warned me not to be hurt by the thorns. On another occasion, she filled a session with her own illness, coughing and sneezing without shielding her mouth, and with near gusto. She then worried guiltily that she had made me sick, when I had a flare soon after.

Although I watched myself and my work carefully as my illness became a growing presence, I felt at times that I was losing hold of my therapeutic position. I especially felt my grasp of my unconscious was tenuous. It was a terribly uncomfortable feeling. Eventually, I simply had to relinquish the security and familiar feeling of control that theretofore came of being attuned to a consistent and relatively steady inner world. My inner world was in chaos. I was not losing my grip, but it seemed so to me internally. One unconscious may speak to another in the therapeutic dialogue, and I was used to keeping tabs on mine. I wondered what it was up to now that it had more free rein. What if my unconscious was telegraphing what was inside of me—my feelings, preoccupations, self-perceptions—unbeknownst to me? What if my inner state had created some filter of which I was unaware, that limited what got through to me, and distorted what came out? There were many questions I had, for instance, about ways that I may have depended on my patients, and whether I unknowingly conveyed this to them. I knew that I relied financially on my private practice patients—and that this swayed me to keep appointments that every other shred of me wished to miss. Similarly, I dragged myself to perform clinical and supervisory functions in my job, believing I would lose something I depended on there if I did not manage to stay vital and responsible.

My life narrowed during periods of illness. I was increasingly alone, and the relationships with my patients became more primary. I continued to involve myself with them, while I was less available in all ways to be among friends and colleagues. My obligations to patients transcended the importance of my commitment to other relationships in my life. I gained from them a feeling of involvement, of being at the heart of something with someone—a feeling that was otherwise diminished or absent in my life. Being a therapist was a retreat to a relational haven at such times. Unfortunately, immersion in the material of my patients also served to remove me yet further from those anchors of reality that one can keep hold of through contact with the external world. This only deepened my disorientation as the therapist.

Very early in my illness, when it was so frightening and such an unknown, my need to deny was strong. Under the circumstances, denial was not such a bad thing, but it contributed to a feeling that I was losing the boundaries between myself and my patients. I felt at times that I was swimming in a sea of patient material and personal associations. These seemed so intermixed I feared I was basing my therapeutic strategies on massive projections. I encountered more parallel process during times of crisis with my illness, such that what I heard myself grappling with in my own analysis was an awful mirror of aspects of process and content with specific patients. This alone reflected my struggle with the job of being a therapist. My clinical edge slipped during some of the periods I was ill; I heard a verbal clumsiness in my interventions and felt a mental inefficiency in my efforts to conceive. I turned increasingly to my trusted intuition when I felt my capacity to reason erode. It made me fear that I was the central patient and that I was finding my own unresolved conflicts in my patients.

As I suggested earlier, I sensed that several of my patients were unconsciously aware of my trouble before it was overt, and before I had said anything about it. I was never quite sure of this, but the associations of certain patients suggested an unusual perceptivity. Three patients in particular were distinct, all of whom had developed in their childhoods extremely sensitive antennae for the emotions and needs of those around them. All had been groomed to respond to their mothers with singular devotion: one by a needy alcoholic woman, one by a mother who was masochistically burdened, and one by a mother who was infantile and devouring.

I was perhaps 6 months into a weekly treatment with one of these women when I had a first crisis with a surge of MS symptoms that at the time were not diagnosable. I was experiencing bizarre sensations in my legs and feet, much numbness, and increasing awkwardness walking. But for my clumsy gait, none of this was observable. A number of serious things had been tentatively ruled out by my doctors, but it was a mystery what was wrong, and I was hardly at ease about my well-being. In a session during this time, my patient brought with her one day a large shopping bag, from which she pulled a towel and small cage. As she set these on the floor of my office, she explained in rather graphic but blithe terms, that her pet bird had fallen on its neck and she had brought it with her on the way to the veterinarian's. She pulled the bird, wrapped carefully in another towel, from her shoulder bag and laid it down on the floor, inside the cage, talking unperturbedly all the while and saying she hoped I did not mind. The session unfolded, and at the end, she gestured to the motionless bird and asked me, could I see, was it dead? She determined its heart was still beating, continued talking as she carefully swaddled it, and then was on her way.

I had never before encountered the scepter of death so vividly in the space of a session, and to be drawn into its presence by such a companionable and laissez-faire attitude on my patient's part would have shaken me under the best of circumstances. In this case, I was left thoroughly rattled. The collision of reality and fantasy around the picture of infirmity, incapacitation, and mortality left me unnerved and therapeutically unbalanced. There were three wounded creatures in that room, myself included, and I could scarcely believe I was the one in charge of rescuing. Could my patient have sensed my illness, some decline, my fear, my diminished availability to care for her? Did she think, at some level, that I would die? A coincidence seemed too uncanny to be possible; I guessed that she had sensed something and that it stirred deep feelings and anxieties for her about the extinction of loved ones. She in fact had survived the prolonged terminal illnesses of several people she loved deeply, including her mother.

It was this patient's style to speak in anecdotes that sketched vivid and detailed images for me of her inner world and its workings. A different patient, whose verbal style was perhaps less rich and complex, instead conveyed the most to me of her unconscious awareness of my illness through her behavior and bearing. The transference-countertransference channel of communication, which had always been my most sure route to understanding her, was the means by which I heard that she was perceiving something. In subtle ways, she began to treat me with care and caution, holding herself back from asking much. Sessions felt easier and lighter, she told more stories, did not move as deep emotionally. It felt as if she was giving me a break; I was not having to work so hard. She simultaneously, however, began to come to sessions obviously sick and talking about how ill she had been. She avoided going for medical attention, and continued to drive herself without respite in her demanding work life. In complicated fashion, she seemed at once to be endeavoring to spare me her needs and let me know she felt neglected. We began to talk about matters of self-care, an issue I silently acknowledged to myself we shared at that point.

It was never easy to put myself first. Although I became better at discerning where my limits were, in terms of physical and mental energy, I frequently felt torn about whose needs to attend, mine or my patients'.

They had vested in our work considerable personal risk and faith, and my commitment to them was quite real. But I had to learn equal respect for my body's unusual needs with its illness. These included limiting my hours of work and activity each day, and building in much time for rest. In the end, I found it did no one good for me to neglect myself in sacrifice to my patients. Stretching myself even in small ways typically made me more sick. And I recognized that being a martyr would affect the security of the therapeutic relationship just as does anything else that denies or distorts the reality of the present and the fundamental needs of those involved.

This story is not over. I cannot know what events are to come, or what kind of ending there will be. I have known my diagnosis for two years, my patients have known it for one. The future is not predictable with MS, beyond the harsh fact that the disease is chronic and progressive. Fortunately, its effects on cognitive functioning are usually minimal or occur late in the disease course. The drugs used to treat MS create a larger problem on this score than the illness itself, but at least they are administered only intermittently.

And in regard to what the future will be for my patients and their treatments? I do not know. But I have the sense we have done the hardest of the work in making room for my illness, by laying a ground of permissiveness and inquiry that will allow for continued exploration and acknowledgment of its impact and meaning. For now, it has enriched the quality of relatedness my patients and I experience with each other, and it has clarified the bounds of such relatedness—those that are unique for each patient, as well as those unique more generally to the unusual enterprise of psychotherapy. The bounds are larger and more flexible than I once would have thought.

PART THREE

The Emotional Impact of the Work

CHAPTER 10

Public Exposure of Shame in the Group Leader

R. TRACY MACNAB, PHD

Whence the shadowy light? What company in the dark!

–BECKETT, *1980*

THE SETTING

It is Tuesday, at 7:10 P.M., the group session has been going on for less than 10 minutes, and I am already hopelessly lost. Tension creeps up my back, through my neck, and settles into my shoulders and jaw. A rapid scan of consciousness for clues to the source of this malaise reveals a dull blankness of mind. The group members appear unconcerned, the conversation flows along touching on one person's fears of losing his job and another's visit with her difficult mother. My perception is that I am the only one in the room experiencing distress. As time wears on, I desire only to be far away from this room. By 7:15, time seems to have stopped altogether; I am exhausted and in need of sleep, and I wonder how I will endure the remaining hour of the group.

This response to the ordinary process of the group appears to be overdetermined and out of context. I mentally scan the recent events in the group to search for clues to my acute distress. In the prior week's session, a significant event had occurred. After weeks of preparation and ambivalence, there had been a long-awaited and promising encounter between two group members. Tim, a very quiet, withdrawn, and narcissistically brittle man had, after much hesitation, confronted Louise on her domineering and emotionally flat manner of speech. He pointed out that she frequently complained about the lack of progress in the group, but that she did not talk about her own life experiences or feelings, preferring instead to be solicitous of others. Meanwhile, her own depression and somatic complaints related to her obesity went unattended. Louise responded to Tim's comments with an extended silence and the subject was dropped.

The group itself is composed of four men and four women whose constant preoccupation must be the maintenance of a fragile and tenuously intact self. Interpersonal interactions pose a constant challenge to this task. All relationships at work or play are potential threats to the preservation of this sense of self that imagines and contains life's good and hopeful possibilities. The group treats intimate social contacts as potentially damaging intrusions. The air of the room is often filled with unspoken terrors, threats, grudges, and potential disruptions of the fragile psychological membranes of the group members. Therefore, each member of the group has felt the loneliness, despair, and hopelessness of a life lived in avoidance of human contact. But any empathic appreciation of this dilemma can be so filled with suffering that it is often regarded as the enemy of hope. The fire at which the group warms itself often burns the very flesh that seeks the warmth. At the same time, it often seems to be a fire that has no warmth at all.

In my efforts to understand my peculiarly strong reactions to this night's group session, I think about Ogden's (1982) description of projective identification as both a defense and a form of communication. As a defense, this moment in the group's struggles may be the group's efforts to preserve itself by asking the group leader to assume responsibility for the alarming affects associated with the unresolved conflict between Louise and Tim. The group might be saying to the leader, "We don't know what to do with this toxic stuff, *you* keep it." I speculate that I may have taken receipt of this message without being aware of it. As a communication, this moment in group has both emotional power and the capacity to compel belief that it is my role to hold the dread of the group. I may not have known that a communication was being received, I simply *became* the message. In one seamless moment, I moved from an empathic appreciation of group members' struggles to a full-blown merger with them. Only in retrospect can the motives for this powerful and disturbing condition be comprehended.

If my speculations are correct, the group is now facing a difficult dilemma. The members can either ignore and attempt to forget the efforts of one of the frailest of their number to make a closer connection, or they can acknowledge the courage involved in raising the issue. Either choice is fraught with difficulty. If they choose the former, they preserve the illusion of intactness in the unbruised insulated self, but remain isolated and discouraged with the work of the group. If the choice is for the latter, a vast array of injurious and intensely critical outcomes can be envisioned.

In the avoidance of these unpleasant and apparently unresolvable alternatives, projective identification is a familiar defensive choice. In this dynamic, I am appointed (and I unconsciously volunteer) to be the battleground on which the tension between these forces is to be resolved. I have always liked the descriptive power of this concept, but I seldom find that it entirely explains the experience. Among the unexplained aspects of the phenomenon is the perfect agreement between the fantasies of the group (sender of the projection) and group leader (receiver and container of the projection). Is there some kind of democratic principle that operates in the soul of the human community? It is as though the group had declared the results of a secret election: "We have met and agreed that you are best suited of all of us to suffer this misery, so here it is and you're welcome to it." The group then goes on about its business as though nothing had occurred. The group leader finds the requisite set of matching conflicts and defenses in his or her own unconscious, and agrees to the contract. But how can an exchange as complex as this one occur at such a high rate of speed? Can any group of people really agree on anything so rapidly? I have often thought that it would be as useful to conceptualize the entire matter as a form of magic, trance channeling, or soul possession.

THE CONFRONTATION

I have entered the group room on this evening with the enthusiasm of a leader who looks forward to the clinical challenges that the meeting might present, confident that I am providing an environment in which group members could work toward an encounter with significant truths about themselves and one another. Now I struggle to remember what could possibly have made me so wildly optimistic. As I try to grapple with the group's conflicts using the vehicle of projective identification, I discover that my discomfort has not lessened one bit. I am still feeling lost, alone, and incompetent to help the group with its troubles. The discussion of difficult bosses and mothers grinds to a halt. The connection between this material and difficult group leaders seems worthy of some attention, and I tell the group of this thought. The response is a long silence. I think to myself that the transference interpretation may be too close to forbidden and intolerable affect, and so I attempt to refocus the group on a reparative emotional experience. I mention the unresolved conflict between Tim and Louise, and ask if there may not be some lingering feelings that need discussing. Another polite but emphatic silence ensues. For a few moments I have the sense that no one has heard a word I said. Possibly I spoke inaudibly? As the silence continues, I am aware of an urgency within myself to demonstrate to the group my abilities as a conscientious group leader. The group's silence thwarts this desire, and I can feel anger building within me.

The next topic for the group is selected by Louise, the object of Tim's comments in the previous week's meeting. She airs a litany of complaints about group therapy and its irrelevance to her life. I mention that she seems to have some feelings on this matter. She counters that she has no personal feelings, but that she sees no positive change in any of the group members and is concerned that they are spending time and money on group therapy that could be more profitably spent on making friends or finding a new job. As for herself, she has long ago given up hoping for change. She has tried everything and everything had failed. She then describes a previous effort to lose weight. After losing about 10 pounds, she had been rewarded with a series of horrendous panic attacks. She claims she then swore off self-improvement forever and goes on to attribute her entry into this group as another foolish episode of hopefulness. She has learned, she says, that she has remained a member of the group (for more than two and a half years) as a kind of bad and unbreakable habit.

Knowing that resistance is the energy that drives the engine of change, I imagine that I have come upon a therapeutic moment in which I can offer an effective group intervention. I can confront Louise with the contradiction between her defensive cynicism and her continuing efforts to improve her life. Perhaps this can unlock her defenses against having immediate emotional experiences and allow her to see that there are things that matter to her. So, I remind her that the group is not an unbreakable habit, but a risky choice for change. I further emphasize that her presence in the group is testimony that she is working toward a change in her life.

Louise is unmoved. She continues her complaint. The group listens in a silence that I imagine signifies extreme discouragement. My level of irritation rises as I watch Louise ride roughshod over any germ of hope that the group may be attempting to preserve. Her behavior seems to me to be an attack on Tim for his confrontation of the previous week, on the hopeful feelings of other group members, and on myself as the creator of this doubtful group enterprise. Her onslaught seems to point directly at my growing professional anxieties and uncertainties about the progress of the group and about my usefulness as a group leader. How can I call myself a competent group leader when members have spent so much time and energy on group therapy in return for so little reward?

Louise completes this chapter of her lament with a direct question to the leader, "What, after two and a half years of my time, energy, and money, would you say I have gotten out of this group?" I respond, with considerable anger in my voice, "You have gotten to the point where you can bring the problems you have outside the room, into the room." Rolling her eyes heavenward, she rebuffs this comment with a shrug. To this challenge to my ability and competence, I snap, "There you go again, avoiding the issue! If you want to get better, you've got to stop running away from these emotions and learn to bear them." I notice after I have spoken that I am gripping the arms of my chair as though I were going to launch myself from it.

Louise responds to the anger in these words. She says she has never met a therapist so insensitive or uncompassionate, she considers my remarks a breach of professional ethics, and she feels that I have brutally insulted her. She feels that her efforts as well as her suffering have been belittled. Hasn't she been trying to be honest about her feelings? This is the final straw. Despite encouragement from me to discuss these reactions and some entreaties from the group not to leave hastily, she retreats into stonelike silence for the remainder of the group and leaves, never to return.

THE LETTER

I spend the day after the group preoccupied with the astonishing power of my own reactions to the group. I experience a growing and painful impression that I have been intolerant and negligent as a therapist. I repeatedly analyze the bind in which I find myself with the group. Have I become impatient with Louise's suffering and departed from empathy into the language of expectancy and demand? In so doing have I enacted the transference role of the repressive mother/boss that the group was talking about? Certainly, these would seem to be the case in varying degrees, but my emotional response to my behavior in the group continues to be that of the hunted criminal rather than overzealous and impatient therapist.

My ruminations are interrupted midweek by a letter from Louise. In the letter, she elaborates on my failures as a clinician, talks about how hurt she has been by my words, and describes how this hurt has made her doubt the usefulness of psychotherapy altogether. As I read the letter,

I again find myself agreeing with her critique of my intervention. I feel that I have allowed my own desire for therapeutic potency to become confused with compassion. I begin to feel that I have punished Louise for the honesty of her complaints. I perceive my intervention to be an unempathic harangue that has entirely missed the preverbal territory in which she and the group struggle for cognitive and affectual mastery over traumatic life events.

This perspective on the problem is accompanied by a shameful view of myself as a failed therapist, group leader, and human being. I accuse myself of missing the point that some complaints are a statement of the impossibility of action rather than a call to action. Havens (1986) describes patients who, when asked, "Are you there?" respond, "No, I'm not here." In this group, I am outnumbered by people who often do not want to be there. I feel the demand to have some dramatic therapeutic impact on their lives, to bring them, alive and present into this moment of their lives, and to help them to tolerate the unbearable realities they face and have faced. The more prolonged the exposure to the withdrawal, passivity, and misery of the group, the more I feel called into action and hopefulness. This pressure for results meets the equal and opposite force of resistance to change. My ambitions to save the group from its distress collide with a growing sense of failure and anxiety about my professional competence. I feel that I am publicly exposing the most damaged aspects of my own preverbal self, where articulating experience occurs only in the most blunt and primary language: posture and facial expression, movement and touch, voice tone and silence. Words seem useless and impossible, and simple presence woefully inadequate. My sense of shame intimates an awareness of a reality so profoundly dreary that human hope apparently cannot survive there. Nathanson (1986) talks about an "empathic wall" that shields the self from such affective experiences. My attitude toward Louise, which I perceived at the time as an effort to breach such a wall, proved to be just the opposite.

Monday night, I have a dream:

> I have made a scheduling error, and all my groups surprise me by arriving at my office simultaneously. My office has been relocated to my home, but the construction is incomplete and there is a partially built wall between the office and the living room. I have not expected the arrival of the groups, but hastily scramble to assemble a circle of chairs in a large circle that crosses the boundary between office and living room. I make an effort to appear calm and to lead the groups as though there were nothing wrong, only to discover that I am dressed in my underwear. The

group appears to proceed successfully for a while, but then Louise points out that I am not adequately prepared to be a group leader and denounces me as a charlatan. She leads a faction of the group in an uproarious departure from the group.

The next day is group day. It is my practice to read all written communications from group members aloud in the next group session. However, my strong countertransferential feelings and the residue of the dream leave me filled with trepidation and dismay at the prospect of reading this particular letter. I keep remembering the words of Elvin Semrad, "Patients do not quit helping situations . . . they get thrown out, but they don't quit" (Rako & Mazur, 1980). The reading of the letter seems a public acknowledgment of my failures as a therapist, a reenactment of the dream. I imagine that the group will see through my grandiose claims of competence and that I will be naked and vulnerable under the unfriendly glare of the group's critical regard.

The day of the group session dawns, and I dread the arrival of the group hour. At the start of the session, I read the letter aloud, from time to time looking around the room to gauge the reaction of the group members. My palms sweat, and my heart rate accelerates as though I were in the presence of judge, jury, and executioner.

I finish the letter, restraining my impulse to editorialize. I await the verdict of the group. The majority response is silence. Then, in an uncharacteristic act, Tim laughs softly to himself. He says, "Boy, she is *really* angry with you." I inquire what he has heard in the letter. He continues speaking in a fashion that is looser and more direct than he has ever allowed himself to be in the group. He observes that Louise has been angry at me for a long time, and that he has often wondered why she stayed in the group. He is also solicitous about my feelings, wondering how badly I must have felt in the face of this onslaught. In the weeks to follow, he takes a more active and openly empathic stance toward other members of the group, making it clear to all of us that our presence in the room is important to him. I note with a continuous sense of surprise that Tim, and the group along with him, have tolerated my failure to help Louise and to hold the group together. They have not only survived the crisis but begin a discussion of their own thoughts about termination from the group, and the work they must do to be ready for that time. They have weathered a sense of hopelessness that I feared none of us could survive. Further, I feel free of the plaguing anxiety to rescue the group. I experience a sense of reprieve from the cloud of guilt that has for weeks accompanied my work with the group.

RESOLUTION

Why my excessively strong reaction to this event? Clearly, the concrete events described here are not as momentous as my life-and-death affect about them. It has become a matter of the greatest importance to me that the group affirm that I am an effective group therapist who can provide a beacon of hope, light, and human warmth. This yearning for effectiveness becomes grandiose when it grows to include either promoting hope where none exists or changing the personalities of other people by sheer force of will. To overcome my perceived deficiencies, I believe it necessary to perfect myself, to create a grandiose self that can overwhelm, outperform, and overmaster any obstacles that stand in the path of the therapy. This grandiosity is intended to bridge perceived inner voids where I feel vulnerable and unable to sustain my hopeful enterprise. The grandiosity signifies that I have a long way to fall when I cannot make Louise happy.

The dream reveals the underpinnings of my struggle with the group. In it, the boundary between family and work is only partial. The group has become my family. I am cast in (and immediately volunteer for) the role of family savior. Subsequent analysis reveals that the countertransference drama derives from my own childhood effort to deal with my mother's traumatic illness and its deteriorative impact on my family. Therefore, I feel I must save the group, though I soon find I am not clothed in the worthy attributes of my adult life. The more I attempt to prove my worth as a group therapist, the more I am lost to the group as an empathic presence. As failure of therapeutic hope looms, my compulsive heroic effort reaches crisis proportions.

Eventually, I am reprieved from the countertransferential condemnation in three stages. First, I am forced by the severity of my emotional response to examine the role of projective identification in the process of the group. This cognitive tool proves to be useful for mapping the terrain of the response, but it provides little relief from the compelling believability of the projected illusion.

Then, I endure a public humiliation of my reputation as I read Louise's letter in the group. This event, complete with sweaty palms and racing heart, is a visceral reminder that my early life history has been engaged by the process of the group. I read the letter because it is an established ritual of the group, but the experience has more of the flavor of an act of contrition than a clinical strategy. Finally, I am offered forgiveness by Tim and by the group. In this last stage of the process, members of the group demonstrate that they can acknowledge and survive the avoided affects. The catastrophe predicted by my own unconscious does not occur, and the group, along with its leader, survives.

The countertransference dilemma described here is a relatively commonplace occurrence for group leaders. Each clinician has some developmental lacunae, and in certain situations these difficulties can be activated. What is interesting to ponder, however, is the means through which the resolution of the countertransference is attained. Despite all my cleverness and training, I became enmired in a hostile dependency bind with the group. I then endeavored to resolve the situation by demonstrating irrefutable proof of my skill as a group leader. The reality of the group's profoundly painful life struggles confronted my grandiose expectations, and I experienced myself as a failure. Only after this experience of failure could I again assume a clear-headed appreciation of the situation facing Louise, Tim, and the group. No amount of self-study, supervision, or consultation could have replaced the heuristic value of the in vivo experience of loss and powerlessness.

A poem by a 12th-century Sufi poet named Rumi begins, "Today, like every other day, we awake empty and afraid." I am reminded that at the core of human experience there is an empty and scared aspect of ourselves that we do not often embrace. It is the gift of this group that they remind me that interpersonal sophistication, professional status, and clinical skill are merely adequate protective clothing around this vulnerable core of self. An empathic connection with the work of the group requires a shedding of the impermeable armor of the family hero.

Groups outnumber leaders demographically and affectively. In the contagion of the group process, I am caught up in my own impossible and irreconcilable conflicts. Then, instead of enacting the role of savior, I am in need of salvation. And salvation arrived in the form of failure.

The use of the concept of salvation in psychotherapy is a controversial issue. The doctrine of separation of church and state applies in our field as elsewhere. However, there are resonances with Psalms 34:18, "The Lord is close to those whose courage is broken; he saves those whose spirit is crushed." Or consider the Tao te Ching:

If you want to become whole,
let yourself be partial.
If you want to become straight,
let yourself be crooked.
If you want to become full,
let yourself be empty.

If you want to be reborn,
let yourself die.
If you want to be given everything,
give everything up.

My illusions of masterful control were humbled by the confrontation with the reality of the group. My shameful sense of public failure as a heroic savior led me to experience myself as partial, crooked, and empty of promise. The apparently necessary and grandiose self suffered a death, but with this death came also a rebirth. The new self regained the resilience to withstand direct experience of empathy with affects, associations, and events in the room. Where I had encouraged members to get *out* of their predicaments, I could now join them *in* their predicaments. If the Lord or the Tao in this instance is expressed as an empathic understanding of the truth within each group member, then this transition in the group and especially in the group leader is a form of awakening or salvation.

These events were not turned to therapeutic advantage only by the clever application of technical interventions. Nor was the change in perspective achieved largely through the vehicle of theoretical study or collegial consultation. What caused the empty to be seen as full was the vivid countertransferential enactment of the experience of emptiness. And what, finally, made that enactment real and immediate, and the subsequent enlightenment effective, was a nearness to courage that had been broken and to spirit that had been crushed. Since this event, the group has been through many similar cycles each of which has yielded new learning, and each of which has renewed my appreciation that to be broken is to open the possibility of being made whole.

REFERENCES

Beckett, S. (1980). *Company.* New York: Grove Press.

Havens, L. (1986). *Making contact: Uses of language in psychotherapy.* Cambridge: Harvard University Press.

Nathanson, D. L. (1986). The empathic wall and the ecology of affect. *Psychoanalytic Study of the Child, 41,* 171–187.

Ogden, T. H. (1982). *Projective identification and psychoanalytic technique.* New York: Jason Aronson.

Rako, S., & Mazur, H. (1980). *Semrad: The heart of a therapist.* New York: Jason Aronson.

CHAPTER 11

Unexpected Encounters: The Wizard of Oz Exposed

GINA ARONS, PsyD and RONALD D. SIEGEL, PsyD

It was a hot, sweaty, Friday afternoon in July. I was glad to get out of my clothes and strip down to my bikini. I stepped into the cool, clear pond water—it felt so good. My boyfriend swam over to me, gave me a passionate kiss, and held me in the water. We played there for a long while. I unwound and for the first time in days felt really relaxed and peaceful. The world had become a cozy blur as it often is when my contact lenses are out.

I stepped out of the pond. As I squinted to look for my towel, my body tensed. I rushed to cover myself. I felt sick. I felt exposed. I was scared.

A family I had been treating for the past six weeks was sitting together watching me as I emerged from the water. "Hi" called out the mother who proceeded to introduce me to her friends. "By the way—we need to change our appointment next Tuesday." I tried to smile and mumble something coherent. I wanted to get out of there as fast as I could.

When we sit in our consultation rooms, we often try to present a carefully sculpted image to our patients. Our therapeutic persona is formed of many parts, some of them consciously designed to support therapeutic work, others coming from our own histories and emotional needs. At times, we are much like the Wizard of Oz, trying to make an impressive presentation while hoping that the curtain we hide behind won't be pulled aside to reveal more vulnerable parts of ourselves.

When we bump into patients outside the clinical hour, we have an opportunity to learn something about ourselves and the therapeutic process. Some encounters feel comfortable and mundane, whereas others can be very difficult. Why is this? What does this say about our personal issues? How can these experiences teach us something about our therapeutic stance and professional persona? What do they say about our attitude toward our work?

In this chapter, we will explore imagined and real extratherapeutic encounters as tools therapists can use to improve their craft. We were drawn to this topic after being disturbed by an encounter much like the one described earlier. It inspired a doctoral dissertation studying experienced psychologists' and psychiatrists' feelings about such encounters (Arons, 1985), which, in turn, led to the development of workshops for therapists using these experiences to better understand themselves and their work.

At some point in their development, most psychotherapeutic traditions have come to see the therapist as the central tool of psychotherapy. They have also observed that a therapist's wishes, fears, conflicts, and unresolved issues can easily interfere with treatment. This difficulty goes by different names in different theoretical systems. Psychoanalysts, who have studied the phenomena extensively, speak of many varieties of "countertransference" and "blind spots" that interfere with analysis. Family systems theorists describe therapists becoming "inducted" into the family system and losing their flexibility. Behavior therapists write of "observer bias" disrupting their objectivity. Client-centered therapists describe a "lack of congruence" in the therapist interfering with the patient's growth. Interpersonal theorists warn of "parataxic distortions" impairing the therapist.

Therapists' emotional responses, when conscious, are important sources of data, as they can help to reveal subtle processes in the patient and the treatment relationship. Problems arise, however, when our emotional responses are based on personal issues and unresolved conflicts of which we are unaware. To be effective tools, we need to recognize and understand the sources of our emotional reactions. Only with such awareness can we practice our craft effectively.

Various therapeutic schools use this insight in different ways to support therapeutic work. Personal awareness allows for using projective identification in psychoanalysis, joining the family system by family therapists, good interobserver reliability in behavior therapy, empathic listening for client-centered counseling, and interacting without distorting in interpersonal schools.

Since remaining aware of our own issues is key to using our emotional reactions productively rather than having them interfere with treatment, it is not surprising that therapeutic traditions have developed a variety of techniques to foster such awareness. It is common for therapists to use their own individual therapy or analysis, and supervision focused on the exploration of countertransference, incongruence, or parataxic distortion, to heighten conscious awareness of the personal issues that they bring to their work. From different angles, systems therapists use family of origin work to avoid being "inducted" into family systems, and behavior therapists devise structured measurements to minimize observer biases.

Interestingly, therapists have written little about using real or imagined extratherapeutic encounters as potential tools to heighten our understanding of our reactions to patients. When such encounters are mentioned in the professional literature, the emphasis is on how they affect patients and threaten treatment alliances, not on what they stir in the therapist (e.g., Flaherty, 1979; Searles, 1979). The closest analogies to our subject that we found in the literature involve traumatic events and visible transitions in the therapist's life, such as pregnancy (Rubin, 1980), losing a loved one (Givelber & Simon, 1981), illness (Chernin, 1976; Dewald, 1982; Halpert, 1981), or injuries (Cottle, 1980). In these circumstances, therapists describe their discomfort at being exposed to their patients.

We have found that studying therapists' reactions to real and imagined chance encounters with patients reveals a treasure trove of information about their therapeutic stance, professional persona, and attitudes toward therapeutic work. It also helps to illuminate personal wishes, conflicts, and concerns related to particular patients.

To help therapists increase their awareness of these issues, we have designed several exercises centered around real and imagined extratherapeutic encounters. In the original study (Arons, 1985), a structured interview was conducted with 10 experienced clinicians, 5 men and 5 women, affiliated with Harvard Medical School. The interview presented guided fantasies of extratherapeutic encounters with patients, questions about actual chance meetings that therapists have had with their patients, and therapists' descriptions of themselves inside and outside the clinical setting. Since this study, other therapists have tried the exercises in workshops and supervision, and the format has gradually been refined.

We invite therapist readers to try the exercises themselves before reading about others' reactions to them. The exercises appear at the end of this chapter.

THE WIZARDS EXPOSED

The great and powerful Oz stood behind his cloth curtain while his subjects were full of awe and respect for the image he projected. As therapists, we use different sorts of curtains. In the safety of our offices where we control the time, the decor, the seating arrangement, the fee, our dress, and our manner, we often seem so sane, so calm, so wise. When we meet our patient outside the clinical hour, the curtain begins to slide open. Many therapists are surprised to see how uncomfortable extratherapeutic encounters can be.

The Wizard of Oz seemed pretty uncomfortable himself when Toto showed him to be human. As it turned out, he still had plenty to offer as he helped the Scarecrow, Tin Woodman, and Cowardly Lion to recognize their brain, heart, and courage, but he was clearly mortal. The Wizard knew he was involved in deception before Toto came along. As therapists, we're not always so self-aware.

Two therapists, stirred by the exercises, remarked:

> I get most upset when a patient sees a part of me that I don't like about myself. I wonder what there is in me that needs to perpetuate the myth of the perfect ideal therapist.
>
> It aroused a lot of feeling in me. I'm surprised I never think of it.

Two other therapists were struck by what they suspect may be well-established defenses:

> I suppose my responses suggest that I'm more blasé than I feel. I act like an old pro and some of it may be denial.
>
> I'm thinking that 20 years of experience makes a difference. . . . Am I pretending or am I beyond this?

The limited existing clinical literature on extratherapeutic encounters focuses on their effect on the patient's transference and treatment alliance. We found, however, in both guided fantasies as well as memories of actual encounters, that most therapists report being more concerned with how they themselves feel and appear than with the effect of the encounter on the patient or on the therapeutic process.

Often therapists are surprised to realize how vulnerable they feel. For example, one female therapist explained:

> Right now at this moment there are certain social situations that would make me feel uncomfortable. Seeing a patient when I'm feeling most alone . . . would be difficult. I'd feel I was exposing the patient to that most vulnerable side of myself. . . . Something makes me uncomfortable with anyone seeing. I'd feel . . . like I might not be able to assume my professional stance in the same way. . . .

Therapists generally report the most discomfort where they feel most exposed. Many therapists describe fear that their personal foibles will be revealed, causing feelings of vulnerability, inadequacy, shame, and humiliation.

Because therapists—since the time of Freud—have been reputed to deal directly and openly with sexual feelings and fantasies, it is especially interesting that many therapists seem to dread most that their sexual feelings will be seen. For example, one male therapist struggled with concerns about his sexuality and professional persona as he described his worst case fantasy of an extratherapeutic encounter:

> In a sexual situation—lying on the banks of the Charles [River], and a patient comes along in the midst. I just wouldn't feel great. I have guilt feelings about sex and rage. If the patient saw me in some sexual situation, I'd know I'd have to go into it and I wouldn't fit it. I think my patients have an image of me somehow having everything in order and this just wouldn't fit.

Another male therapist responded to the guided fantasy of encountering a patient while waiting to see an art film many consider to be pornographic (see Exercises on pp. 134–137). He reported that, externally, the patient "wouldn't see much but might judge me to be cool, distant, and unfriendly. . . ." Meanwhile, internally, his thoughts would be quite different:

> I'd feel anxious and embarrassed. I'd be in turmoil wondering should I explain. I'd feel that somehow this event would open up the therapy to personal events and fantasies in my life that I wouldn't be willing to share. My fantasy about how the patient would interpret this situation is that they'd think I'm unhappy, lonely, and that I have perverse fantasies. He might think that I'm neurotic and I'd feel exposed in a way I wouldn't want.

Therapists also report discomfort about their bodies in exploring fantasies of extratherapeutic encounters. One female therapist imagined:

> I'm in a changing room trying on a string bikini. A client walks up to me from behind and says, "Oh, I love that one." I'd feel so exposed, imagining that she'd think I wasn't attractive.

Other therapists reported similar uncomfortable fantasies dancing in a sexy way, swimming at nude beaches, kissing erotically in public, and watching sexy women or men walk by.

Along with their reputation for directness and openness in sexual matters, therapists are known for helping patients to become comfortable with angry feelings, particularly toward loved ones. Many a parody centers on the therapist "helping" a patient to hate their parents. It is thus ironic that therapists are often afraid of being seen getting angry. They fear that their difficulty handling anger will be exposed, and their patients will judge them harshly. Responding to a guided fantasy about encountering a patient while having a painful public argument with a loved one (see Exercises), a female therapist reported that outwardly, she would just "say hi quickly" and walk on. However:

> Inside I'd be embarrassed, especially if the patient overheard. I'd be particularly upset if a patient saw me angry or nasty with my children, more upset if it were with my husband . . . and I'd die if it was with my mother, which puts me back to being a child. I'd seem infantile and out of control and I'd worry that my patient would think "Oh, she can't even manage her own life; how can she help me?"

Along with concerns about sexuality and aggression, the exercises bring up discomfort with being seen in a myriad of other activities, including displaying public playfulness, being unkempt or dirty, drinking alcohol, engaging in religious or political activities, getting therapy themselves, shopping at "cheap" stores, shopping at "fancy" stores, and enjoying a variety of "unsophisticated" entertainment.

During the exercises, therapists are often surprised to see how much they worry that the image they try to maintain in their professional role will be tarnished by an extratherapeutic encounter. They discover concerns about no longer being viewed as a "paragon of functioning." For example, a male therapist remarked that he would dread being seen:

> When in the course of normal life if I'm acting in a way I don't want others to know—If I got drunker than I should. Really I hope people whose esteem I want to hold don't see me like that.

Some therapists are confused about why they are so uneasy about shattering the myth of the perfect therapist. A female therapist reflected:

> I don't really understand. I get most upset when a patient sees in me a part I don't like about myself. But rationally it doesn't make sense. I certainly say to my patients that their feelings are OK. I don't judge, so why am I afraid to have them see me?

In our experience leading therapists through these exercises, we repeatedly find that therapists are far more accepting of their patients' humanity than they are of their own. They can be quite harsh in their self-criticism and are often ashamed of the same human foibles that they try to help patients to accept in themselves.

Therapists are, of course, also concerned about the effect on their work of an unplanned encounter. Some report worrying that they will no longer be experienced as useful by their patients if they are seen as they really are. A male therapist mused over what he hoped would not be exposed in an encounter:

> A million things. It's consistent with personality things. I don't think I want my patients to discover them. Little psychoses—antitherapeutics—it might frighten off the patient—some fragile patients might never come back. What's most valuable might be lost.

This idea that patients might leave treatment after seeing their therapist as he or she really is surfaces repeatedly. Like the Wizard of Oz, we therapists often believe that we need an impressive persona to keep our patients believing that we can help them.

For most therapists, the fear that patients would leave treatment if they saw their therapist's foibles extends beyond concerns for their patients' well-being. It could be bad for business. One female therapist commented:

> My clients aren't particularly open-minded. I fear their rejection. Many wouldn't like me if they really knew me, and that wouldn't be very good for my practice.

Therapists' concerns about their patients' closed-mindedness become acute in realms where the therapists may be comfortable but fear that their patients are not. For example, many gay and lesbian therapists are particularly concerned about their patients' attitudes regarding sexual orientation. While some are explicit with their patients about this, others are not and worry about being discovered. They report fears of being rejected by their patients if they are seen at activities such as gay clubs or homosexual rights marches.

Some therapists report similar concerns about having their social or political views exposed. One politically active therapist commented:

> I've spent a lot of time obsessing about whether to put bumper stickers on my car. While I want to support the movements I believe in, I'm sure

that many of my patients would see me as the "enemy" if they knew my beliefs.

It is not surprising, given the feelings that arise during these exercises, that therapists typically do not wish to encounter patients outside the clinical hour. The feelings of shame, vulnerability, and inadequacy that often arise are obviously unpleasant, and most therapists would rather avoid them. Concerns about "losing" patients are similarly compelling. However, there are other, less obvious reasons that they dislike extra-therapeutic encounters.

Therapists report that they resent the intrusion into their private life. This can take many forms. Therapists may dislike feeling exposed and having their family and friends "on display" for their patients. They also often remark on the lack of control they experience in an extratherapeutic encounter compared with a scheduled session. Whereas many therapists feel comfortable revealing aspects of themselves or their family when they choose to do so as part of treatment, they feel intruded on when involuntarily exposed. One female therapist commented, "I do draw on my personal experiences in the treatment setting," but there's a "difference between choosing to reveal something and being exposed." Another therapist described an evening in which she knew that both she and her patient would be at the same concert. The therapist was anxious to spot her patient in the crowd before the patient found her, so as to maintain a feeling of control.

Another source of discomfort in extratherapeutic encounters involves resentment of having to work when "off duty." Therapists feel a responsibility to be therapeutic in their responses to patients outside the clinical hour. Perhaps more than other professionals, therapists feel a need to act professionally when encountering their clients outside work. As one therapist put it, "they have the power on the outside—we can't be ourselves, we're committed to not have a regular social relationship." This same therapist highlighted another common concern when he added, "I wouldn't want my patients to see how much I prefer not working."

Psychotherapeutic work requires the therapist to exercise careful, thoughtful control of his or her behavior. This is particularly challenging outside formal sessions, when other people may be participating in the encounter, the therapist hasn't had time to formulate a therapeutic strategy, and there is no time to process the feelings that arise. There are limitless opportunities during extratherapeutic encounters to do the wrong thing, to hurt the feelings of your patient, to seem insensitive, to be too friendly or too distant. Therapists thus report feeling resentment along with inadequacy, resenting having to work after hours and feeling unable to do an adequate job under adverse conditions.

Perhaps because we feel uneasy in extratherapeutic encounters and resist exposing our vulnerability, therapists have done little to help each other figure out how to handle these moments effectively. We Wizards would probably have less difficulty with extratherapeutic encounters if we discussed them more freely.

In view of therapists' reactions to fantasies of extratherapeutic encounters, it is not surprising that when they do the descriptive exercises (see Exercises), they see themselves as rather different people inside and outside the clinical hour. Interestingly, most therapists view this difference in their presentation as a sign of inadequacy. In contrast, they describe "ideal therapists" as far more similar inside and outside the hour than they are themselves. ("Ideal therapists" are, however, expected to be more affectively expressive outside clinical hours than inside.)

Therapists generally see their own behavior inside the hour in positive terms but use far more negative adjectives to describe themselves outside the hour. In our experience, male therapists give their behavior outside the clinical setting the most scathing reviews. Most therapists seem to share the view of well-known psychoanalyst Roy Schafer (1983), that "within the clinical setting we are often better people than in our personal lives" (p. 291).

In contrast to their views of themselves, therapists imagine that their patients have very high opinions of them outside the clinical setting. They imagine that their patients see them as mature, balanced, sensitive, caring, intelligent, happy, and secure. While most therapists see themselves as actually embodying these qualities at times, they describe themselves (when not working) as often acting in ways that are immature, unbalanced, narcissistic, confused, and anxious. The contrast between how we imagine our patients see us and how we at times see ourselves contributes to therapists fearing involuntary exposure to their patients.

Much has been written about how therapists should conduct themselves within the clinical hour to maximize their effectiveness. Our experience exploring extratherapeutic encounters suggests that while studied therapeutic postures often facilitate treatment, they may also represent defensive stances designed to protect the therapist from difficult feelings of exposure and shame. By reflecting on our images of ourselves inside and outside the clinical hour and our feelings about chance encounters, we can gain insight into which parts of our professional persona are there to support our work and which parts stem from our fears, self-criticism, and difficulty accepting unexamined aspects of ourselves.

In the end, the Wizard of Oz was probably most helpful to Dorothy and company once his curtain was pulled aside. While therapists' self-disclosure is a therapeutic tool that should be used judiciously, self-deception is rarely useful. We hope that other therapists can add the exploration of extratherapeutic encounters to their repertoires of awareness-enhancing activities. We hope, too, that reading about other therapists' fantasies and feelings can help us all to feel less ashamed and to support one another in exploring our own hearts and minds as well as our therapeutic relationships.

EXERCISES

Please take a few moments now to close your eyes, attend to your breathing, and relax. As you approach the following exercises, try to be open and honest with yourself—nobody else will see your responses. We all know how to focus on our patients' difficulties. This is an opportunity to focus on our own. While your first response to an exercise may be, "This doesn't apply to me—I've worked these things through," try to stay with each image for a little while to examine any subtle reactions that may arise.

Guided Fantasies

Imagine yourself in the following situation with a patient whom you would feel particularly uncomfortable encountering:

> You've decided to go see a very controversial film. Some critics consider it art, others state that it is pure pornography. While you're waiting for the film to begin, your patient walks over, says hello, and sits down near your seat.

(Please take a few moments to close your eyes and experience the scene.)

Now take out a piece of paper and jot down the following:

1. Your patient's name.
2. Your inner feelings during the imagined encounter.
3. Your outward behavior during the imagined encounter.

How do you understand your feelings? What do your reactions to this fantasy suggest about your personal issues vis-à-vis your patient? Please take a few moments to consider these questions and jot down your answers. When you are finished, please read on.

* * *

Now imagine yourself in the next situation with a patient whom you'd feel particularly uncomfortable encountering:

> You have recently joined a health club. After a heavy workout, you undress and head to the sauna. Once inside, you notice your patient lying down on a nearby bench.

(Again, please close your eyes to experience the scene.)

Now, again, take out a piece of paper and jot down the following:

1. Your patient's name.
2. Your inner feelings during the imagined encounter.
3. Your outward behavior during the imagined encounter.

How do you understand these feelings? What do they suggest about your personal issues vis-à-vis this patient?

* * *

Please follow the same instructions for the following situations, choosing patients whom you would rather not encounter outside the clinical hour:

> Imagine that a close relative of yours has died. Your patient reads the obituary in the paper and decides to attend the funeral service. As you are leaving the service, your patient approaches you.

* * *

> Imagine that you are walking in a busy public place with a close friend or family member. The two of you are having an argument that is escalating painfully. As you pause to make a point, you notice that a patient of yours has been walking just behind you.

* * *

> Imagine that you are in a store with your child who is having a loud tantrum. You are getting more and more agitated as your attempts to calm your child fail. You are finding yourself saying things that therapists advise

their patients not to say. You notice that a patient of yours has been standing nearby, apparently watching.

* * *

For the final situation, recall the most uncomfortable actual encounter you had with a patient outside the clinical hour.

Again take out a piece of paper and jot down the following:

1. Your patient's name.
2. Your inner feelings during the encounter.
3. Your outward behavior during the encounter.

How do you understand these feelings? What do they suggest about your personal issues vis-à-vis this patient?

* * *

Now consider all your patients:

1. Which patients would you generally not like to encounter outside the therapy hour?
2. What about encountering these patients feels uncomfortable?
3. Are there other patients you would not mind encountering outside the therapy hour?
4. What about encountering these patients feels more comfortable?

* * *

Now take a few moments to imagine one or more particular places or activities in which you would especially not want to encounter patients:

1. What about encountering a patient in these places or activities feels especially uncomfortable?
2. Are there other places or activities in which you would generally not mind such encounters?
3. What about these places or activities makes you feel more comfortable?

The Therapist's Image

You may have noticed in the previous exercises that real or imagined extratherapeutic encounters illuminate concerns about the images we wish to present to patients. The following exercise is designed to explore this realm.

Please fill in the following grid using a few descriptive adjectives in each box:

	Inside a Clinical Hour	Outside a Clinical Hour
An Ideal Therapist		
Your Patients' Image of You		
Your Image of Yourself		

1. How do your images of the ideal therapist, your patients' views of you, and your view of yourself inside the clinical hour compare?
2. How do your images of the ideal therapist, your patients' views of you, and your view of yourself outside the clinical hour compare?
3. Do these comparisons help to illuminate any issues or concerns for you?

REFERENCES

Arons, G. (1985). An examination of extra-therapeutic encounters: A route to increasing therapist awareness of blind spots (Doctoral dissertation, Rutgers University, 1985). *Dissertation Abstracts International, 47,* 1709.

Chernin, P. (1976). Illness in a therapist—loss of omnipotence. *Archives of General Psychiatry, 33,* 1327–1328.

Cottle, M. (1980). An accident and its aftermath: Implications for therapy. *Psychotherapy: Theory, Research and Practice, 17*(2), 189–191.

Dewald, P. A. (1982). Serious illness in the analyst: Transference, countertransference, and reality responses. *Journal of the American Psychoanalytic Association, 30,* 347–363.

Flaherty, J. A. (1979). Self-disclosure in therapy: Marriage of the therapist. *American Journal of Psychotherapy, 33*(3), 442–451.

Givelber, R., & Simon, B. (1981). A death in the life of a therapist and its impact on the therapy. *Journal of Psychiatry, 44*(2), 141–149.

Halpert, E. (1981). When the analyst is chronically ill or dying. *Psychoanalytic Quarterly, 51,* 372–389.

Rubin, C. (1980). Notes from a pregnant therapist. *Social Work, 62,* 210–214.

Searles, H. S. (1979). *Countertransferences.* New York: International Universities Press.

CHAPTER 12

AIDS: The Therapist's Journey

MICHAEL SHERNOFF, MSW, ACSW

I am a person, a social worker, who has been living with AIDS since 1982. Although I do not have AIDS myself, the disease and all the personal and professional issues surrounding it have profoundly influenced my life for over a decade. In 1984, my oldest brother died as a result of AIDS, followed by my best friend and partner in my practice in 1989. Six men who lived in my apartment building have died from AIDS in the past 12 years, as have numerous acquaintances, colleagues, and several close friends. Four of my closest friends are currently seriously ill with complications from AIDS. The man I love and share my life with has AIDS. When patients and therapists are dealing with virtually identical life crises simultaneously, the potential for therapeutic mistakes is enormous. Therapists must be highly skilled and self-aware to avert such dangers.

As a therapist with a largely gay male practice, I work with people who are living with AIDS or who are intimately affected by it every day. Before the onset of AIDS, active alcoholism, drug addiction, and Hepatitis B were the only life-threatening illnesses likely to kill my patients. My first professional experience with AIDS was in 1981 when a psychotherapy client began exhibiting symptoms of what we now know is HIV illness. At that time AIDS was unknown but shortly thereafter, the syndrome was labeled "Gay Related Immune Deficiency" (GRID). It soon became clear to me that the men who were sick with this new disease had lived no differently than I had for many years. I assumed that if these people were getting sick, there was an excellent chance that the same thing could or would probably happen to me. In 1983, I began to volunteer at Gay Men's Health Crisis (GMHC), working with people with AIDS, and supervising other volunteers. I still volunteer at GMHC. In the past 12 years, over 100 patients in my private practice have died from AIDS. My purpose in relating the preceding experiences is to attempt to describe how I, along with so many others, am able to survive and thrive emotionally, psychologically, and spiritually in the midst of this plague and how I continue to do this work without becoming burned out.

Colleagues and friends often ask me how it is that I've been able to work in AIDS for so long, dealing with all the pain and suffering endemic to this patient population. Others ask whether it's overwhelming to have intimately known and worked with so many people who have died or who are dying.

As an action-oriented person, I have had to struggle to learn that I am indeed *doing something* by simply sitting with clients, caring about them, and encouraging them to share any and all their feelings about what is happening to them. Of course, I am unable to change the outcome of their illness. Accepting this reality, more than anything else, has taught me how to tolerate discomfort.

The discomfort I experience is about many things. Often, it arises from a genuine empathetic connection with clients who are honestly experiencing feelings about their loss of health, career, lover, and their own imminent death. Once I have grown to care about a person comes all the accompanying discomfort about losing that person. Sometimes, there is simply the uneasiness of being close to a person who is very ill or who is dying, simply because this reminds me of the fragility of my own good health.

The case examples in this chapter illustrate the challenges inherent in attempting to provide competent treatment while living and practicing under the shadows of HIV/AIDS. The following case illustrates how the HIV status of the therapist can emerge as an important clinical issue.

DISCLOSING THE THERAPIST'S HIV STATUS

I injured one of my hands and had to cancel several patients' sessions. One of my partners telephoned these patients and told them that I had an emergency and would phone them later to reschedule. One of the men I was scheduled to see was Lawrence, a 32-year-old referred to me by his AA sponsor. Lawrence's last two therapists had both died of AIDS within 2 years of each other. Lawrence himself is seronegative. In addition to wanting to work through his feelings about the deaths of his previous therapists, he wanted to explore his own fears of intimacy that were making it difficult for him to form romantic relationships with other men.

I telephoned Lawrence that evening to reschedule the session the following day. Knowing that his last two therapists had died of AIDS, I assumed he might be anxious about the cancellation. With this in mind, I felt it was important that Lawrence either speak with me in person or hear my voice on his machine rescheduling the appointment. When I saw him the next day, he began the session by telling me he thought I was in the emergency room and he had panicked thinking I too had AIDS and was going to leave him. While he said this, I was thinking that I hoped I didn't get sick any time soon and provide him with one more reason why he shouldn't trust other gay men.

Lawrence went on to say that the phone call from my colleague had reawakened all his feelings about the deaths of his previous therapists as well as several close friends. He told me he realized he didn't even know what my sero-status was, and he felt that perhaps he was holding back from telling me everything out of the fear that I, too, might die. He then said that his feelings at this point concerned how he would be affected if I were to become permanently disabled and then asked me how I would react if he asked me about my sero-status.

I told him how glad I was that he was able to share those feelings with me. I then explained that at the present time I wasn't sure how I'd respond to a request from him regarding my HIV status. Before answering, I'd want us to spend time exploring all his feelings—what it would mean if I was seropositive, and what it would mean if I was seronegative. I also said that before I made any decision about whether to answer this question, I would spend time thinking about where we were in his treatment. I explained that I wanted my response to be in the best interest of his therapy. I then asked him how he felt hearing this answer to his hypothetical question.

After thinking for a few moments, he told me he was very comfortable with my response—it made him feel well taken care of. He had been afraid I wouldn't tell him my HIV status because of concerns about confidentiality. He then said he wasn't even sure he really wanted to know what my HIV status was anyway.

While I believe I handled this with sensitivity, it was a difficult session for me because it raised some anxieties and questions I had not spent much time considering. Suppose Lawrence had insisted on knowing my HIV status. Did he have a right to know this information? What if he refused to continue treatment unless I assured him I was HIV negative? This would not have been paranoia, a simple avoidance of intimacy, or resistance to treatment on his part. I viewed Lawrence's concerns to be well founded and an appropriate attempt to be self-protective. He chose not to ask what my HIV status was, and he remains in treatment more than 2 years later.

A CASE OF COUNTERTRANSFERENCE

Ernie had been a patient of mine for 5 years when John, his best friend of 25 years and roommate for the past 8, became acutely ill with AIDS and decided to return home to the Midwest. Ernie felt guilty that he had not tried to talk John into continuing to live in New York in their small studio apartment. I fully supported his decision about the impracticality of John's continuing to live with him but this proved to be a mistake. I had not explored Ernie's feelings thoroughly enough. Two weeks after John left, Ernie came to session enraged at me. Appropriately, he yelled at me for not having urged him to explore options about having John continue to live with him. Ernie was overwhelmed by guilt that he had abandoned John in his time of greatest need.

As I listened to Ernie and encouraged him to tell me all his feelings, I knew I had "messed up" and would need to examine this. During supervision, I discovered why I had behaved as I did in not attempting to explore Ernie's ambivalence.

My failure was largely a result of my experience with my older brother Henry, who was also gay. As adults, we were not close and, in fact, our first conversation after a 3-year silence was his announcement that he had been diagnosed with AIDS and was going to return to New York to live. My decision to allow Henry to move in with me was impulsive—I did not like him and did not relish the prospect of having him live with me. I also did not want to become his primary-care partner, but being an AIDS activist, I didn't see how I could refuse to offer my destitute and homeless brother a place to live. Henry lived with me for 14 months until he died in my bed.

At the time I was working with Ernie on this issue, my brother had been dead for 2 years. It was while exploring my reactions to Ernie that my supervisor reminded me that, years ago, I had waited to tell her my brother was moving in until the day before he arrived. I had neglected to discuss this with her and did not explore my own ambivalent feelings and possible options before offering to let Henry move in. Because this had occurred years before Ernie became my patient, I was unaware it was influencing me. In my unconscious desire to protect Ernie from the horrors I experienced as I watched my brother deteriorate, I had not been neutral in my role as Ernie's therapist.

DISCUSSING DEATH

I have grown increasingly comfortable talking with terminally ill people about impending death, and about the corresponding losses and feelings they experience. It is remarkable to ask someone very near to dying why he still clings to life. The answers I elicit are often extraordinary in their clarity and show an understanding that an important issue needs completion before each person can finally let go.

In the final week of my best friend's life, he was at home and every breath was a struggle. During that time, his lover Dennis repeatedly told Luis it was all right to die, that he loved him very much, and he thanked him for the wonderful years they had shared. Dennis wisely urged me and others also to tell Luis that it was all right for him to let go. This was the first time I'd ever said this kind of thing to anyone, and it was excruciatingly painful. Yet, it was only after we had all given Luis permission to die that his breathing became less labored and he died peacefully the following morning.

I thought of this as I sat at the bedside of my patient Cal and listened to him say how worried he was about his lover Stan. Cal had done most of the caretaking in the relationship prior to becoming ill, and even though their roles were now reversed, he worried that Stan would have trouble taking care of himself.

Cal was so ill that Stan did not understand why he was still alive. I urged him to ask this question, and Cal told him he was hanging on because he was worried that Stan wouldn't be able to take care of himself. With a laugh, Stan reminded him that he had taken good care of himself for the 30 years before they met and had subsequently learned even better from all the ways that Cal had nurtured him. "Every time I do one of the things for myself that you used to do for me, I'll think about you and feel you inside of me," he told Cal. "I'll miss you like hell, yet your body is no longer useful to you and hasn't been for some time. The most loving thing you can do for me and yourself is to stop fighting and move on." Cal died that night, in his bed, at home, surrounded by the people who loved him most.

The therapist's experience of death and dying will shape his or her work with patients at risk for the same illness. Does the therapist believe that death is the end of it all, or does he or she envision some kind of life following death? Therapists who have not examined their own beliefs and feelings surrounding death, and have not faced their own fears, will not be able to initiate discussions about this with patients. A therapist's inability to discuss these issues creates a sense of secrecy or shame in the patient who may not have anyone else to talk to about these issues.

Living with AIDS has forced me to face and grapple with many of life's most profound issues. For instance, I have learned how to question clients about some of the most personal areas of their lives. This includes asking about individuals' personal faith experiences and how they integrate spirituality into their lives. Although some people do not find that spirituality or traditional religion meets their needs, it is surprising how many people are hungry to talk about this subject once asked. Many people living with AIDS find meaning and comfort in New Age spirituality. Not believing in either New Age teachings nor in an afterlife, I have had to contain my own skepticism and disbelief in order to encourage patients to discuss how meaningful and comforting these beliefs are.

Whereas I acknowledge how difficult it can be for any of us, patient or therapist, to face the reality of our own death, being forced to confront this on a daily basis, both in my work and personal life, has helped me demystify death and dying and move these issues from the abstract into the concrete realm.

PERSONAL AND PROFESSIONAL GROWTH

I used to confront patients' defenses quicker and push them more if they were symptomatic with HIV disease than I would have if I felt there was more time to work with such patients. When I explored this in supervision, I realized that it came from my need to feel something tangible was occurring during treatment, and not from the soundest clinical decision for the individual patient. It became clear to me that it was neither fair to my patients nor was it good therapy if I did not customize the treatment to meet each individual's needs, defensive structures, and psychodynamics.

I find many rewards in doing this work. Each time I have helped a client explore a painful or difficult area there is no choice but to explore these same issues in my own life. Working closely with so many people who have subsequently died has helped me to be more completely present while my own friends and loved ones are gravely ill or dying. My work has provided valuable training that enables me to help those in my personal life discuss and deal with emotionally charged situations such as faith experiences, beliefs about death, feelings about dying, and practical issues such as medical proxies, living wills, and plans for burial or cremation. Similarly, by not remaining a stranger to the process of dying, I have grown more comfortable confronting my own mortality.

When I had less experience doing this work, I would find myself becoming numb, glazing over, and nodding in what I hoped was an empathic way when a client discussed something that was deeply disturbing to me. I was not proud of the way I responded, but there were many times when it was the only way for me to tolerate being in the same room with someone sharing such intensely painful feelings. When I tune patients out during a session, my own narcissistic injuries are being triggered, and I regress to a less developed way of being. I am not able to put aside my own reactions to be present for my patients, encouraging them to share their feelings. I would rather not listen to their feelings, since they are so similar to the ones I struggle to defend myself against.

Recently, Jeffrey became my psychotherapy client following the death of his lover of 8 years. Jeffrey was actively and appropriately grieving and was also mourning the deaths of most of the men with whom he and Richard had been friends. As he began to discuss being a widower, being single, and his fears about how he would meet men once he felt ready to date again, I felt compassion and a deep connection to him. I recognized that much of this feeling was present because I empathized with him and spent hours in my own therapy discussing related issues.

After a session with Jeffrey I reflected on why I was able to hear the things he said, remain empathic, and not need to distance myself from him and those distressing feelings I also struggled with. During my lover's recent illness, we both have awakened in the early morning hours. At those times, we talk about whatever is on our minds, share our nightly dreams, and hold on to each other tightly. As I lay there with him, trying to take in each touch, odor, and taste of him, I can't help but think about the approaching time when I will not have Lee to hold, talk to, and meet the dawn with. We are growing closer, even as the end of our relationship approaches.

Sometimes, I think that allowing myself to get ever closer to Lee will only increase my pain after he dies. At times, I feel a strong pull to distance myself from him in a misguided attempt to protect myself. When I withdraw from him, one of us invariably notices and we discuss the situation in that moment. My increased ability to be present in my personal life has enabled me to remain more present with clients, and not distancing from my clients has helped me stay closer in touch with my friends and my lover.

Being closely involved with so many people who were ill and who have died has made me learn not to take any part of life for granted. I no longer assume that I have enough time to do everything I want to do; the preciousness and fragility of life are much more apparent now. My priorities also have shifted so that I increasingly savor my relationships with friends and loved ones on a daily basis. I no longer shy away from telling a friend, family member, or my lover that I love them or that I appreciate something specific about them.

SUPPORT

The potential for burnout in AIDS service providers is a serious reality. My experience is that burnout happens largely when people ignore their feelings. Thus I share in this chapter what it is like for me to do this work, in the hope that other therapists doing similar work will find it helpful to read about my struggles. The challenge remains how do we sustain ourselves and each other for this reality: AIDS will likely be with us for the rest of our professional lives.

It would not have been possible for me to live through all of this, without losing whatever serenity I had, if I had not been in my own active psychotherapy and supervision with a remarkable woman who has been my professional mentor for the past 15 years. In addition, for 5 years, in the early to mid 1980s, I attended a support group for health care professionals who were working in AIDS. We met regularly and provided ourselves with a "safe space" to ascertain what each needed to continue to do this draining yet exhilarating work.

From supervising therapists working in AIDS and facilitating support groups for AIDS professionals, it has become increasingly clear to me that the only way any of us are able to continue to expend the prodigious amounts of energy demanded by this work, is by feeding and nurturing our many needs as individuals. When I ask the professionals I work with what they do to nurture themselves, they often look at me as if I were crazy. I have been told on more than one occasion, "I don't have time to do my work, have a life, and take care of my own needs as well." This is a poignant conflict. Similarly, a large part of my work with care-partners of people with AIDS is to encourage them to take time for themselves and to give themselves much-needed breaks from their routine. I am amazed at how resistant both colleagues and clients are to the notion of building in time for play and fun in the midst of the horror.

* * *

I find that my work in AIDS, and living surrounded by AIDS for the past 12 years, has increased my appreciation for and my capacity to enjoy the richness of life. While of course tremendously saddened, instead of finding myself drained, I am increasingly nourished and inspired by working with people living with HIV and AIDS, as devastating as it is. The inspiration comes from their courage.

As a gay man living in the midst of a community ravaged by AIDS, the issues I have discussed take on an obvious immediacy and urgency to me, personally as well as professionally. Although the content of this discussion has been living and practicing psychotherapy in the face of a particular plague, the dynamics are universally relevant to all therapists. Which of us has not had to face our own fears and losses, or grapple with our own mortality? This is the core of human pain and triumph. How we manage these issues defines our personhood. How we help our patients manage these issues defines us as therapists.

CHAPTER 13

Lifeline

GLORIA GARFUNKEL, PhD

There is an old saying that the person who saves a life is then responsible for that life.
—*Linehan, 1993*

Who saves one life, saves the world.
—*The Talmud*

I am interviewing my new outpatient, Lisa, a fidgety young woman with darting eyes that avoid contact with my own. She perches on the edge of her seat, seemingly ready to bolt, her left leg jiggling fervently as she describes to me the circumstances leading up to her most recent psychiatric hospitalization.

"I sat on my bed in the dark with a loaded gun to my head, completely numb, just getting the courage to pull the trigger. And then, out of nowhere, my cat jumped on my lap! I dropped the gun and just started crying. And then I called my boyfriend. I couldn't even talk, but he just knew it was me. He came right over and drove me to the hospital."

When I suggest that her cat could have just as easily startled her into pulling the trigger, Lisa's leg motions cease and, for the first time, she meets my gaze head-on.

"That would have been OK, too."

My adrenalin gives a mild surge, but my eyes meet hers unflinchingly. We have our work cut out for us, I think. "So what do you imagine would have to change in your life for you to feel differently about that?" I say out loud, alert to every nuance, verbal and nonverbal. She meets this question with a long, thoughtful pause.

* * *

As Lisa ponders her response, I marvel at the social and historical forces that have propelled the two of us together: she the help-seeker, semiattached to her life as if it were a half-severed limb, and I, the salaried healer, paid to be committed to her life, at least within the allotted time, until the next patient takes her place and I focus on that person's anguish. A clock silently logs the minutes on my desk, its glowing red numbers managing the procession of patients in and out of my office in this busy HMO health center, where a multitude of lives in turmoil intersect with my own. My time is a semiprecious commodity to the insurance company that pays for it. My patient's time? She clearly puts no value to it at all.

So how did it come about that I am in this position of being paid to care more about whether or not this stranger lives than she herself cares? If my profession did not exist, would she just die? Would her problem be defined as spiritual rather than medical? A crisis in faith or meaning, to be discussed with a priest, nun, or rabbi? Would she interpret her misery as a deficiency in vitality or just loneliness, either way something to discuss with a nurturing woman in her social network, a local wise woman?

There have always been women healers. Only since the industrial revolution and the rise of the power of the medical profession has healing become a commodity to be measured and sold, originally only by men, in discrete parcels of time and procedures (Ehrenreich & English, 1978). Before that, most healing was continuous with the female role of tending to others' needs. The spiritual, social, and physical aspects of healing were bound into the seamless fabric of domestic life.

My life, on the other hand, is so rigidly scheduled and compartmentalized that if one thing is off, the whole day can unravel, along with my nerves. My children are in daycare as I tend to the relentless stream of patients who wander into my office all day like lost souls. Trying to give enough attention to everyone's needs at home and at work, I am usually late for everything.

Yet I cannot imagine giving any of it up. All my labors and connections with others, both personal and professional, enrich and balance my life. While I have to conserve my energy and have found myself over the years shedding some of my needier friends, being a healer of many fulfills something deep inside me—emotionally, spiritually, and intellectually.

My mother, Ilonka, and her sister, Ibike, are wise women to whom others informally turn for help. They are role models for me in their insight, compassion, and strength. Their mother, my grandmother Gittel, was also a caretaker of others in her family and community. She lived in a tiny rural village in Hungary, where the rolling farmland blossomed with new life in the spring of 1944, just after Passover, as she and her family were sucked into a cesspool of Nazi horrors and her life was stolen from her in a pesticide-filled gas chamber with her four youngest children. She was just about the age I am now. I was named after Gittel, which means Good. Most of the people Gittel nurtured so well were also murdered by the Nazis. Even her dog died of grief waiting on the doorstep for her family's return, refusing food from neighbors. But Gittel's love, passed along through my own mother's fine nurturing, remains alive in me and my children.

My grandfather, her husband Chaim, survived the cataclysm, and lived with us on a farm during my childhood. "He saved many lives," my mother would say, but not in ways usually associated with male heroism. He nurtured the young and frail survivors of the camps after the liberation. He made for them a special broth of caraway seeds, garlic, and some oil and flour that my mother also made for us as children whenever we had upset stomachs. Many concentration camp survivors died soon after they began to eat again: Their starved bodies were overwhelmed by the sudden food. No one Chaim cared for with his special broth died. His name means Life, and he cherished whatever he had left. His blue eyes sparkled with laughter whenever he saw me, though sadness had permanently etched deep lines around his eyes as well, like a frame around all he saw.

I carry on Chaim and Gittel's lifeline that the Nazis tried to sever and with this the tradition of helping that both my maternal grandparents were so good at, a tradition I hope to pass along to my two sons in whatever form they choose to use it. I also carry a frame of sadness around my own eyes that places everything I see and do—both professionally and personally—in the larger context of massive past losses and possibly future ones, if our species does not begin to place more value on caretaking. As with my grandfather, this frame (although painful), like a pair of glasses, helps me to see better. In this case, I view the whole cycle of life and death over the generations, and the preciousness, transience, and interconnectedness of all life on this planet, past, present, and future.

And so human history, with the gruesome torment some people are capable of inflicting on others, has swept the remnants of my family across an ocean and landed me at this moment with this hurt human being whose will to live is threadbare. My job is to help her reconstruct her lost will and bolster it with coping skills that enable the best of the human spirit to overcome the worst of calamities. In so doing, I will make a small but significant contribution to Tikkun Olam, a Hebrew expression for "repairing the world."

* * *

I bring to my work with suicidal patients the resources of my family legacy. I understood, from an early age, that the worst imaginable horrors could happen to anyone, but that if one was lucky enough, inner strength (coping skills), optimism, and connection to a relationship with either a person or God, could sustain one through terrible tragedy and oppression.

Compared with my parents, I admittedly felt weak as a child, with no confidence that I could ever survive a calamity. Both of my parents had survived the worst of Hitler's concentration camps, while I could barely tolerate the homesickness that swept over me in summer camp. Their belief in a benevolent, comforting God had miraculously survived intact, while I felt constantly judged by a stern, angry God who had shown no mercy to little children more virtuous than myself. On Yom Kippur, I seemed incapable of fasting, daring God, I suppose, to strike me down dead for this failing. I was always surprised to find myself written into the Book of Life, despite year after year of this secret misbehavior. My mother, on the other hand, had starved for an entire year in Auschwitz and Ravensbruck at the age of sixteen. My mother seemed superhuman: While she appeared outwardly feminine and fashionable, I knew that her small body was as strong as any man's and that her inner self could withstand anything. I felt weak and sickly next to her. My view of my mother did not fit any of the images of women in the American culture around me. I felt our whole family were foreigners in this strange land where no one discussed the Holocaust and we alone seemed riveted by its power. I believe that this societal denial was at least as damaging to me and my siblings as the legacy we carried.

But as an adult, I have come to have a greater respect for the strengths that have arisen in me from this legacy, and what I have to offer others, not the least of which is my ability to see the whole picture in people's stories of despair. I can easily find the thread of hope and empathize without drowning. Having been inoculated at an early age, a little at a time, by my mother's stories of what and who had been lost, and how, I am a steadfast but nonprying witness who finds the concept "secondary trauma" inappropriate. Comparing the hearing of trauma stories with the actual experiencing of trauma is to belittle the enormity of the latter experience. Although Holocaust stories would greatly upset me, I always felt that bearing witness was the least I could do in a world full of such stories. I still feel that is the least we can do for victims of the world's violence, rather than shutting our ears because we want to believe in a just and safe world. The most we can do is work collectively to prevent future destruction. Hearing my mother's stories, I always felt incredibly lucky to have been spared the actual events and believed it was my duty to pay back in some way for my good fortune. Admittedly, these stories have also left me with a sense of vulnerability, a pervasive sense of dread and vigilance about potential future calamities that might befall me and my children. But I would rather my eyes were open, so that I can take steps to change what I can change, rather than just waiting passively for the inevitable.

In one of the stories my mother told me, she wanted to kill herself in Auschwitz. It was a particularly cold and rainy day, the sort of day on which sadistic Nazis loved to force prisoners to stand in lines for hours in their flimsy dresses while the Nazis counted them, over and over, selecting for the gas chambers those too weak and sick to remain standing. The heavy smoke and ashes of the crematoria permeated the grey fog, so that the inmates were in effect breathing in the dead. My mother, a dazed and depleted adolescent, lost all hope that particular day. "I don't know what I was thinking. I just thought the whole world was like this, one big concentration camp. I thought 'We will never get out of here.' I was just so cold and so tired. I started walking toward the electrified fence and began to reach out my hand when I heard Ibike cry, 'Don't leave me, Ilonka! Please don't leave me here alone!' Then I realized what I was doing, and I went back to her. We kept each other alive. If I had died, she would have died, too." My mother was sixteen and Ibike, her sister, was fifteen at the time. They both survived to have children and grandchildren. I owe my own existence to my mother's tenacious will to live and to her life-giving connection with her sister.

I thus bring to my suicidal patients a strong belief that coping with trauma and grief is possible, that humans are resilient, and that authentic human bonds are healing, even life-saving forces. Connections are essential, both with those in the present and those from the past who continue to give us strength. I carry in me a great sense of loss for my grandparents, their murdered children, and their rural Jewish community. My clinical work draws on this yearning for community by emphasizing the connection of patients to social networks: their own family and friends, religious and self-help organizations, and/or to therapy groups I create for people with similar problems. I do not allow myself to become the center of my patients' lives: It would not be healthy for them or for me.

I have always preferred working in communities of health care providers—hospitals, clinics, and health centers. Both individual therapy and isolated private practice have never held much appeal for me. I am puzzled by the feminist "relational" theorists coming out of a psychoanalytic tradition, who continue to emphasize individual rather than group or family work with their women patients. I have always viewed feminism as a collective endeavor, with collective "consciousness-raising" roots. In my current setting, we treat all our patients, both male and female, "relationally" or "systemically" (depending on the lens), both through family and group therapy, and as a mutually supportive team of health care providers, both within mental health, as well as across medical disciplines. The frequent collegial consultation across disciplines enhances both the quality of the treatment and our own ability to sustain a high level of productivity and creativity without burning out. Dyadic healing is an invention of the modern doctor-patient relationship, with its inherent imbalance of power. Long ago, and in other cultures, most forms of religious and magical healing drew upon the power of group and family rituals (Frank, 1974).

In addition to validation by bearing witness and emphasizing connections to others, I also bring to suicidal patients the confident optimism that life is unpredictable and can take amazing turns for the better, not just for the worse. Where there is life, no matter how miserable, there is hope. Optimism, no matter how false it may seem, is necessary for species survival at a time when the ozone layer is disintegrating, mass extinctions are rampant, wars are as plentiful as ever, toxins pervade every meal and every breath, and nuclear power plants function near populated areas with human error as likely there as anywhere else. Communicating optimism while validating suffering is a complex dialectical and ethical stance, requiring hopeful eyes looking out of a sad frame. This stance is not neutral or passive by any means, and it requires that the therapist be able to actively grasp these contradictions. A despairing therapist and a suicidal patient can be a deadly combination.

Finally, I bring to suicidal patients the ability to teach new coping skills, expanding their problem-solving repertoire beyond suicide. I help them recognize the many strengths they already have and just need to expand upon, a technique that might be called "solution-focused" or "ego-strengthening," depending on one's theoretical orientation.

To help others see their own strengths, however, I had to find my own among many weaknesses I could easily tally. I had to search my own experience that ran counter to the early psychoanalytic literature on Holocaust survivors and their offspring which seemed to dismiss us as hopelessly neurotic. We were tainted by a horror story no listeners really wanted to hear or to imagine took place in the same world in which they lived, to people not unlike themselves. I began to realize that a great many offspring of survivors pervade the helping professions as highly competent clinicians. And I learned to appreciate more and more the dilemma faced by Holocaust survivors regarding whether and how much of their stories to convey to their children in the service of good parenting. From my mother's point of view, not telling me about her Holocaust experiences was to not warn me of dangers in the world that could harm me, and to not have me know her and understand that her profound sadness at certain times of the year was not my fault. But telling me her stories was "to allow Hitler to hurt you, too." Either way, she lost, for both choices meant passing along pain, something good mothers are not supposed to do. Weingarten (1994) discusses this common dilemma in mothers who have been sexually abused or those, like herself, with life-threatening illnesses such as cancer. This world is full of pain, as we parents and healers in the real world know too well. To not pass along trauma and suffering narratives, to not integrate them into our collective consciousness, is to split off the traumatized, the sick, the dying, from the rest of us. It renders their experiences invalid, invisible, meaningless, and even contaminated, and it promotes the repetition of traumatic events themselves through their nonacknowledgment by the culture at large.

My mother told me her stories, which included both joy and agony, to connect me to my family's past. There were no heirlooms or photographs to pass along, only her vivid memories of who and what had been lost, and how that had occurred. She conveyed her stories to strengthen and protect me, which they did, giving me a powerful positive legacy, as well as warning me about the dark side of the world. I learned how dark parts of the human heart—jealousy, greed, racism, anti-Semitism, sadism, dehumanization—can lead to dark horrors in human history, linking the individual psyche with collective experience. She transmitted to me, her eldest daughter, the family lifeline. I am often astonished to realize that I have inherited her sense of inner strength, which has been both challenged and nurtured by my own motherhood. And through my profession, through helping others reconstruct more hopeful life stories, that encompass rather than deny or dwell on suffering, I have found ways to honor the legacy of my family that both validate and alleviate the suffering of others.

* * *

To sustain my ability to do clinical work, I need clear boundaries between my time at home and my time at work. I try hard not to think about my patients when I am at home. Not thinking about patients in pain is often difficult; not thinking about suicidal patients seems at times impossible. There is often the nagging doubt that a little more thought could save someone's life. And my resulting emotions run the gamut from a protective anxiety to angry resentment over this intrusion into other parts of my life.

Suicidal patients captivate my catastrophic imagination, my excellent ability to vividly visualize worst-case scenarios, honed through years of thinking, hearing, and reading about the Holocaust. Suicidal patients often provoke my worst fears for both them and for my own career should I ever be found negligent. When a patient fails to show up for a session, my stomach sinks. I wonder if she is alive, and I have to decide how active to be in locating her, and how much time to wait. Sometimes it feels like a game of hot potato: If I was the last person to see a patient, I feel much more anxious than if it was the psychiatrist I work with. No one wants to be the last contact prior to a suicide, the most likely target for the wrath, grief, and projected guilt of surviving family members.

Treating suicidal patients can become an emotional high-wire act: One false move, a bad judgment call, and the patient could end up dead. I could be sued, my career could be ended, my name could appear in the *Boston Globe* under some photograph of me looking like a madwoman. But most of the time, I try not to worry. I know that I am always doing my best and documenting meticulously. As I have matured as a clinician over the past fifteen years, I have realized that false moves are usually self-corrected quickly if I remain receptive to the feedback patients readily give. Being attuned, responsive, nondefensive, appreciative, and encouraging of patient feedback is essential in maintaining an alliance with all patients, but especially with those who are suicidal.

Once suicidal patients have crossed our thresholds, they are ours, in certain intangible as well as legal ways. They can seem like emotional black holes, often sucking up more energy than we had intended to expend, both on and off hours, tempting us to breach boundaries and make exceptions we ordinarily would not make. My own tendency has been to extend the therapy hour while a pileup forms in the waiting room. This then creates hostility on the part of other patients toward me, which I may then transfer back to the suicidal one whose needs did not neatly fit into the allotted time.

One particularly theatrical and chronically suicidal woman persistently persuaded me to extend the hour by raising the specter of imminent suicide as she was about to leave my office. I recall saying to colleagues after one extremely backed-up day, "I wish she would just do it already and leave me alone." In fact, I would have felt horrified and guilty if she had. I was simply feeling mistreated by her, due to my own lack of skill. I had let things go too far. We therefore spent the next session setting ground rules we should have set down at the beginning, making it clear what was her piece and my piece in keeping her alive. If she were suicidal, we needed to address it right at the beginning of the session. Otherwise, it would undermine treatment. She acted more responsibly after that. And I stopped feeling hostile.

Marsha Linehan (1993) offers a helpful metaphor for this tenuous balance a therapist must keep in working with chronically suicidal patients:

> Another extended metaphor for therapy is learning how to swim in all kinds of conditions. The patient is the swimmer; the therapist is the coach, sitting in a rowboat circling the patient, providing directions and encouragement. The tension often is between the swimmer's wanting to get in the boat so the coach can row her to shore and the coach's wanting the swimmer to stay in the water. If the coach rows the swimmer to shore, she will never learn to swim, but if the swimmer drowns in rough seas, she will never learn to swim either. Clinging to the boat and refusing to swim, and swimming underwater to scare the coach into jumping in after her, are instances of patient therapy-interfering behaviors. Refusing to hold out an oar when the patient is clearly drowning, and rowing the swimmer to shore every time a black cloud comes by, are examples of therapist therapy-interfering behaviors. (pp. 210–211)

As managed care has shortened hospitalizations, it has become necessary for outpatient therapists like myself to become even more agile masters of this balancing act. It is no longer so easy to take a break from a highly demanding patient through her hospitalization. I once spent an entire three-week vacation worrying about a chronically suicidal patient who had seemed especially miserable as I was leaving, despite contracting for safety, with many contingency plans in place. I would have felt better with her in a hospital, but more for my own peace of mind than for her clinical needs. When I returned, I found myself both relieved and annoyed at her buoyancy and animation; she had had a wonderful three weeks. I thought of my children crying during daycare drop-off and then playing happily the minute I was out of sight, while I cried on my way to work. Although separation is one of my Holocaust issues, usually I master it pretty well. This time, I felt angry at myself, angry at my patient, and angry at the Holocaust for making me feel so often that I must tithe my pleasure in life to someone else's misery, fearing that if I let down my guard and do anything purely pleasurable, I will return to a disaster.

* * *

I know that at times the extra effort I have put into worrying about a suicidal patient has had less to do with the patient than with me. When I just cannot let go of thinking about a suicidal patient, despite following all the professional ground rules, it often has to do with my discomfort with helplessness: the recognition that in spite of my best efforts and doing all of the right things, this person may in fact take her own life. This resurrects in me some old guilt about never doing enough, my second-generation survivor guilt about not being able to rescue my relatives who were murdered by the Nazis less than a decade before I was born. After all, I will never save six million lives, no matter how good a therapist I am. I will never treat anywhere near that number of patients, no matter how time-effective I manage to be. I will never even touch that many lives—though this last I still reserve as a possibility through my writing. All these limits have been difficult to accept, for growing up, I felt it was my calling to somehow make up for the Holocaust, to correct it, to retroactively change its course.

Of course, I cannot do this lacking magical and God-like powers. (Even God did not rescue my grandmother and her children.) I am human and imperfect, something it has taken me several decades to begin to accept. The best I can do is learn how to thrive on this planet with what I have, and share what I learn with others who feel stuck and unable to go on with life at all. And I can try to contribute in some way to the solving of societal problems that will decrease the likelihood of ecological and human-violence Holocausts in my children's lifetime. This makes me a good enough, rather than perfect, daughter of survivors of the Holocaust. Perfection, the ability to undo history, would erase me, for my very existence is the result of my parents' displacement.

Nazis believed in perfection, but if they had been perfect in their extermination attempts, I also would not be here. The Nazi love of perfection makes it easier for me to relinquish perfection as a life goal, something I strongly urge my patients to do as well—something many suicidal patients seem to have particular difficulty with. I recall one suicidal patient referred to me after he broke a safety contract with his therapist and shot himself in the chest, missing his heart by mere centimeters. He had been obsessed with perfection, doing everything right, and felt like a failure when he could not. But his imperfect aim had saved his life. His survival transformed him: He now owed his life to a mistake. Thus, failed suicide attempts, near-misses, are opportunities for both the patient and the therapist to reassess the life and the treatment, and frequently change directions in both.

This story resonates for me because my father's life was saved by a Nazi guard's imperfect aim. My father was shot by a guard who thought my father was trying to escape from the labor camp where they were digging up Jewish gravestones to pave roads.

"I have perfect aim. I never miss," said the astonished guard, when the bullet went through my father's hat instead of head. "That I missed is a sign that you will survive."

"Prophecy is often given to fools," thought my father, who took courage from the event and did escape soon afterward, to spend the next two years in hiding.

My Holocaust legacy and my patients have also taught me to be cautious about the good times, not to take them for granted. Successful suicides often occur when patients are doing better. Something bursts the bubble—an event, anniversary, memory, or relationship crisis—and the distress is intolerable, so the old impulse sets in. For some, a certain sense of invulnerability may be a factor: Having tried to kill themselves so many times before and been rescued, some people actually succeed at suicide by accident. Others, unfortunately, are successful on the first attempt, startling everyone with the lack of signs. A patient in our practice who had not been sober since adolescence entered an inpatient program after his wife threatened to leave him. He was in a day hospital program, clean and sober, doing great, when his wife announced that she would still not take him back. He jumped out a window.

I therefore harp on the issue of suicide with my formerly suicidal patients: I never become complacent. We rehearse relapse prevention strategies (Marlatt & Gordon, 1985) and distress tolerance skills (Linehan, 1993) ad nauseum, even when they are feeling better, often in the context of helping others in group therapy. I attempt to establish a trusting alliance so they will tell me the truth and reach out for help when a part of them is planning to exit life. But I cannot rescue those who do not at least partially try to rescue themselves, who do not give signals to me or friends or family members that the precipice is near, who impulsively resort to substance abuse at their lowest moments, thus clouding their judgment and diminishing their capacity for self-protection. I can follow certain professional guidelines and my best instincts, but there are no guarantees. I cannot be a guardian angel or choose life for them. I can just try to be a benevolent influence pointing out options they cannot see and looking for signs of drowning.

Recognition of the limits of my profession's ability to rescue patients from themselves is difficult to accept, but also comforting as a mental health care provider to so many: It absolves me when, despite my best efforts, I fail to prevent the disasters adult humans plunge themselves into unwisely. In my heart, though, having made contact with that person, there remains the inescapable tug of "what if?"

* * *

"You would have to be able to change my whole life history," Lisa finally says. "And you can't do that. You can't change all of the times my father molested me, called me stupid, beat me up, threatened to kill me. I still hear his voice in my head all the time. You can't change that."

"Your past doesn't have to determine your future, Lisa," I reply. "Psychotherapy is a partnership, and if you and I each do our own part, I can help you transform your life. I wouldn't be doing this work if I didn't constantly see people with horrible pasts go on to lead happier lives. And leading a happier life is of course, by far, the best revenge of all."

She looks at me again, this time with the hint of a grim smile. "Well, OK, I'll give it my best shot."

And while I cringe at the double meaning, I am pleased that my foot is in the door and a contract for treatment has begun. I know that in spite of my best efforts, Lisa may indeed die at her own hands. But the chances are much greater that she will not, and that my experience as a lifeline, both personally and professionally, will serve her well if she chooses to use me as a resource. In turn, being instrumental in the transformation of her desire to live will bolster my own belief in the healing power of human connection, and it will give me hope for my own children's future in this crazy, violent, and beautiful world.

"You can't save the world," my mother frequently said to me during my years of fervent adolescent idealism. She may have been right, but because of her example, I have never really stopped trying, one person at a time.

REFERENCES

Ehrenreich, B., & English, D. (1978). *For her own good: 150 years of experts' advice to women.* New York: Anchor/Doubleday.

Frank, J. (1974). *Persuasion and healing* (rev. ed.). New York: Schocken.

Linehan, M. (1993). *Cognitive-behavioral treatment of borderline personality disorder.* New York: Guilford Press.

Marlatt, G. A., & Gordon, J. (Eds.). (1985). *Relapse prevention: Maintenance strategies in the treatment of addictive behaviors.* New York: Guilford Press.

Weingarten, K. (1994). *The mother's voice: Strengthening intimacy in families.* New York: Harcourt Brace.

PART FOUR

Clinical Dilemmas

CHAPTER 14

*Cracks in the Mirror: When a Psychiatrist Treats Physicians and Their Families**

MICHAEL F. MYERS, MD

Over the past 21 years of psychiatric practice, I have become a doctors' doctor (Myers, 1992a, 1994). My interest, however, in physicians and their emotional and psychiatric difficulties, began much earlier, and tragically, when one of my roommates in medical school committed suicide in 1962. I didn't really deal with his death at the time—I buried myself in anatomy lab, biochemistry experiments, and fraternity activities. It was only during my residency in psychiatry (1969–1972) when I began to look after hospitalized physicians (and their spouses and children) that I began to examine how caring for these patients affected me personally. I recall a mixture of emotions—but mainly anxiety and feelings of self-consciousness. Because of all the insecurities of being in training, I know that I felt more professionally confident treating patients who had nothing to do with the medical field.

When I completed my residency in 1972, I pursued two equally engaging career paths—academic psychiatry and private practice. They have complemented each other in many respects. Teaching medical students and residents in psychiatry and family practice has kept me abreast of the myriad interface issues between professional and personal development in medical school and postgraduate training. Being the director of undergraduate education in psychiatry has given me access to students' concerns about not only pedagogical matters but the learning atmosphere of our medical schools and hospitals. How can a teacher-administrator of

* The clinical vignettes in this chapter are composites of many cases with similar themes. They have been altered and disguised to protect the identities of my patients.

future physicians not be affected by reports of poor instruction, medical student abuse (Richman et al., 1992), sexual harassment (Charney & Russell, 1994), or the rampant demoralization in so many clinicians in our medical centers (Belkin, 1993; Wehbe, 1994)?

In my private practice, as both an individual therapist and subspecialist in marital and divorce therapy, I have had the opportunity to treat a large number of psychiatrically distressed medical students, physicians, and their families. This has been a privilege—for I am party to a vast range of biological and psychosocial vulnerabilities with which today's doctors live. It is gratifying to be able to help people in medicine to get feeling better again and to regain optimal functioning. But this kind of work also hits very close to home and generates a plethora of unsettled emotions in me.

With this background, what follows is a range of feelings, reflections, and insights that characterize my work as a doctors' psychiatrist, a psychiatrist for approximately 500 medical students and physicians who have consulted me over the years. The problems range from major psychiatric illness (bipolar disorder, schizophrenia, recurrent mood disorder, dementia) to milder concerns such as adjustment disorders, sexual dysfunctions, and phase-of-life problems, including many individuals with relationship, marriage, and divorce concerns. However, underlying these diagnostic categories, or arising from them, are many painful emotional conflicts in physicians (e.g., guilty feelings for being on medical leave, shame for being dependent on narcotics, anxiety about living with AIDS, feelings of failure if one's marriage is ending). All therapists know that psychiatric labels, and cold diagnostic categories do not capture the inner turmoil with which our patients struggle. This is the "stuff" that touches the heart of the therapist.

SHOCK

Shock is a strong emotion that most psychiatrists do not feel often, especially as they age and become more experienced. There is this sense that "I've seen it all." But I have certainly felt this emotion as a doctors' psychiatrist, more than occasionally, despite my becoming seasoned and battle-scarred. Here is an example:

> When Dr. A called my office and asked if I would be willing to see him as a patient, I was initially hesitant. Why? For three reasons. First, we were on the clinical faculty of the same teaching hospital (although in

different departments) and served on an AIDS Policy committee together. Second, our wives were friends, although we never socialized as couples. Third, our children knew each other through various sports teams. My temptation to temporize with Dr. A was preempted by his saying to me over the phone: "It's been very hard for me to make this phone call—it's embarrassing to admit that I need help—I called you quite deliberately, because I've met you, know you a little bit, and respect you—more than I can say about most psychiatrists on staff here or ones I know personally." Flattery aside, I agreed to meet with Dr. A later that week.

Because I knew through my wife that Dr. A's father had died recently and that this had been quite difficult for him, I thought that that was why he was calling me. Wrong! He started his first visit with: "Thanks for agreeing to seeing me. Let me get to the point. I don't love Sarah. I never have really. I began to fall in love with my secretary about 2 years ago and we began seeing each other. She has now left her husband and I'm planning to leave Sarah as soon as I get up the nerve to tell her. Monica and I are going to live together. I know you do a lot of marital and divorce work. Can you help?"

I was shocked when Dr. A told me his reasons for coming to see me because of my prior knowledge, and erroneous assumption, about his marriage. Had he been a complete stranger to me, I wouldn't have felt shock. Empathy yes, shock no. Dr. A was so nervous and self-absorbed in that first visit, that I don't think my shock was visible to him. If it was, he didn't say anything. Had he said something, I would have acknowledged my surprise, given him a brief explanation, and continued with my assessment. I found that after that first visit, I had much less difficulty being a therapist to him. I was able to regain my usual sense of professionalism and to reach out to him with concern, support, suggestions, and guidance. When he disclosed to his wife his plans to leave, he told her that he had consulted a psychiatrist but didn't tell her whom he was seeing. I continued to see him individually and recommended another therapist, a social worker unknown to both of them, that he and his wife could see for separation therapy.

SHAME

As a physician and psychiatrist, I see myself as a member of a group of individuals with a common goal or commitment. Therefore, I feel something, for better or for worse, when a member of my profession—

my reference group—is in the midst of a struggle of conscience. The shame I have is a mixture. Some is from my physician-patients and what they project onto me. Some is my own. Here is a recent example:

> Dr. B, a senior and highly respected psychiatrist at our medical school, came to see me about one year ago for depression. Because I treat a number of medical students and psychiatry residents (who would know Dr. B) and because I also treat some of Dr. B's patients (whom he refers to me for marital therapy with their partners or spouses), I began to become very anxious about my waiting room. More specifically, I worried for Dr. B's privacy that he might run into colleagues, students, or patients there. As I attempted to juggle his appointments with me all over the map, he asked what was going on. I explained my dilemma and he laughed. "You're the one with the problem Mike—I'm not ashamed coming here—why should I be?—we'll never eradicate stigma against people with mental illness if we remain in the closet ourselves."

Many conflicts, behaviors, and incidents that physicians bring to psychiatrists have shame as an accompanying emotion (Myers, 1992b). Some examples are a doctor who talks about sexually molesting his younger sister when he was a teenager; a medical student who confesses that he cheated on a pathology examination and agonizes over his behavior; a male gynecologist who describes sexual arousal while doing pelvic examinations on certain patients; a woman psychiatry resident who recalls going home with one of her patients, a college student, after unexpectedly running into him at a party; an intern who lies to his attending supervisor that he has dictated up an operative report (which no one can find so stenographic services are blamed); an anxious urology resident, uncertain of his sexual orientation, who becomes excited when a young male patient develops an erection during a testicular examination; an anesthesiologist who describes an incident in the operating room wherein his patient "goes flat" and almost dies; a medical student who recalls that his divorced mother, naked and drunk, once spread her labia in front of him to teach him "some real anatomy."

ANXIETY FOR ONE'S FAMILY

As mental health professionals, we can do our best to observe rules of conduct and respect the boundaries of the doctor-patient relationship. Yet, other variables may occasionally come into play when psychiatrists treat physicians (or their loved ones) in their living and working communities.

One of these is the insularity and smallness of some medical worlds. At times, the boundaries between professional and family life might be quite porous.

> When I was asked to treat Colleen for an eating disorder, I had no idea that my work with her would make me so nervous. She was 21 years old and her parents were both physicians. I had observed the conventional rules (i.e., I had never met her before and had been introduced to her parents only briefly at a party). I had no preexisting or ongoing relationship with them. What I didn't know was that Colleen and my 21-year-old daughter had something in common—the same boyfriend Garth. He was my daughter's first "real boyfriend" between ages 17 and 18. One year later, he became Colleen's boyfriend for about a year and a half. They "broke up" about 6 months before Colleen became my patient.
>
> After hospitalizing Colleen and getting her through the crisis of her severe weight loss and depression, I began to work with her in psychotherapy on some of the contributing dynamics of her illness. In one session, she discussed her relationship with Garth and her rage at him. She went on to describe how abusive he had been—verbally, emotionally, physically, and sexually. He put her down a lot, called her "stupid" when he was angry, swore at her, and accused her of "cheating" on him. Often he'd make a date with her and not show up. He'd promise to call and "forget." On two occasions, he struck her—once when he didn't like what she was wearing and she refused to change—and again when he felt that she was talking to his best friend too long at a party. He also raped her once when she didn't want to make love during her period. She told no one about this—including her family doctor who treated her the following week for PID (pelvic inflammatory disease).
>
> It is never easy for a therapist to listen to his or her patients' descriptions of abuse. But this was different and much harder for me. Was Colleen describing the same young man I thought I knew and really liked? Who was polite, respectful of my daughter (I thought) and my wife and me? Was this the same man who I had considered would make a terrific son-in-law had my daughter and he met when they were a few years older? Was my daughter as self-confident and secure in her relationships with men as she seemed? Suddenly I was doubtful and full of paternal worry.

This vignette illustrates one of the painful realities of doing psychotherapy—the ethical constraints of the doctor-patient covenant. I couldn't probe into my daughter's relationship with Garth. I couldn't disclose to her what I had heard in psychotherapy. I couldn't tell her that Colleen was my patient. All I could do was process this information in my own way and hope that whatever had happened between my daughter and Garth wasn't like what poor Colleen had experienced.

LIVING WITH SECRETS ABOUT PHYSICIAN-PATIENTS

Whenever possible, I try never to be in a conflict-of-interest situation with my physician-patients. For example, I do not accept as a patient a medical student or a resident whom I am currently supervising. I do not write letters of reference for my physician-patients. When I served on the resident selection committee, I excused myself (tactfully I hope) from any evaluation or decision on an applicant who was or had been my patient.

Yet despite these safeguards, I am not uncommonly in situations that disrupt my equilibrium. One example: I am supervising a medical student seminar on childhood sexual abuse. The student giving the seminar touches on incest and its consequences. One of the five other medical students is a woman who was my patient for two years before she entered medical school. She is a victim of father-daughter incest. I am acutely anxious. I can recall as if it were yesterday her painful recollections in my office. I am afraid to look at her and to reexperience the shame that I felt as a male when I was her therapist so many years earlier.

Here is another example: A medical colleague of mine called me into his office and said: "Hey, did you hear that Dr. A (a high-profile clinician at our medical school) just got fired—he's been screwing one of his patients!" I responded with outrage: "That's a nasty rumor and I don't believe it. It's mean-spirited. Don't spread it around." What my colleague didn't know was that Dr. A and his wife were patients of mine. I felt extremely defensive and protective of them—and the agony that they were experiencing. Dr. A, during a period of depression and marital unhappiness, did have a brief relationship with one of his patients. This had ended now. I had him on antidepressant medication, and he and his wife were in marital therapy with me. Dr. A was suicidally depressed and deeply ashamed for the pain and dishonor that he had caused his patient, his wife, and his children. This man was not a sex addict or sexual predator. He was a psychiatrically impaired physician whose usual impeccable judgment was affected by mental illness. For his medical colleagues to gossip about him made me feel nauseated—and terribly dispirited about how cruel we can be toward each other.

Being a doctors' psychiatrist means that I also learn information about other physicians who are not patients of mine but who are intimates of my physician-patients. In the course of their therapy, my patients may discuss matters about physicians with whom I work or serve on committees or teach. I'm used to having a "head full of secrets" and feel no sense of judgment toward these individuals. But I feel strange knowing things about physicians without their knowledge or permission. Many examples come to mind: learning that Dr. B has genital herpes, that Dr. C had an affair with my patient last year, that Dr. D has erection problems, that Dr. E has been treated for substance abuse, that Dr. F is a married father of four but a frequent sexual partner of one of my gay physician-patients, that Dr. G is HIV-positive, that Dr. H is infertile, that Dr. I and her husband are about to separate, and on and on.

SUICIDE OF A DOCTOR-PATIENT

When my patient Dr. S committed suicide 5 years ago, his death was unexpected and shocked his medical colleagues and friends. He was newly separated—his wife and children had left—and this loss, on top of his bipolar illness and alcoholism was too much for him. As his psychiatrist, I knew his prognosis was not good. He had been hospitalized twice and had made two serious suicide attempts before I became his doctor. In fact, I had not seen him in several months. He canceled his regular 3-month appointment and told my secretary he would call after vacation to rebook. It was purely accidental that I heard about his separation. I learned this from another patient of mine, who worked with him, late on a Friday afternoon. Indeed, it was the mention of Dr. S's name that jogged my memory that he hadn't been in to see me in a while. I made a note to myself to call Dr. S on Monday. It was too late. He was found dead of carbon monoxide poisoning on Sunday.

How did I feel? Sad—and guilty. Regretful? Yes. I wished I would have called him Friday before I left for the weekend. I might have prevented his death at that time but given his deteriorating health, and his personal and professional decline, he was at high risk for suicide eventually. Reaching out to his wife and children and attending his funeral were therapeutic for me.

What I found difficult was the criticism of his friends and colleagues. They didn't know that I was his psychiatrist nor did they know about his mood disorder or his chemical dependency. He concealed all this from them. Even though I know that people lash out and blame others when someone commits suicide, I still felt that I had let his friends down in some way by not preventing his death. That I had failed them—not Dr. S!

That maybe I should have been able to see this coming and to intervene sooner.

Ironically, about 6 weeks after Dr. S's death, one of his residents who had been my patient off and on for about 3 years came in to see me. In this session, he had just finished telling me about how much he missed Dr. S as a mentor and teacher when he said: "I don't know who Dr. S's psychiatrist was but I'm lucky to have you looking after me. I feel I'm in good hands. There are a lot of lousy shrinks out there."

I was touched by his words but felt only half-deserving of his kindness. I remember smiling at him, but it was forced and awkward and weak. I also felt flushed (my visible shame) and I know I didn't look him directly in the eyes. Afterward, I reflected on how much easier it would be if I could have blurted out: "I was Dr. S's psychiatrist! Yes he was a wonderful physician, teacher, and mentor to many young physicians! But he was a very sick and troubled man! He fought a lot of demons! I tried my best. I'm sorry you've lost someone so special to you."

TREATING PHYSICIANS FACING DISCIPLINARY CHARGES OR LAWSUITS

A range of emotions and questions arise in me when I am asked to treat physicians who have been charged with ethical breaches or medical malpractice. As I listen to the physician and review documents from attorneys and licensing bodies, I question my tendency to deny, rationalize, and minimize the alleged trauma to the victimized patient(s) of my physician-patient. Did he or she really commit such acts? Was it really that bad? Was the patient really harmed? Is this feminist backlash against this poor doctor? When we look after physicians, we are wanting to be their advocates as well as their physicians—but we must be careful in our quest to be fair and to correct possible injustice.

I find that I must also resist a tendency in me to collude with the physician-patient against the victimized patient. It is easy to identify with my patient, we are both physicians, perhaps both psychiatrists. He or she really didn't mean any harm. Why is this patient charging this physician? Vindictiveness? Is she a spurned lover? Is it doctor-bashing? Financial compensation? Is her new therapist putting her up to this? Is it interprofessional rivalry—a psychologist against a psychiatrist, or a chiropractor against a physician?

At other times, I find myself identifying with the victimized patient: "I feel really sorry for her—all she wanted was to be helped, not used—I know what it's like to be exploited—I was a patient once myself, I know how vulnerable you can become and how frightened of authority figures you can be—I don't think my therapist respected my boundaries—what an abuse of power!"

Another challenge for the psychiatrist looking after physicians who have been charged is processing strong emotions (e.g., rage, disgust, abandonment) that may arise. "How could any physician be so cruel, so self-serving, sick, perverted, disgusting, sexist? How am I going to hide my anger and disdain for this physician and use professional judgment? I don't feel my usual warmth or empathy toward physician-patients, I feel cool and stiff and rather stylized. This makes me feel self-righteous and guilty to have this kind of attitude. I wish I could just get rid of this patient."

Finally, treating physicians who have charges against them may lead to the arousal of memories and feelings (anxiety, shame, sadness, guilt) about one's own previous unethical (or possibly unethical) mistakes and transgressions. An inner dialogue may run something like this: "This patient is making me very nervous. He is talking about things that hit very close to home. How can I suppress how I behaved toward some of my patients during my internship, during my residency, or during my early years of practice? This subject wasn't talked about in those days or if it was, in only a titillating manner. Boundaries were different 20 years ago, weren't they? I'm feeling ashamed and guilty the more he keeps talking about what went on between him and his patient. There but for the grace of God go I. Why wasn't I sued as an intern when that 25-year-old man with meningitis died unexpectedly under my care? Was I negligent and just got away with it? Or that distraught female patient I hugged 23 years ago when I was a resident. The one who never came back. Why didn't she lay an ethical complaint against me? I've obsessed about that day ever since and about who needed that hug—me or her? And how much I breached the covenant, her trust in me, and let her down as a physician."

FEAR OF ONE'S OWN MARRIAGE DISSOLVING

Because I treat a lot of medical students and physicians with stressful relationships or marriages, it is not uncommon that I see my own marital dynamics in the couples who come to me for help. At times when my own marriage has been strained, I find it hard to separate myself from my patients' marital problems. Further, I begin to wonder if my wife and I are in the early stages of marital breakdown and maybe don't recognize it as such. How can I keep perspective?

Here is an example of a couple whose marital separation represents a type of marriage breakdown that is not uncommon in the 1990s. As a professional man with a dual career marriage, and as a middle-aged psychiatrist who sees sadness and fear in his office five days a week, I cannot help but identify:

> Dr. W is a cardiologist and Mrs. W is a businesswoman. They are both 50 years old and came to see me on their 25th wedding anniversary. Their two children are both living away from home attending university. Two weeks earlier, Mrs. W told her husband that she wants to separate. He was shocked and begged her to at least try marital therapy before leaving. She agreed but didn't feel very optimistic. This was the background to our first visit together.
>
> What I learned was that Mrs. W had been unhappy for at least 5 years. She had tried to talk to Dr. W about her loneliness and boredom with him, and her belief that his whole life was his work. He argued that he would cut back and they would begin to do more together. This made things better for a few months but soon they were back to old habits. Their sexual life together became less frequent but neither really complained. When Mrs. W suggested a marital enrichment group, Dr. W scoffed. A couple of years later, when she wanted to go to marriage therapy, he thought that was silly and unnecessary. He booked a cruise instead, which was fun, but Mrs. W continued to feel unstimulated with her husband. Years passed until she finally decided that she wanted to be on her own.
>
> Mrs. W's only hesitation about separating was living with her friends' and family's disapproval. They all loved Dr. W and thought he was an ideal husband—hardworking, successful, conscientious, well-respected in the medical community, and fit. He was never violent. He wasn't alcoholic. He was a good father. He was kind and trusting—she managed the money. On the surface, he was wonderful. However, he was a perfectionist and never relaxed. He was driven, self-centered, and subtly controlling. And as she said, boring.
>
> Dr. W was devastated and panicky. He was terribly regretful about the way he had led his life and how much he had given to medicine and to his career advancement. He decried how much he had underestimated his wife's unhappiness and loneliness. He wished he had gone for help years earlier.
>
> Dr. and Mrs. W's attempt at marital therapy was sincere but to no avail. After four visits, it became clear to Dr. W that his wife was very closed off and quite psychologically separate. It was too late to try to patch things up. I began separation therapy with them and after two

months, Dr. W took an apartment and moved out on his own. He remained sad about his marriage ending but much more accepting.

How did my therapy with Dr. and Mrs. W affect me? In lots of ways. I remember bringing flowers home in the evening! I remember listening more carefully to how my wife's day had been at work. I remember suggesting walks after dinner. I remember being much more conscious of my wife's degree of happiness and unhappiness with me. And I remember striving to get beyond my "knee-jerk" defensiveness when I'm criticized for working too hard.

Being a therapist is both humbling and enriching. Humbling because society's dramas are portrayed in my office daily and we are all part of society (even though many of us in medicine try to fight it and deny that we are human too); enriching because I learn a lot from my patients and their challenges and struggles. Dr. W (and so many others over my career) taught me not to take my marriage and children for granted and not to put my patients, my students, and my research ahead of them. Mrs. W taught me to pursue hobbies and other forms of relaxation. They both taught me the importance of spending time together, of humor, of good communication, of being creative.

CONCLUSION

In this chapter, I have described some of the more common issues for psychiatrists when they look after physicians and their families. Much of my commentary is idiosyncratic and personal; not all psychiatrists will have the same inner emotions and conflicts precipitated by their therapeutic work with physician-patients. My message though is universal: Physicians and their families are a mirror to the psychiatrists who treat them. We have a duty to look in that mirror.

REFERENCES

Belkin, L. (1993). Sensing a loss of control, more doctors call it quits. *New York Times,* March 9, A1, C2.

Charney, D. A. & Russell, R. C. (1994). An overview of sexual harassment. *American Journal of Psychiatry, 151,* 10–17.

Myers, M. F. (1992a). Treating physicians with psychotherapy. *Directions in Psychiatry, 12,* 1–7.

Myers, M. F. (1992b). Fighting stigma: How to help the doctor's family. In P. J. Fink and A. Tasman (Eds.), *Stigma and mental illness* (pp. 139–150). Washington, DC: American Psychiatric Press.

Myers, M. F. (1994). *Doctors' marriages: A look at the problems and their solutions, Second edition.* New York: Plenum.

Richman, J. A., Flaherty, J. A., Rospenda, K. M., & Christensen, M. L. (1992). Mental health consequences and correlates of reported medical student abuse. *Journal of the American Medical Association, 267,* 692–694.

Wehbe, M. A. (1994). A father's advice: Don't become a physician, my son. *American Medical News,* April 25, 22.

CHAPTER 15

*Psychotherapy with Therapists: Countertransference Dilemmas**

NANCY A. BRIDGES, LICSW, BCD

Historically in psychodynamic circles, personal treatment for therapists has been recognized as a prerequisite for becoming a competent clinician (Baum, 1973; Buckley, Karasu, & Charles, 1981; Burton, 1973; Strupp, 1955). However, despite the frequency with which psychodynamic psychotherapists enter and undergo treatment during their training or professional years, little has been written about the special characteristics of treatment or the experience of the treating therapist. Psychotherapy with therapists raises intense and complicated countertransferential feelings for the treating therapist and presents unique problems around recognition and management of identification issues. Strong, often unconscious feelings of envy, competitiveness, exposure, and vulnerability, together with a particularly close sense of self-identification and a powerful wish to be helpful, threaten to intrude into the treatment. Fears of criticism, issues of therapeutic narcissism, and protection of one's professional self-esteem are likely to accompany any treatment with a therapist-patient.

Psychotherapy with therapist-patients provides unique opportunities for treating therapists to wrestle with themselves and the intense feelings generated in the treatment process. The danger and difficulty lie in the treating therapists' avoidance, denial, and refusal to honestly confront themselves. In those cases, psychotherapy may indeed be hazardous.

What follows are common countertransferential dilemmas, specific to treatment with therapist-patients, as described by practicing therapists. Heightening treating therapists' awareness and understanding of the potential countertransferential feelings involved in treating therapists may

* This chapter is a revision of a paper published in the *American Journal of Orthopsychiatry, 63*(1), January 1993 (pp. 34–44), and has been reprinted with permission.

enable their fruitful use in the treatment process. This discussion will enhance the treating therapists' capacity to observe themselves in the treatment process. The creative use of the inevitably rich and varied countertransferential responses may be beneficial to both therapist and therapist-patient.

CASE MANAGEMENT ISSUES

Self-Esteem and Professional Development

Psychotherapists treating therapists often face a host of self-esteem issues that threaten to intrude into the therapeutic relationship. As one psychotherapist put it, "the first one is the hardest," meaning that the therapist's sense of increased vulnerability, awkward self-consciousness, fears of exposure, and feelings of specialness may be mastered and diminished with repeated experiences. These feelings may remain, however, if the treating psychotherapist is recently out of training or not well-grounded in beliefs concerning competence and professional self-worth.

One of the major tasks for therapists is to learn to appreciate thoroughly the power and therapeutic value of a treatment relationship and the use of the therapist's self in the process of treatment (Rubin, 1989). This developmental task often remains an open and ongoing struggle for therapists because the feelings associated with being so important to a patient are difficult to bear. The capacity to bear painful feelings and contain intense urgencies while maintaining a therapeutic balance is a crucial treatment skill that the therapist acquires through experience, supervision, and personal treatment. Inexperienced therapists commonly manage this sense of responsibility and specialness by questioning their usefulness and their knowledge, and by devaluing the treatment, imagining that a more seasoned therapist would do a better job (Sank & Prout, 1978). The following case example illustrates the management of such issues:

> A psychiatrist, recently out of training and just beginning a private practice, accepts into treatment a newly trained staff psychologist, employed at an institution where the psychiatrist had previously trained. In the course of treatment, as the psychologist struggles with issues of self-esteem, he becomes dismayed by his choice of a psychiatrist for a therapist and is very devaluing of his treatment and his therapist. At work, he liberally shares his anger and disappointment about his treatment, and he receives informal, ambivalently solicited, one-sided consultations about his treatment from his professional colleagues.

> The therapist becomes aware of increased anxiety about this case, feels open to scrutiny by previous mentors, and worries about his professional reputation in the community. Self-doubts arise about his clinical judgment, and he begins to view the patient's informal consultations with colleagues as disruptive. The patient's negative transference, combined with the therapist's inexperience, threaten to derail the treatment and abort the crucial therapeutic work of exploring and understanding the dynamic meaning of the outside consultations.
>
> Through his own consultations, the therapist struggles to manage his personal, developmental, and professional self-esteem issues around feelings of exposure and self-worth that intersect and are potentiated by this patient's self-esteem issues and transference. With assistance, the therapist returns to the task of examining the symbolic meaning of these behaviors and explores the patient's terror around dependency, intense affect, and therapeutic regression.

Therapists who treat other therapists acquire, by nature of these experiences, special status with all the attendant dilemmas that accompany specialness (Greenberg & Kaslow, 1984). The seductive allure of such status may be simultaneously pleasing, terrifying, and burdening. Being such a therapist may be a role to which the professional aspires, but if undertaken prematurely, self-expectations may remain disproportionate to clinical experience and comfort. This honor may be unexpectedly accompanied by quite intense countertransferential dilemmas.

In treating therapist-patients, therapists commonly struggle with feelings of exposure and fears of criticism by colleagues. In all treatment, therapists recognize countertransferential phenomena as providing vital and crucial information about the therapeutic dyad and the treatment process (Lang, 1978). They rely on such phenomena to deepen their understanding of the work. However, when clinicians treat therapist-patients, these predictable countertransferential phenomenon intersect and are enlarged by the therapists' own self-esteem issues, and the treatment process may suffer. If not well attended to, the therapists' focus may shift toward their own developmental struggles, and a clear focus on the clinical issues at hand may be lost. All treatments reliably contain therapeutic errors of varying size and nature that chart and inform the process (Lang, 1978). Therapists must deal with their own professional self-esteem issues elsewhere and be open and available for detailed processing of moments of disconnection, countertransference errors, and therapeutic mistakes. Exploring the dynamic meaning of treatment errors with patients requires as much attention as considering the therapist's blind spots and identifying errors.

The feelings of specialness and honor about treating a competent professional like oneself may create difficulties around power issues and boundary maintenance, even for the seasoned therapist:

> A charismatic, bright, interpersonally, and intellectually compelling psychologist prided himself on filling his practice with therapists and therapists-in-training patients. Enjoying the exercise of power and being well-respected in the professional community, he made up his own rules of conduct and treatment. He viewed his therapist-patients as protégés, inviting them to attend his public lectures, read his papers, and tour his house to view his rare furniture and private gardens. A therapist-patient painfully recalls that an hour of therapy was a success if she was the focus for part of her session.

Therapist-patients who idealize and aspire to be like accomplished treating therapists may not object to exploitative treatment practices. Therapists' personal vulnerabilities, such as grandiose entitlement, may match or intersect with the usual countertransferential feelings produced by the treatment of therapist-patients and result in the magnification of these issues and the violation of commonly understood treatment practices (Epstein & Simon, 1990).

Even with experience and feelings of expertise, a number of variables may create professional disequilibrium for the therapist and encroach on the treatment:

> An accomplished therapist was referred a therapist-patient by the chairman of the department. He found the treatment particularly difficult, feeling intimidated and psychologically burdened as he imagined his boss's displeasure and his loss of professional esteem if the treatment was unsuccessful.
>
> With peer discussion, the therapist discovered his feelings of intimidation and fear of failure also reflect the experience of his therapist-patient who has unrealistically high hopes and fears about the therapeutic power and potential of their relationship. Understanding the possible meanings of these feelings to his patient, the therapist integrates this information onto the treatment process asking his patient about his wishes and fears about their beginning treatment relationship.

Limits of Responsibility

The therapist's ability to recognize clinical and professional limitations while maintaining ethical standards becomes easier with experience.

However, the potential for role confusion, with the inevitable tension it generates, is inherent in the treatment of therapist-patients. One treating therapist comments, "It was unclear who was the therapist and who was the patient. Maybe I was too close to the work." Treating therapists hear compelling clinical material about their patients' patients. They may have more experience and wish to be helpful by offering clinical tips or supervisory comments to their therapist-patients. Professional paths may cross at conferences or with mutual colleagues, making it necessary to choose the tone and amount of interaction. In the following case example, some of these issues came to the fore:

> A newly licensed social worker began treating a medical student who was quite impaired; she experienced deep depressions with chronic suicidal ideation, had severe difficulties around self-esteem and disturbances of the self, and was socially isolated. After several years of treatment and further training, the student applied for and was accepted into a psychiatric residency training program. The therapist viewed her patient's choice as a behavioral expression of her identification with the therapist and consequently felt concern, conflict, and powerlessness.
>
> As the patient began practicing psychotherapy and used the treatment to share her serious difficulties, the therapist became increasingly anxious about her patient's clinical work and deeply divided by issues of loyalty, ethics, and the limits of her responsibility. Plagued by the notion that she was helping to create an incompetent, potentially destructive therapist, she found it ever more difficult to remain empathic with her patient, while she felt increasing empathy and identification with her patient's patients. Preoccupied with these concerns and unable to comfort herself, the therapist wondered whether she alone was seeing pieces of her patient's clinical work to which no one else had access.

Therapist-patients may travel in close social or professional circles and may see and know much about the treating therapist (Ordway, 1976; Kaslow, 1984). They may be well liked and, under other circumstances, might be colleagues or friends. Alternatively, therapist-patients may be incompetent, causing professional concern among their treating therapists.

Discipline Differences and Competitiveness

Issues of competitiveness, envy, and fears of criticism are commonly part of the countertransferential package for treating therapists. An experienced therapist tells of her conscious wish to "blind her therapist-patients with her clinical brilliance" or another of his efforts to remain nondefensive when criticized by therapist-patients. Some situations may be difficult to accept and integrate; for example, if therapist-patients charge higher fees for psychotherapy, are paid higher salaries, hold coveted positions, or are supervised and admired by mentors beloved of the treating therapists.

Public speaking and teaching provide unique arenas in which issues of competitiveness in relation to therapist-patients can arise. Feelings of exposure and fears of criticism may be embodied in the therapists' conspicuous self-consciousness about the presence of patients in the teaching audience. Therapists wonder if they are "smart enough" when unmasked behind a lecture podium, feel they can't "stand the scrutiny" of being observed by therapist-patients, or choose their words carefully, aware that their teaching can affect therapist-patients and the treatment process. Therapists acquire idiosyncratic ways of dealing with the anxiety involved in feelings of exposure and competitiveness vis-à-vis their patients. One therapist commits himself to "never say anything publicly (in lectures) I wouldn't share with my patients," while another therapist deals with her anxiety by instructing therapist-patients, "You may not come to hear me teach. I believe it would compromise your treatment." Under the guise of protecting patients and the treatment process, these therapists attempt to regain control over situations that produce feelings of anxiety and vulnerability.

Therapists become accustomed to dealing with their own and their patients' grief, anger, disappointment, frustration, and ambivalence. However, feelings of envy and competitiveness toward a patient may disorient the therapist and be denied or expressed as reaction formation. Therapists treating therapist-patients of other disciplines may discover such feelings in themselves after handling clinical material in an uncharacteristic manner:

> A psychologist, while completing his dissertation, was in treatment with a nurse. The therapist was very fond of this patient viewing him as smart, confident, astute, and emotionally steady. As the patient's graduation grew closer and his entry into the professional world was imminent, he began to wonder why he had chosen a nurse for a therapist. These discussions left the therapist feeling devalued and unimportant. When the patient needed subjects for his dissertation research, the therapist, in an uncharacteristic intervention, helped him by placing notices at her place of employment and soliciting subjects from colleagues. These interventions alerted the therapist to the existence of unacknowledged feelings about this patient and herself. With self-examination, the therapist realized this patient evoked her own ambivalence about her choice of discipline and private regrets about

> not being a doctor, a profession she viewed as consonant with authority, respect, and power. This patient held special transferential meaning for the therapist around her professional and self-identity, which was out of her awareness and became transformed into helpfulness outside the therapeutic contract. These unconscious feelings overshadowed the therapeutic work and were enacted before the therapist identified them.

Uncharacteristic treatment of material and behavioral enactments signal to the therapist the need for further self-scrutiny and reflection. In such instances, it is likely the therapist is struggling with previously unacknowledged, perhaps personally unacceptable, feeling states.

Therapists may be startled by the intensity of competitive feelings with therapist-patients and unsure of how to make the best therapeutic use of such feelings. If unexamined, these feelings may be expressed by harsh, controlling, or sadistic treatment of material:

> A therapist treating a talented young psychologist struggles with feeling threatened and harshly critical of his patient when she discusses her feelings of admiration and respect for idealized mentors. As she continues to elevate her mentors with praise, her therapist feels compelled to correct her misperceptions of his colleagues. Abandoning clinical restraint, he discloses unflattering personal and professional information about these colleagues. His patient, upset and angry, experiences her therapist's unsolicited personal opinion of idealized mentors as hurtful and self-serving.
>
> In this situation, the therapist's harsh unhelpful interventions led him to focus his clinical inquiry toward his intense competitive feelings with this patient and his colleagues. A consultation with a colleague revealed the subtle manner in which the patient's idealizations served, in fact, to criticize her therapist. With this information, the therapist refocused his attention on the patient's unacknowledged and unspoken disappointments and criticisms of her treatment and their treatment relationship. With supervision, the therapist prepares to tolerate personally and manage therapeutically the self-esteem issues around his personal, competitive feelings toward colleagues.

Identification with Therapist-Patients

Very quickly, but often unconsciously, therapists imbue treatment with a therapist-patient with special expectations and meaning. These are often intense and deeply personal, and they may spill over into the treatment in ways the therapist does not notice or anticipate. The tug of intense identification often leads to creative, innovative therapeutic interactions. But it can also lead to interventions with unintended effects that derail treatment or which are harmful.

Some of the most dangerous countertransference errors can occur when the therapist-patient is ill, impaired, or in need of protective care. At these times, the treating therapist's identification with the patient may be a disservice:

> A therapist treating a depressed and suicidal therapist patient struggled with the issue of involuntary hospitalization as the therapist-patient refused inpatient care. The therapist-patient, although ill and desperate, was adamantly against hospitalization, believing it would ruin his reputation and take away his livelihood as a practitioner. The therapist, swayed by the power of the patient's argument and sensitive to the stigma attached to psychiatric illness among mental health professionals, decided not to hospitalize. While an outpatient, the patient committed suicide. Retrospectively, the treating therapist felt his identification with this patient as a therapist had obscured his judgment about hospitalization.
>
> A consultation to the therapist revealed the meaning of his intensely personal identification with this patient extended beyond feelings of professional sameness, as is often the case. The therapist's younger brother suffered from a major mental illness and was repetitively hospitalized against his wishes. The therapist had once participated in the decision to hospitalize his brother for which his brother never forgave him. His conflicted and unresolved feelings toward his brother and this history intersected with his patient's feelings about hospitalization, his professional identification with his patient, and resulted in flawed decision making.

The need for involuntary hospitalization is an extreme example. However, less dramatic cases of illness among therapist-patients routinely confront treating therapists:

> A therapist treating a clinically depressed psychiatrist consulted a psychopharmacologist who concurred with the therapist's recommendation that the patient obtain a psychopharmacology consultation for medication to alleviate his depressive symptomatology. The patient was appalled at the idea of taking psychotropic medication, angry at his therapist's suggestion, and frightened as he imagined how this would be perceived by colleagues. The treating therapist prematurely abandoned his exploration of the possibility of a medication consult because he privately agreed that the act of taking medication would potentially diminish the patient's credibility and professional standing in the community.

The therapist's task is to acknowledge the multiple and overdetermined feelings and meanings involved in such moments in treatment and to supervise their unconscious and therapeutic expression. Although these identifications may present therapeutic challenges and opportunities for the therapist's increased self-awareness and understanding, their intensity and richness can enhance treatment and are invaluable:

> A psychologist began treating a young psychologist at an uncomfortably reduced fee because the patient was recently out of training, looking for employment and reportedly unable to afford treatment. It was a challenging treatment case with many issues around self-identity, entitlement, idealizing and devaluing relationships, neediness, and rage. The patient spent a portion of each therapy hour criticizing the therapist's technical handling of material and his personal style. After 3 years of arduous, devaluing, self-doubting, enraging treatment, in which the therapist frequently felt he was not paid enough and wished he had not accepted such a low fee, the patient casually revealed that many years ago he had inherited a large estate from a distant relative and was quite wealthy. The therapist was enraged, felt swindled, and demanded that the patient begin to pay full fee. The patient felt that they had made a contract and that it should remain binding. The therapist was unable to contain his anger, deal with his countertransference outside the treatment, and engage the patient in working with the symbolism involved in this exchange while negotiating a more equitable fee. Berating himself for this clinical confusion, the therapist was convinced that the fact that the patient was a psychologist, and the subsequent feelings of identification, had clouded his clinical judgment at the beginning of treatment resulting in his agreement to an unusually low fee without exploration of the other financial resources available to his patient.
>
> In addition, as the therapist reflected further on the meaning of his identification with this patient, he associated to his own treatment experience and remembered his therapist had charged him a reduced fee as a professional courtesy. Beginning treatment with a therapist-patient stimulated his unconscious wish to be like his admired personal therapist and to extend a professional courtesy he otherwise would not do.

Ruptured Treatments

In the business of psychotherapy in which a therapist's practice and thus livelihood may thrive or suffer by the reputation enjoyed among peers, a dissatisfied customer, who is also a peer group member, can provoke anxiety. This is especially true in the current climate of numerous public legal actions brought against incompetent and abusive therapists. Anxiety and feelings of increased vulnerability to patients' dissatisfactions and accusations are ubiquitous in professional communities today. When treatments with therapist-patients go poorly, long-lasting feelings of humiliation and professional overexposure may continue to threaten the therapist's self-esteem and make it difficult to regain therapeutic balance.

Professional communities are small, even in urban settings, and it is likely that professional paths will cross at lectures and professional meetings or through mutual colleagues or friends. Therapists who have experienced a ruptured or derailed treatment with a therapist-patient speak of the intense shame, feelings of exposure, and dread that they will, when they least expect it, encounter the therapist-patient. Therapists continue to scrutinize and review the treatment in an attempt to understand further the etiology of the difficulties, accept their contribution to it, and forgive themselves. Often, consultations with a senior admired clinician are necessary to facilitate and hasten the therapist's recovery from the injury. If such consultations are avoided, the time-honored tradition of pathologizing the patient may be invoked as therapists add new and previously unthought-of diagnostic labels, in an effort to manage overwhelming feelings of shame.

Ethical Dilemmas

It is not surprising that therapists can develop deep, special, and complicated attachments to therapist-patients. The opportunities for multiple identifications and meanings are many. What is often unexpected is how unaware the treating therapist can be of these processes:

> A therapist had successfully treated a young psychotherapist in what they both agreed was a valuable and transforming psychotherapy for the patient and a gratifying experience for the therapist. As the patient was completing her treatment and moving on with her life, she was in crisis around a credentialing issue, the specificity of certain requirements, and the panic she felt at having to wait to fulfill the requirements. The therapist, who admired and deeply cared for this patient, offered to sign the necessary forms. The patient was both touched and frightened by her therapist's unorthodox, perhaps unethical, offer and struggled to understand what motivated her beloved therapist to offer to violate a professional standard. After the patient's termination, the therapist came to recognize this offer as an error arising from her identification with this patient's issues, her own sadness around termination, and her unconscious wish to offer a lasting gift.

Few therapists would be startled by a compelling wish to help a beloved patient, even with a credentialing process. The challenge of maintaining boundaries and managing powerful unconscious identifications with therapist-patients is illustrated by the preceding example. Consultations with colleagues and mentors may assist treating therapists in managing their own process and identifying countertransferential issues.

USING PERSONAL TREATMENT LEGACIES

Therapists commonly report their personal treatment experiences as particularly instrumental in shaping their views, values, and orientation, and as offering crucial modeling and information about how to conduct themselves as practicing therapists. Most professionals agree that having the experience of being a patient expands and deepens empathic understanding of self, patients, and the process of treatment (Ford, 1963). To a far greater extent than is usually or publicly acknowledged, therapists learn how to conduct treatment through the process of identification and internalization of their personal treatment experiences (Buckley et al., 1981). Therapeutic posture, approach, sensitivity to issues of power, mutuality, respect, and openness around personal disclosure, as well as the specifics of how particular dilemmas should be handled technically, are all learned and shaped by the therapist's own treatment experiences. The policies around the practice of psychotherapy that represent our important mentoring relationships are far easier to catalog than is the subtle yet crucial learning that takes place around the handling of particular dilemmas in treatment. Becoming a psychotherapist is a painstaking endeavor similar to mastering a craft or becoming a fine artist. Who has been the therapist's master/mentor makes all the difference. Empathic identification with patients is crucial to all successful treatment. However, when the patient is a therapist, the burden of multiple, intense, unconscious identifications is all the more important.

Therapists' identification with their own therapists, and personal treatment, and the inevitable repetition of significant aspects of those treatment relationships hold the potential for enriching therapeutic relationships as well as for iatrogenic harm. The potential for difficulty is exacerbated if the repetition is out of the therapist's awareness, if the importance of the event to the particular patient is not fully understood, or if its importance in the therapist's own treatment is not fully integrated.

Integration of valued aspects of personal treatment into the therapist's practice seems inevitable. Therapists commonly acknowledge that they make a conscious effort to remember that the therapist-patient is a colleague and that techniques experienced in treatment will be employed by these patients in their own practices. Treatment with therapists involves a sacred trust that may enhance the therapist's commitment to therapist-patients and to the success of their treatment. Therapists who treat therapists express a particular interest in being helpful because of the impact that treatment may have on these patients' practices. With clear memories and ideas from their own treatments of what was particularly helpful and what was not helpful, therapists are frequently aware of trying both to incorporate the positive dimensions and to avoid the harmful or negative aspects experienced in their own treatment.

Therapists believe in the importance of an authentic and empathic therapeutic relationship. Harmful therapeutic experiences include competitive or controlling treatment relationships with an absence of warmth, mutuality, and a feeling of defensiveness. Therapy experiences with therapists who are theoretically correct but emotionally absent signal to the therapist-patient that affect is dangerous or that vulnerability and genuine feelings involve shame and humiliation, and are to be avoided. It can be argued that all patients experience therapists with such characteristics as unhelpful (Grunebaum, 1986). Therapist-patients, however, understand the importance of the real relationship and realize that education through modeling takes place in treatment.

Boundary maintenance difficulties of various types are also experienced as unhelpful. When therapists break treatment contracts around issues of touch or use therapist-patients for self-serving needs, whether it be for adulation, patient referrals, sharing professional gossip, or as an object of criticism, harm is done. Therapists struggle not to abuse power or "blame the patient" in ways they themselves may have experienced.

CONCLUSION

Psychotherapists treating therapists confront a myriad of challenging and sometimes painful clinical dilemmas that may catch them by surprise. Difficult countertransferential issues facing a treating therapist include managing self-esteem, overidentification with therapist-patients, and ethical dilemmas. Because of the deeply felt and often unconscious countertransferential phenomena common to therapy with therapist-patients, therapists are well advised to seek consultations with peers or mentors to help manage their experience treating other therapists and to make informed decisions about how to use these phenomena in the treatment. Without adequate self-observation and outside consultations when necessary, treating therapists may unknowingly act on the inevitably strong and varied countertransferential feelings evoked by treatment with these patients. When countertransference or identification errors occur, as they will, the crucial therapeutic task is to attend to the meaning of the event and the dynamics of the therapeutic process. The conscious use by the treating therapist of the rich and powerful identification issues present may enliven and advance treatment.

REFERENCES

Baum, O. E. (1973). Further thoughts on countertransference. *Psychoanalytic Review, 60,* 127–140.

Buckley, P., Karasu, T. B., & Charles, E. (1981). Psychotherapists view their personal therapy. *Psychotherapy: Theory, Research, and Practice, 18,* 299–305.

Burton, A. (1973). The psychotherapist as client. *American Journal of Psychoanalysis, 33,* 94–103.

Epstein, R., & Simon, R. I. (1990). The exploitation index: An early warning indicator of boundary violations in psychotherapy. *Bulletin of Menninger Clinic, 54,* 450–465.

Ford, E. (1963). Being and becoming a psychotherapist: The search for identity. *American Journal of Psychotherapy, 17,* 472–482.

Greenberg, S., & Kaslow, F. W. (1984). Psychoanalytic treatment for therapists, residents, and other trainees. In F. W. Kaslow (Ed.), *Psychotherapy with psychotherapists* (pp. 19–30). New York: Haworth Press.

Grunebaum, H. (1986). Harmful psychotherapy experiences. *American Journal of Psychotherapy, XL(2),* 165–176.

Kaslow, F. W. (Ed.). (1984). *Psychotherapy with Psychotherapists.* New York: Haworth Press.

Lang, R. (1978). *The technique of psychoanalytic psychotherapy.* Vol. II. New York: Jason Aronson.

Ordway, J. (1976). Transference in a fishbowl: A survey of rural psychoanalysis. *Comprehensive Psychiatry, 17*(1), 209–216.

Rubin, S. (1989). At the border of supervision: Critical moments in psychotherapists' development. *American Journal of Psychotherapy, XLIII(2),* 387–397.

Sank, L. I., & Prout, M. F. (1978). Critical issues for the fledgling therapist. *Professional Psychology, 9,* 638–645.

Strupp, H. H. (1955). The effects of the psychotherapist's personal analysis on his techniques. *Journal of Consulting Psychology, 19,* 197–204.

CHAPTER 16

The Therapist as Recipient of the Patient's Relentless Entitlement

MARTHA STARK, MD

I see many patients who never had the experience of a "good enough mother." These patients find themselves hoping against hope that their love objects in the here and now will be able to provide the "good mothering" they never received as a child. They have never really mourned the mother's failure of them; instead, they have spent a lifetime defending themselves against the pain of their grief. They cling to the hope that perhaps someday, somehow, someway, if they are good enough and try hard enough, they may yet be able to extract from a current object (a stand-in for the mother), the love they never got.

These patients relentlessly pursue their love objects, unwilling to take no for an answer. By way of their relentless entitlement, they defend themselves against their grief. Their refrain is that they themselves "cannot" (distortion), the object "can" (illusion), and the object "should" (entitlement) provide the good mothering for which they feel starved.

The patient's need for objects to be other than who they are addresses something I describe as the "defense of relentless entitlement." It is a defense I have observed often in my work with women. It may also be employed by men, but it seems to figure more prominently in women than it does in men, so my focus will be on women—and on what it is like to work with these women.

For the therapist who is the recipient of a patient's relentless entitlement, the challenge is great. It is hard to be at the receiving end of a patient's insistence that you be the good mother, the perfect mother she never had. It is all the more difficult because you often share the patient's illusion that you can and should make up the difference to her. You may believe that, since the problem arose in the context of the mother's failure, you must come through for your patient now—the relationship with you, a compensation for the patient's early relationship with the mother. You may feel that you should be able to gratify the patient's infantile need to have you be her perfect mother.

Although you may want to say yes to the patient's insistence that you be that perfect mother, you must eventually say no. As much as you might wish to, you will never be able to compensate the patient entirely for the damage done early on. To believe that you can, and should, is to collude with the patient's defensive need to deny the truth about her mother, to reinforce her refusal to grieve, and to rob the patient of the opportunity to confront her grief about her actual mother.

But if you can tolerate being in the position of breaking the patient's heart, then she will have an opportunity to do now what she could not possibly do as a child. Within the context of the safety provided by her relationship with you, she will be able, finally, to feel the pain against which she has spent a lifetime defending herself. She will be able, at last, to confront the heartrending reality of just how flawed and imperfect her mother really was and of just how great a price she has paid for that. She will be able, at last, to grieve, to access her outrage and her devastation that her mother really was not good enough and that she has therefore been scarred.

As the patient becomes aware of the extent to which she protects herself against her grief by way of clinging to her defense of relentless entitlement, it becomes more and more difficult for her to maintain her attachment to the defense and to deny the truth about the infantile object. Belatedly, she grieves for the vulnerable little girl she once was, a little girl whose heart was broken by her mother.

As part of the grieving she must do, she must come to accept that she is ultimately powerless to do anything to make her objects, both past and present, different. She must feel, to the very depths of her soul, her anguish and her outrage that her mother was as she was, her therapist is as she is, and her other love objects are as they are. Such is the work of grieving, such is the work of coming to terms with disappointment and moving on, sadder perhaps but wiser.

THE DEFENSE OF RELENTLESS ENTITLEMENT

Let me now spell out the circumstances that can engender the defense of relentless entitlement.

A little girl needs the experience of being cherished, in a nondemanding, loving, accepting way, by a mother who is emotionally present and empathically attuned. At least for a while, the girl must experience being the center of someone else's world, having her every need, her every gesture, recognized and responded to.

If the little girl is denied this experience, the need for a good mother becomes reinforced and intensifies over time. Unable to confront the truth about just how unavailable her mother really is, the little girl defends herself against her disappointment by taking the burden of her mother's badness on herself. By so doing, she creates a distorted sense of herself as bad (that is, as unlovable), but she is then able to hold on to the illusion of her mother as good (that is, as loving)—and as ultimately forthcoming if she, the daughter, could but get it right.

The little girl defends herself against facing her pain; it hurts too much to acknowledge the truth about her mother's limitations. She protects herself against the pain of such knowing by deciding that it must have been she who was bad, her mother who was good. To go on living, she must deny the reality of what, on some level, she really does know to be the truth.

Meanwhile, the need for a good mother persists. Even as an adult, she brings to relationships a little girl's desperate need to be known, understood, and loved in the ways that a perfect mother would love her young daughter. Hoping against hope, she looks to each new love object to offer her the kind of empathic attunement, emotional availability, and unconditional love that her mother should have been able to offer but did not. In essence, to subsequent love relationships, she brings her illusions about what could be and her entitlement about what should be. She brings her need for her objects to be other than who they are; she does not accept them as they are but asks that they be who they are not, namely, perfect mothers.

Until her infantile need becomes transformed into a mature capacity to accept her objects as they are, she will be destined to feel ever frustrated and helpless. As long as she locates the responsibility for change within others, as long as she experiences the locus of control as external, her experience of her love objects will be one of bitter disappointment, angry dissatisfaction, and painful defeat. As long as she refuses to grieve, refuses to confront the early reality of just how limited her mother really was, she will continue to look to her love objects in the here and now to be something they are not.

The patient is deeply convinced that her love objects could be her good mother if they were but willing. She is sure that they have it to give but choose to withhold it, that they have the capacity to offer it but refuse to. She experiences it as essential to her survival and so feels that she must have it.

When such a need is delivered into the treatment situation, an idealizing transference emerges in which the patient comes to expect that you will be this perfect mother she never had as a child. On some level, it is not unreasonable that the patient should find herself looking to you to be ever sensitive, understanding, empathic, and responsive. In fact, this may not be too different from what you yourself strive to be. So too, it is not unreasonable that the patient should find herself wanting unconditional love and total acceptance, that she should find herself wanting to be special, wanting exceptions made, wanting you to know without her having to say, wanting magic, answers, and guarantees. It is easy enough to understand the patient's desire for such things.

The situation, however, is complicated because, when she is caught up in her relentless insistence that you be her good mother, it is always with respect to something that, on the surface, is not all that unreasonable but, as it happens, is not something you feel in a position to offer. Inevitably, what the patient wants is something you could conceivably offer—under other circumstances, or if you had received different training, or if you had another orientation, or if that were your specialty, or if you had different skills, or if you were someone else.

Inevitably, the patient will find herself wanting the very thing you are not comfortable offering. For example, the patient demands that you hold her, that you give her advice, that you tell her you love her, that you reassure her she will get better, that you give her your home telephone number. Perhaps the patient has a friend whose therapist holds her. Perhaps the patient was given answers by a previous therapist. Theoretically, you too could do these things. But, as it happens, these are things you do not feel comfortable offering—and the patient comes to know this but insists anyway.

The patient may demand that you be her advocate with the welfare department, that you write her a letter of recommendation, that you testify on her behalf in court, that you get her husband to recognize the ways in which he has wronged her, that you side with her against a previous therapist. Again, these are things you could conceivably offer but, for whatever the reason, do not—and, here too, the patient knows this but will not take your no for an answer.

It is the patient's insistence in the face of being denied that demonstrates the defensive nature of her desire. More generally, it is the relentlessness with which the patient pursues her quest and the intensity of her outrage in the face of its being denied that speak to her need to defend herself against the pain of her disappointment. She is unable to tolerate the disappointment experienced in the face of the object's failure of her. Unable to bear her heartache, she pursues the object of her desire with a vengeance, absolutely unwilling to take no for an answer.

Ordinarily, a patient who has been told no must confront the pain of her disappointment and come to terms with it. In other words, she must grieve.

But a patient who is relentlessly hopeful does something else. She refuses to confront the pain of her disappointment; she refuses to grieve. And she feels entitled to a yes.

What is it like to work with a patient who is relentlessly demanding, insistent, entitled, ever refusing to accept the reality of things as they are, ever needing her objects to be something they are not, ever needing you to be something you are not? What is it like to work with a patient who feels entitled to have you gratify her need for a perfect mother and who, in those moments when she sees that you are not going to be forthcoming, is outraged that you refuse?

When faced with this, it is easy to become defensive, to get caught up in trying to demonstrate that what the patient wants is unrealistic or inappropriate. You may even find yourself protesting, in response to the patient's accusations that you are incompetent, unethical, heartless, that the problem lies not within you but within her. Whether your protest is implicit or explicit, the message to the patient may well be that she is wrong to be wanting so much and that it is right for you to be denying her gratification of her infantile needs.

Alternatively, in the face of the patient's relentlessness, it is easy to get caught up in feeling that you are wrong and the patient is right. If you are insecure and live in fear of being found out, shown up as a fraud, an impostor, then, in the face of the patient's insistence that you come through for her, you may find yourself struggling to preserve your good feelings about yourself and your abilities as a therapist. Or if you have unresolved narcissistic issues and a need to be the patient's perfect mother, you may find it particularly difficult to be cast in the role of the bad, withholding, unempathic mother. More generally, if you tend to lack self-confidence or can easily be made to feel guilty, you will have an especially difficult time saying no to this patient.

In point of fact, neither you nor your patient is wrong. Because you are not able to be the perfect mother the patient would have wanted you to be, you are, however, letting her down. If the patient is ever to be able to experience this disappointment, then you must be able to tolerate being the disappointment, being in the position of failing the patient, of not coming through for her, perhaps even of breaking her heart every now and again. You are not bad; nor are you as good as you (and the patient) would have hoped you could be—and you need to be able to live with that.

In other words, if you yourself have cherished the illusion that you can and should make up the difference to the patient, then you must be able to make your peace with the reality of just how limited you actually are. You do the best you can, but you will never be able to be the perfect mother, much as you might have wished you could. If you need to see yourself as the mother the patient never had, it will be more difficult for you to help the patient master her disillusionment, harder for you to help her come to terms with her disenchantment. Ultimately, you and the patient must both face the reality that you will never be able, entirely, to compensate the patient for the damage she sustained early on.

Many of us entered the mental health profession because we wanted to offer our patients what we ourselves had never received from our mothers. We had a need to give what we had never gotten. But we must eventually be able to relinquish that dream, must ultimately be able to come to terms with our very real limitations, which is exactly the work the patient must do as well. Together, patient and therapist confront the reality that things are not always as one would have wanted them to be—and both must grieve.

CLINICAL VIGNETTE

To demonstrate the importance of being able to come to terms with the reality of the therapist's limitations, I offer the following clinical vignette. For seven years, I saw a woman in analysis, five times a week. Her mother was an emotionally aloof woman who had never been terribly available to her daughter but who defected totally once her son was born. And father was a man who spent most of his time on the road; when he was home, he was usually sleeping. As a child, my patient did well in school and had a few friends, but she was unhappy and lonely much of the time.

As an adult, my patient had managed to construct a life that worked somehow (marriage, child, part-time work), but she lived always with the pain of her loneliness and frustrated longing.

Over the course of our first years of work, my patient came gradually to trust me. At first she was hesitant, but eventually I came to matter the world to her. As she lay on the couch, she would experience herself as a little baby, my baby. I was her good mother, and she loved me dearly. And when she was with me, the chronic ache inside was eased. She spoke often about how much she looked forward to coming and about how comfortable she felt being in the room with me.

Sometimes, she would tell me about what she was doing in her life or how she was feeling about different things, but often she would spend the entire session in silence, lying on the couch, comfortably ensconced in the soft blanket I provided. When she would speak, her thoughts were often fragments, her sentences incomplete. Interestingly, I found myself often able to finish her sentences, which I would do when it felt right to do so. We were very much attuned to each other—and it felt wonderful to us both.

But there came a time, in our fourth year, when I had to tell her that I would be away for a week over Thanksgiving. In previous years, my weeklong vacations had been difficult, but not impossible, for my patient to manage. There was, however, something different this time. When I told her about my plan to be away for the week, she was devastated. How could I really care about her if I could leave her for a whole week? What good mother left her baby for that length of time? She had never before asked of me that I not go, but, this time, she told me that she needed me to stay, not to leave her, not to abandon her. She screamed out her pain, told me that were I to leave her, she wouldn't make it.

It troubled me greatly to be causing her such anguish. I couldn't stand being in the position of breaking her heart.

I knew that she was experiencing me as her bad, unloving mother, but deep within my heart, I felt (somewhat defensively, I might add) that it was not really true that I was being a bad mother. I knew that I loved her; I knew that I would miss her; I knew that I would be so happy to see her on my return. But I did not want to think of myself as an abandoning, heartlessly unconcerned mother. I told myself that I needed to take my week off; I was so tired and so in need of a rest.

And so it was that I had some difficulty listening to my patient berate me for being a bad mother; nor did I like it that she was accusing me of not really understanding; and it upset me that she was demanding that I not go.

Yes, my patient had an intense need for me to be her good mother, but I had an equally intense need to be that good mother.

What was happening? On some level, I was not really able to tolerate being in the position of breaking her heart, letting her down, failing her. I did not want to acknowledge the truth in what she was saying. Fair enough that I be *experienced* as her bad mother, but I did not want to think that I was actually *being* her bad mother.

In this instance, I am proud of my patient for having persisted in her relentlessness, because eventually there did come a time when I was able to let go of my defensive need to see myself as her good mother. It took longer for me to admit than, in retrospect, I would have wished that it had—but I was finally able to see that, indeed, I was not being a good mother in leaving my little one for a week. What she was saying was true—good mommies don't leave their babies when their babies are little and need them.

What did I do? I went on my vacation, but now I understood, where once I had not, that I really was being bad by going away for a week. I had to relinquish my investment in being a good mother and had to come to terms with my own very real limitations. As I came to know and to accept that truth, I became more available to my patient and it became easier for her to deal with her disappointment in me and to grieve my inadequacies.

The weeks that followed (both those before my vacation and those on my return) were not easy ones, but my patient courageously confronted her heartache, her devastation, and her outrage. And I was able to be with her in that. Together, we faced and grieved the reality of my very real limitations as the good mother we both would have wished I could have been.

In coming to terms with her disappointment in me, she was able, eventually, to replace her illusion that I would be for her the good mother she had never had with a reality, namely, that she would have to become that good mother. Her need for illusion and her entitlement were replaced by a capacity to experience and to accept reality.

In this situation, my patient was able to work through her defense of relentless entitlement and to access her grief once I was able to relinquish my need to be the good mother she had never had.

ANOTHER CLINICAL VIGNETTE

Let me now present another situation in which I had to struggle hard to be available to my patient so that she would eventually be able to let go of her unrelenting hope. I worked with a depressed young woman who, after some years and much hard work, became insistent that I be willing to hold her when she was feeling alone. She was the only child of a profoundly depressed, narcissistic, and alcoholic mother who loved her daughter but was so caught up in her drinking and her own pain that she was unable to provide nurturing and support. As a child, my patient (to comfort herself) would retreat to her room and to her stuffed animals, all of whom had names and elaborate histories.

Over the course of our first several years, the patient, initially withdrawn and inaccessible, gradually dared to entrust herself to the relationship with me. It was a deep and fulfilling experience for me to bear witness to her coming more and more into her own, as she became enlivened through her connection with me.

But there came a time when she felt that she needed actually to be held by me. She said that she was so starved for physical contact in her life (she lived alone, had friends but no romantic involvements) that she felt she would die without it. Over and over, she told me that she had come to feel so close to me and longed for me to be the comforting mother she had never had. My heart would break as she pleaded with me to hold her, promising me that one good hug would last her an awfully long time.

For me, it was excruciatingly painful and heartrending.

On the one hand, I wanted to be able to hold her. I was very aware that it was through the relationship with me that she had come alive; it was easy to understand why she would look to me for actual physical contact as well. I felt very close to her; I did love her. I knew how much it would mean to her were I to hold her. I knew that she had been starved all her life for that kind of contact.

On the other hand, my immediate gut response to her request to be held was one of discomfort; it made me very anxious to think about actually hugging her. In my psychoanalytic training, I had been taught to avoid physical contact with patients under all circumstances. It had been made very clear to me that the appropriate response to a patient's request for physical contact was to explore the wish, not to provide gratification of it. I had been warned about the dangers of becoming physically intimate with a patient, of stirring the patient up in ways that were inappropriately stimulating and seductive.

I was truly conflicted about my patient's request. But, at least initially, I was aware of feeling more anxious and confused than anything else—and I did not want to hug her.

As time went on and my patient continued to plead with me to hug her, ever striving to convince me that it would be so healing for her to be able to get that hug, I found something shifting within me. I began to allow myself to enter more fully into her experience and to join with her as the subject (and not the object) of her desire. I was now able to listen more empathically—and less defensively.

Although, with time, she had become increasingly insistent that she be held, at least initially her wish to be held had arisen from her need for contact. She was not trying to be difficult or to make me uncomfortable;

she was simply feeling the need to be touched and held by someone she had come to love. And so, although my initial response had been a no, my next response was to pause.

I was now able to recognize that certainly a part of me wanted very much to embrace her, to hold her close, to comfort her with my physical presence. I began to entertain the possibility of hugging her, imagined what it would be like to have her in my arms, holding her, comforting her, soothing her, perhaps stroking her gently, perhaps rocking her—and it felt good.

But I was also aware that it still made me very anxious. It really did seem to me that holding her would create a confusing blurring of boundaries. It did seem too seductive. Perhaps it was my training, but although my heart was willing to consider a yes, my gut was telling me that, bottom line, to give her a hug did not feel quite right.

I began to realize that, as much as a part of me wanted to hold her, I did not really feel comfortable having physical contact with her. It really did seem that it would be too tantalizingly seductive and, ultimately, not fair to my patient. I must admit that part of my reluctance also had to do with my annoyance that she was being so persistent, despite my obvious discomfort.

But it also seemed to me that, were I to gratify her need, we would then be losing an opportunity to understand what was fueling the intensity of her need and the relentlessness with which she was pursuing me. As painful as it might be, here was a chance for her to come to terms with the fact that her objects might not be all she would have wanted them to be.

I knew from her history, that she had always, in every relationship, eventually come up against something in the other person that was deeply disappointing to her, something in the other person that she wanted different. Inevitably, she would end up feeling dissatisfied, frustrated, unhappy. Eventually, all her objects failed her.

By denying her the hug, I would now be just like all the others who were withholding something she wanted. But, by denying her the hug, I would also now be in a position to help her come to terms with just how disappointing her objects (past and present) have always been. She had never really grieved her mother's unavailability but would now have an opportunity to grieve in relation to me (a stand-in for her mother). Although I had offered her many things, I would not be able to give her the hug she so desperately sought. In coming to terms with that painful reality, she would be doing some belated grieving.

What did I do? I decided, finally, to share with her my dilemma. I told her that, on the one hand, I wanted very much to hold her and to comfort her but that, on the other hand, I did not feel completely comfortable with the idea of actual physical contact, because it seemed to me to be too seductive—and I was not willing to risk that in our therapy.

I knew that a no was a no, no matter how I explained it. But my hope was that, by sharing with her both my wish to be able to respond to her need and my concern about how confusing such gratification might be, I would be enabling her to contextualize the no.

It was hard to say the actual no, but, as I became more comfortable with that position, I began to see more and more clearly how my refusal was a necessary catalyst for the grieving my patient would need to do before she could relinquish her need for her objects to be something they were not. As I came to see ever more clearly the opportunity this presented, it became a little easier for me to be in the position of thwarting her desire. I recognized that what she needed to do was to deal with the disappointment, hurt, and outrage she felt in the face of my refusal to comply with her need.

It still made me sad to disappoint her, but I also found myself feeling a little bit hopeful that I would be able to give her the opportunity to discover that she could survive the experience of her disappointment.

The work was not easy and took several years to get done, but once I became clear that I was not comfortable gratifying my patient's need to be held, she was able to begin grieving. She cried for the hungry little girl she had once been and cried for the starved woman she had then become. But there did come a time when she began to make her peace with the reality of what we were now both able to describe as my limitations—that I was a pretty good mother but, even so, had some very real limitations.

My inability to gratify my patient's infantile need for the perfect mother recreated her mother's failure of her. All the old hurt, all the old pain, was revived; she raged, she wept. But it was as she confronted the reality of just how limited I was and just how limited her mother had always been, that she was able to let go of her defensive need to deny reality and to face just how disappointed she really was.

It is this work of grieving—the constant, repetitive raging and sobbing that accompany disillusionment—that is the process whereby patients eventually let go of their illusions and their entitlement. As the patient grieves, her need for illusion and her entitlement will be replaced by a capacity to experience and to accept reality. Her infantile need for the external provision of good mothering will become transformed into a mature capacity to provide for herself this good mothering.

It was a very powerful piece of work that we did. Had she never done it, she might well have continued to deliver into each of her relationships her need for something that she would never be able to have, thereby consigning herself to a lifetime of chronic frustration and angry dissatisfaction with respect to each of her subsequent relationships.

CONCLUSION

Although the patient who employs the defense of relentless entitlement may contend that her pain will not go away until her needs have been gratified, my belief is that the patient's pain will not go away until she has worked through her disappointment when it turns out that her needs may not always be gratified. The patient must have the experience of working through optimal disillusionment; she must be able to tolerate the devastation and outrage she feels as she begins to confront, head on, her object's limitations (whether the object is the infantile object, a contemporary object, or the transference object). She must face such limitations, grieve them, and master them. Ultimately, she must move beyond the need to have reality be a certain way, transforming such a need into the capacity to know and to accept reality, the hallmark of mental health. As the patient finally confronts just how limited her mother really was and grieves it, then she can let go of her relentless hoping and move on to a deeper, richer enjoyment of her life and her relationships.

For therapists who are at the receiving end of the patient's relentless entitlement, it means an ability to confront the reality that we will never be the perfect mother both we and the patient would have wanted. We must grieve the reality of our own very real limitations. We will then be able to tolerate being in the position of saying no. But our ability to say no in the face of the patient's unremitting insistence that we say yes will give her the opportunity to come to terms with the reality that things are not always as she would have wanted them to be.

REFERENCES

Fairbairn, W. R. D. (1954). *An object-relations theory of the personality.* New York: Basic Books.

Stark, M. (1994a). *Working with resistance.* Northvale, NJ: Jason Aronson.

——. (1994b). *A Primer on working with resistance.* Northvale, NJ: Jason Aronson.

Winnicott, D. W. (1958). *Collected papers: Through paediatrics to psycho-analysis.* London: Tavistock.

——. (1965). *The Maturational processes and the facilitating environment.* New York: International Universities Press.

CHAPTER 17

The Hazards of Treating Suicidal Patients

DAVID A. JOBES, PHD and JOHN T. MALTSBERGER, MD

Case Study

A psychologist with 15 years of experience in private practice was wakened at 2:30 A.M. when the roommate of a patient telephoned. Coming home late from a party, the roommate had discovered the patient dead, hanging by the neck in the hall closet. The patient's two-page, handwritten suicide note was found on the desk. It said he could bear the "endless depression" no longer. He wrote that the efforts of family and friends, the medicines, and his "futile psychotherapy" (in particular) had simply not worked.

The disturbing call marked the beginning of what proved to be a long-lasting, living nightmare for the clinician who had to endure months of intense professional and personal anguish. The patient's parents seized on the suicide note reference to "futile psychotherapy," as a full explanation of their son's death; they filed a malpractice lawsuit against the therapist charging him with wrongful death secondary to a failure to diagnose and safeguard. The therapist, devastated by the death of his patient, felt ashamed and guilty. Despite extensive efforts to help his severely depressed and chronically suicidal patient (including countless crisis calls taken at home, multiple hospitalizations, professional consultations, and three different medication trials), the therapist, falling into a depression, blamed himself.

In the two years following the suicide, the clinician was tormented by the litigation and grew obsessed with the perception that colleagues and friends condemned him for the suicide. As his mood darkened, he experienced recurring episodes of suicidal ideation.

Among the various psychotherapy hazards discussed in this volume, the death of patient by suicide may perhaps be the ultimate peril for the psychotherapist. The suicide death of a patient in active treatment is commonly taken as prima facie evidence that the therapist, somehow or another, has mismanaged the case. Whether this perception arises from a widespread professional prejudice, pressure from the general public, or the exigencies of law, it has not always held sway, though throughout history society has sought somebody to blame in suicide's wake.

Litman (1988) has discussed the long-standing social attitude of fixing on a scapegoat after purposeful death. For years, natural and accidental deaths were regarded as operations of "God's will"; homicide and suicide, on the other hand, were regarded as heinous sins wherein a wicked person intruded on God's designs. In 18th-century England, trials of suicide were held posthumously in a Coroner's Court to determine whether the suicide had been insane and therefore innocent (*non compos mentis*), or a criminal against the self (*felo de se*), guilty of a crime, and subject to forfeiture of property to the crown and desecration of the body (Colt, 1987). If someone were to blame, then someone must be punished. Since the actual person responsible for the suicide was beyond the reach of the law, a surrogate had to be chosen. The suicide was thus punished by public defilement of the corpse before it was cast aside as unfit for Christian burial. The surviving family was often punished through seizure of property and social ostracism. Though with the passing of time, suicide has come to be perceived as the consequence of mental illness, society at large and the legal system in particular still seek someone to blame in its wake, and too often, the scapegoat selected is the clinician who was trying to treat the illness and prevent the suicide, but failed. Increasingly, modern social attitudes reflect concern for survivors and the need for some form of compensation for their loss. In recent years, mental health professionals have become ripe targets for modern acts of retribution (and compensation) in the form of malpractice litigation, the process of which must be endured even in cases where there is clear evidence that there has been no negligence (Maltsberger, 1993). Juries can be fickle and are often ready to identify with the surviving family, sometimes finding against clinicians when the evidence has shown a suicide was not preventable.

Whatever the historical lineage, or the morality of "playing God" with another's life, the hazards inherent in treating suicidal patients are ever present and troublesome, personally and professionally. This chapter first addresses the risks by exploring the various clinical issues that make the treatment of suicidal patients so professionally challenging. Its focus then shifts to countertransference issues that can make this work so personally challenging. Finally, ways of working through the various hazards will be explored and discussed.

CLINICAL CHALLENGES

Unlike the surgeon or emergency room physician who may lose a patient through a variety of circumstances and causes, psychotherapists ordinarily lose patients only through suicide. Although such a loss is rare in comparison with losses encountered by certain kinds of physicians, survey data nevertheless suggest that more than one in five psychologists and half of all psychiatrists will lose at least one patient to suicide over the course of their careers (Chemtob, Hamada, Bauer, Kinney, & Torigoe, 1988; Chemtob, Hamada, Bauer, Torigoe, & Kinney, 1988).

To treat a suicidal person inexorably entangles psychotherapists in life-and-death issues that cannot be avoided. The problems of empathically engaging with a patient bent on dying pose the most significant barriers to their effective treatment. Beyond personal and existential issues lie other barricades unique to clinical work with suicidal patients that can make the endeavor formidable.

Assessment Issues

From a legal perspective, practicing at a reasonable "standard of care," with regard to assessment, requires clinical "foreseeability" (i.e., an adequate assessment of suicide risk has been performed). Suicidologists know risk assessment is not synonymous with prediction. No clinician can validly and reliably *predict* suicide. The prediction of suicide (a low base-rate phenomenon) is statistically impossible at present because we lack sufficiently specific predictive correlates. Any predictive attempts we may make at present result in a prohibitive number of false-positive identifications (Berman & Jobes, 1991; Pokorny, 1983).

Even though suicide cannot be predicted, the clinician is nevertheless legally bound to determine whether a patient is in "clear and imminent danger to self." While the legal duty is unequivocal, the clinical assessment of suicide risk is invariably uncertain. Suicidality by its very nature tends to wax and wane. Frightened suicidal patients may suddenly change their stories when their civil liberties are threatened. Furthermore, even a well-conducted assessment may yield results that do not match the patient's inner reality (Eddins & Jobes, 1994). It is beyond the scope of this chapter to discuss the details of suicide risk assessment, but the clinician must keep in mind that the competent assessment of that risk is a considerable, often difficult and stressful task. It requires specific knowledge about suicide and specific clinical skills that many workers do not possess (Jobes, in press; Maltsberger, 1986; Maris, Berman, Maltsberger, & Yufit, 1992; Shneidman, 1985).

Intervention Issues

After navigating through the tricky waters of suicide risk assessment, the competent therapist must endeavor to initiate clinical interventions that neither do too little nor do too much. In the worst-case scenario, when too little is done (e.g., a patient who needs to be hospitalized is not), the patient may die. Alternatively, when too much is done (e.g., a patient is involuntarily committed to a hospital, secluded and restrained, or given electroconvulsive therapy), basic civil liberties may be compromised, the therapeutic alliance may be irreparably damaged, and the patient may never again seek out what might be lifesaving treatment.

Ethical and Moral Issues

Over the years, there has been a great deal of controversy and conflict about ethical and moral issues embedded in clinicians' protecting their patients from their suicidal impulses (Maltsberger, 1993). Compelling arguments can be made in favor of the legal position requiring clinicians to protect patients from themselves. Most people who kill themselves do not in fact want to be dead. Suicidal patients often tell others about their deadly feelings and have diagnosable mental conditions that are treatable. These observations have led to several suicide aphorisms: Suicide is a permanent solution to a temporary problem; nobody should kill him- or herself when feeling suicidal (Shneidman, 1993). The thrust of the interventionist perspective speaks to long-held beliefs that by definition suicide is crazy, life is sacred, and doctors know what is best for their patients when they are mentally ill.

On the other hand, it can be argued that protecting patients from themselves undermines their ability to take responsibility for their own lives. Inherent in the act of involuntarily committing a suicidal patient to a hospital is the abrogation of the patient's personal freedom and civil liberties. Characteristically, within the privilege of the therapeutic relationship, the patient is encouraged to talk openly and honestly about thoughts and feelings. In turn, the therapist is expected to be worthy of the patient's trust and, where life and death are not at stake, can assure the patient that innermost secrets will remain confidential. The trust between therapist and patient, which is built on a foundation of confidentiality, can thus become something of a sacred but conditional trust. Yet ethical regulations and rules of law pertaining to confidentiality require the therapist to break the seal of confidentiality when suicide becomes a clear and present danger. Thus it is that the patient's trust must sometimes be violated. Psychotherapeutic circumstances in work with suicidal patients are wrought with conflicting, even paradoxical, requirements respecting trust, responsibility, and control.

The debate related to the preceding issues is not new. West (1993) recorded a famous debate on the ethics of suicide prevention between the pioneering suicidologist Edwin Shneidman and the iconoclastic psychiatrist Thomas Szasz that took place in San Francisco in 1972. In that debate, Shneidman argues persuasively that doctors *should* have a sense of responsibility for suicidal patients because those who talk about suicide are by definition ambivalent and suicidality is usually a symptom of a treatable frame of mind. Szasz countered by arguing that suicide is a civil right; the therapist-patient relationship should be one of equals such that therapist meddling in the patient's personal liberty is inappropriate interference.

While the ethics and philosophical issues between the merits of providing lifesaving treatment and the inappropriateness of playing God with another's life remain open to debate, the relevant law is unambiguous. In every state in this country, psychotherapists have a legal duty to hospitalize a patient who is at clear and imminent risk for suicide voluntarily or, if necessary, involuntarily (Nolan, 1988).

Malpractice Liability

Beyond the clinical issues of assessment, intervention, ethics, and morality, the threat of malpractice liability can haunt clinicians who treat suicidal patients. Jobes and Berman (1993) have pointed out that while malpractice related to suicide is the sixth most frequent claim brought against psychologists, it has nevertheless become the second most costly. Even though most suicide-related malpractice claims do not reach the courtroom (the vast majority are either settled or thrown out before this), in recent years there has been an exponential increase in the number of malpractice claims brought against outpatient clinicians.

Invariably, malpractice lawsuits are expensive, literally as well as professionally and personally. The reality or even the threat of malpractice litigation can create a tremendous amount of personal stress for clinicians and may ultimately affect good clinical judgment. Excessive fears related to malpractice liability prompt some therapists to practice defensively; good clinical judgment and human needs may become secondary to overriding legal concerns.

COUNTERTRANSFERENCE ISSUES

Confronting possible suicide in the seriously lethal patient can generate a variety of nontherapeutic reactions within the psychotherapist. Sometimes these reactions are quite primitive, tapping into the therapist's deepest narcissistic needs or most hidden conflicts (e.g., therapist-savior vs. therapist-killer). As Bongar (1991) has noted, any consideration of treating suicidal patients would be incomplete without explicitly addressing the reactions that therapists have toward these patients.

As previously noted, clinical encounters involving suicide are wrought with complex therapist-patient issues and conflicts related to freedom, responsibility, choice, and control. The bottom-line (life vs. death) existential dichotomy fundamental to suicide can evoke the best and the worst of reactions in psychotherapists. In the best scenario, the gravity of working with a person who is teetering on the edge of life can motivate some clinicians to perform determined, creative, even inspired, lifesaving work. In the worst scenario, however, the suicidal patient's sense of utter despair, worthlessness, and hopelessness can provoke countertransference mistakes that may ultimately contribute to a fatal outcome.

Countertransference responses to suicidal patients are always a problem once treatment is underway. But errors arising from countertransference may occur in the first clinical encounter (Maltsberger, 1986). Clinical judgment is often clouded by the countertransference hate that suicidal patients arouse in those who are responsible for their care (Maltsberger & Buie, 1974). Malice and aversion, the two components of countertransference hate, can interact in complex and destructive ways unless the psychotherapist is aware of these feelings and has them under control. Suicidal patients can also evoke a strong countertransference wish to do something active, powerful, and healing so that the therapist will not have to endure the empathic pain of experiencing the patient's despair; we want our patients to get better quickly, to help ourselves (Maltsberger, 1989). Therapist aversion to the suicidal patient's despair may be thought of as "empathic dread."

Personal Challenges

As noted throughout this volume, psychotherapists face numerous personal challenges in the course of practicing their profession. Arguably, the personal challenges embedded in clinical work with suicidal patients are among the most daunting.

Death Anxiety. Within philosophy and psychology, issues related to death have long been a focus of scholarly examination (Becker, 1974). Indeed, questions related to existence, being, nonbeing, life, death, and suicide are central considerations of existential philosophy and psychology (Binswanger, 1963; Boss, 1963; Camus, 1955; Sartre, 1956). Broadly stated, within the tradition of existential psychology, one's current existence can only be understood in relation to one's mortality. Facing death invariably causes anxiety, dread, and avoidance. Ultimately, the philosophers conclude, when we are unable to face death, we are unable to embrace life; death anxiety interferes with our ability fully to live.

With relevance to the clinical setting, the suicidal patient's preoccupation with death may tap into the therapist's own death anxiety (countertransferentially). When therapist death anxiety enters the clinical situation, dread and avoidance may cause the clinician to hold back from fully engaging in the suicidal struggle.

Alternatively, recognizing the influences of one's own death anxiety enables the therapist to approach and engage in the struggle (which may require the clinician to risk his or her own vulnerability). The therapist who is able to engage can become an active participant, a partner, in the patient's existential struggle. While a transference relationship is inevitably present, the therapist who is aware of his or her own death anxiety (i.e., the "therapist-participant"), can become a *real* object to the patient (Guntrip, 1968)—a healing presence in the suicidal patient's phenomenological world.

Control Issues. A number of control issues, the roots of harmful power struggles, are unique to clinical work with suicidal people. From the patient's perspective, suicide may come to represent the ultimate, and final, "treatment" option. Conversely, therapists must discourage the exercise of this very option. Within this paradoxical standoff, patient and therapist are pitted against each other and cruel truths underlying the very nature of psychotherapy emerge.

Psychotherapy patients, by definition, have problematic thoughts, feelings, and behaviors for which they retain (typically at considerable expense) clinical experts to help them address their problems. In response, to address patients' problems, these experts employ the only tools they ultimately have to heal: influence and persuasion, which transcend all theory, research, and practice (Frank, 1980).

When a patient resists, or outright fights, a therapist's efforts to influence and persuade, he or she may act out life-long issues within the therapeutic relationship through transference. The successive mutual efforts to work through these moments often lead to therapeutic insights and emotional healing. However, in the imminently suicidal patient, the stakes are high. Suicide will leave no patient behind to work through anything. In dire cases, the therapist may feel that influence and persuasion are not enough to keep the patient alive. A threshold is reached, the therapeutic alliance is abandoned, and influence and persuasion may quickly give way to therapist coercion, intimidation, and dominance. Szasz (1986) refers to extraordinary "heroic" efforts by therapists to save patients from themselves as "coercive intervention."

When the battle of wills deteriorates to this level, patients may cling to their right to determine their own fate. In turn, the determined therapist usually must employ legal means to impede such patients whether they like it or not. Deeply embedded in such a therapist-patient standoff are two essential truths: First, most therapists, if they are honest, fear and hate the helpless experience of being unable to influence and persuade. Second, no one can ever ultimately control others' lives and therefore their deaths (Berman, Jacobs, & Jobes, 1993).

Survivor Issues. A final personal challenge inherent in treating the suicidal patient involves the potential experience of losing a patient to suicide. Among suicidologists, "surviving" is the term used for the grief and bereavement experience that follows the suicide death of a significant other. As Berman and Jobes (1991) have noted, the suicide of a patient in therapy is one of the most difficult personal and professional experiences that a therapist may ever encounter; the differentiation of personal versus professional issues can become quite unclear. Indeed, survey data suggest that surviving a patient's suicide is similar to experiencing a death in one's family (Chemtob, Hamada, Bauer, Torigoe, & Kinney, 1988; Litman, 1965).

That losing a patient to suicide should be so traumatic is not surprising; skilled therapists tend to develop intense, close relationships with their patients and care deeply about their progress and survival. When self-expectations become omnipotent or grandiose, the therapist may take it upon him- or herself to be the savior of a particular patient. To embrace the seductive role of therapist-savior may set the therapist up for a devastating personal loss should the patient choose death over life. Among therapists, survivor issues are often intimately entangled with savior issues. It follows that few experiences may be so sobering and deflating as losing a patient to suicide; that threat will haunt psychotherapists who expect themselves to perform therapeutic magic both before and after a patient dies (Maltsberger, 1992).

WORKING THROUGH THE HAZARDS

Thus far, we have delineated the varied and considerable clinical and countertransferential issues that make clinical work with suicidal patients so professionally and personally challenging, even perilous. It is our belief that the various hazards of treating suicidal patients may lead some therapists to practice in dangerous ways. In the remainder of this chapter, we hope to provide guidance for the clinician in working with, and through, these professional and personal hazards.

Empathic Fortitude

As noted earlier, empathic dread may arise from the therapist's reluctance to endure the empathic pain of a suicidal patient's profound despair. Most therapists who choose to work with suicidal individuals are aware of it from time to time, but sometimes it operates unconsciously and out of awareness, slowly transforming the therapist into emotional wood, so that interactions with patients become stilted and lifeless. In the worst case, empathic dread may imperceptibly transform the psychotherapist into a detached "therapist-voyeur," able only to watch the patient's suffering from the relative distance and safety of the professional role. Suicidal patients demand a different kind of involvement from the therapist (Federn, 1952; Shneidman, 1993). Healing work with suicidal patients requires *empathic fortitude.* It is not enough that the clinician become a therapist-participant in the patient's existential struggle between the "siren song" of death (Clark & Fawcett, 1992) and the remaining fragments of hope that sustain life. He or she must also empathically persevere.

Metaphorically, imagine that the patient lives in an interior suicidal cave. The cave may be a cold, dark, and lonely space, buried deep inside the patient. It may be a hell, fixed inside the patient's essential core, where he or she lives a tortured existence. Some patients are caught in the cave only from time to time, and others are perpetual prisoners there. It depends on the nature and severity of the disturbance.

In moments of deep suicidal despair and crisis, a patient occasionally permits a therapist to enter this cave of suicidal anguish. On such occasions, therapist-participants, guided by empathic fortitude, may carefully step into the patient's inner experience, asking the patient to describe the air, the walls, the floor, and the ceiling of the suicidal cave, an inquiry that will enable genuine connection and ameliorate the patient's experience of aloneness (Adler & Buie, 1979).

Successful treatment with suicidal patients demands the therapeutic preparedness to step into the cave where they live. We must offer the patient a real relationship, not only a transference relationship, if we are to be of any use. Retaining professional balance, taking care not to overstep boundaries, we are called on to be emotionally generous and to offer our struggling patients the full benefit of all the vitality and engagement we can offer. They need neither lectures nor pep talks. Ultimately, interpretations and clarifications are not enough. Narcissistically depleted, suicidal patients need the therapist's genuine warmth, interest, and respect. Most emphatically, these patients *do not require* harmful erotic entanglements with their therapists. The therapeutic interest and respect to which we refer is *agape:* that unselfish, nonerotic unexploitative concern that loyally accepts others and seeks their well-being.

The honest, kind, empathic, and respectful therapist will ordinarily succeed in engaging suicidal patients and may be invited to visit the horrors of patients' inner world, or cave. That is where real psychotherapy begins. Only there may the therapist expect to begin the deeper negotiations that can enable the patient to defer suicide and to try for a life.

At the heart of these negotiations lies this inquiry: What fantasies, impulses, deprivations, injuries, and disappointments caused the patient to turn away from hope, love, and investment in work? As Birtchnell (1983) has asked, If the patient has never claimed these things for him- or herself, what has stood in the way?

Empathic fortitude is the ideal toward which we reach. Even for the experienced clinician, the encounter with intense suffering and despair is a painful, difficult undertaking. Our own journeys with our patients, and suicidological study, have impressed us that empathic devotion and perseverance are essential in achieving any therapeutic movement. Our patients live on the edge between life and death, and there we must join them fully, not detachedly, if progress is to be made.

It was said of the therapeutic style of the late John Murray, a preeminent Boston psychoanalyst, that while others might stand on the riverbank and shout advice to a drowning man, "Jock," as he was known, would strip down, swim out, and throw the fellow a lifeline. Murray was too wise to get caught up in ill-considered omnipotent acting-out with patients, but he was not too timorous to give from his heart to patients sinking in despair.

Clinical Suicidology

From a professional standpoint, it is remarkable that most therapists (across professional disciplines) typically receive little, if any, formalized training in clinical suicidology (Bongar, 1991). Generally speaking, most clinicians learn about working with suicidal patients by finding themselves responsible for such a person and perforce having to decide what to do. The lack of suicide prevention training may perhaps reflect an unconscious, deeply rooted, discomfort that mental health professionals may have toward suicide. Professional avoidance of suicide training is ironic, given the prevalence of suicidality in clinical practice and the considerable challenges related to assessment, intervention, ethics, and malpractice.

To address deficits in training, and adequately rise to good clinical and legal standards of care, most practitioners must increase their knowledge in clinical suicidology and related legal issues. To this end, there are a number of excellent scholarly works in clinical suicidology that consider in depth the topics of assessment, treatment, and management of suicidal patients as well as legal standards of care (Berman & Jobes, 1991; Bongar, 1991, 1992; Maltsberger, 1986; Maris, Berman, Maltsberger, & Yufit, 1992; Shneidman, 1993). The intellectual pursuit and development of mastery in clinical suicidology can have a remarkably soothing effect on the suicide-anxious psychotherapist.

Consultation and Supervision

Regrettably, reading is not enough to prepare therapists for the clinical challenges outlined here. The importance of consultation cannot be overemphasized; it is crucial, not only for the development of clinical skill, but for forensic reasons as well.

Even seasoned suicidological clinicians make regular use of consultation in treating suicidal patients. The stresses involved are too great for one person to shoulder independently. Under intense life-and-death pressure, judgment is easily skewed and perspective is difficult to maintain. During phases of painful treatment intensity or heightened suicide danger, even the most experienced therapists initiate weekly consultations with a colleague. When inexperienced workers undertake the treatment of suicidal patients, regular consultation over many months (supervision) cannot be too strongly recommended. Close consultation with a colleague of greater suicide experience, combined with selected reading in suicidology, will go far to improve skills.

In the event a patient commits suicide, full case notes reflecting the details of regular consultation sessions will go far to deflect any potential charges of negligence should a malpractice action ensue.

Dealing with Personal Issues

Working with suicidal people is always difficult, and for the inexperienced, it is often terrifying. Countertransference hate, empathic dread, or personal conflicts pertaining to empathic disconnection, death anxiety, control, or surviving the suicide of patient are but a few of the potential therapist problems that may impede the effective treatment of a suicidal patient. When therapists fail to examine these (and other) problem areas, their practices are likely to become fear-based. Ultimately, fear-based treatment of suicidal patients leads to clinical paralysis, therapeutic bondage, compensatory grandiosity, denial, and avoidance that may prove to be tragically fatal (Hendin, 1981).

Simply stated, the best way to address countertransference feelings and personal issues is to acknowledge, examine, and work them through. Good supervision and consultation with a trusted colleague is essential in this connection. We all have blind spots.

Experience has taught us that personal psychotherapy or psychoanalysis is enormously helpful and much to be recommended in undertaking this work. Without it, the modifications in the therapist's self-expectations so necessary for success are most difficult to achieve. Psychodynamically oriented therapies offer the further advantage of working through the defenses involved in warding off full awareness of some of the subtleties of countertransference.

CONCLUSION

We have discussed some of the hazards in treating suicidal patients—the crags of suicide risk assessment are hard to negotiate, the chasms of the law are menacing. Suicidal patients demand more of us than we may wish to give at first; their treatment promises empathic pain and narcissistic knocks; it calls for courage and perseverance. Such treatments threaten loss of balance and require inner investigation, consultation, and sometimes, personal analysis. In short, these treatments are daunting enterprises. They can be fairly compared to mountain climbing.

"All things excellent," said Spinoza, "are as difficult as they are rare." Those who strike out to master the challenge of treating suicidal patients in the best way may expect to help many, and to save some lives. They will not save all their patients; some will fall. But as therapists go forward and up, growing personally richer in therapeutic skill and experience, they may further expect to grow in wisdom and perspective in their work and in their personal attitudes. To see life fully and whole from the pinnacles, it is first necessary to experience the blindness of the cave.

REFERENCES

Adler, G., & Buie, D. H. (1979). Aloneness and borderline psychopathology: The possible relevance of child development issues. *International Journal of Psycho-analysis 60,* 83–96.

Becker, E. (1973). *The denial of death.* New York: Free Press.

Berman, A. L. (Ed.), Jacobs, D. G., & Jobes, D. A. (1993). Case consultation: Tillie. *Suicide and Life-Threatening Behavior, 23,* 268–272.

Berman, A. L., & Jobes, D. A. (1991). *Adolescent suicide: Assessment and intervention.* Washington, DC: American Psychological Association.

Binswanger, L. (1963). *Being-in-the-world: Selected papers of Ludwig Binswanger.* New York: Basic Books.

Birtchnell, J. (1983). Psychotherapeutic considerations in the management of the suicidal patient. *American Journal of Psychotherapy, 37,* 24–36.

Bongar, B. (1991). *The suicidal patient: Clinical and legal standards of care.* Washington, DC: American Psychological Association.

Bongar, B. (Ed.). (1992). *Suicide: Guidelines for assessment, management, and treatment.* New York: Oxford University Press.

Boss, M. (1963). *Psychoanalysis and daseinanalysis.* New York: Basic Books.

Camus, A. (1955). *The myth of sisyphus and other essays.* New York: Vintage Books.

Chemtob, C. M., Hamada, R. S., Bauer, G. B., Kinney, B., & Torigoe, R. Y. (1988). Patient suicide: Frequency and impact of psychiatrists. *American Journal of Psychiatry, 145,* 224–228.

Chemtob, C. M., Hamada, R. S., Bauer, G. B., Torigoe, R. Y., & Kinney, B. (1988). Patient suicide: Frequency and impact of psychologists. *Professional Psychology: Research and Practice, 19,* 421–425.

Clark, D. C., & Fawcett, J. (1992). Review of empirical risk factors for evaluation of the suicidal patient. In B. Bongar (Ed.), *Suicide: Guidelines for assessment, management, and treatment* (pp. 16–48). New York: Oxford University Press.

Colt, G. W. (1987). The history of the suicide survivor: The mark of Cain. In E. J. Dunne, J. L. McIntosh, & K. Dunne-Maxim (Eds.), *Suicide and its aftermath.* New York: W. W. Norton.

Eddins, C. L., & Jobes, D. A. (1994). Do you see what I see? Patient and clinician perceptions of underlying dimensions of suicidality. *Suicide and Life-Threatening Behavior, 24,* 170–173.

Federn, P. (1952). Psychoanalysis of psychoses. In E. Weiss (Ed.), *Ego psychology and the psychoses* (pp. 117–165). New York: Basic Books.

Frank, J. D. (1974). *Persuasion and healing: A comparative study of psychotherapy.* New York: Schocken Books.

Guntrip, H. (1968). *Schizoid phenomena, object relations and the self.* Madison, CT: International Universities Press.

Hendin, H. (1981). Psychotherapy and suicide. *American Journal of Psychotherapy, 2,* 238–294.

Jobes, D. A. (in press). Psychodynamic treatment of adolescent suicide attempters. In J. Zimmerman & G. M. Asnis (Eds.), *Treatment approaches with suicidal adolescents.* New York: John Wiley.

Jobes, D. A., & Berman, A. L. (1993). Suicide and malpractice liability: Assessing and revising policies, procedures, and practice in outpatient settings. *Professional Psychology: Research and Practice, 24,* 91–99.

Litman, R. (1965). When patients commit suicide. *American Journal of Psychotherapy, 19,* 570–576.

Litman, R. E. (1988). Psychological autopsies, mental illness, and intention in suicide. In J. L. Nolan (Ed.), *The suicide case: Investigation and trial of insurance claims* (pp. 69–82). Washington, DC: American Bar Association.

Maltsberger, J. T. (1986). *Suicide risk: The formulation of clinical judgment.* New York: New York University Press.

Maltsberger, J. T. (1989). Discussion of Leston Havens' interview. In D. G. Jacobs & H. N. Brown (Eds.), *Suicide: Understanding and responding: Harvard Medical School perspectives on suicide* (pp. 357–360). Madison, CT: International Universities Press.

Maltsberger, J. T. (1992). Implications of patient suicide for the surviving psychotherapist. In D. G. Jacobs (Ed.), *Suicide in clinical practice* (pp. 169–182). Washington, DC: American Psychiatric Press.

Maltsberger, J. T. (1993). A career plundered. *Suicide and Life-Threatening Behavior, 23,* 285–291.

Maltsberger, J. T., & Buie, D. H. (1974). Countertransferential hate in the treatment of suicidal patients. *Archives of General Psychiatry, 30,* 625–633.

Maris, R. W., Berman, A. L., Maltsberger, J. T., & Yufit, R. I. (Eds.). (1992). *Assessment and prediction of suicide.* New York: Guilford Press.

Nolan, J. L. (Ed.). (1988). *The suicide case: Investigation and trial of insurance claims.* Washington, DC: American Bar Association.

Pokorny, A. D. (1983). Prediction of suicide in psychiatric patients. *Archives of General Psychiatry, 40,* 249–257.

Sartre, J. P. (1956). *Being and nothingness.* New York: Pocket Books.

Shneidman, E. S. (1985). *Definition of suicide.* New York: Wiley.

Shneidman, E. S. (1993). *Suicide as psychache: A clinical approach to self-destructive behavior.* Northvale, NJ: Jason Aronson.

Szasz, T. (1986). The case against suicide prevention. *The American Psychologist, 41,* 806–812.

West, L. J. (1993). Reflections on the right to die. In A. Leenaars (Ed.), *Suicidology: Essays in honor of Edwin Shneidman* (pp. 359–376). Northvale, NJ: Jason Aronson.

PART FIVE

Professional, Ethical, and Legal Issues

CHAPTER 18

"I Didn't Think I Was Speaking Chinese"

DONALD L. NATHANSON, MD

So said a clinical supervisor to one of my colleagues. The colleague, a 45-year-old masters level psychologist with 15 years' experience and an excellent reputation for his work with chaotic adolescents, believes in the tradition of our field. He sees psychotherapy as a dialogue evolving between patient and therapist that mirrors the evolving dialogue among therapists that characterizes our domain. He acts as preceptor for younger therapists, and is a happy purchaser of personal preception.

He had accepted this particular supervisor at the suggestion of the senior colleague who was at that time his personal therapist. Both of these individuals, supervisor and therapist to my friend, work together as teachers in an organization devoted to a particular brand of psychodynamic psychotherapy. They are preternaturally pleasant people who exude a sense of competence and love for their work. Yet, everybody I have met who is associated with their organization seems ill at ease socially, reticent to speak about anything other than their therapeutic system, and somewhat furtive in their gestures and attitudes.

During the supervision session in question, my colleague had raised a question about something the supervisor had said. It was a fair question, based on the therapist's need to know how to integrate into his work with a particular patient the idea brought up by the supervisor. The supervisor's answer ("I didn't think I was speaking Chinese") caught him off guard, and he was unable to think clearly for a couple of moments. Suddenly he felt awkward, inadequate, stupid, ungainly, incompetent, and, worst of all, unworthy of the services for which he was paying. Briefly unable to speak, he stumbled and bumbled through a paraphrase of his original question. She smiled benignly at him for this verbal incoordination, which made him feel all the more like a professional cripple, and launched into an answer that seemed at once overly simple and a bit to the side of what he had tried to ask.

Something clicked into place for me when I began to think about that story. It reminded me of the plumber who has defended our home from leaks and strange noises for the generation we have occupied our home. Fred demonstrated rare talent and ability as a plumber from childhood. At 16, just as soon as he got the learner's permit that allowed him to drive legally, he had his own business with its own plumber's truck. In his 20s, he oversaw the work of several assistants and a fleet of four trucks; now, nearing 50, he is comfortable with two. A new customer cannot call on his services for an emergency, and he will only accept new business when someone has sold a house and moved out of our area. Usually it takes between 3 and 6 months for him to find a place in his schedule for a referral.

Stories about Fred are legion, like the time he walked into the basement of the senior colleague who referred me to him, glanced at the maze of pipes while gesturing toward various sections of the house, and said "I bet you've got a problem with too much heat in that area of the house and never get this area warm enough." My colleague reports that instantly he felt loved and safe. He had not mentioned that problem to this new, young plumber because a generation of specialists had failed to optimize his heating system, and anyway, he had been called in for something else. "Yeah," said Fred, "some idiot reworked your heating system about 25 years ago and connected it wrong. All you have to do . . ." Given the nod, he did the work, and my neighbor's house was reliably and evenly contoasty warm thereafter. Fred just sees things like that with ease. His conversation is similarly intelligent, and his sense of humor is legend among his friends. Not surprisingly, Fred's older brother is a successful cardiologist who, of course, works with another system of pipes that get clogged, leak, and cause uneven heating. We have always suspected that had Fred not been dyslexic he might have gone into some field that required book study rather than this artisan's life that has been so gratifying and remunerative.

Yet it is Fred's behavior with his employees that was called to mind by the psychotherapeutic supervision anecdote mentioned previously. No matter what they do, his underlings get the big picture neither as quickly nor as easily as their boss, and simply cannot work as swiftly and simply as he. Fred watches them, working alongside them, describing their pitiful attempts at joining and welding in a high-pitched, squeaky voice that resembles the characters Mel Blanc created for two generations of cartoons. Fred, who is treated with respect and accepted as an equal in my home, treats only with derision those who work for him. Eventually all of them leave to form their own businesses, all proud to say that they trained with Fred, and all quite happy to be out from under his control.

Garth Zimke,[1] one of my classmates in medical school, was so far and away the most brilliant of our group that there was no question that he would be our valedictorian. Youngest in the class, eager to study anything placed in front of him, respectful of anybody who would teach or demonstrate this magic world of medicine into which we were being inducted, he was universally loved rather than the subject of envy. (Somebody like Zimke is so far above you that there is no sense of competition and thus no reason to compare your own performance with his; he is in a different league. Only invidious comparison makes for envy, jealousy, and greed.) In sequence, he became professor of medicine at one prestigious university, department chairman at another, and a respected leader of several national societies charged with the responsibility of guiding the entire field of medicine into its next era.

But then, in 1959, we were junior medical students learning to scrub with the surgeons, grateful for the menial tasks of holding retractors so the big guys might do the important work, and immensely proud when we were given the privilege of cutting suture material above the knots with which the surgeon tied off the myriad of small blood vessels responsible for leakage and therefore reduced visibility in the operative field. Garth reported to me his experience as assistant at a segmental resection of bowel, an operation in which a tumorous section is removed from the long tube that we call the colon and the remaining ends anastomosed—stitched back together so the colon is once again a tube. That done, the only task remaining was to sew up the belly so the patient might be allowed to emerge from anaesthetic sleep and ushered into the phase of convalescence. At that point, the surgeon (who knew quite well the reputation of this remarkable student) turned to Garth Zimke and said, "Time to check the anastomosis. Let's do a Zimke test." Suddenly alert to the possibility that one of his ancestors had been so celebrated a surgeon that his way of checking the patency of an anastomosis had earned permanence in the lore of medicine, Garth asked, "What's that?" Palpating carefully the remainder of the large bowel, the surgeon located a large piece of fecal material and moved it along the now repaired colon. "We just take this little piece of Zimke and move it back and forth across the anastomosis to make sure it is patent." Now, nearly 35 years later, when we are all senior physicians known and respected for something or other, Garth Zimke still remembers the day that particular surgeon "got" him.

[1] Not his real name.

In each of the preceding scenes, teaching did go on. The gifted psychologist did learn a new piece of clinical technique, the younger plumber did learn an easier and more efficient way of repairing bathroom piping, and the medical student came to understand better the mechanics of the body. Yet in each scene, there was a subtext, an undercurrent quite unrelated to the information imparted. Each instance of professional teaching was colored by powerful messages about the differences in rank between teacher and student. It is as if teacher must say to student that there is now and probably will always be a gulf between us; you will achieve only to the extent that you remember my ascendancy over you.

Some version of this theme may be detected in any relationship between apprentice and master. The expression "bald as a novice's knee" refers to the time spent in genuflection by young women studying to become nuns. Even the kindest of mothers superior must test the devotion of the otherwise free-spirited girls under her charge so they learn proper reverence and respect for authority. Only those young men who are able to handle the hazing intrinsic to boot camp are turned into full-fledged marines. Those who cannot accept frequently repeated sequences of demeaning and irrational demands made by the drill sergeant will not be able to learn how to respond instantly and perfectly to commands given during the chaos of war. Accusations of sexual misconduct are legion today, as the population at large becomes aware that those in authority often take several kinds of pleasure from those immediately beneath them.

I took a residency in internal medicine and endocrinology before my formal training in psychiatry, and remember the peculiar attitude with which some of his colleagues viewed one of the leading physicians in our training program. One might have thought that the immensity of his practice, and the near awe in which his patients held him, would have defined his character for all. But a senior colleague told me that this "superdoc" had been apprentice to the most famous cardiologist of the immediately preceding era, accompanying him when he taught the medical students. On several occasions, the great man would shake his head in disbelief at something this gifted apprentice had said, and literally tell him to sit on a stool in a corner of the medical student classroom. "And he actually did it," said my own teacher. "He actually did sit in the corner, in front of all those medical students, absorbing all that abuse just so some day he could take over G's practice. He disgusted me then, and I can't stomach him now, no matter how great a clinician he is."

During my psychiatric residency, one supervisor always blew cigar smoke in my face while waiting silently for my response as if I were an analytic patient. The office of another was arranged with a chair directly opposite the glowering presence of this famous psychoanalyst, and an analytic couch just to his left. "Why did you bring an apple for yourself and nothing for me?" he demanded during one early supervision session, his eyes never leaving my face. One longed for the safety and security of the couch, which would allow freedom from his unflinching gaze. It was an era during which only the psychoanalyst might have ascendence: "Even though you are only doing psychotherapy, there are still some things you can do for your patient" said still another supervisor.

What is this subtext? Where does it come from? Can we, should we do anything about it? Does the ubiquity of this attitude of condescension and derision common to the relationship between apprentice and master influence in any way the doing of psychotherapy, and is it good for our patients? The answer is to be found not in an analysis of the words exchanged, but in the emotions they evoke. Scenes characterized by put-down, disgrace, being singled out for derision, the feeling of incompetence and incoordination, the experience of public humiliation or private embarrassment in moments of invidious comparison, all these are manifestations of shame. One good place to investigate the failures and foibles of the supervision process might be the arena of this complex family of emotions. I suggest that shame teaches more about our relationship to the teacher than the material under consideration. If we are to improve our field, protect those colleagues who come to us for improvement, and offer our patients a better opportunity for growth, we had better know a great deal more about this painful emotion.

In a way, the current state of the study of shame, and the discrete body of psychopathology associated with it, is an artifact of the psychoanalytic revolution. Simply stated, Freud realized quite correctly that the people of his era suffered a wide range of discomforts that he could trace to hidden ideas about sex; exposure of the history of one's sexual ideation seemed likely to bring relief. But each time the explorer steered his ship in the direction of sexuality, his progress was impeded by defenses thrown up to block his access to the inner world of the patient. There were two choices available to him—investigation of the nature of this impediment to disclosure, or the development of a series of techniques for the removal of impediments. By labeling this quite natural form of embarrassment "The Resistance," Freud opened to view all we now know about sexuality; resistance analysis is a major part of classical psychoanalytic technique.

Lost in the scuffle over sexual ideation was the emotionality associated with its investigation and revelation. Earlier, Freud had found that he could not elicit memories of embarrassment occurring before age 3, and decided that shame did not exist before that period of development. The emotion was said to emit from a realm of the unconscious called "the superego," (an emotion machine that came on line just about the time that the libido force became truly sexual) and remained with us through life as just punishment for exhibitionistic impulses. This was an unfortunate decision on the part of the founder of psychoanalysis, for even though our field became masterful in its study of the problems associated with sex, the study of shame was blocked for approximately 50 years.

Careful review of taped therapy interviews convinced Helen Block Lewis (1971) that much of our case failure stemmed from our tendency to overlook shame. Wurmser pointed out that the experiences of being put down, of ridicule, embarrassment, mortification, humiliation, denigration, disgrace, and public failure might be appraised more effectively were we to group them as examples of the shame family of emotions. He was the first to recognize that through the defense called "turning the tables" we produce shame in others when we cannot detoxify it by other means.

Recently, I suggested that shame starts as a physiological mechanism best defined in the affect theory of Silvan Tomkins, but that no matter what triggers shame, we respond in one of four distinctly programmed sets of responses assembled as the Compass of Shame. It is the physiology of shame that causes the bowed head, averted gaze, sudden cognitive shock that makes us stammer, and the blush that exposes us even more to the awareness of others. Immediately as we recover from the cognitive shock that makes it difficult to think at all, we enter the psychological phase and begin to remember a lifetime of similarly shame-filled moments that involve such categories as dependence/independence; agility and skill; personal attractiveness; sexuality; closeness and intimacy; the feelings of superiority or inferiority occurring as the result of comparison with others through competition; issues about seeing and being seen; and the sense of self. No matter what our highly individual path through life, we will respond to the current moment of shame by using one of the script libraries found in the compass of shame; this is the reactive phase that completes the sequence we know as shame emotion.

The Withdrawal pole of the compass involves all those times that we allow the affect itself to take over; it is when we augment the tendency of shame to force our gaze away from whatever had only a moment ago seemed so interesting or enjoyable. When we withdraw, we are less hurt by the gaze of others, even though we are, for the moment, shorn from the herd.

Some of us find it particularly difficult to remain alone for more than a moment—those who abjure abandonment will accept humiliation in order to get some other person to take responsibility for their safety. This is, of course, a precarious safety in that it places us in the care of one who is quite likely to treat us as an inferior; these scripts define the Attack Self pole of the compass. None of these poles is intrinsically pathologic. In this library, the script for normal deference is filed next to that for masochism; the degree of overt psychopathology is proportional to the degree of damage to our self-esteem we are willing to endure for this safety.

Most of us can handle momentary experiences of mild embarrassment, else how could we ever play golf or try on clothes at the store? Nevertheless, all of us some of the time, and some of us all of the time find the experience of shame literally unbearable and strive to avoid it at all costs. In the Avoidance pole of the compass are all the scripts through which we call attention to whatever brings us pride, distracting the viewing eye of the other away from that which might trigger shame. Other methods of avoidance involve the use of alcohol (a powerful shamolytic drug), the amphetamines, cocaine, or other drugs that bring excitement to one who has been reduced by shame. Everything we think of as narcissistic is really a defense against shame that is handled through avoidance scripts.

One of the categories of shame mentioned earlier references the tendency for the affect to be triggered by any experience of inferiority, and, conversely, to create the feeling of inferiority when the affect has been triggered for other reasons. For those to whom any experience of inferiority brings with it the idea of danger at the hands of others, shame becomes so toxic that they flare angrily at anybody available to mitigate this moment of incapacity. It is through the scripts assembled as the Attack Other pole of the compass of shame that we develop methods for the reduction and humiliation of others. What Helen Lewis called "humiliation fury," and what we all know as the response to "frustration" are parts of this script library. Everything we have been led to see as sadistic is really an Attack Other defense against shame best handled in therapy by discussion not of the resultant behavior but of the underlying shame.

With this brief outline of shame in hand, we are able to revisit the discomfort of clinical supervision with much more sophistication. Several generations of psychoanalysts or psychoanalytically trained psychotherapists were taught that shame was only a mild and quite proper punishment meted out by the superego in situations of sexual exhibitionism. Few, if any, of our teachers and therapists were ever treated or trained in the area of shame psychology. All of them were exposed to the personalities of their own teachers and therapists, none of whom knew nearly enough about their own defenses against shame. Unwittingly, we therapists perpetrated, transmitted, validated, enshrined, codified, taught each other to increase shame in our patients and our students. James Anthony said once that uncovering psychotherapy is an arena of shame in which everything that is revealed must produce shame that remains painful until we work it through. Ours is now an era of discovery in which what has been uncovered about the nature of psychotherapy now seems to be our own ignorance of shame as we have magnified it during the processes of supervision and preception.

To an apprentice plumber, the shame experienced at the hands of the master is of little consequence when compared with the lessons to be learned about plumbing. Nevertheless, this attitude of Attack Other defense against shame will appear in that apprentice's treatment of spouse, children, and any others who "get in the way." Undiagnosed and unrelieved shame conflict is ubiquitous in our society. Our society no longer emphasizes deference and withdrawal as "proper" methods of expressing shame, but celebrates narcissistic avoidance and explosive attack. Modern society is discolored at every level by the angry pole of shame.

The experience of humiliation at the hands of clinical supervisors is so common that some believe it both natural and unavoidable. There is, of course, little we can do about the moments of incompetence natural to any clinical training program. To be a beginner at anything is to be subject to shame. But if the supervisor does not recognize this moment of shame, and with it the tendency to behave in ways governed by scripts stored in the libraries of the compass of shame, then the process of supervision must fail its consumers. When we as supervisors have failed to deal with shame as a personal matter, we are poorly able to deal with the shame experienced by those who come to us for training; indeed, we will most certainly use them as vehicles for the expression of our own defenses.

Read through the pages of this multiauthor book on the perils and hazards associated with clinical practice, looking for evidence of shame as it appears in matters of self-esteem, personal competence, difficulty in our own problems of intimacy, accusation of malpractice, any intimation that we are less than wonderful. Shame underlies much that makes our field perilous. The study of shame rewards our practice as much as it brings to our own personal lives new confidence and safety.

REFERENCES

Lewis, H. B. (1971). *Shame and pride in neurosis.* New York: International Universities Press.

Nathanson, D. L. (1992). *Shame and pride: Affect, sex, and the birth of the self.* New York: Norton.

Tomkins, S. S. (1962). *Affect, imagery, consciousness.* New York: Springer.

Wurmser, L. (1981). *The mask of shame.* Baltimore: Johns Hopkins University Press.

CHAPTER 19

A Career Plundered*

JOHN T. MALTSBERGER, MD

Margaret Bean-Bayog, a 49-year-old Boston psychiatrist, resigned her license to practice medicine last September after a former patient's suicide set off a fire that burned down her reputation and her career. It started when the family sued her, their attorney inflamed the press, and the Board of Registration in Medicine joined the persecution. The damage was done before she ever had a day in court. Yet Dr. Bean-Bayog's side of the story has not been heard. I have decided to speak to you about this case because I think she was brutalized without justification, and because it shows what hazards and risks therapists must endure in the current climate: Our society is hostile to the mentally ill. The government and the courts often deal harshly with those who try to help them.

I was called into the case a year ago as an expert and reviewed the extensive records which became public after they were filed in court before the trial that never took place. Most of you will recall the sensational reports that heated up national newsmagazines and television at the time.

This controversial four years' treatment was a psychiatrist's nightmare. The record documents endless telephone calls, emergency interviews, consultations, and hospitalizations as the patient careened through months of living on the edge. I think the most likely diagnosis was manic-depressive illness complicated with intermittent delusions, or else schizoaffective illness. At one point, he connected himself to an intravenous apparatus and injected a dangerous drug. He revisited the 13th-story ledge, abused drugs and alcohol, and refused to cooperate in taking the medicines prescribed for him. There is little doubt in my mind that

---

* Presidential Address to the American Association of Suicidology, April 15, 1993. Reprinted with permission of the Association.

This chapter first appeared in *Suicide and Life Threatening Behavior,* 23(4), Winter 1993 (pp. 285–291), and has been reprinted with permission.

the patient would have committed suicide long before he did without Dr. Bean-Bayog's extraordinary dedication and tenacity. I think she did not know she was living out Hippocrates' famous axiom: "Life is short, the art long": She had trained for years to prepare herself to treat the desperately sick, and she was making an all-out effort for this man. "Opportunity fleeting," continued Hippocrates, "Experiment treacherous, judgment difficult."

There is no doubt that Dr. Bean-Bayog felt forced into several unusual therapeutic undertakings. Yet I would have you understand that these steps were not motivated by an intent to exploit or misuse Mr. Lozano. Ed Shneidman has written that in treating suicidal patients extraordinary involvements are sometimes necessary, and I agree with this. But experiment *is* treacherous.

She learned in the second week of the treatment that the patient already had a stuffed puppy with which to soothe himself when he was overwhelmed. It is not the case that Dr. Bean-Bayog "regressed" this man, as the newspapers have reported. He had regressed already. She tried to help him with his shame about this and, borrowing from her knowledge of child psychiatry, gave him the blanket he found in her office and which he had spontaneously adopted as a comforter. He was to bring this blanket to subsequent sessions and used it at home when, away from his doctor, he felt terrified and suicidal. Later, she gave him children's books and, at his request, wrote "Love, Mom" and similar now notorious inscriptions in them, though not without misgivings. Her treatment notes show that she repeatedly reminded the patient that she was not really his mother and could not be his mother. He seemed to understand this but claimed he found it comforting when away from her to pretend some mother had really given him the books, loved him, and wanted him to be comforted. The much deplored cards described by the press had the same origin. These were written at the patient's dictation, and when they were being written, he was reminded that they represented fantasies, not facts.

The card memorializing "the phenomenal sex" was also written at the patient's dictation, and it referred not to Dr. Bean-Bayog, but to another woman with whom the patient had been intimate.

There is no evidence in the record that any sexual intimacy ever took place between her and Mr. Lozano. She has repeatedly denied it. She estimates that in the four years she provided care—during which he was hospitalized several times—some 117 mental health professionals (nurses, social workers, psychiatric aides, psychologists, psychiatrists, and the like) were engaged with him in one way or another. The patient could have complained to any of these were he being abused, but he did not. In April 1988, the treatment notes record the patient's chagrin that Dr. Bean-Bayog was not in reality sexually available to comfort him. He repeatedly thanked her for supporting him and saving his life when he was less frenetic. Months after she had terminated the treatment and the patient was in a rage at her, he told other doctors that she had been sexually intimate with him, falsely, I believe, and this is why the matter was reported to the Board of Registration in Medicine which later behaved so badly, as you will hear. I think Lozano lied about the treatment to avenge himself on Dr. Bean-Bayog for declining to see him any longer. The record shows that he had lied about her before: In June 1987, he told another psychiatrist, consulted about antidepressant drugs, that she discouraged his taking what was prescribed. The records demonstrate the contrary: She had done all she could to get him to take his pills, and it was he who was consistently unwilling.

Dr. Bean-Bayog has been assailed with the charge that her treatment invited disastrous therapeutic regression and promoted a psychotic transference reaction. There is no doubt that during periods of her treatment with him the toys, the blanket, the books, and the cards (so-called transitional objects) were fixtures in profoundly regressed periods and that the patient was psychotic in the transference. I would not have written those inscriptions nor those cards. Read out of context, they do indeed sound too tender, too intimate, like a mother speaking to a frightened child. Yet I am a man, and Dr. Bean-Bayog a woman. She was there and I was not. Furthermore, she repeatedly consulted with several other psychiatrists about her use of transitional objects as the treatment progressed. The patient was frantic in his distress on many occasions, and he claimed to find the writings and toys useful. Bear in mind that the patient had convincingly reported repeated episodes of childhood sexual intimacy with his mother. Remembering those experiences pitched him into fits of suicidal anguish. He seemed to have been afforded little maternal soothing and comforting. Dr. Bean-Bayog repeatedly tried to make the line between fact and fantasy plain to this patient. The record shows that the patient invented the "Mom" of the cards and the children's books and the toys. Dr. Bean-Bayog reminded him time and again of the difference between fact and fantasy. She repeatedly consulted other colleagues about this somewhat unconventional treatment, the thrust of which was to meet the patient at the level where he was already functioning. He quickly began presenting himself to her as a child. The worst that can be said about the technique is that it invited him to tarry in an infantile regression and intensified the transference. Fairness demands that the record be set straight: She did not force him into the regression in the first place. Furthermore, as their work together continued, the patient became less reliant on the transitional objects, and to a great extent laid them aside. *There is evidence in the treatment record that they had their usefulness.* The patient's worst symptoms belonged to the first 18 months of the treatment, after which he began to improve. The transitional objects were of urgent usefulness only for about six months, after which the patient said he no longer needed them. Quieting down, he was able to stay out of the hospital from December 1987 until March 1990. His sister found the transitional objects when she searched his apartment during the last Boston hospitalization. They were the principal faggots used to build the bonfire with which Dr. Bean-Bayog's reputation and career were burned.

There was a phase in the treatment when the transference became intensely erotic, and in a most unpleasant way. Mr. Lozano became obsessed with sexual torture and bombarded Dr. Bean-Bayog with graphic, brutal sadomasochistic fantasy. He presented her with a hideous book picturing cruel instruments designed to mutilate women's breasts and vaginas, with detailed descriptions of how they were to be used. In an effort to keep her balance, she wrote many of his torture fantasies down. Experiencing reciprocal countertransference fantasies of a disturbing nature, as many therapists would, she wrote these down too, and kept them in a separate file, using her notes to sort out her inner reactions to this formidable patient and to help her keep her balance. She consulted other psychiatrists about her countertransference experiences with Lozano as a further aid in maintaining her distance from the response the patient was stimulating. Then, in October or November 1987, the patient broke into her office and stole many of his records. At some juncture, maybe then, or maybe at another time, he also stole the personal notes of her own countertransference responses as well. She did not know he had stolen, copied, and secretly replaced the countertransference fantasies until the family and their lawyers began their pursuit in 1990. When she learned of the theft of his personal records on 20 November she demanded the patient return her papers, which he did, but he secretly photocopied them first.

I would have stopped the treatment at this juncture, but as Hippocrates said, judgment is difficult. Stopping would have been perilous at that juncture. The patient was homicidal, threatening to shoot physicians and other staff at one of the hospitals where he had been confined. There was the distinct risk termination at that juncture might have provoked not only suicide, but murder as well. Furthermore, the patient was in a paranoid state about psychiatric hospitals and would have taken flight if urged to go into one; involuntary commitment would have spelled the end of the therapeutic relationship. He had nothing but that to sustain him. Appropriately sensitive to the patient's profound horror of abandonment, Dr. Bean-Bayog persevered.

Late in autumn 1987, a sinister theme arises in the treatment notes. The patient began to threaten Dr. Bean-Bayog that he would kill himself and leave written materials behind for his family to discover, so they would sue her and ruin her reputation. Thus he began not only to torture her in fantasy, but with direct threats of action.

In December, he was psychotic, convinced that apparatus in the laboratory where he worked was measuring his worth and finding him wanting, but this was transient. He seemed to improve in 1988. Dr. Bean-Bayog had by now begun to see him for little or no fee because his resources were exhausted. Later, in 1989, when it appeared he could again afford a small fee, the patient was enraged when asked to resume modest payment. In early 1990, having been on leave from medical school, he was preparing to resume clinical studies and the patient responsibilities that go with it. Because he had been so irregular in taking his medication, and because of his tendency to drink and abuse drugs, Dr. Bean-Bayog was concerned. Furthermore, Lozano had reported fantasies of becoming a "monster doctor," a pediatrician who would sexually abuse the children coming under his care. She recommended that Lozano should voluntarily put himself under supervision by the Massachusetts Medical Society's monitors of impaired physicians for the protection of his patients. This advice threw the patient into a rage and he refused. In March, just before he was to return to hospital work, he took an hallucinogen, began to hear voices, and to think delusionally. He went to her house in the night when she was out for the evening, banged on the windows, shouted for her, and terrified her children who were home alone.

Readmitted to the hospital for the fifth time, the patient reported that he had injected himself with ketamine (an hallucinogen) and lidocaine (an anaesthetic) in a suicide attempt, and that he was hearing voices ordering him to kill himself. Later that spring Dr. Bean-Bayog at last decided to get out of the case. She carefully arranged the transfer of Lozano's care to another psychiatrist during yet another psychiatric admission. She was not willing to continue when he refused to submit to monitoring by the impaired physicians' committee.

Five more hospitalizations followed. Not until the autumn of 1990 did he tell another psychiatrist that Dr. Bean-Bayog had been sexually intimate with him. Lozano's sister was alerted and found the stuffed animals, the papers, the cards in the cache that he had so carefully saved for this occasion. As required by Massachusetts law, the psychiatrist then in charge wrote a letter to the Board of Registration in Medicine, detailing what the patient alleged, and describing the materials. His letter stated, "If Dr. Bean-Bayog's conduct of his treatment has indeed been as [Lozano] describes it, she has done this patient great harm."

After temporary improvement following a course of electroconvulsive treatment, the patient went to Texas to visit his family and to continue with some medical work that would have been credited toward his degree. He came under the care of yet another psychiatrist. After a brief overnight hospitalization in El Paso, his home, Lozano died of suicide by injecting himself with a massive dose of cocaine.

The family brought a malpractice action against Dr. Bean-Bayog on September 11, 1991. Their attorney took an extraordinary step: he filed some 3,000 pages of documents with the court in March, 1992, including the treatment notes and the books and cards inscribed "Love, Mom." The newspapers seized these and the fire began to burn in earnest; soon all the media, local and national, were aflame. The Massachusetts Board of Registration in Medicine had a series of hearings and a well-known trial lawyer, John Fabiano, emerging from the Boston firm Hale & Dorr, stepped forward to volunteer his services to assist the Board in its scrutiny. The Board of Registration in Medicine was under the supervision of Gloria Larson, the consumer affairs appointee of Governor William Weld. Hale & Dorr was the law firm to which the governor belonged before his election; he must have been acquainted with Mr. Fabiano. Never before had the Board felt it necessary to appoint a special lawyer for one of its disciplinary proceedings.

The Board next announced its intention to conduct several days of public hearings in a large auditorium to which the press and television would be invited. Five television stations and cable television as well were to be present with lights and cameras aimed. European reporters were expected also. The Japanese were coming. The government of Massachusetts was preparing an extravaganza.

Dr. Bean-Bayog's position was terrible from several points of view. In the first place, the law provides that after a patient's death the rights to confidentiality do not lapse but pass to the heirs; the treating physician is not allowed to disclose details about a treatment without their permission, even in the course of an ethics inquiry. To do so invites severe penalties. The Lozano family refused to grant permission, so Margaret Bean-Bayog was gagged and would have been forced mutely to point only at the papers their lawyer had already filed with the court. She was forbidden to speak out about her side of the story. The press knew this, but elected not to report it. Perhaps doing so might have lessened the savor of the breakfast dishes they were regularly serving up in the morning papers at Dr. Bean-Bayog's expense.

In the second place, the legal costs of defending herself before the Board and the national media promised to be enormous, in fact, ruinous. Though she had understood that legal costs could be kept within reasonable limits, in less than a fortnight before the Weld administration's circus was to begin, her lawyers informed her she would have to pay them between three-quarters and one million dollars in fees and costs if they were to proceed. She would have been crushed with overwhelming debts for the rest of her life had she agreed to such a demand

Third, the emotional cost of a gagged appearance before the Board, a large auditorium filled with sensation-hungry spectators, reporters, and cameras promised to be overwhelming. She had already taken an emotional beating from Paul Lozano and suffered the expectable pain of losing a patient to suicide. She was being assaulted by the press. Now she faced the prospect of public humiliation as Paul Lozano reached from the grave to fulfill his promise—that he would kill himself and ruin her career and reputation. The Board offered to resolve the matter if she would sign a statement admitting to wrongdoing she had never committed—she was invited to perjure herself.

It was in this context Margaret Bean-Bayog elected to resign her license to practice medicine. This step put her beyond the reach of the Board of Registration in Medicine and the prospect of a trial in the media, but it meant she could never again practice medicine anywhere in the United States. She had already been suspended from the staff of the Cambridge Hospital, and the Harvard Medical School, where she had held an academic appointment, had hastened to drop her from its faculty. Only the Boston Psychoanalytic Society and Institute, where she was a psychoanalytic candidate-in-training, the Massachusetts Medical Society, and the American Society of Addiction Medicine refused to abandon her until she had had her day in court.

The malpractice case continued to loom. A number of experts reviewed the records on her behalf and on behalf of her malpractice insurance company. In spite of contrary opinions of experts for the Lozano family, the experts on her side, among whom I had the honor to be included, believed that Dr. Bean-Bayog stood a good chance to win her case. We did not believe her treatment caused Lozano's suicide.

The malpractice insurer advised Dr. Bean-Bayog to settle out of court. Though their experts were of the opinion her treatment of Lozano had been within acceptable standards and that her work was not a proximate cause of his death, it was feared that the enormous newspaper pressure and public hysteria might significantly affect the outcome of the trial. She was warned that an unsuccessful outcome at trial would leave her liable to enormous expenses for which they were not obliged to pay. Faced with the prospect of a punishing public trial coupled with the strong possibility that going through with it would ruin her financially she elected to settle. Thereupon, the insurance company paid the Lozano family a million dollars, and Dr. Bean-Bayog went home.

She has now retired from practice, but she has read what I am saying to you and sends her greetings to the American Association of Suicidology. She expresses her regret that she is unable to be present today; she was invited to attend our meeting by your executive committee.

I hope that what I have said to you serves to put some fairer perspectives on what I believe was an act of arson by the press. Nothing that I have said was hidden from the newspapers, yet they chose to say nothing about her side of the story, nor did they choose to report that she was gagged by the law's blind rules. What the press did in this case reminds me of what it did to the Scottsboro Five, and what it did to Dreyfus. You will remember how the press and the courts and the government of France sent an innocent man to Devil's Island. Something like that has just happened in Massachusetts, where the principal actors have been the Massachusetts Board of Registration in Medicine, the administration of Governor William Weld, certain lawyers, the *Boston Globe* and the *Boston Herald.* J'accuse!

Though malpractice insurance will pay for the defense of a lawsuit, it will not pay for costs incurred before regulatory agencies such as the Massachusetts Board of Registration in Medicine. Typically, these agencies are not bound by the strict rules of evidence that govern court proceedings. A physician challenged before the Massachusetts Board must prove to its satisfaction there was no deviation from ethical standards, and not the contrary: The person who challenges a physician does not have to prove there was an ethical lapse. It is a matter of guilty until proven innocent. A license to practice medicine is not a right, but a privilege, and such agencies have enormous discretion in what they do. They are much influenced by public opinion, and they are most certainly not above politics.

A number of psychiatrists have very properly been disciplined by the Massachusetts Board of Registration in Medicine for sexual misconduct with patients in recent years, but the Board has not been evenhanded, and sometimes it has been capricious. In one case, a prominent academic psychiatrist was shown to have been sexually involved with a patient, but his license was not revoked, and his tenure was not interrupted by his medical school, where he continues to enjoy a professorship.

The Boston newspapers have taken these cases up and they have been widely reported. The Bean-Bayog case was the first involving a woman, however, and the publicity blown up around it was far greater than for any of the other cases. There was no evidence here of sexual misconduct except for what a dead patient, known to lie and bent on revenge, said about her.

This scandalous assault on Dr. Bean-Bayog has done more than to knock her out of the practice of medicine. It has had a profound negative effect on others who have been treating deeply disturbed suicidal patients for years. Many of the finest psychiatrists and psychologists in Massachusetts have told me they will no longer accept such patients for treatment. Others of us have not given up, but I would not accept a patient as disturbed as Paul Lozano unless long, continuous hospitalization were possible. Some years ago, it might have been possible to keep Mr. Lozano in a psychiatric hospital continuously for several years, but this is no longer the case. Dr. Bean-Bayog tried to arrange for long-term inpatient care for Paul Lozano more than once, but nobody would pay.

We joke in Boston that it is easier to get somebody into Harvard College than into the state hospital. The state system discharges patients like Mr. Lozano quickly after the first symptomatic improvement, blinding itself to the fluctuating nature of such illnesses as his, taking no interest in the possibility of lasting therapeutic improvement a long stay might afford. They cannot: They are very overcrowded. Private hospitalization for long periods is impossible except for the fabulously rich; insurance companies and the health-maintenance organizations will not pay. The average length of stay in good private hospitals is now about two weeks.

So I leave you here among the embers and ashes of Margaret Bean-Bayog's career. I hope the smell of smoke will linger in your nostrils as a reminder of what happened to a doctor who did her best, made some regrettable judgments under great pressure, but who certainly never exploited her patient for a personal end.

CHAPTER 20

The Therapist as Dragonslayer: Confronting Industrialized Mental Health

PETER GUMPERT, PhD and SUSAN SCHOLFIELD MACNAB, MSW, PhD

As the middle of the decade approaches and the health care reform movement keeps growing, many dynamic therapists are distressed and in shock. They feel caught in the dizzying pace of the changes being imposed on the health care delivery system and the changes they are being asked to make in their work. They are frightened that there may be no room for them in the new world of health care they hear about. The rallying cry of the new health care industry is that private practice is soon to be a thing of the past, and that if health care providers (including therapists) want to survive, they must climb aboard and endorse the bandwagon of change. The process is reminiscent of how artisanry was replaced by machine production during the industrial revolution. In this case, however, it is not the making of shoes that is under discussion; we are talking about the complex processes involved in helping people who have sustained psychic damage.

What is the nature of the change that is being demanded? By most accounts, we therapists are being asked:

- To organize into provider groups and sell ourselves to the preferred provider panels of managed care companies, or to accept jobs in health maintenance organizations.
- To comply assiduously (and without complaint) with the treatment protocols and information demands of case managers, thus compromising patient confidentiality and other ethical standards.
- To adopt a perspective that favors short-term, issue-focused treatment that relieves symptoms, and to enjoy this problem-solving approach.

- To use groups as the primary modality for cases that may require longer-term work.
- To cooperate with any quality-assurance methods that may be introduced by case managers, even though we may feel certain that these are conceptually empty and designed primarily to restrict care.
- To assume the financial and legal risks of doing treatment while giving up the deeper rewards of participating in the growth of our patients.

We are asked to treat patients as if we had a simple, effective set of diagnostic categories in which they fit and solid treatment protocols that can be tied to each diagnosis. In mental health, diagnostic categories are little more than an insurance convenience. By and large, they are not (and, for the foreseeable future, will not be) good indicators of how treatment should proceed. Research on DSM-III-R, for example, indicates that Axis II categories are very difficult to separate from one another, and if a patient meets the criteria for one category he or she is likely to meet the criteria for at least four (Bower, 1994). It is abundantly clear that within a given diagnostic category, patients vary enormously and require very different treatment. Patients diagnosed with borderline personality disorder are an excellent example.

We are also being asked to violate our ethical codes. We do not know what harm we are causing for the patient's future when we reveal sensitive information about the patient and the treatment to a reviewer—despite signatures on informed consent forms. We are asked to accept the dual relationship of working for the patient, who needs treatment—and also working for the insurer, whose primary agenda is cost control. We are asked to abandon patients before their work is done, and to tell them they require no more treatment. We are implicitly or explicitly asked not to treat patients who have severe personality disorders, are victims of childhood sexual abuse, and so on—or we are tempted to lie about diagnosis to provide them with the treatment they need.

The alternative we are offered to complying with the industrializers is not pleasant. We are told that if we operate independently, we will be forced to compete frantically with colleagues for the few private patients who may remain outside the mainstream system being formed, with uncertain results. Even this alternative is questionable, since the federal health care legislation that is being written may severely limit private practice.

Thus, control of mental health treatment, which used to be in the hands of the individual therapist-patient dyad, is being transferred to third parties. Therapists have lost control of many aspects of treatment. In many cases, the decision about whether outpatient treatment is medically necessary and therefore indicated is made by an evaluator employed by the managed care company. The traditional patient choice of referrer (friend, physician, or member of the clergy) and choice of psychotherapist and treatment method are being replaced. Patients in search of a referral are now asked to call an 800-number and explain their problem, or are asked to make an appointment with a gatekeeper who will, if he or she believes it is indicated, make a referral believed to be appropriate. Thus the patient's choice of treatment modality and treatment length, and the patient's choice of the gender and discipline of the therapist, are being lost. In some cases, patients are being forced to be evaluated for medication as a condition of continued coverage.

The *ideology* that is being put forth by the industrializers of mental health care seems to involve several assertions. Mental health care, we are being told, has been very expensive for the nation, and the nation can no longer afford the expense. We are also told that there have been many abuses of the older system by providers and patients alike, and these have resulted in medically needless expenditures that line the pockets of providers while providing narcissistic gratification for worried-well consumers. The very idea that unconscious processes are important is discredited. Long-term treatment is considered ineffective as well as wasteful, at least as compared with short-term treatment. We are told that a medical-model conceptualization of mental health and substance abuse treatment is both appropriate and necessary, and that we must develop treatment protocols that are clearly tied to diagnoses. We are asked to push treatment goals that simply return the patient to his or her precrisis level of functioning. The point of all this is to induce providers to begin treatment only if an effective brief treatment for a condition is known to exist and, if treatment is begun, to terminate it as soon as possible. Mental health care is thus conceived as a set of technologies that can be applied to any patient by any modern-day person who is properly trained in their use. As the insurers and care managers see it, the application of this technology set is our proper work.

The newly emerging ideology of mental health care plays nicely into the uncertainty and guilt of many psychotherapists. There are many times when we doubt ourselves, and feel unworthy of what patients (and the insurers who hold their money in trust) pay us. The work is hard and the hours are long, but we have been making a good living, and every apparent failure of psychotherapy is painful and undermining. So we are predisposed to worry that the people who say that our work is self-serving and ineffective may be correct in their judgment. A prominent colleague who has joined the managed care business often asserts that it is criminal to practice long-term psychotherapy. We wonder how many therapists secretly worry that he is right or will convince the public that he is right and that they are the "worried well" who should get on with their lives without burdening the mental health care system.

In the past, there have indeed been abuses of third-party payment, particularly in respect to inpatient care. At one time and in some hospitals people were sometimes hospitalized up to the limit of their insurance coverage when less restrictive treatment might have been better as well as less costly. Much of the present ideology about mental health costs, however, is based on distortion rather than truth, and the distortions seem to us to be part of a deliberate marketing effort. We can confront some of the distortions easily; in some cases, the truth is a matter of record. Outpatient mental health and substance abuse treatment is anything but a major expense; it accounts for about 3% of the nation's health care bill, a figure that has been measured quarterly by the government and has remained stable for 15 years (e.g., Letsch, Levit, & Waldo, 1988). Furthermore, outpatient treatment is effectively self-regulating, and needs no micromanagement. Psychotherapy is not entertainment; the evidence is very strong that people stop treatment as soon as they can, regardless of how generous mental health benefits are (Ackley, 1993; Pollak, Mordecai, & Gumpert, 1992; Ware, Manning, & Duan, 1984).

In fact, the untreated "worried well" (a particularly pernicious notion) are likely to cost the nation enormous amounts in lost productivity and overuse of expensive health care facilities (Greenberg, Stiglin, Finkelstein, & Berndt, 1993a, 1993b; Robert Wood Johnson Foundation, 1993). The experience with Germany's health care system indicates that providing virtually unlimited access to psychotherapy for people who ask for it is anything but wasteful; indeed, it is known to save a great deal of money (e.g., Reinhardt, 1993).

THE BUSINESS MOTIVE BEHIND THE NEW IDEOLOGY

Behind the ideology we and the public are being urged to accept, there is a simple business motive. Baldly stated, our business has provided many of us not only with hard and rewarding work, but with a good living. Other people—insurers, care managers, and provider businesses—want as big a piece of our business as they can get, preferably all of it. In the language of finance, private practice psychotherapists are being subjected to a hostile takeover of one business by another. In some states, community mental health clinics are also being disbanded and "privatized" (their contracts given to for-profit businesses). We are witnessing the formation of a number of vertical trusts—large health care businesses that sell insurance, provide care (or own the businesses that provide care), and define, manage, and evaluate the care provided.

The effort simply goes against a broader national trend toward smaller, more flexible, autonomous businesses. In the current business climate, big and bureaucratic is no longer considered beautiful. Paradoxically, industrialized health care is more likely to be an economic anachronism than the wave of the future.

THE HEALTH INSURANCE BUSINESS SINCE WORLD WAR II

The White House health care reform initiative of 1993 has helped elevate the commercial insurance industry to leadership status in the delivery of health care to the nation. How did this come about? According to some pundits, because President Clinton knew he could not get a Canadian style single-payer system adopted because of the probable opposition of powerful interest groups, he decided to work with "the politics of the possible" to get a comprehensive reform package through the Congress. The package depends heavily on commercial insurance companies and large health maintenance organizations.

Surprisingly, commercial insurers have only been in the health insurance business for a relatively short time—since World War II (Bak & Weiner, 1993). Prior to their entrance, the task of insuring the broad community had been given to certain nonprofit insurers: the Blue Cross/Blue Shield companies in various localities. This method worked reasonably well because the risk that the "Blues" took on was spread widely, and people of every health status were covered. Commercial insurers saw the opportunity to insure healthier segments of the community through the businesses that employed them. They sold insurance to these subgroups for less than it would have cost through the Blue Cross/Blue Shield companies (since the risk was smaller). Thus they left the community insurers with the less healthy segment of the population, and the Blue Cross companies had to raise their rates. The government found itself caring for an increasing number of people who were too poor and too infirm to buy insurance of any kind. So the nonprofit insurance companies and the government took on more and more high-risk patients, and the commercial insurers continued to cherry-pick the healthiest subscribers.

The HMO experiment, which really began in the 1970s, introduced the idea of cost control through preventive care and through the management of care delivery. The health insurance industry learned from this model and began to offer managed insurance products at lower rates by restricting the number of providers they had to deal with and monitoring (reducing) the delivery of services through direct management practices. Thus, two new layers of profit making have been introduced into the system since the 1940s: the insurance layer and the cost-management layer. As the profit-making health corporations grew and went public, they came under the usual shareholder pressure to grow and to enhance profit, and reduce expenditures.

Blue Cross/Blue Shield was made to appear noncompetitive, and the myth grew that the Blues were in trouble because of their nonprofit status—not because they had a mandate to serve the community. In self-defense, they finally began to climb on the commercial bandwagon and to offer managed health care policies.

Today, insurers are buying a large number of medical practices and hiring their former owners to deliver care. They are positioning themselves to profit most handsomely from a huge business windfall provided by the government—and the devil take the hindmost provider and the consumer with a health problem. This, in short, is the politico-economic context in which we dynamic therapists are trying to continue to do the work we trained to do.

Therapists are confused, frightened, and conflicted about how the art and the science of our "quiet profession" will survive. How much will we be forced to become marketers who offer only short-term, behavioral treatments? Will we disappear as the industrializers choose to use more docile paraprofessionals to provide direct service (see Christensen & Jacobson, 1994)? What is happening to the healing aspects of listening over time that we and our patients know is essential for creating lasting intrapsychic change?

LISTENING: THE WORK OF PSYCHOTHERAPY

As Stanley Jackson has said, "Listening is central to learning about and coming to understand a sufferer, and those steps are crucial to being a healer. The healer learns about the sufferer in direct proportion to the quantity and quality of his listening" (1992, p. 1631).

From Freud's elucidation of the powerful effects of unconscious wishes and fears through the more interpersonal focus of object relations and self-psychology, psychotherapy has used the therapeutic relationship to learn about the patient's needs and conflicts, and to effect change. This perspective on psychotherapy treats the work in part as an educational and developmental process. Thus it may not conform well with the traditional medical model of disease, technologically oriented diagnosis, and technologically oriented treatment. On the other hand, much of medicine itself is not fully suited to this traditional diagnosis-treatment model. Diagnoses in medicine are often not so straightforward, and medical treatment does not always lend itself to a standardized treatment-protocol approach. The recent research of Roter and Hall (1992) on the effects on therapeutic outcomes of how doctors and patients communicate makes the point very clearly: relationship seems critical in all healing.

Psychotherapists work in the context of a private, intimate, confidential relationship in which patient listening and learning occurs at many levels and in many ways. These include exploration of the patient's past, and the patient's conscious and unconscious wishes, hopes, and terrors; exploration of defenses that have distorted the patient's understanding and his or her present functioning; and respectful exploration of the pain, shame, rage, and grief that underlie a wide range of symptoms that have a different meaning, however subtly, in each treatment case. Anxiety and depression are appreciated as long-standing responses to past and present trauma or deprivation, or to insufficient support for the developmental needs of the child or developing adult. Dynamic therapies use the developing transference and the working alliance to provide the patient-therapist dyad with the data that illuminate the patients' intrapsychic and interpersonal struggles. There is less emphasis on "cure" and "fixing the problem" than on the patient's growing understanding of his or her inner world and the acquisition of greater freedom to make changes. The intricacies of psychic functioning are revealed over time in an atmosphere of developing trust. In such relationships, the most difficult characterological patterns can be changed. Narcissistic, borderline, and schizoid patients are successfully treated; victims of severe childhood trauma gradually begin to live satisfying, productive lives (Lazar, Hersh, & Hershberg, 1993). For us as therapists, the complexity of these treatments, like parenting, is far from being reducible to a technology.

This highly abbreviated description of some of the important aspects of dynamic psychotherapy is worlds away from the symptom-focused brief treatment that third-party payers wish to make universal as a key to minimizing costs and maximizing profits. The industrializers of mental health care do not want to support more open-ended therapies in which the therapist and the patient agree on goals that may take considerable time to reach, such as improved ability to conduct intimate and work relationships. In addition, the privacy that more exploratory therapy demands is compromised by a solution-oriented model of care that is managed on behalf of a for-profit insurance company. Finally, according to some managed care protocols, people with personality disorders and disorders related to severe trauma should be seen as *untreatable.* Certainly, it appears more cost-effective to define them out of the treatment universe than to treat them the slow and difficult—and effective—way.

Thus, not only providers but patients suffer under the system being promulgated. By many accounts, people have already been suffering from restricted access, violations of confidentiality, heightened stigmatization, and truncated treatment.

The treatment *relationship* suffers as well. A convincing presentation by a colleague (Smith, 1994) recently detailed a number of serious countertransference problems that are introduced by managed care intrusions into the treatment relationship. The exacerbation of the therapist's moment-to-moment self-doubt, for example, has effects on the treatment as well as the treater. The case reviewer sits in judgment of my work. Is it going fast enough? Well enough? Will I be able to "do the job" in the sessions allotted? Should I exaggerate or dissemble a bit to obtain approval for additional treatment we know the patient needs? Or, if I am being asked by the reviewer to discontinue the treatment, am I tempted to present the patient with a distorted view of his or her readiness to end treatment? Smith suggests that such lies gradually erode our self-respect and our relationship with patients. If we have compromised the patient's confidentiality through a case review over the phone and suspect we might have done some harm to the patient's future, how is the relationship affected? If we have agreed to accept a very low fee from the managed care company, does the anger and entitlement that may follow hurt our relationship with the patients involved? In sum, does the managed care process erode our ability to provide the safe holding environment that is necessary to support the patient's exploration? Does the increasing attention managed care forces us to pay to risk management keep us from writing good, informative notes in which we allow ourselves to play with feelings and ideas? We are convinced that these intrusions erode the treatment in many ways.

PRESERVING PATIENT WELFARE, OURSELVES, AND OUR WORK

The professional guilds in many states have tended to respond to the circumstances we have described by working at insuring the place of their members in the new health care system. In some cases, members who complain that this is the wrong tack are not heard, or are seen as uncooperative and unrealistic "radicals" or "dinosaurs" who are unwilling to change. The possibility that the future may hold alternatives to managed care psychotherapy is not taken seriously, and the traditional interdisciplinary rivalries continue. At the same time that psychotherapists are encouraged to remain passive and compliant, they are driven into further isolation by the intense competition they assume exists "out there." The prevailing wisdom is that the pie is getting smaller and smaller, and there is no alternative but to engage in deadly competition for what remains. We are being conquered through isolation, internal division, and the illusion of an overwhelming opposing force.

Indeed, the pie will shrink—if we do nothing about it. The industrializers of mental health and their bedfellows will prevail—if they are able to keep us divided and keep us passive. Thus far, aided by an economic downturn, they have done a pretty effective job.

But cracks are beginning to appear in the illusion that the industrializers have impregnable armor and irresistible power. Employees are beginning to complain, despite the stigma attached to accessing mental health treatment. Human resource professionals in some large companies are concerned and even angry about what their employees fail to get from managed care mental health. Professionals who work in internal employee assistance plans say increasingly often that they do not like the managed mental health care that is available to the employees they work with and refer out. Psychotherapists are getting together outside their disciplinary associations, and in a few cases, the professional associations are listening to them.

In mid-1992, we began to organize an interdisciplinary group of psychotherapists in New England; we called it the Consortium for Psychotherapy. It was conceived as an information and support system for its embattled members and soon began to be involved in educating consumers and the public about psychotherapy, influencing public policy, and making contact with similar groups elsewhere. There has been an interesting parallel between what we have gone through in forming the Consortium and what we witness in our clinical work. Dynamic therapies, despite their many differences, value the "putting into words" of private, problematic wishes, fears, and conflicts. They generate a dialectic process in which certainties are questioned, confusion is tolerated, and new perspectives and ideas are synthesized. The experience of talking to one another, disagreeing, writing, and speaking to various groups has pushed us to examine our ideas and values, and has expanded the range of choices that will be available to us as we practice in the future.

The Consortium now has more than 500 members. It grows daily and has increasing numbers of people eager to do the work that needs to be done. Members have written a consumer education booklet about psychotherapy and informative brochures about insurance. They write letters and editorials, appear on TV, and give presentations to professional and lay audiences. They work to initiate and generate support for legislation at the state level to protect patient freedom of choice of provider and patient confidentiality. They make and maintain contacts with local consumer groups, and with groups of psychotherapists in other states. Perhaps most importantly, they support one another, help one another market, and refer patients to one another when they can. The Consortium is now creating a cooperative nonprofit mental health care plan that is not a managed care "clone," and thus it is getting ready to compete directly in the marketplace with managed care companies. Groups in other states are investigating similar ideas; the groups are in touch with one another and are actively sharing information.[1]

We have noted from this remarkable experience that we and other members of the Consortium no longer feel depressed and powerless. We have learned that we must avoid being divided by external forces, avoid the temptation to see relationships with colleagues as competitive, and work very hard to counter the efforts of businesses to control ideas about psychotherapy and to restrict access to treatment. Many of us have turned away from working with managed care companies.

The task we face is, however, both major and daunting. Some might suggest that the "dragonslayer" image we chose for the title of this chapter should have been a Don Quixote image instead. The enemy is diffuse,

[1] The work of preserving our discipline is partially national, partially state by state, and partially local. We are developing a "Consortium-Cloning Kit" for interested psychotherapists in other states—a way of sharing what we have learned about how to organize both ourselves and our work. Other organizations are also doing good work (e.g., the Coalition of Mental Health Professionals and Consumers, P.O. Box 438, Commack, NY 11725-0438, tel. 516-424-5232). Write to the Consortium (or to one of us) if you think we can be of help. The address is: Consortium for Psychotherapy, P.O. Box 717, Brookline, MA 02146, tel. 617-739-7083.

and its vulnerable regions are hard to locate. Indeed, the two greatest dangers we face are very indirect. First, the public can easily adopt a new view of mental health care and can forget altogether that psychotherapy is a viable way for troubled people to create a different future for themselves. Second, psychodynamic training for psychotherapists is already in trouble and is disappearing from graduate programs. Psychiatry residencies increasingly concentrate on biological approaches. Postgraduate training institutes are dependent on private practitioners, and many are experiencing a loss of enrollment; these could disappear as well. Even more than dealing with managed care itself, then, our greatest challenges are creating a public understanding of psychotherapy and preserving good training for the future.

We must emerge from our offices and make a concerted effort to speak clearly and *repeatedly* about the realities of change as we have learned about them, personally and professionally. Our emphasis on the term "repeatedly" is important: The message must be articulated again and again, and yet again. People must be helped to understand that there are few if any "quick fixes" for those who desire to make durable changes in their lives, and that the more gradual, developmentally oriented methods of psychotherapy are truly effective. We must create a strong, collective voice that can be heard by consumers, governmental bodies, and the business world, whose interests are not being served by the technological approaches they are, in ignorance, accepting. Corporate and union officials must be helped to understand that managed care and quality mental health treatment are not compatible (e.g., Fendell, 1994), and that the characteristics of good mental health care can be specified.

If we wish to preserve the profession, therefore, we must truly become dragonslayers. The task ahead is certainly difficult—but together we can prevail.

REFERENCES

Ackley, D. C. (1993). Employee health insurance benefits. A comparison of managed care with traditional mental health care: Costs and results. *Independent Practitioner, 13*(1), 159–164.

Bak, J. S., & Weiner, R. H. (1993). Issues affecting psychologists as health care service providers in the national health insurance debate (Part I). *Independent Practitioner, 13*(1), 30–38.

Bower, B. (1994). Piecing together personality. *Science News, 145*(10), 152–154.

Christensen, A., & Jacobson, N. S. (1994). Who (or what) can do psychotherapy: The status and challenge of nonprofessional therapies. *Psychological Science, 5*(1), 8–14.

Fendell, S. (1994, Spring). Mental health managed care: MHMA report card mixed; conflict between profits and consumers. Advisor: *Notes from the Mental Health Legal Advisors Committee, 40,* 4–12.

Greenberg, P. E., Stiglin, L. E., Finkelstein, S. N., & Berndt, E. R. (1993a). Depression: A neglected illness. *Journal of Clinical Psychiatry, 54*(11), 419–424.

Greenberg, P. E., Stiglin, L. E., Finkelstein, S. N., & Berndt, E. R. (1993b). The economic burden of depression. *Journal of Clinical Psychiatry, 54*(11), 405–418.

Lazar, S. G., Hersh, E. K., & Hershberg, S. G. (1993). The Long Term Psychotherapy Needs of Psychiatric Patients: Executive Summary. Unpublished review of literature. Copies may be obtained from the first author of Dept. of Psychiatry, George Washington University School of Medicine, Washington DC.

Letsch, S. W., Levit, K. R., & Waldo, D. R. (1988). National health expenditures, 1987. *Health Care Financing Review, 10*(2), 109–122.

Pollak, J., Mordecai, E., & Gumpert, P. (1992). Discontinuation from long-term individual psychodynamic psychotherapy. *Psychotherapy Research, 2*(3), 224–233.

Reinhardt, U. (1993). *The German health system: Providing equitable, universal access to health care and controlling its cost.* Paper delivered at the Senior Policy Seminar in Health Financing in China. Beijing, China, July 19–31, 1993.

Robert Wood Johnson Foundation. (1993). *Substance abuse: The nation's no. 1 health problem.* The Robert Wood Johnson Foundation, P.O. Box 2316, Princeton, NJ 08543-2316.

Roter, D. L., & Hall, J. A. (1992). *Doctors talking with patients/Patients talking with doctors. Improving communication in medical visits.* Westport, CT: Auburn House.

Smith, J. W. (1994, January). The extinction of the 20th-century psychodynamic psychotherapist during the ice age of managed care. Grand Rounds presentation, Boston Institute for Psychotherapy. (Available from the author, 520 Commonwealth Avenue, Boston, MA 02215.)

Ware, J. E., Manning, W. G., & Duan, N. (1984). Health status and the use of outpatient mental health services. *American Psychologist, 39,* 1090–1100.

CHAPTER 21

The Importance of Risk Management in a Managed Care Environment*

ERIC A. HARRIS, EdD, JD

THE NEW CLIMATE OF INCREASED RISK

These are hard times for mental health professionals, particularly those in private psychotherapy practices. The recession, managed care's increasing market share, and the possibility that national health insurance reform will not adequately cover outpatient psychotherapy have most mental health professionals concerned about their professional and economic futures. As if this weren't bad enough, a number of developments have combined to create an additional threat to professional practice.

The most obvious manifestation of the increasing litigation exposure faced by mental health professionals is escalating malpractice insurance premiums. This exposure may have been greatly increased by a recent California court decision in which a father who was accused of sexual abuse by his daughter on the basis of memories recovered in therapy successfully sued his daughter's therapists for damages. In addition to opening the possibility of a large number of actions for the implantation of false memory, this decision, if upheld on appeal, could make it possible for parents of patients to sue therapists if they feel damaged by the results of the therapy.

In addition, the incidence of consumer complaints to the Licensing Boards and Professional Society Ethics Committees has increased dramatically. The capture of the health delivery system by managed care makes such complaints as likely to damage one's career as a malpractice action. For reasons discussed in this chapter, if a mental health provider

* This chapter first appeared as a series of columns in *Massachusetts Psychologist* (May, June, and July, 1993), and has been reprinted with permission.

is found to have violated the Ethical Principles and receives a disciplinary sanction, however minor, there is a good chance that he or she will be permanently barred from managed care participation. The frequency of these complaints seems to be growing exponentially. In fiscal 1992, in Massachusetts, more than 80 complaints were filed with the Social Work and Psychology Boards.

This increase can hardly be a surprise to anyone who has followed the intense media attention to therapist-patient sexual misconduct both nationally and in Massachusetts. One of the offshoots of this publicity about such cases is that consumers are becoming more informed and sophisticated about available disciplinary remedies if they are aggrieved by their therapeutic treatment. The recent Massachusetts Legislative Task Force on Therapist-Patient Sexual Abuse on which I served recommended distribution of a brochure to all clients that describes in detail all the disciplinary remedies available to aggrieved consumers. Although the brochure focuses on sexual abuse, it will clearly be read by those with other grievances.

In addition, the increase in disciplinary complaints is an indirect result of the explosion of knowledge about the etiology and treatment of Post-traumatic Stress Disorder, particularly complex PTSD. Many providers feel that trauma theory presents a better model for explaining and understanding most cases that had previously been diagnosed as DSM-III-R Axis II Borderline Personality Disorders and other character disorders. Many experts in the treatment of PTSD caused by early physical and sexual abuse have asserted that public confrontation of the traumatizer/victimizer is an important stage in a victim's recovery. A side effect of this process has been the filing of disciplinary complaints against former therapists by patients who perceived failures in the treatment as retraumatization.

A number of "victim" self-help organizations have sprung up to assist aggrieved individuals. One of the services they are providing is relatively sophisticated consultation about consumer complaints. Many of these groups have, as one would expect, a very broad definition of victimization. Estelle Disch, a codirector of BASTA, Boston Associates to Stop Therapy Abuse, has written that "Taking action against the therapist is in most cases an effective form of empowerment and healing once the pain and frustration of the complaint process is over."

The nature of the professional disciplinary process creates enormous risks for accused mental health professionals. The primary responsibility of a licensing authority is to protect the consuming public, not to protect licensees. This means that there is at least a finger on the scale in favor of the complainant-patient in any licensing board disciplinary proceeding. Further, professional disciplinary bodies have been appalled by the data that has been put forward concerning the extent of therapist-patient sexual abuse and the public criticism that this is, in part, the result of the failure of the profession to exercise its self-regulatory responsibilities. Many lawyers have observed that licensing boards have developed a far more prosecutorial perspective, which slants the process unfairly toward consumers. Some have described the professional's task as proving that the presumption of guilt is unjustified. Since a license to practice a profession is a privilege, these bodies have considerably more leeway and are less bound by due process and evidentiary restrictions in prosecuting and sanctioning providers who they feel are violating professional standards. Unlike in a malpractice case, one need only prove that the standard of care was breached or that one of the Principles was violated. There is no need to prove damage occurred or that the damage was related to the breach. In fact, the disciplinary body is free to sanction a provider for conduct that had nothing to do with the complaint. Further, the disciplinary bodies have overlapping jurisdiction. Thus, representation is relatively expensive and is often not covered by malpractice insurance.

Obviously, there are things to applaud about this new trend. Therapist sexual abuse of patients is a major problem that needed to be forcefully addressed. There are many other types of therapist intentional misconduct and gross negligence that clearly cry out for tough enforcement actions and severe disciplinary sanctions.

The problem is that many of the complaints do not involve this kind of serious misconduct. They are brought by patients who are dissatisfied with the results of their treatment and are asserting that their therapist mishandled the case. Many of the complainants have DSM III-R Axis II diagnoses and have been the victims of serious trauma, usually physical or sexual abuse. They are among the most difficult patients in the therapist's caseload. There is considerable variance between their perception of what happened and that of their therapist. When one retrospectively examines these cases, it is usually possible to find some things that could have been handled differently. Often, there are clear mistakes, even negligence. However, there is nothing that indicates any intent to harm or exploit a patient. Usually, the opposite is true. Often, these are what I call "there, but for the grace of God, go I" cases. They could happen to any of us. These are not people who deserve to have their careers seriously damaged or destroyed. But in the managed care environment, this can easily be the result.

For those who feel that managed care participation is important to their future practices, disciplinary complaints are anathema. To simplify a complex subject, one of the few sources of "corporate negligence" for a managed care company is "negligent credentialing." If a managed care panel accepts a professional it knew or should have known presented a risk to the public, it can be held liable for that person's future misconduct. To lawyers who represent managed care companies, past disciplinary sanctions present a red flag. Since there are still far more applicants for managed care panels than places, it makes sense for managed care panels to extrude providers who have been disciplined and this is exactly what they are doing. Any disciplinary sanction, whether formal or informal, whether serious or minor, puts most providers on a permanent blacklist.

Professional disciplinary bodies have either been slow to recognize this problem or unwilling to confront it directly. They still think of the complaint process as having a primarily educational and not punitive agenda. This educational orientation means that many of these complaints are resolved by a warning letter and/or informal agreements for supervision and/or therapy between the disciplinary body and the practitioner. These informal agreements are not seen as serious sanctions, so disciplinary bodies impose them more liberally than would otherwise seem justified. In the past, these informal disciplinary arrangements were difficult and inconvenient, but could be handled without much interference with one's professional career. But managed care has changed that.

There are steps that professionals can take to manage these risks, which can reduce the possibility of both complaints and sanctions. But this is also a structural problem that needs to be addressed by the profession.

THE DEVELOPMENT OF A RISK MANAGEMENT STRATEGY

Since any disciplinary sanction could have a potentially devastating impact on a psychologist's professional career, it is crucial that we all develop and integrate "risk management" strategies into our professional practices. In this section, I would like to focus briefly on some basic risk management steps a psychotherapist can follow that will minimize the risk that a complaint will be filed and minimize the possibility of an adverse consequence if such an unfortunate event occurs. Obviously, the space restrictions of this chapter make it impossible to do more than give brief, simplified descriptions of what often are complex processes.

In my experience, disciplinary complaints that do not involve intentionally harmful conduct or gross negligence have two similarities. First, with the benefit of hindsight, it is usually possible to identify the factors that led to the problems in treatment, which then led to the complaint. It is then possible to identify ways the case could have been handled more effectively, which might have alleviated the problem. Second, the complaint usually presents a very different version of events than the one remembered by the practitioner. Often the practitioner will firmly believe that the complainant has "grossly distorted" what actually happened. The complainant is equally firm in his or her belief in the "truth" of the presentation. Thus, the practitioner's task is to demonstrate, to the extent possible, that (1) whatever went wrong in the treatment was not the result of unprofessional conduct, but, at worst, the kind of good faith mistake that is often unavoidable in our business and (2) that his or her version of events is the most credible. Practitioners can best demonstrate credibility by showing they handled the case professionally and that they generally practice in a competent and professional manner.

RECOGNITION AND CONTROL OF RISK IN ONE'S PRACTICE

Obviously, the first step in any risk management strategy is the ability to recognize risk before it becomes a problem. This requires a good working knowledge of one's ethical and legal responsibilities. It includes studying the published Ethical Principles and Professional Standards and the laws and regulations that govern professional practice. It also includes a good working knowledge of causes and frequencies of malpractice and disciplinary complaints.

A mental health professional should also be aware of clinical situations that involve high risk. To oversimplify, the four highest risk situations are (1) working with a client who has a primary diagnosis on Axis II of DSM-III-R and/or who has been the victim of a serious trauma, particularly physical or sexual abuse in childhood or adolescence, (2) working with a potentially violent or suicidal patient, (3) working with a patient who is involved in a contested divorce or custody case, and (4) working in a case where there is an unusually rapid or intense transference or countertransference. In each of these situations, the mental health professional should be certain that he or she has the training and experience necessary before undertaking treatment. The practitioner may also wish to try to limit the number of this type of cases in his or her caseload at any one time. In order to preserve the opportunity to appropriately select their patients, mental health professionals should make a formal division between evaluation and treatment. Patients should be informed that one of the purposes of the evaluation period is for both parties to determine whether or not the therapist is the best professional to provide the requested treatment. If the mental health professional decides not to undertake treatment during the evaluation period, it would be difficult to accuse him or her of abandonment. If one is participating in a managed care system, with its short-term, problem-oriented treatment focus, the evaluation period will have to be limited to one or two sessions.

INFORMED CONSENT

This structured information about the nature of the evaluation process is one component of an informed consent process, which is a central part of any risk management strategy. All practitioners should develop an informed consent policy that either is given to the patient in written form or is delivered orally and noted in one's records. That statement should include specific ground rules of therapy, the risks and benefits, the business aspects, limits to confidentiality and the implications of third-party management of insurance benefits. On first hearing this suggestion, many mental health providers express a fear that providing this information will damage the therapeutic relationship, cause patients to be more anxious than necessary, cause them to abandon needed therapy, and diminish willingness to reveal important data about themselves. Anecdotal information from those who have adopted and used a 5-page contract that I developed indicates that, for the most part, these adverse consequences do not occur. Most patients are grateful to receive the information, and many consider it an aid, rather than a detriment to the therapeutic process.

Informed consent clearly has an ongoing clinical component. Certain aspects of informed consent cannot be standardized nor can they be meaningfully communicated at the onset of treatment. Both the substance and the timing of certain information has to be tailored to the particular dynamics of the patient and the dynamics of the therapy. Even when the therapist knows the particular risks and benefits of treatment of a specific client, the client may not be able to tolerate their explication until there is a firmer alliance. With trauma victims in particular, informed consent is not a one-shot event, but rather an ongoing process of mutual information sharing and evaluation of risk.

Many trauma experts emphasize the important role of cognitive psychoeducation as part of the treatment strategy. Part of the rationale includes the recognition that patients need to be intellectually warned and prepared for what they are going to experience so the experience will not be as overwhelming. It is a method of normalizing that which does not feel normal. Informed consent can be seen as a part of the psychoeducational process. The rationale for informed consent is really quite similar. It is to help clients intellectually understand what they can expect from the treatment and what the risks and benefits are. If patients are warned of the risks in advance, they are likely to feel more control and, conversely, less anger and betrayal when risks occur.

CONSULTATION

In my judgment, any mental health professional, no matter how senior or experienced, who accepts a case in one of the high-risk categories would be wise to be involved in a formal consultative-supervisory relationship where that case is regularly discussed and notes are taken of the discussion. If consultation is properly used, it will often prevent a complaint by avoiding or responding to the problem before it reaches crisis proportions. Even if a complaint is filed, it provides real corroborative support for the mental health professional's version of events, and professional support for the clinical interventions that the mental health professional undertook to resolve the problems which were developing in the therapeutic relationship. The form and content of consultative relationships can vary considerably, depending on the practitioner's experience, expertise, and practice situation. It can be a peer supervision group made up of one's colleagues, or a more formal, one-on-one consultation. It can take place once a week, once a month, or on a PRN basis.

In addition to ongoing consultation, the mental health professional should seek additional consultation when substantial problems in the treatment can be foreseen or are developing. The optimal consultation will consider the problem from both a clinical and legal perspective, examining the risks and benefits of a number of interventions. The "best" solution is the one that minimizes interference with clinical goals and reduces risk to a level acceptable to the clinician. Obviously, acceptable levels of risk will vary from individual to individual. One should periodically consider consultation in all difficult cases. If the thought of consultation makes you anxious, that is one of the best reasons to do it.

Unlike the ongoing consultation relationships, the pre-"crisis" consultation should be with a senior expert who is not professionally involved with the mental health professional and/or the particular case. The consultant should be paid for the consultation and careful notes taken. The mental health professional should present not only what he or she is doing and why, but what he or she has considered and rejected. If it is clinically and financially possible, the patient should be seen by the consultant. Once the case has been carefully explored with the consultant, the advice given should be followed, or else the mental health professional will place him- or herself at high risk. If the mental health professional disagrees with the consultant's judgment, he or she may seek additional consultations.

RECORDS AND RECORD KEEPING

The mental health professional has to have competent, complete contemporaneous records of the treatment which present a picture that is internally consistent and allows one to demonstrate both professional competence and corroboration of one's version of events if it is necessary to respond to a complaint or lawsuit. This should include an accurate diagnosis and appropriate treatment plan. If the mental health professional is going to assert that the patient's version of events is distorted, this needs to be consistent with the clinical analysis of the client's problems that is contained in the records. The mental health professional also should be able to demonstrate how he or she attempted to resolve the problem if the client presented it to him or her during the treatment process. The style of the record should be progress notes as opposed to process notes, clear unequivocal statements about what happened and why, and clinical conclusions supported by empirical observations from the treatment and statements made by the patient. Have a relatively complete treatment plan that includes an adequate history, complete with answers to questions designed to elicit evidence of high risk, such as "Have you ever thought of harming yourself or someone else?" If these questions are answered in the affirmative, they should be thoroughly and completely followed up. The treatment plan should also contain clear goals for treatment, which have been discussed with and consented to by the patient. If there is any evidence of affective disorders, or other conditions that have been effectively treated with medication, there should be notes of a discussion of the possibility that a medication evaluation might be valuable. If a practitioner has a thorough treatment plan, session notes can be very brief if therapy is proceeding smoothly. If a situation develops in the treatment which suggests that a situation or crisis with a high level of risk attached is likely to develop, the session notes should become complete risk/benefit analyses of available options. In addition to a description of what the therapist does and why he or she does it, these notes require a thorough explication of other strategies or actions considered and the reasons they were rejected. Risk management notation is a lot like ninth-grade algebra. If someone is filing a complaint or a lawsuit against you, your answer is going to be suspect. If you "show your work," you may still be able to get at least partial credit.

UNDERSTANDING AND COPING WITH THE PROFESSIONAL DISCIPLINARY PROCESS

Since even the best risk management strategy may not protect a mental health professional from disciplinary complaints, this section will focus on how a mental health professional should respond if such a complaint is filed against him or her. Much of this advice also applies to a complaint filed with a Professional Association Ethics Committee, although there are some basic differences between the two procedures. This section is based on experience in Massachusetts and direct knowledge about several other New England states. There is obviously a great deal of variety among the 50 states and between licensing boards of different mental health disciplines.

A mental health professional will first officially learn of a complaint on receipt of a certified letter from the Investigation Unit of the Boards of Registration announcing that a named person has filed a complaint. The letter will enclose a copy of the complaint and will instruct the licensee to respond in writing, usually within 10 days. A formal complaint, no matter how frivolous, distorted, or unfair it may appear to the mental health professional, is serious and should be treated as such. The first thing a mental health professional should do is consult an attorney who has real experience with disciplinary complaints, particularly in the mental health arena. A mental health professional who believes that it is too expensive to consult an attorney or who refuses, on principle or out of anger, to let this patient impose those costs upon him or her is taking an enormous risk with his or her career.

Usually the attorney will call the investigator assigned to the case and ask for additional time to prepare a response. In my experience, the investigators are uniformly reasonable and extensions are routinely granted.

A great deal of care should be exercised in preparing a written response to the complaint. In addition to defending oneself against the specific allegations that have been made, the response is also the mental health provider's first opportunity to demonstrate his or her professional competence and professionalism. In most cases, the complainant's version of events will appear quite distorted to the mental health professional. In those cases, the professional should first present a thorough description of the treatment, including the initial treatment plan, and then respond to specific allegations in conclusions. This presents the mental health professional's behaviors in the most positive light, rather than purely in reaction to the allegations. While the professional should include his or her clinical explanation for the distortions and his or her understanding of why the patient may have filed the complaint, the clinician should treat the patient with appropriate professional respect and avoid appearing to blame the client or his or her pathology for the complaint. A good response would develop three or four themes and cite facts or ideas in support of each one.

After the Board considers the written response, in most cases it will ask the mental health professional to attend an informal hearing with a committee of the full Board. For reasons discussed in the balance of this section, this informal hearing is often the most crucial factor in determining the outcome of the proceeding, so great care should be taken in preparing for it. The complainant is not present but has usually met with the committee sometime before the hearing takes place. This hearing is labeled informal because it is part of the investigative process and no final legal action arises from it. It gives the Board the chance to see the mental health professional, assess his or her skills, and take his or her measure as a practitioner. Since the Board considers that its primary responsibility is to protect the public from inappropriate psychological practice, many who have experienced this proceeding consider it to be "prosecutorial" in nature. Very difficult questions may be asked which feel quite accusatory in both tone and content. It is often the case that the complainant has raised additional concerns, and these can also be a subject of inquiry, even when the mental health professional has no prior notice. The clinician will often be asked questions that require subjective judgments and that often go beyond the specific complaint to more global questions about one's practice and techniques. Almost everyone I have represented has described the procedure as provoking serious anxiety.

The mental health professional should be thoroughly prepared substantively, tactically, and emotionally for the informal hearing. It is helpful to engage in several practice sessions to become comfortable verbalizing the themes from the written response. To the extent possible, the licensee should also practice responding to anticipated questions. The mental health professional should also have spent some time processing his or her feelings about the complainant so that they will not be acted out or otherwise interfere with the professionalism of the presentation.

Unless the mental health professional has actually engaged in serious misconduct, I believe that it is unwise to employ an adversarial, legalistic strategy at the informal hearing stage. The mental health professional should attempt to answer all questions professionally, honestly, and fully. Although this means that the role of legal counsel at the hearing is somewhat limited, it is nonetheless very important that one's lawyer attend. First, my clients have stated that it is very reassuring and supportive to have an advocate present who understands the procedure and who can speak up if there is a problem or a need for clarification. Second, since the procedure is so anxiety provoking, even the best prepared mental health professionals may require prompting about some of the most important points. Finally, one's counsel can raise some points independently, ask clarifying questions and in other ways add to a mental health professional's defense, including making legal points and substantive arguments.

There is some dispute as to the best strategy for responding to complaints. Some attorneys feel that if the provider admits even minor mistakes or retrospective misgivings, the Disciplinary Body will feel compelled to take some disciplinary action because of its responsibility to consumers. Although it varies depending on who the practitioner is and what he or she is charged with, I believe it is often valuable at the informal hearing for the mental health professional to acknowledge good faith mistakes and/or identify issues that, in retrospect, might have been handled differently. However, this should only be done in a planned manner, after consultation with one's attorney and at least one clinical consultant. This is particularly true when the complaint has been filed by a very difficult client where dissatisfaction was quite likely, if not inevitable. Ours is not a profession which provides one with the opportunity for perfection. All mental health professionals make mistakes in treatment. Being able to recognize problems in the treatment and develop strategies to cope with them is one of the indicators of a competent psychotherapist. This is particularly true if one recognized the problem and sought consultation during the treatment and has good notes to prove it.

If the Board believes that there has been a violation of the law or of its regulations, which include the ethical principles of mental health professionals, it may either refer the matter for a formal administrative hearing to revoke or suspend a license, or it may seek to negotiate a mutually acceptable solution called a consent agreement. Except for the most serious ethical violations, such as sexual misconduct or indicators of gross incompetence, the vast majority of cases are resolved through such consent agreements.

Consent agreements typically require the acknowledgment of a violation. Because a consent agreement is a public document, these admissions can have adverse consequences and care should be taken around the precise wording. Consent agreements can also require that the mental health professional accept a sanction such as a reprimand, have supervision, enter therapy, or all three. Consent agreements are just that—agreements—and a mental health professional, or counsel, can negotiate the terms with the Board or his or her attorney. Both parties should be looking for a fair and equitable solution. There is pressure on both sides to settle the matter. A formal hearing is quite expensive for the complainant, and also takes considerable time and energy for a volunteer Board with limited resources.

Unfortunately, the complaint process takes a very long time to sort itself out. The Board consists of volunteers with very little staff support and its resources are stretched in a way that seriously limits its ability to operate in a timely manner. This is the fault of the state funding system, and not the members of the Board, who I believe are most uncomfortable with the shortcomings imposed on them by this resource shortfall. The Board can only meet once per month to deal with complaints. Thus, it can take a year or more after the informal hearing for a consent agreement to be proposed. In the interim, on managed care applications and malpractice insurance applications, a mental health professional has to include information about the complaint in its unresolved form.

Note. Much of the information in the last section was developed collaboratively with Barry Mintzer, Esq., of Deutsch, Williams, Brooks and DeRensies. Some of it appeared in an article that he wrote for *Focus,* the publication of the Massachusetts Chapter of the National Association of Social Workers. Most of the information about trauma was developed out of discussions with Dr. Stephen Krugman, Ph.D., with whom I consult if confronted with a PTSD patient.

CHAPTER 22

Female Therapists and the Search for a New Paradigm

JUDITH V. JORDAN, PHD

The Stone Center relational approach to therapy was born not from some abstract idea of how developmental and clinical theory "ought" to be. Nor did it grow from some carefully researched body of empirical data. Rather, it grew originally from the dialogues of a group of four clinicians (Jean Baker Miller, Irene Stiver, Jan Surrey, and myself) who felt that existing psychological theories frequently led to misunderstanding rather than understanding of women. In these models, women were seen as "too dependent," "too emotional," not rational enough, "too needy," "hysterical," "masochistic." These judgments arose in a system that defined "normative maturity" by male standards: autonomous, self-sufficient, rational, objective, and task oriented rather than relationship oriented. We felt, instead, that life is characterized by movement in relationships and that psychological growth occurs in human connections rather than apart from them. Our process as a theory-building group reflected our message: our ideas and models arose among us, in connection, and our thoughts, values, and convictions are woven together, with particularity, but are part of a common, jointly created pattern.

As therapists, supervisors, and at times, as clients, we were paying attention to our own subjective experiences of what felt wrong with existing clinical attitudes and techniques. Slowly, we began to examine how our models could be different, pointing to what we hoped would be a better understanding of women's experiences. Following the lead taken by Jean Baker Miller in her visionary book *Toward a New Psychology of Women* in 1976, we sought to clarify our value orientations and to look at women clients in their social context rather than as solely intrapsychic beings to be changed by psychological treatment.

Briefly, the core ideas in our model suggest that (1) women grow through and in connection, (2) for women, especially, connection with others is central to psychological well-being, and (3) movement toward relational mutuality optimally occurs throughout life, through mutual empathy, responsiveness, and contribution to the growth of each individual and to the relationship (Jordan, 1983; Miller, 1986; Stiver, 1984; Surrey, 1985). Our model focuses not so much on "self-development" as on "relational development." The primary unit of interest and study for much of Western psychology has been the "separate self." We are suggesting that a woman's sense of self is formed in relationship, what has been called "self-in-relation," "relational self," or "relational being." We are also suggesting that the relationship and relational processes become central in our clinical and developmental theories.

In keeping with this emphasis, the relational approach points to disconnection and isolation as major sources of human suffering. Jean Baker Miller has used the phrase "condemned isolation" (Miller, 1986) to capture the sense of immobilization and self-blame that characterizes the terrible pain of being disconnected from others. I have spoken about the sense of being cut off from "empathic possibility" (Jordan, 1989). This involves the inner conviction that another person could not possibly be empathically attuned to me because my being is so profoundly flawed, putting me "beyond the pale" of human acceptability.

The thrust of therapy that grows from this model is to help the client reestablish a sense of empathic possibility and movement or growth in relationship. This involves the establishment of mutual empathy and empowerment. We focus on disconnections occurring in the person's life as well as in the therapy setting itself. And we work toward the emergence of what I have called "relational resilience" (Jordan, 1992). In a relationship, there are inevitable failures of connection, with ensuing movement into disconnection. Disconnections are the expected consequences of empathic failures, misunderstandings, and other sources of hurt. Therapy allows us to bring awareness to these disconnections, creating the possibility of moving back into connection. Not only is this particular relationship strengthened in the process of building relational awareness and competence, but all relationships are potentially enhanced when we become more aware of our own patterns of disconnection. We build skills in repairing and enhancing relationships, leading to transformation of relational patterns.

For the therapist, this attunement to movement through gradations of connection and disconnection involves a heightened awareness of his or her own propensities to move into disconnection as well as to the client's difficulties. While traditional theories of therapy emphasize the dangers of a countertransference that involves "overinvolvement" or "loss of distance," we point to the equally damaging effects of the therapist who distances too much, who hides in unarticulated and unexamined power, or who sees therapy as a one-directional relationship.

Movement away from traditional patterns of therapeutic practice inevitably creates tensions, vulnerabilities, and potential hazards for the therapist. Our theory suggests there is mutuality in therapy in the sense that, in addition to the more obvious goal of the client being changed by the contact with the therapist, it is important that the client have an emotional impact on the therapist as well. But many traditional approaches to therapy have warned us about the dangers of moving away from therapeutic "neutrality." At the extreme, they prescribe a "blank screen" presentation from the therapist, with a dearth of emotional display or personal responsiveness. We suggest, instead, the development of mutual empathy. What exactly do we mean by mutuality and mutual empathy in therapy? By definition, empathy is about being emotionally "moved"; when we empathize with people, we are "touched" by them. They influence us, stir a response in us, possibly transform us. We are vulnerable to being changed in directions we might not be totally in charge of. And for empathy to make a difference, the client must also see the impact she or he has on us and be affected, be touched by it in return. Mutual empathy means we are *both* affecting each other and we are aware of this mutuality. Empathic attunement that resides only in one person does not effect change (and perhaps it should not really be called empathy as we use the term). Change happens only when that emotional resonance is experienced and known by both people. This is what we mean by "mutual empathy" in the therapy relationship.

We are not suggesting the relationship between therapist and client is equal or symmetrical; the therapist has a goal to provide a certain kind of attention and care, and the client is there to get help with suffering, to change in some direction that will bring about a greater sense of well-being or "health." Each has a role that carries different responsibilities; each also has a different kind of power. The therapist carries the power of the professional, the so-called expert; he or she actively sets certain parameters of the treatment (location, ground rules of what gets talked about, confidentiality, financial constraints, timing). There is also a power that resides for the therapist in being less seen or known, often mystified; transference confers additional power on the therapist. Although the client carries less of this structural or social power, he or she often carries a kind of emotional power: what gets discussed, how intense the affect is, whether or not there is movement around certain areas of pain often depend on the client. This emotional power, however, is generally less validated. Whatever the configurations of power, we are suggesting that it is essential to take them into account, to try to be aware of power dynamics in the way that one is aware of the other forces in therapy.

UNCERTAINTY

In embracing any new paradigm, one moves from behind the protective armor of the accepted theory and dogma. Often in the field of psychotherapy, the professional is not buttressed with solid scientific data to support the models of practice that one is building. Support from a group of respected colleagues, while essential, can sometimes feel insubstantial when compared with volumes and volumes of clinical literature expounding on the virtues of one of the more established approaches or another. And we forget that often these practitioners and theoreticians once stood on very similar, uncertain ground advocating courageous, revolutionary but unsubstantiated models for psychological treatment in their own time. Often the first response to new theory is "This is outrageous, crazy, and even dangerous!" These same people, years later, will frequently attest, about the very same theory, "We've known all this all along. We've been doing it this way for years. This is nothing new. It is so obvious that this makes sense!"

Using a relational model, therapists are invited to be more real, more vulnerable, more mutual than many traditional psychodynamic models advocate; I am suggesting that dogma, and even much of good theory, is often used to protect and mystify the therapist rather than assist the client. In our model, the therapist must assume a responsibility to regulate and modulate mutuality in such a way that the client's interests are at all times at the core of the treatment. Respect and appropriate protection of the client's vulnerability are essential.

In working from a new theory, the therapist is always struggling with issues of uncertainty and vulnerability. A quote from the poet Keats regarding negative capability is one of the most useful guides I have come across in doing psychotherapy, particularly psychotherapy that departs from more traditional theory. Keats writes about "the capacity to be in uncertainties, Mysteries [sic], doubts, without any irritable reaching after fact and reason" (1987, p. 43). In moving from the more traditional theories of therapy in which I was trained, I had to surrender the certainty that they provided. But that very certainty often felt wrong, and sometimes destructive to the clients I was working with. It sometimes kept me from really hearing and knowing them; it kept me locked in a position or image of myself or them. At times, it led to wrong understanding. I did not really allow myself to see the world from their perspective or know their pain or respond to it. I was too busy explaining them to myself (or an imagined supervisor); or I was feeling ashamed that I could not find a way to apply the old esteemed theories in a better way. I assumed initially that any difficulties I had in using these theories were due to some problem within me. Supervisors sought to convince me that when the theories didn't work, it was because the patients were "resistant" or untreatable in some way. Between my own personalizing of failures and the system's tendency to "blame the victim," it took a long time to gain the insight that perhaps the theories were in error.

In a relational approach, we are moving away from a model of therapy as a mechanistic approach to one which acknowledges that the whole being of the therapist is crucial to the movement and understanding of the relationship. How we do therapy is a lot about how we are as people. The therapist must be ready to experience a fair amount of vulnerability in this process. Relational therapy does not rely on a clear set of skills that can be easily mastered and then carried from client to client. Rather, therapists are challenged to stay in connection, to stay in awareness and open to learning in the face of their own vulnerability and limitation. This often leads to the experience of doubt, uncertainty, and potentially shame, the sense that our very "being" has failed us, the process, and the client.

VULNERABILITY

Our culture tends to overemphasize problem-focused, instrumental coping styles; these approaches often denigrate the lack of control and potential sense of vulnerability inherent in many situations of personal pain and crisis. As a culture, we tend to value highly task-oriented coping styles. Emotion-focused problem solving (Lazarus & Folkman, 1984) is more characteristic of women's coping styles, and women are socialized to be more comfortable with vulnerability and emotional responses rather than with instrumental responses to difficult situations. Openness to being affected is essential to intimacy and growth-enhancing relationships for all people; without it, people relate inauthentically, adopting roles and coming from distanced and protected places. Open sharing of our need for support or acceptance is essential to developing close connections. The relational model suggests we need to transform an illusory sense of self-sufficiency and a tendency to deny vulnerability toward a realization of supported vulnerability, that is, vulnerability in a supportive or benign context (Jordan, 1992).

As therapists, we must be willing to be in our own vulnerability. This can occur in admitting mistakes or owning temporary lapses in attention (Jordan, 1993). I see one client who is exquisitely sensitive to my levels of stress. This is a woman who grew up in an extremely invalidating and violating family and she had to develop extreme hypervigilance to try to protect herself from frequent, unanticipated abuse as a child. When I began seeing her, several years ago, I often took refuge in a more traditional analytic posture when she would pick up on the lapses in my attention: "You feel I'm not interested in you now? What are your thoughts about why I might be so out of touch with you today?" As my theory and approach shifted, I found myself waiting for her observation of my stress; then I would suggest there might be a kernel of truth in her observation but would ask why was it bothering her so much on this particular occasion. Now as I have moved into a mode of therapy based more in mutuality, I often anticipate her observation of my occasional emotional unavailability during a session and note, "This is one of those times when my stress level is high. I just wanted to let you know. I'll do the best I can to be here for you but you will probably notice that I'm not as present as I sometimes can be. This is about me, not you." This allows her not to personalize my failure in a way that in the past always led her to feel either ashamed or enraged. She still has a right to her anger at me for not being there for her in a better way, but it does not leave her feeling like "the bad one." As a therapist, I no longer feel comfortable pretending that exploring her fantasies about my inattention is the most useful thing for her, although at times it might be of some use. It also might obscure my own inadequacies both from her and from me. Nor do I need to go into a lengthy or detailed description of exactly what is causing my failure in that moment; I simply have to validate her experience of me as less present. A part of what I want her to learn from and with me is that we can both be fallible and still connect. In fact, in naming the disconnection and locating responsibility for it in my failure, we actually begin the movement back into connection. The typical mystification of the therapist in these situations leaves the therapist "looking good" but also leads to inauthentic connection and the illusion of a perfectible human being who is above stress, moods, uncertainties, and mistakes. The inevitable result in such obfuscation is invalidation of the client and further disconnection.

A relational model suggests that we must move out of models of narcissistic perfection if we are to become whole, productive, and connected beings. As a therapist, then, I must be ready to surrender the investment in my own image as "the expert," perfectly empathic human being, or whatever else I am attached to as a positive image of myself as therapist. One client I saw for several years, another sexual abuse survivor, tested my investment in an image of myself as a "good" therapist by phoning many of my colleagues and former supervisors to report each empathic failure or stupid thing I said to her in our therapy sessions. She was a highly accurate reporter! Each time I failed in understanding her in some way that she found intolerable, she called one of these other people to complain in excruciating detail about my mistakes. Initially, again using an old model, I tried to interpret this as "acting-out." Only slowly did I come to see that she had figured out a very wise way to keep our relationship public, and thus safe. This was someone who had been abused behind the closed doors of her bedroom as a child, and she was making sure that abuse in a supposedly close and caring relationship would not happen again. At the same time, she was able to ascertain whether I would "really be there for her," or whether I would betray her as her childhood violators had, to take care of my own needs rather than hers. One of the clear hazards of working from a relational model that stresses authenticity and looking at our own responsibility for disconnections is that we as therapists really do have to come face to face with our own limitations. We cannot assume that the client is the only one who connects in less than perfect ways. And at times, we have to let others, including clients and colleagues, see these difficulties and flaws as well.

Vulnerability of another kind, involving sadness, arose when I was in deep grief following the death of my mother and I was occasionally tearful in sessions. One client was a particularly nonaffective individual who had not cried with me or her two previous therapists; she described being separated from the world by a Plexiglas shield. On one occasion, I began to shed tears as she spoke unemotionally of her grandmother's death the year before. She suddenly stopped and said "You're crying about your mother right now aren't you? I've felt so bad for you . . . I'm so sorry." In my obvious and palpable vulnerability, I genuinely thanked her for her caring. She too began to cry. She and I shared these tears quietly. All my traditional training would have suggested that I had "lost my boundaries" or made the mistake of letting my client take care of me. Obviously, if we had moved into her actively and persistently comforting me, this would have been problematic. But this human, mutual exchange became a turning point in our work together. She grew into more emotional authenticity, and I came to better appreciate both her possible responsiveness and the awful pain of disconnection that she had emerged from. I saw how very difficult it had been for her, how ashamed she was of her cutoffness, and how my vulnerability really allowed her to move into a new place of connection with herself and with me.

BOUNDARIES

The mention of mutuality in psychotherapy often creates misapprehension and anxiety for many who are traditionally trained. They protest: "But what about the maintenance of boundaries? Aren't you worried that therapists will violate clients? Doesn't this open the door to the therapist abusing the client in subtle ways, by asking for psychological assistance from the client? Doesn't this put the therapist at risk for being too vulnerable?"

Therapy is not a meeting of two people who have complete freedom to define their relationship. Goals and expectations accompany the roles of therapist and client. The therapist is committed to helping; the client is committed to getting help. The therapist belongs to a profession that has a set of standards of care. Protective limits are crucial to this relationship; there should never be sexual interaction between therapist and client; the therapist's needs should never become the focus of treatment; confidentiality of the client must be protected. I feel it is essential to respect the client and that there be clarity regarding the therapeutic task. Respect, clarity, and responsibility for the well-being of the client on the part of the therapist capture better for me the values that are often tagged with the word "boundary."

The concept of boundaries has become a particularly complicated one in psychotherapy. Any approach that challenges old models of nongratification or neutrality and suggests the importance of mutuality must address the issue of boundaries. What is usually implied in the concept of the need for boundaries in therapy is the need to protect the vulnerability of the client, not to transgress, not to violate the client by using the client for our own needs; it also underscores the need for clarity about what feelings and thoughts are arising in which person. Additionally, it is thought to be useful for the client to learn that the therapist has a need to maintain his or her "boundaries" as well.

I strongly support the need for protecting the client's vulnerability; furthermore, therapists should never use the client for their own needs (I deplore the subtle and major violations that occur and I have actively sought to bring some accountability to our profession around the issue of sexual abuse of clients by therapists). I think it is essential that therapists have clarity about what are their issues and what are the concerns of their clients; *clarity,* rather than boundedness feels important to me. And I am equally convinced of how essential *respect* is for the client. My problem with the concept of boundaries is that it builds on the individualistic notion that safety lies in being "armored against," shut off from other people. This derives from the "separate self" paradigm which suggests that safety occurs in the development of self-sufficiency, autonomy, and power over others. A relational model suggests that real safety, growth, and development occurs through relatedness not separation.

Mutuality is based on respect, personal and relational clarity, and principles of nonviolation and empowerment. With all of these forces operating, we do not need an additional concept of "boundaries" that connotes a molecular, containment model of self. Both people must have the right to say no, to state their limits as well as to seek responsiveness in the other. I prefer to talk about "stating limits" rather than "setting limits"; the latter suggests a powerful person is dealing with a powerless and demanding person (like a spoiled child). The former acknowledges the necessity to be clear about one's personal limitations and to feel the right to state them. Part of being an adult in relationship is learning to respect the other person's limits and flaws. This feels like a better route to genuine and mature relatedness than basing relationship on one "powerful," "in-charge" person setting limits on an "out-of-control" other who is reined in by force or superior power. It is important to see that the concept of boundaries is laden with power inequity and does not support the client in her development of new relational patterns.

Another problem with the traditional notion of boundaries is that it often leaves the client feeling abandoned. And it is invoked with just those clients who are most sensitive to abandonment: often those people who have suffered major violations in their early relationships (e.g., sexual abuse, physical abuse, or traumatic abandonment). When applied to these populations, a heavy emphasis on "limit setting," boundaries, working on the negative transference, and seeing the person as "manipulative" can in fact exacerbate their sense of isolation and lead to increasingly maladaptive efforts at making connection.

Thus I think it is important for clients to learn about personal limitations in terms of what we can give and how we can respond; and it is important to learn to grapple with yearnings and needs in the face of another's unavailability. Much can be learned in the course of these struggles and explorations. I do not see what is gained, by the implication that this client is "too needy," "demanding," or "manipulative" in the face of what treaters feel is perfectly "reasonable" and necessary boundary maintenance, a stance that is often taken with the so-called borderline personality. I have taken to referring to this diagnostic category as "so-called" because I find the diagnosis so damaging for the people to whom it is applied. When used, it often alerts me to anger and a sense of helplessness on the part of the therapist that would perhaps be better grappled with more honestly by the treater rather than in dismissive and distancing diagnostic labels. And furthermore, this diagnosis seems to lead away from an empathic stance into a more confrontive and adversarial one. And such a stance, in my experience, is iatrogenic: further cut off, invalidated, and judged, the client increases maladaptive efforts to establish a real and safe sense of connection.

MUTUALITY

Mutuality in therapy does not mean personal disclosure on the part of the therapist, particularly of details of one's life. It certainly does not involve the therapist turning to the client for support or help in handling any of the therapist's life problems. It also does not involve equal emotional involvement or display, although the therapist's emotional responsiveness is a part of mutuality. But it is always a modulated responsiveness, an emotional presence that is filtered through the therapist's caring attention to the well-being of the client.

The invitation to be real, while appealing in the abstract and often deeply satisfying in reality, can also be frightening and challenging. When we as therapists engage in therapy in a way that suggests we are open to being emotionally touched or changed, we move into uncharted territories. While we maintain a commitment to protection and positive change in the client, we cannot be sure of our own paths of growth or pain in this deeply interpersonal process. We have a responsibility to make sure that whatever our responsiveness, we remain in good connection to ensure the therapeutic goals. But within those parameters, we may also discover new, possibly painful, truths about ourselves. We may also come upon new and wonderful possibilities in ourselves.

But if I take seriously the task of mutuality, I must open myself to being influenced by my clients, not just in the pleasant moments of empathic joining or of watching them move from some place of pain or paralysis. I must feel their pain resonate with my own pain. I must look at shutdown places in myself. Sometimes, I must bring to life memories I would rather leave in darkness. I must take certain risks, become vulnerable as a human being. All this I must do, as I continue to hold fast to my primary goal of helping this person change and grow. This is no easy task.

CHARTING NEW TERRITORY

In a field that aspires to scientific objectivity but often appears more truly allied with the arts, and in which the skills learned are very subjective, it is not surprising that practitioners experience a high level of insecurity about the validity of their practices. In such situations, consensus and precedent weigh heavily. Although these often steer us in useful directions, they also can create huge blind spots and failures of creativity (witness the profession's failure to grasp the reality of sexual abuse of children for so many years). Most steps forward in the field of psychotherapy have occurred when one or several creative and courageous individuals dared to state a view of reality that differed from the mainstream theories. Often these individuals were subject to ridicule, rejection, or harassment. To continue to follow a particular course in the face of such reactions is not easy. There is often a real sense of risk and uncertainty.

To chart new territory in psychotherapy is difficult at best, hazardous at worst. One is always cautious about making generalizations. Each generalization is fraught with complexities and pitfalls; yet trainees and young clinicians are hungry for guidelines, which so often must take the form of generalizations. Once ensconced in established theory (which often has not been demonstrated to be of particular use with certain populations but which nevertheless carries the authority of years of usage), the clinician feels safer. The dictums flow more easily despite the questionable helpfulness of them in many cases. As a woman, I question so many of the theoretical guidelines for doing therapy with women, and yet they stand squarely at the center of much established practice. But to move outside these sturdy and buttressed practices leaves the professional often feeling lonely, potentially vulnerable, and open to shame.

NEED FOR COLLEGIAL SUPPORT

The pursuit of a new model of therapy brings with it many places of discomfort and risk; as a therapist, I often feel I am out on a limb. Although my colleagues and I knew in our hearts and minds that the traditional modes of treating women clients were not working, and sometimes were actually destructive, these old ways of doing things had loyal followers and intimidating dogma. Breaking from these traditions also meant being exposed to doubt, possible criticism, and censure. Facing these doubts and criticisms in a purely academic way is hard; but when people's lives and hopes are brought into the picture, the responsibility becomes even more daunting. I am painfully aware that how I work on these issues in therapy has an impact on the people I am working with; they can be helped, they can be hurt. There are no airtight answers. Even though I feel the integrity of the relational approach in a deep way, I must constantly test my beliefs against valued colleagues' wisdom. The need to get support and validation, so integral to the theory of therapy I am doing, then, also becomes imperative to my practice in this model. I must constantly check with other practitioners. While I attempt to steer a steady course, remaining true to the healing relationships I am building with my clients, I must be respectful of critical feedback. The truth I am building with these clients is not a truth in a vacuum; it is a relational truth between us and between us and a larger context. This can become very complicated.

Without this incessant dialogue with others, however, I would not have the courage or the strength to pursue a less traveled path. The work of therapy often feels lonely and treacherous. Backed by well-worn theory, the practitioner can feel an illusory sense of comfort and control. Blazing new trails, the practitioner can feel downright stranded at times. But this very need of others, this belief in a truth built in relationship, this sense of creating in connection is the substance of the theory. It only makes sense that it would also nourish the process of therapy. When uncertainty arises, I bear it, study it, and learn from my interaction with my client and often with valued colleagues. I also learn in the many workshops and lectures I give and with my many students; they, too bring back new insights, validations, questions, pointers where inconsistencies in approach may lead to disconnection or stasis rather than growth.

And most of all, I learn with my clients, my greatest teachers. They keep me honest and focused on the work. They sometimes cause me personal discomfort as they push me to grow or confront split-off places in myself. They sometimes provide me moments of great joy, as they burst into some new freedom or depth. They sometimes vex me or worry me. They seldom bore me. In fact, I am, more than anything else, interested and curious with my clients. Learning lies at the core of my meaning system; I come alive in the questions, in the honest movement toward discovering and creating personal relational truths together. While I am not always comfortable in learning since it involves "not knowing," potentially looking foolish, or feeling anxious, I really believe that it is what life is about. So therapy, for me, is a gift: a place to learn and to help others learn or to rekindle their desire to learn . . . about themselves, about the world.

I have often commented that I'd rather be in a good therapy session than in almost any social situation I can imagine. Some have suggested I am revealing too much of my own personal social limitations in this admission (that may be true), but I feel that, at its best, therapy is about helping people come into their most real and deep places. That is true for both therapist and client. To me, that is a core privilege of being human; to witness and encourage the development of personal truth and the sense of well-being that ensues from that deep connection to oneself and others. And in those places of personal truth, I think we are most clearly connected to a sense of the universal. I suppose that one of the greatest hazards of doing psychotherapy is that we will veer from the emerging truths that we are allowed to know in this powerful and unusual relationship and in that avoidance we will lose contact with ourselves, the other person, and ultimately fail in our pursuit of truth.

REFERENCES

Belenky, M., Clinchy, B., Goldberger, N., & Tarule, J. (1986). *Women's way of knowing: The development of self, voice and mind.* New York: Basic Books.

Gilligan, C. (1982). *In a different voice.* Cambridge, MA: Harvard University Press.

Jordan, J. (1983). Empathy and the mother-daughter relationship. *Work in Progress, No. 2.* Wellesley, MA: Stone Center Working Paper Series.

Jordan, J. (1986). The meaning of mutuality. *Work in Progress, No. 23.* Wellesley, MA: Stone Center Working Paper Series.

Jordan, J. (1989). Relational development: Therapeutic implications of empathy and shame. *Work in Progress, No. 29.* Wellesley, MA: Stone Center Working Paper Series.

Jordan, J. (1992). Relational resilience. *Work in Progress, No. 57.* Wellesley, MA: Stone Center Working Paper Series.

Jordan, J. (1993). Challenges to connection. *Work in Progress, No. 60.* Wellesley, MA: Stone Center Working Paper Series.

Jordan, J., Kaplan, A., Miller, J. B., Stiver, I., Surrey, J. (1991). *Women's growth in connection.* New York: Guilford.

Keats, J. (1987). Letter to "My dear brothers." In R. Gittings (Ed.), *The letters of John Keats.* Oxford: Oxford University Press. (Original letter dated 1818.)

Lazarus, R., & Folkman, S. (1984). *Stress, appraisal and coping.* New York: Springer.

Miller, J. B. (1976). *Toward a new psychology of women.* Boston: Beacon Press.

Miller, J. B. (1986). What do we mean by relationships? *Work in Progress, No. 22.* Wellesley, MA: Stone Center Working Paper Series.

Stiver, I. (1984). The meanings of "dependency" in female-male relationships. *Work in Progress, No. 11.* Wellesley, MA: Stone Center Working Paper Series.

Surrey, J. (1985). Self-in-relation: A theory of women's development. *Work in Progress, No. 13.* Wellesley, MA: Stone Center Working Paper Series.

PART SIX

The Therapist's Renewal

CHAPTER 23

*Prevention: Avoiding Burnout**

WILLIAM N. GROSCH, MD and DAVID C. OLSEN, PHD

Overwork is the curse of our time. Working long hours has become almost a badge of honor among professional people, whose complaints about overwork are often mixed with a sense of pride in their dedication and importance—and perhaps a sense of entitlement, namely that their hard work justifies avoidance and indulgence in other areas of their lives. Nowhere is this ethos of overwork more prevalent than in the helping professions, where the overwhelming demand for service has made long hours expected and honored.

Burnout is reaching epidemic proportions in the helping professions. It is an insidious and complex problem caused not by any one factor but by a combination of environmental and work circumstances, emptiness and drivenness, and an exaggerated need to shore up the self at the expense of real communion with friends and family. More specifically, as we have shown (Grosch & Olsen, 1994), it can be understood from a variety of theoretical frames, including Self psychology, general systems theory, and the multigenerational perspective of Murray Bowen.

All too often, when mental health workers attend conferences or seminars on preventing burnout or dealing with stress, they receive simplistic formulas and advice: exercise more, develop outside interests and hobbies, balance work and play. Such advice is easier to give than to follow. Unfortunately, such commonsense solutions usually do not work and frequently leave people feeling even more frustrated and guilty.

A theory of prevention must take seriously personality issues within the professional, wrestle with the complexities of working in the mental health system, and help the professional find ways of defining him- or herself within that system, as well as finding balance and meaning in life.

---

* This chapter has been modified from Chapter Five of *When Helping Starts to Hurt*, New York: Norton, 1994, by the same authors, and has been reprinted with permission.

Professionals can take several important steps to help prevent burnout. These include realistic self-assessment, investigation of the impact of their family of origin, understanding their own narcissistic issues, utilizing support groups, finding effective supervision, and finally, finding balance in their life.

RECOGNIZING THE SIGNS OF BURNOUT: SELF-ASSESSMENT

Spotting the signs of burnout is rarely as easy as it sounds. Differentiating normal tiredness, tension, and occasional exhaustion from the gradual debilitation of burnout is difficult. To prevent burnout, professionals must learn to distinguish between normal tiredness or tension and the early signs of burnout. Ongoing self-assessment will help them recognize both the early stages of burnout and signs of their susceptibility to it.

Self-assessment in this case has several levels. On the first surface level, helping professionals need to scan their experience periodically, using their observing ego to transcend themselves and their experience and realistically assess how they are doing in several areas of their lives. This involves questioning how much enjoyment and satisfaction they are getting from their work, as well as checking for feelings of enthusiasm and optimism. It includes being sensitive to feelings of dread of going to work, or excessive boredom, or feelings of flatness, tiredness, and pessimism about the future. It means being aware of how often they fantasize about finding a new position or even a new career. These fantasies are often related to perceiving some sense of personal control and a sense that their talents are being put to use in a way that leads to a sense of feeling appreciated. In addition, it means assessing the balance in their activities, and whether they are becoming one-dimensional, thinking, reading, and studying only what is relevant to their profession and neglecting different interests, people, and ideas. Finally, it means honestly assessing their family life, how their spouse and children are doing, and how they fit into the daily family system. Asking for feedback from the spouse and children can be revealing.

When mental health professionals begin to feel flat, tired, or bored, or report many of the same type of symptoms athletes report when they have overtrained, they may try "cross-training." This may involve study leaves, conferences, reading novels, getting away for a long weekend or vacation, or rearranging schedules to allow for hobbies. But perhaps the best idea—and most like cross-training—would be varying the jobs they do at work. Although most bosses are less than enthusiastic about staff refusing assignments, most are quite receptive to staff who initiate requests to try different things. If this works, it is fair to assume that tiredness or perhaps a very early stage of burnout was the problem. If it does not work and feelings of apathy, flatness, and irritability continue, then burnout is more than likely the culprit. People who are burning out do not usually bounce back.

Distinguishing, in self-assessment, between burnout and tiredness can be difficult. Symptoms of burnout could simply mean that a vacation is long overdue; a couple of weeks on a beach might reverse the feelings. It could mean that the therapist needs more variety or flexibility at work. It could also indicate that marital and family problems are exacerbating work-related stress. Self-assessment may identify proactive steps that can be taken to prevent burnout. For example, an alcoholism counselor was able to reverse early burnout by becoming more selectively involved at work. She was able to increase her control by cutting out things that were optional and no longer (if ever) rewarding. She took herself off a few committees. She reinvested in her clinical work by starting up a special therapy group, which turned out to be greatly satisfying, even exciting. She said she felt better because she had expanded the scope of her effectiveness.

If symptoms persist, however, then a more advanced stage of burnout should be diagnosed. A sure sign of burnout is ennui that does not disappear after weekends and vacations. When you come back without feeling refreshed, it may be a sign, not that you need a longer break, but that something more than just a break is needed. At this point, you need to move assessment to two additional levels: family of origin issues, and your own narcissistic vulnerability.

FAMILY OF ORIGIN WORK

When we address significant problems in our lives, we naturally focus on where the hurt is. We want the pain to go away quickly. In the case of professional burnout, we zero in on our disillusionment with work, or on our exhaustion, or maybe on the disappointments or strain on our home life and the way they compound our work stress. In the midst of this pain, the idea of examining the way in which the families we grew up in influenced our roles and scripts for living may seem far removed from the primary problem. Unfortunately, not examining those issues in the interest of solving the problem quickly is much like putting a Band-Aid on an injury that needs more thorough attention. The imprint of our families sets up both roles and unconscious expectations that continue to be played out in our marriages and in our work environments. Only when these patterns, roles, and unconscious expectations are understood and dealt with can we avoid getting trapped in narrow and self-defeating approaches to love and work.

To begin understanding your family of origin either a genogram (McGoldrick & Gerson, 1985) or an informal family map can be used as a springboard for exploring several important issues. The goal is not an exhaustive review of family themes but rather a simple understanding of several key issues. An important theme to consider involves the family rules about dealing with conflict. Was open conflict permitted? If so, what were the rules of engagement? Was it ok to argue? To raise your voice? Or was it imperative to remain "calm" and "be reasonable"? Was challenging your parents allowed? Fighting with your siblings? All these questions have obvious relevance for how the therapist handles conflict at work.

If in your family of origin arguing was not allowed and no tools for dealing with conflict were developed, then you will avoid confrontation and find it difficult to be appropriately assertive. The boy who didn't learn to fight in the family becomes a man who doesn't know how to stand up for himself at work; the girl who learned that being "good" (long-suffering) was the way to get rewarded may discover that this strategy doesn't work very well for grown-ups. Learning to say no and to set firm boundaries about how much responsibility to take on at work is hard enough for most of us. Those who grew up in families where there was no example of assertiveness or healthy confrontation find it even more difficult.

Another important family legacy pertains to the spoken or unspoken rules about the value of work. Was overwork encouraged and rewarded? Were you encouraged even as a child to believe that achievement or selfless dedication was more important than having fun? Or, even if children in your family were allowed to be children, did either or both of your parents set an example of all work and no play? For some, whose families lived through depressing economic times, overwork can become a way of dealing with the anxieties of past generations. Ironically, those of us who were favored in our families or scripted to be "the successful one" often feel the mantle of success as a burden. Living up to the legacy of being the successful or favored child can become exhausting, and it is easy to feel driven by something bigger than ourselves. Bowen called the process whereby a theme or role is passed on over several generations "multigenerational transmission" (1978, p. 477).

Other professionals will find in exploring their family histories that there were consistent messages, given out both subtly and not so subtly, about perfectionism and the need to be compulsive about doing things right. This script frequently plays out in compulsive overfunctioning and a need to do everything perfectly, without always knowing the source of that anxiety. Discovering in ourselves neurotic habits that turn out to be like our parents' can make us feel fatalistic and discouraged. But sometimes just seeing ourselves playing out certain scripted roles can inspire us to experiment with changing the script.

Finally, in some families, work functions like an addiction that prevents underlying emptiness from manifesting itself. Like other addictions, overwork tends to be passed on generationally. This predilection for overwork is particularly common in families who have experienced substantial loss, economic depression, or financial reversals.

Patterns of overfunctioning and underfunctioning in the family of origin should also be tracked. Systems theory suggests that there is a predictable feedback loop between over- and underfunctioning. Whenever one person in a family underfunctions, someone else will overfunction to compensate. The more one overfunctions, the more the other will underfunction, and vice versa. In dysfunctional families, parents frequently do not take charge in appropriate ways, which sets up a pattern of underfunctioning. This results in someone, usually one of the children, having to overfunction. Thus, for example, a girl who grows up with a mother who often seems depressed or overburdened may take over much of the housework or care of her brothers and sisters. The child is parentified and does far more than is appropriate or even reasonable. This pattern of overfunctioning is not easily overcome, not only because it's familiar but also because it is so well rewarded. Too often it reappears in work settings, which all too easily become yet another family and a new arena for overfunctioning. As in families, the more a person overfunctions at work, the more his or her coworkers will underfunction. Overfunctioning at work is particularly common because, for every person ready to do more than his or her share, there are several others quite willing to do less.

The first steps in prevention, then, are to understand the messages we received in our families, comprehend patterns of overfunctioning frequently driven by dysfunctional family structure, and clarify the roles that were played in the family. Only by understanding these patterns and the ways they are replicated in current work situations can we begin to prevent burnout.

Not only must we understand the legacy of our families, but Bowenian theory suggests that we need to understand our level of differentiation of self. Differentiation is conceptualized on a scale of 0–100 with 100 representing the totally differentiated person (a theoretical ideal that is never achieved), and 0 representing complete undifferentiation or "no-self." According to Bowen, "The ability to be in emotional contact with others yet still autonomous in one's emotional functioning is the essence of the concept of differentiation" (Kerr & Bowen, 1988, p. 145). Undifferentiated people deal with their families with one of two extremes: cutoff ("the immature separation of people") or fusion ("ways the people borrow or lend a self to another") (Kerr & Bowen, 1988, p. 346). Persons who cut off attempt to stay distant from family and deal with family tensions by having as little contact as possible. Those people who deal with their family by fusion or enmeshment do just the opposite. In response to chronic anxiety, they remain enmeshed in the family, preventing any sense of a differentiated self from emerging.

Differentiated persons can be with the family and still be free to be themselves without either cutting off or fusing. They can maintain a sense of what E. Friedman calls nonanxious presence (1985, p. 208). In other relationships, they are able to maintain their own identity while at the same time allowing for intimacy without feeling overwhelmed by it. In work settings, they can sustain their own sense of differentiation by maintaining their own sense of self, setting appropriate boundaries, and saying no when necessary. Persons with little differentiation, on the other hand, will have great difficulty setting appropriate boundaries at work and may wind up doing much more than is appropriate. Such persons often claim that, when they are asked to do something unpleasant, their head says no but their mouth says yes. They wind up taking on too many responsibilities or tasks for which they do not wish to be responsible.

What are some of the signs of differentiation? It means being able to separate thinking from feeling and to think about what you are feeling. When we do this, we can maintain a calm, nonreactive stance even in the midst of difficult situations, such as those times our parents do those annoying things that tend to push all of our buttons, or when we are in the midst of one of those staff meetings that deteriorate into blaming and withdrawal. During times of stress or transition, our anxiety is bound to be elevated. Awareness of this can help us step back, look at the big picture, and avoid making bad decisions when our thinking processes have been overwhelmed by our emotions.

Another part of self-assessment involves evaluating how differentiated we are at home and at work. Can we go home and visit our parents and have a one-to-one conversation with each of them, without becoming reactive when they annoy us or engage in old games? Can we be ourselves and talk about a range of subjects, without hiding who we are or becoming overly defensive? Can we disagree either at home or at work without attacking or remaining mute? Do we find ourselves becoming paralyzed in the face of disagreement, or else unreasonably angry and unable to think clearly?

In therapist's-own-family groups, professionals wrestle with the impact of their families of origin on their present relationships. This is one context in which mental health professionals can explore patterns of differentiation in both family of origin and work settings and receive some "coaching" as to how to achieve greater differentiation in both places. As mental health professionals achieve greater differentiation, they can define themselves more appropriately in their work systems. This might include learning to set more appropriate boundaries at work, particularly in terms of hours worked and extra assignments accepted. It might also include learning to ask for more compensation or advocate for better working conditions, such as more support staff, better supervision, or additional in-service programs.

Many professionals have discovered in these groups an invaluable resource for growth. Too often, it is easy to assume that because we know a great deal about family systems theory, we have achieved a measure of differentiation within our own families. When we finally begin to understand how undifferentiated we are, it is far from easy to make changes. The support and coaching of a therapist's-own-family group help us make these changes. Through coaching around being nonreactive—not getting "hooked" in predictable ways, getting out of difficult triangles, and building genuine one-to-one relationships with our own relatives—exciting changes can be achieved that result in far greater levels of differentiation of self. These changes in turn can generate other types of changes in other systems such as work systems, leading to greater differentiation of self in those systems as well. The unique combination of practical coaching and support that these groups offer can facilitate tremendous changes in differentiation, which can be of enormous value in preventing burnout.

ASSESSING THE COHESIVENESS OF THE SELF

In addition to evaluating family of origin issues, we must realistically assess our fundamental need for appreciation and meaning, that deep desire to be liked and admired which can easily drive us to overwork.

The great paradox revealed by professional burnout is that, although helping others can and should be a way to transcend ourselves, many of us embark on helping careers not out of a genuine concern for others but rather out of a need to be appreciated by them. For all too many professional helpers, the real motivation is getting love, not giving it. Here, Kohut's concept of the selfobject is quite useful. The idealization of dependent clients, admiration of our colleagues, and positive feedback from our supervisors serve selfobject functions in enabling us to feel better about ourselves or, as Kohut put it, to feel more cohesive. As long as we can secure this admiration and feedback by working hard (usually not difficult to do since overwork is often rewarded), we will tend to overwork.

Gratification of the idealizing transference can lead to emotional entanglements with clients. Many of the therapists who become sexually involved with their clients do so because they need the idealization of clients to build their own self-esteem; it is easy to confuse this with "love." Dealing with the power of these abusive relationships is not as easy as describing them.

To achieve balance and find satisfaction in love and work, we must accept our own need to be appreciated and admired, and then learn how to express it. Working on this issue in isolation can be difficult. While simply gaining insight into this explosive issue can be helpful, it is frequently not enough; consequently, professionals may want to explore several options for further treatment. Individual or group growth-oriented therapy may be one way to come to grips with narcissistic vulnerability. A less intense option would be a safe support group of peers.

Whatever the context for exploration, knowing our vulnerabilities is an important part of self-assessment and prevention. In safe contexts, professionals can begin being honest about themselves and sharing their private issues. When professionals are aware of their weaknesses, as well as their desire for appreciation and admiration, they are less likely to begin the slow and painful descent into burnout. They are also less likely to abuse the therapeutic relationship, using it to build their own self-esteem, or to overwork as a way of bolstering their sense of adequacy.

SUPPORT GROUPS FOR MENTAL HEALTH PROFESSIONALS

An excellent place to begin dealing with the difficulties of self-definition that have been a product of our upbringing, as well as our unmet needs for appreciation, is a professional support group. Groups can provide us with the opportunity to get to know ourselves as individuals and as individuals with-others.

These groups must be structured to ensure trust and confidence. Frequently, this means finding a support group outside the primary work setting. In some of the clergy support groups we have run, several clergy have commented on the importance of having a safe group outside their own church, and even denomination, so they can open up and talk about their feelings without fear that their words will get back to their bishop or denominational executive. The same need for confidentiality and anonymity applies to psychotherapists. Exploring issues around countertransference, personal struggles, and difficult clients apart from the work setting is an invaluable experience. Professionals working in a mental health agency may wish to talk not only about problems with clients but also about agency structures, bureaucracy, and administrative concerns. Safety and confidentiality are essential in this regard. The ideal situation may be to meet with groups of people from a variety of agencies doing roughly similar kinds of work. It is ideal because this configuration combines personal anonymity with professional familiarity, and it allows a cross-fertilization of ideas. Meeting with other professionals from other settings but with similar interests and problems may be optimal.

EFFECTIVE SUPERVISION

Another key to prevention of burnout is receiving good supervision on a regular basis. While this may seem obvious, it is rare to find mental health professionals who are satisfied with the caliber of supervision they receive. Agency-based supervision frequently has problems including paradigm clashes (e.g., trying to provide psychodynamic therapy in an uncongenial setting, or using a family systems approach in an agency whose supervisors work only with individuals) and conflicts between administrative supervision and clinical supervision. If the supervisor has administrative responsibilities, then the clinical supervision will most likely not feel safe. How many people are going to reveal how stuck they feel with certain clients, or acknowledge that they are attracted to a client, to a supervisor who is then going to write their evaluation and has the power to fire them? Unfortunately, those therapists who do open up to their administrative superiors (often with such people's active encouragement) often find out later what a mistake this mixing of roles can turn out to be.

The odds of getting high-quality supervision at work are slim. One way to secure effective supervision is to contract for supervision with a seasoned supervisor outside the agency. This person should have no evaluative function and a personal theoretical orientation that is congruent with the supervisee's. Outside supervision provides a safe context in which therapists can work on specific learning goals, distinct from those of the agency, and explore countertransference reactions or why they habitually get stuck or overinvolved with certain types of clients. To many professionals, paying for private supervision seems like a luxury. They may dislike the idea of having to pay, or think that it is too expensive, or even resent their agency for not providing better supervision. One way to lower the cost of supervision is to form a supervision group of three to five professionals, who split the cost. The cost will be further reduced if the group meets only every two or three weeks or even once a month. In the end, it costs far less than might be imagined, and the benefits in terms of growth and prevention of burnout far outweigh the cost.

Supervision can and should be a place where the learning goals of the supervisee are taken seriously. Too often, agency-based supervision is of necessity focused on case management, including checking to see if case notes and files are in order and meet agency standards or if quality improvement standards are being satisfied. Exploration of the goals of the supervisee is not encouraged and frequently avoided altogether. In reality, one of the problems in the mental health field is that many of us are undertrained and feel inadequate with at least some of our cases. Good supervision increases our ability to work effectively and feel more self-confident and self-assured. In addition, when supervision is safe and focused on the theory and technique of the supervisee, the supervisory relationship becomes a selfobject relationship for the professional, which will enhance a sense of well-being and confidence. Although learning theory stresses that the learner should formulate and articulate goals, too often the supervisor's goals dominate. Learning goals are not met, and in worst case scenarios the supervisee feels abused.

Another productive form of supervision is provided by peer supervision groups, where a group of professionals meet together regularly to review cases and provide mutual supervision in an informal context. These supervision groups can be extremely helpful and growth producing. Peer supervision groups can take several forms. One involves professionals meeting regularly to review and discuss video- and audiotapes of each other's sessions, in order to improve their psychotherapeutic techniques. Other groups focus on understanding and utilizing countertransference in work with clients. Still others become study groups; while less personal, these can be a helpful and focused way to learn theory and technique and gain perspective on day-to-day work.

When they have been meeting regularly over time, these groups often can become a safe forum not only for the processing of difficult cases but also for monitoring and review of transference and countertransference material. Within a safe support group, the potential exists for mental health professionals to explore their vulnerable selves, as well as get creative input from colleagues. These groups are only helpful when they meet regularly and consistently and when trust builds among the group members. When meetings are allowed to become irregular, or when one person's needs are allowed to dominate the discussion, the group can stop working. A certain structure, such as a rotation schedule that guarantees each person a turn at presenting material, is essential.

Both good one-on-one supervision and a healthy peer supervision group contribute to the prevention of burnout. In these contexts, mental health professionals experience support that will aid in the development of self-esteem, even while they stay in touch with the vulnerable self. Here supervision is a safe context in which to grow professionally and not become stagnant, as well as to deal with transference and countertransference issues.

BALANCING LOVE AND WORK AND PLAY

A final aspect of prevention is finding balance in our lives. We have deliberately mentioned this last for two reasons. First, it is frequently overused as advice, resulting in very little change or prevention. Second, unless you attend to family of origin themes and how they influence your professional life, and unless you attempt to better understand personal needs for admiration, it will be difficult to find balance.

Balance includes taking care of primary relationships, as well as finding time for your physical, emotional, and spiritual needs. Sometimes this is fairly simple. For instance, one colleague found he could refresh himself by taking long lunches. When feeling worn out and exhausted, he would go to a restaurant for upwards of an hour, often with a book, and return relieved from stress. Sometimes he would do this with a friend, but this required more energy and was not as much of an indulgence, so he would usually go alone. Another preventive is exercise, as long as it doesn't become a compulsion. Much like a hobby, exercise, such as running or hiking, can be a positive resource and a source of satisfaction. Strenuous exercise can also be health enhancing.

The sports analogy is useful here. It is possible to be in vigorous training, such as for a marathon, without getting injured. The athlete can work hard while maintaining vigilance to avoid psychological injury or burnout. A person in training for competition has to maintain a constant awareness of how to avoid injury. If we are going to be good—that is, effective—therapists, we have to remain healthy.

Finally, staying healthy means also nurturing your spiritual self. Who has not felt like a well that clients draw from which is often in danger of going dry? The well must have water continuously flowing into it to keep this from happening. In that regard, finding spiritual refreshment is essential. Taking an occasional afternoon to just sit, taking someone to a play, finding a place that encourages contemplation—an art gallery, park, or country setting—may be one source of refreshment. This can be found in attending weekly services at a place of worship. For others, it may involve learning to meditate or pray or connect with what the late Protestant theologian Paul Tillich called the "ground of all being" (1952). Most recovery groups stress the need for a higher power, and perhaps that is also an important part of prevention and growth. However it is done, spiritual nurture can be an important part of burnout prevention.

SUMMARY

When looking at the issue of prevention, many writers suggest that the work system should provide an environment that is conducive to growth, and so help professionals avoid burnout. Obviously, much could be written about the work system's potential contributions to the prevention of burnout. The issue we are most concerned about, however, is how mental health professionals can define themselves appropriately within these systems so as to avoid the burnout that comes from counterproductive feedback loops.

Being part of a support group that works on family-of-origin issues, differentiation of self, and healthy narcissism can be a very important part of prevention. Securing good supervision outside your agency or being part of a peer supervision group can also be extremely helpful in maintaining professional growth, aiding in appropriate self-definition, and sorting out complex countertransference reactions. In addition, finding ways to balance love and work, as well as periodically expanding and enhancing your skills and sense of competence, through travel, conventions, workshops, reading, supervision, and personal therapy, is helpful. Learning to exchange ideas with colleagues instead of getting stuck in the rut of solitary activity also helps. Finally, when you have done a thorough self-assessment, part of prevention may involve choosing to leave a position that does not permit growth, and then looking for a work setting that offers the best likelihood for using your talents and fulfilling your aspirations.

REFERENCES

Bowen, M. (1978). *Family therapy in clinical practice.* New York: Jason Aronson.

Friedman, E. (1985). *Generation to generation.* New York: Guilford Press.

Grosch, W., & Olsen, D. (1994). *When helping starts to hurt.* New York: Norton.

Kerr, M., & Bowen, M. (1988). *Family evaluation.* New York: Norton.

McGoldrick, M., & Gerson, R. (1985). *Genograms in family assessment.* New York: Norton.

Tillich, P. (1952). *The courage to be.* New Haven: Yale University Press.

CHAPTER 24

*The Spiritual Self: Its Relevance in the Development and Daily Life of the Psychotherapist**

BRYAN WITTINE, PhD

The purpose of this chapter is to discuss the relevance of spiritual experience in the development and daily life of psychotherapists. C. G. Jung, the Swiss psychiatrist whose pioneering work in depth psychology included investigations of spiritual and religious phenomena, believed that psychotherapists need to be open to a transpersonal dimension far deeper than their personal egos if they are to help clients who suffer from meaninglessness and despair. My intention is to discuss how an unfolding awareness of a deep spiritual center in the psyche, which Jung (1966) called the Self, can support and sustain therapists as they encounter inconsolable human suffering and potentially overwhelming unconscious forces. If psychotherapists make contact with the deep center of their being and ultimately realize that they are this Self, and not solely their surface personality, a subtle, yet profound transformation is likely to occur within them and within their clinical work.

Whether we are in private practice, attempting to contain tempestuous unconscious forces that erupt in our patients and in ourselves, or in the trenches with sick and dying, addicted, or other people who are in anguish and despair, psychotherapists are always facing fundamental existential realities. This means we must confront inexorable change, contingency, freedom and responsibility, and our separation from, yet relatedness to others (Bugental, 1981). The threat of pain and destruction, of fate and death, of guilt for actions taken or not taken, of loss of identity, or of becoming isolated—we encounter these existential anxieties every day of our professional lives.

Our psyches are also burdened by vast changes taking place in the health care industry: managed care and other insurance dilemmas, the litigious nature of some clients, the debate over which therapies work and which ones do not. Then, as if relating to anxious and depressed clients all day isn't enough, we get home to our families and once again find ourselves confronted with human need. Our wives and husbands, lovers, and children all require our attention. And all of this takes place in a world where vast sociocultural changes are taking place, where icons and long-held values are cast aside with shocking brusqueness, leaving us feeling unrooted and groundless. With all these forces impinging upon us, it is no wonder that we ourselves are prone to depression, self-doubt, restlessness, and dissatisfaction. Burnout is a significant occupational hazard in our profession.

The question is not whether we can avoid the unconscious or deny the inevitability of illness and death. We cannot. The question is, how do we react to these unavoidable givens? Few therapists do not at times react to existential anxiety by at least partially closing their heart to their own and their clients' suffering and by hardening their egoic defenses. The questions I suggest we ask ourselves are these: "Is there anything we can sense within ourselves—some deeper center of being, awareness, love, wisdom, and power—that we might draw upon to 'keep our seat' and not get blown away by our patients' and our own unconscious forces? What will help us to keep our hearts open, yet remain steady and centered in the face of human suffering? Can we discern some reservoir of stability and strength that can help us to remain steady in the face of existential realities and disturbing unconscious forces?"

THE SELF

In all my years of training in the Western psychological tradition, and in all my years on the analytic couch, I became sharply aware of something missing. For all our richness and creativity, we Western psychologists generally neglect, and in some quarters actively reject, a very vital dimension of human experience—the spiritual dimension. By spirituality, I do not mean orthodox religion with its codices of dogma and creed and rules of morality. I use the term to point to an experience of millions of human beings that there exists within them a deeper dimension of being that feels sacred and full. For some, this dimension seems more real than their physical body. For millions of individuals, direct experience has brought them to the incontrovertible conclusion that they are inescapably a part of and rooted in a greater life, being, awareness, and power. Jung called this dimension the Self.

In addition to Jung, other pioneering psychologists have investigated the link between spiritual experiences and psychological well-being. They include William James (1902), the Italian psychiatrist and psychosynthesist Roberto Assagioli (1965, 1972), the existential-humanistic psychotherapist James F. T. Bugental (1981), and transpersonal psychologists Abraham Maslow (1968, 1972), Ken Wilber (1993), and Stanislav Grof (1985, 1988). In particular, the purpose of transpersonal psychology is to empirically investigate the nature and varieties of spiritual experience, including (1) what people phenomenologically experience; (2) the causes of these experiences, including the techniques that bring them about; (3) the effects of these experiences on the psyche; and (4) the psychologies, philosophies, disciplines, arts, cultures, lifestyles, and religions that they inspire (Walsh & Vaughan, 1993).

Of the various categories of transpersonal experience (Grof, 1988), the one that is central to this chapter is the experience of the Self. The word *Self* spelled with a capital *S* is used to point to one's unconditioned being, one's true nature, the essence of who and what one is. As I will discuss, this concept contrasts with the myriad formulations of the small *s* self of contemporary psychoanalysis (Mitchell, 1993) that refer to one's personal, conditioned, acquired identity.

Equating the Self with essence or true nature is how Jung first used the word. According to Henderson (1990), Jung's early awareness of the Self took shape in response to his fascination with Eastern spirituality. In various writings, Jung compares the Self to *Atman/Brahman* of Hindu philosophy (1958a, 1971), the *Tao* in Chinese philosophy (1967), and *Buddha-nature* in Mahayana Buddhist philosophy (1958b).

To understand what the Self is, it is necessary to understand what it is not. The deep center is not what is usually identified as the self. According to the transpersonal or spiritual psychologies, most persons live in their ego-personalities. The ego-personality is a construction built out of various unconscious organizing principles (Atwood & Stolorow, 1984) that shape the pattern of one's experiencing, the characteristic ways in which one unconsciously sees the world and oneself in that world. In analytical psychotherapy, the therapist seeks to bring awareness to these "distinctive configurations of self and object that shape and organize a person's subjective world" (Atwood & Stolorow, 1984, p. 33).

Jung (1960) used the word "complex" to designate a cluster of these unconscious principles organized around specific motifs, which he called archetypes. He believed the ego-personality is a composite of any number of complexes. Each complex is a structure of identity composed of a self-representation in relation to an object-representation, along with the memories, fantasies, beliefs, and states of mind and emotion associated with them. Normally, we have complexes associated with our mother and father. These are our main complexes, although others may develop in relation to other significant figures. Each person has a whole matrix of psychological complexes that become the determiners of experience.

When we repeatedly ask ourselves the question, "Who am I?" and come up with a long list, we begin to identify the complexes of our ego-personality. We may respond by citing our gender and our sexual orientation. The list might include the roles we play: "I am a father," "I am a psychologist," "I am an airline pilot," and so on. Characteristics of our prevailing self-experience could be added, such as "I am a happy, congenial, fun-loving person with a strong need to help others." Recently, a woman came to me for therapy and described herself in the first session as "I am a woman who runs wild with the wolves," apparently having identified with many of the personality characteristics depicted in a recent best-selling book. Then there are more subtle identifications that were given to us by others in our early years. When a child is regularly thought of as a "wimp," a "weakling," as "mother's little helper," or as "the family's 'shining one,'" unconsciously he or she begins to define him- or herself in these ways.

An exercise of this sort can only begin to illuminate the ways in which we construct ourselves and our world. Anyone who has undertaken analysis can appreciate how varied, how embedded in the psyche, and how unyielding many complexes are. It takes a therapist with keen sensitivity and eaglelike perception to discern them operating "between the lines" of what clients say and how they relate to the therapist and others. As the complexes are brought to light, clients learn that they experience themselves and their external world through the filter of the complexes of their inner world and therefore tend to perceive the present in terms of the past. They also discover the extent to which they are identified with these structures, that the complexes compel them to think, feel, perceive, and act in ways that match those structures, resulting in unique ways of being-in-the-world.

But none of this is what Jung is pointing to when he talks of the Self. The Self is not the ego-personality, with its complexes and unconscious organizing principles. It has nothing to do with self-images, or object-images, or the states of mind and emotion associated with them. Nor does it have to do with gender. This means that Kohut's self, Winnicott's real self, Guntrip's regressed ego, and all the other selves of contemporary psychoanalysis (Mitchell, 1993) are not the same as the transpersonal Self. Rather, the transpersonal Self is what is left when a person has disidentified from the structures of the ego-personality. It is being itself, awareness itself. It is our pure contentless being. It has no habits or patterns, no neurosis, nor for that matter health. It is pure "I"-consciousness, pure subjectivity. Read what Swami Muktananda (1981), a famous Hindu sage, wrote on the Self:

> Even though that "I" exists in a woman, it is not a woman. Even though it exists in a man, it is not a man. That "I" is without form, color, or any other attribute. We have superimposed different notions onto it—notions like "I am a man," "I am a woman," "I am an American." But when we wipe them all away, that "I" is nothing but pure Consciousness, and it is the supreme Truth. (pp. 26–27)

Essentially, then, the Self is free and unconstrained by our complexes and independent of our familiar world. The complexes are more precisely instrumentalities used by the Self, but, as they are mental constructs, they have no fundamental reality, no "be-ing," of their own. Greatly oversimplified, we can say that the complexes are vehicles employed by the Self to express its being in the world, but the complexes are no more identical with the Self than an automobile is with its driver.

Another way to discern the nature of the Self is to use the analogy of a movie projector. There are three principal components in the projection of a movie: the light source, the film, and the screen. The light may be equated to the Self. The complexes are the various films that are shown by the projector. The image on the screen may be equated to the experienced complex of a given individual at any given time. We never experience a complex directly, but only its affects and states of mind as they arise within ourselves, and its image projected onto others. Just as the image on the screen is the light projected through the film, so a person's self-sense and worldview may be thought of as the product of the Self as "interpreted" by a complex or complexes at any given time. Thus, to experience the Self directly, we must penetrate beneath interpretations, reclaim projected images, and disidentify from the corresponding affective and mental states. As I will discuss momentarily, this is precisely the effect of mindfulness meditation as taught in the Buddhist tradition.

SYMBOLS OF THE SELF

Reference to the Self is found in all the world's great religious traditions. Often these traditions use cryptic symbols for the deep center of being and awareness. Symbols of the Self are ways to represent to the human mind a dimension of experience and knowledge that is essentially beyond words, that can only be approximated in concrete, rational terms.

To Chinese philosophers, the Self is sometimes symbolized as a diamond center or a golden flower (Jung, 1967). Tibetan Buddhists (Sogyal Rinpoche, 1992) speak of the jewel in the lotus, a symbol for the inner Buddha who waits to be discovered within the heart (or lotus) of every human being. The Upanishads (Easwaran, 1987), the sacred texts of India, tell of the Atman, the ground of individual being, which is said to be identical to Brahman, the ground of universal being. The Atman is said to be smaller than the small (and so hidden within the depths of the psyche) and greater than the great (thus, paradoxically, as vast as the universe), and is the center within the psyche where a human being and God are said to meet. To Hindus, then, the Self is the essence of the human being and the heart of creation itself.

In Sufism or Islamic mysticism, the Self is known as the Guest, the Inner Companion, and the Beloved, who seeks to be admitted into a person's heart, then decides to stay, and gradually takes over the psyche. This creates a state of consciousness fundamentally the same as St. Paul's when he said, "It is not I who live, but Christ who lives in me." Finally, in the Christian mystical tradition, St. Teresa of Avila (1979) portrays the psyche as a castle with various mansions or dimensions, each representing a different facet of the total personality. At the very center of the castle is the king's chamber, and within it, the king, a symbol for God, the alpha and omega of the Christian mystic's seeking.

SELF-EXPERIENCE VERSUS SELF-KNOWLEDGE

An experience of the Self may unfold spontaneously, as a person listens to a beautiful piece of music or spends time in nature. A Self-experience can also occur during a particularly painful or stressful time in one's life, as a part of the course of thoroughgoing psychotherapy (Wittine, 1989, 1993; Vaughan & Wittine, 1994), or by undertaking a contemplative spiritual practice, such as Buddhist mindfulness meditation. Unless we are particularly gifted and can discern the distinction between ego and Self, however, we can know the Self deeply only by committing ourselves to the practice of contemplative techniques which are designed to help cut through our ego-mind. Thus, we can distinguish between Self-experiences, which are transient moments in which consciousness is dramatically expanded to include the transpersonal dimension of the unconscious (Jung, 1966), and Self-knowledge, which is a more or less permanent acquisition, reached usually by enduring the difficulties of many years of disciplined spiritual practice. When an individual is gaining in Self-knowledge, the characteristics that are more dramatic in Self-experiences are quieter. They are always more or less present, but they operate more as an ongoing hum in the background of daily life. In the sections that follow, I wish to examine some of the characteristics of Self-experiences in people who have made contact with the deep center, then offer some suggestions on how Self-knowledge may be acquired. There are several characteristics of the Self-experience.

Presence

The underlying experience of the Self is of a heightened feeling of presence, of one's reality and substantialness, of being more alive, more real, and more oneself than at any other time. One's senses are heightened; we are more "in" our seeing, smelling, touching, tasting, hearing. We feel our existence, our reality, with greater intensity. Maslow's (1968) concept of peak experiences certainly fits here. He sees them as "acute identity experiences" in which we feel most ourselves, as unified and whole, in which we feel we are an energetic presence, an existence, an "isness," an aliveness, a fullness, all occupying space. We are all of a piece, at one with ourselves and with whatever we are doing. At the same time, we feel more solid, stable, and grounded.

Awareness

A primary experience of the Self is of being a center of pure awareness. As Ramana Maharshi (Godman, 1985), one of India's greatest sages, once said, "You are awareness. Awareness is another name for you" (p. 11). According to Wilber (1980), the Self is an "impersonal witness." It has an objective, "standing above" quality. The experiencer is distinct from what is experienced. Disidentified from the contents of the ego-personality, one takes an "aerial view" and perceives oneself in a more impartial way. One merely observes the flow of physical, emotional, mental, internal, and external processes, without interfering, commenting on them, manipulating them, or in any way defending against them.

Insight

This is a feeling that one's perception is sharper and more acute, that one can see beneath surface appearances, behind the persona and ego-identity of oneself and others, that one can see into the hidden recesses of the human soul, the earth, and its creatures. Very often, Self-experiencers report that God, a divine intelligence, is in everything they see.

Divinity

The heightened experience of being a presence and of being a center of awareness is often accompanied by a feeling that one is in touch with a divinity, with something deeper and far greater than one's personal existence. This feeling can extend also into a feeling of merger with the divinity, of feeling oneself as being a part of it. Often people report a feeling that the world is one, that a divine intelligence permeates the whole of creation, and that their truest identity is essentially identical to this greater intelligence.

Continuity

For many individuals, the experience of the Self carries with it a sense that one's true existence will in all likelihood survive once the body and the ego-personality die. When contact with the deep center is made, people often conclude that continuation, immortality, survival of physical death is not merely a noble hypothesis, but at least very likely.

Love

The experience of the Self is often accompanied by a feeling of profound love and compassion for one's self and others. In some instances, this includes a feeling that one interpenetrates with all living things or at the very least that there is a deep link between one's self and other people, that every stratum of existence is intimately linked with all other strata. As one client put it, "You are one hand and I am the other in the body of a great being."

Peace

This includes feelings of calmness, serenity, and peace—that one's body, mind, emotions, and existence are profoundly relaxed.

Strength

A quiet strength that seems abiding and sustaining is felt to be an aspect of who and what one is. Even though the body and the surface personality are clearly fragile and vulnerable, basic strength is recognized as an intrinsic property of the pure being and awareness of the Self.

Inner Wisdom and Guidance

According to some spiritual traditions, such as Hindu yoga (Aurobindo, 1992) and Tibetan Buddhism (Sogyal Rinpoche, 1992), the Self may be experienced as a guiding function that can teach an individual about him- or herself and the spiritual world. In Christian mysticism, this is sometimes referred to as the Holy Spirit. The principle of inner wisdom has been described throughout human history in religion, psychology, fiction, and myth as a "still, small voice." Often this principle is visualized as a wise old man or woman, an angel, an Inner Christ or Buddha who can answer any question and offer wisdom on all sorts of life problems and concerns (Assagioli, 1965), but the voice can also speak clearly and directly without the need for symbols and imagery. Jung writes that the inner voice is often heard as a call to greater self-awareness:

> What, in the last analysis, induces a man to choose his own way and so climb out of unconscious identity with the mass as out of a fog bank . . . is what is called "vocation." . . . [He] who has vocation hears the voice of the inner man; he is called. . . . To have vocation means in the original sense to be addressed by a voice. (quoted in Assagioli, 1972, p. 115)

In contrast to the voices of various split-off complexes in the psyche or the voices of schizophrenic patients, the voice of the Self never flatters or interrupts, nor is it tyrannical or judgmental. The voice of basic wisdom is impersonal, yet is not harsh. In an extensive study of 30 individuals who regularly heard an inner voice, Heery (1989) concludes that many believe the inner voice is part of a spiritual dimension of being, and can become a teacher for an ongoing interior education about spiritual realities, leading ultimately to missions of selfless service.

Meaning

In profound Self-experiences, one often feels that one's life is full of meaning and purpose, that life itself has extraordinary value, and that the search for meaning itself becomes meaningless.

GAINING SELF-KNOWLEDGE THROUGH MINDFULNESS MEDITATION

Let us now return to psychotherapists. I believe they can be aided immeasurably in their work if they begin to experience the Self and gradually know, in a quiet and intimate way, the deep center of their being. Toward this end, the benefits of practicing mindfulness meditation are immeasurable (Goldstein, 1976; Kornfield, 1977; Levine, 1979). I do not see mindfulness meditation as a substitute for individual psychotherapy, but as an adjunct. In my experience, when psychotherapy and mindfulness meditation are undertaken together, many individuals acquire Self-knowledge with greater facility than when either are undertaken separately.

Mindfulness meditation is essentially two pronged. First, it concentrates and relaxes the mind, producing states of stillness, calm, and tranquillity. Then, it develops clear vision or insight into the character of all phenomena, including the basic nature of the mind and ultimately into how the universe works. It also supports the process of making the unconscious conscious. While meditators are practicing in a retreat setting, it is not unusual for unconscious contents to emerge that are far deeper than the levels probed by many psychotherapies. For example, mindfulness meditation not only accesses the biographical unconscious described by Freud, but the contents of the archetypal unconscious described by Jung. Further, mindfulness helps one to disidentify from all unconscious contents, biographical and archetypal, so that one may directly encounter formless dimensions of mind, realms that are devoid of content. It is here that one may have direct experience of the Self.

There are many approaches to mindfulness meditation. My own preference is to begin by assuming a meditation posture, closing my eyes, and very slowly sweeping the body with awareness, starting at the top of the head and moving down to my feet. This tends to stabilize the mind. Then I can bring my awareness gently to the breath, to the rise and fall of the diaphragm. The movement of the belly on the breath becomes ground zero, so to speak. I then simply note all that goes on within my psyche. Anything that takes me away from the belly and the breath is noted gently—mentally saying "thinking"—then I bring my attention back to the breath.

To this may be added a second technique. Zen Buddhists who practice the technique of the koan (Kapleau, 1968) concentrate on such questions as "Who am I?" "What is my true self?" and "What was the face I had before I was born?" Ramana Maharshi (Godman, 1985) taught a similar method of spiritual practice he called Self-inquiry. A colleague and I discuss this practice at length in another paper (Vaughan & Wittine, 1994). After a meditator has spent several minutes quieting the mind through the mindfulness practice, he or she asks the question, "Who am I?" and fixes his or her attention on the I-consciousness, the consciousness of the one who is asking the question. By keeping attention there, every answer offered by the discursive mind is rejected. If, upon asking "Who am I?" a person hears his or her own name, this is rejected: "No, this is a name I have been given," and inquires again, "Who is the 'I' who has been given this name?" If the next response is a feeling, such as sadness or joy, this too is rejected. "No, this is a feeling I have. Who is the 'I' that is aware of this feeling?" A third response could be a self-image stemming from events in one's past, as in "I am the little girl who was sexually abused by my father." Self-images, too, are rejected: "No, this is an image I have of myself. Who is it that has this image?" None of these questions is meant to be answered by the discursive mind. They simply orient the seeker toward the Self. As concentration increases and intensifies, the person may cut through the socially adapted layers of the ego-personality, unconscious self-images, and the archetypal layer of the psyche to a direct experience of being and awareness. One is specifically taking an introspective stance into the very foundation of identity, consciousness, and life meaning.

Research into the effects of meditation (Shapiro & Walsh, 1984) suggests that disciplined, consistently practiced meditation helps individuals to become less defended, more impartial and even-tempered, and more compassionate and loving. Disciplined meditators tend to become more open and alert, with enhanced perceptual acuity and ability to make choices and take action. Intuition, wisdom, vision, the ability to register psychic impressions, and to discern the value and source of inner guidance—all these are attributes that unfold to one degree or another as meditators become more open to the depth dimension of the Self.

If psychotherapists practice mindfulness meditation and Self-inquiry, the likelihood is that Self-knowledge and a spiritual perspective will gradually characterize their outlook on life and eventually inform their therapeutic work. It is a truism that the state of mind of one individual can affect that of another for good or for ill. The kindly doctor with a soothing bedside manner can help to ease the pain and suffering of a frightened patient through the magnetism of his friendliness and radiance of his good will. The teacher who is open and loving can inspire others to learn far more than one who is controlling and defensive. The therapist who is unfolding awareness of the Self through meditation tends to develop a healing presence along these lines. A therapist whose mind is becoming attuned to the deep Self is gradually more open, spacious, and accepting than one who is not and is likely to have a corresponding effect upon the state of consciousness of the client.

This in no way implies that therapists who meditate will be rid of the complexes that become triggered in their work with clients. Nor does it mean they will no longer need intensive psychotherapy as part of their ongoing training and development. I see mindfulness meditation and Self-inquiry as an adjunct to analytical psychotherapy, not as a substitute for it. Nor does this imply therapists will no longer need the theories of ego, personality, conditioning, personality, behavior, object relations, and psychopathology that are the backbone of mainstream psychology. Self-realization does not take the place of this. Self-realization is the ground out of which comes enhanced awareness, stability, strength, compassion, wisdom, and so on, enabling therapists to use their theories and techniques in a more satisfying way, perhaps with less burnout.

One will also not lose one's shadow, the repressed side of one's personality, although the combination of psychotherapy and mindfulness meditation may enable one to uncover further depths of the repressed unconscious and become more capable of containing one's automatic responses by contacting a wider, more spacious field of mind. Gradually, one may feel a deep center of calm and stability within one, such that one won't be blown about by one's own unconscious complexes quite as easily.

Further, our tendency to stiffen in the face of existential realities may also change in important ways. We are likely to feel greater acceptance of existential realities, that we cannot change these realities, that all human beings are forever subject to change, contingency, impermanence, choice, and periods of aloneness. Therapists can, however, become more present to their own and their clients' suffering. They can gradually become softer, calmer, and more open in the midst of that anguish, to bear grief and distress with greater courage, with a deeply felt strength.

From the perspective out of which I write, these developments are potentially available to us all. It is almost a truism that if a therapist is closed to certain subjects—say, sexuality—clients will rarely bring them up. Therapists who are committed to Self-knowledge are those who can aid their clients to attain the same.

To summarize, when we have significantly disidentified from the unconscious organizing principles that structure our subjective world, we are likely to discover the being and awareness of a spiritual Self. In this way, our usual experience of ourselves and our world is gradually transformed. Our being in the world becomes imbued, enriched, and pervaded by the love, peace, strength, inner wisdom, and meaning of the Self. The context of our experience changes. We see ourselves and the world with different eyes. The realization of the Self brings depth and sacredness to our daily lives, and helps us to become more fulfilled as human beings. That, in turn, allows us to be more present with our clients and to bear inevitable suffering in our daily lives.

REFERENCES

Assagioli, R. (1965). *Psychosynthesis.* New York: Hobbs-Dorman.

Assagioli, R. (1972). *The act of will.* New York: Viking.

Atwood, G. A., & Stolorow, R. D. (1984). *Structures of subjectivity: Explorations in psychoanalytic phenomenology.* Hillsdale, NJ: Academic Press.

Aurobindo. (1992). *The synthesis of yoga.* Pondicherry, India: Sri Aurobindo Ashram.

Bugental, J. F. T. (1981). *The search for authenticity: An existential-analytic approach to psychotherapy* (enlarged edition). New York: Irvington.

Easwaran, E. (Trans.). (1987). *The Upanishads.* Tomales, CA: Nilgiri.

Godman, D. (Ed.). (1985). *Be as you are: The teachings of Sri Ramana Maharshi.* London: Arkana.

Goldstein, J. (1976). *The experience of insight.* Boston: Shambhala.

Grof, S. (1985). *Beyond the brain: Birth, death, and transcendence in psychotherapy.* New York: SUNY.

Grof, S. (1988). *The adventure of self-discovery.* New York: SUNY.

Heery, M. (1989). Inner voice experiences: An exploratory study of thirty cases. *Journal of Transpersonal Psychology, 21,* 73–82.

Henderson, J. (1990). *Shadow and self: Selected papers in analytical psychology.* Wilmette, IL: Chiron.

James, W. (1902). *The varieties of religious experience.* New York: Modern Library.

Jung, C. G. (1958a). Foreword to Suzuki's "Introduction to Zen Buddhism." In R. Hull (Trans.), *The collected works of C. G. Jung* (Vol. 11, pp. 538–557). Princeton, NJ: Princeton University Press.

Jung, C. G. (1958b). The holy men of India. In R. Hull (Trans.), *The collected works of C. G. Jung* (Vol. 11, pp. 576–588). Princeton, NJ: Princeton University Press.

Jung, C. G. (1960). A review of complex theory. In R. Hull (Trans.), *The collected works of C. G. Jung* (Vol. 8, pp. 92–106). Princeton, NJ: Princeton University Press.

Jung, C. G. (1966). *Two essays on analytical psychology.* In R. Hull (Trans.), *The collected works of C. G. Jung* (Vol. 7). Princeton, NJ: Princeton University Press.

Jung, C. G. (1967). Commentary on "The secret of the golden flower." In R. Hull (Trans.), *The collected works of C. G. Jung* (Vol. 13, pp. 1–55). Princeton, NJ: Princeton University Press.

Jung, C. G. (1971). *Psychological types.* In R. Hull (Trans.), *The collected works of C. G. Jung* (Vol. 6). Princeton, NJ: Princeton University Press.

Kapleau, P. (1968). *The three pillars of Zen.* New York: Harper & Row.

Kohut, H., & Wolfe, E. (1978). The disorders of the self and their treatment: An outline. In P. R. Ornstein (Ed.), *The search for the self: Selected writings of Heinz Kohut: 1978–1981* (Vol. 3, pp. 359–386). Madison, CT: International Universities Press.

Kornfield, J. (1977). *Living Buddhist masters.* Boulder, CO: Prajna.

Levine, S. (1979). *A gradual awakening.* New York: Anchor/Doubleday.

Maslow, A. (1968). *Toward a psychology of being.* New York: D. Van Nostrand.

Maslow, A. (1972). *The farther reaches of human nature.* New York: Viking.

Mitchell, S. (1993). *Hope and dread in psychoanalysis.* New York: Basic Books.

Muktananda. (1989). *Where are you going: A guide to the spiritual journey.* South Fallsburg, NY: SYDA Foundation.

Shapiro, D., & Walsh, R. (Eds.). (1984). *Meditation: Classic and contemporary perspectives.* New York: Aldine.

Sogyal Rinpoche. (1992). *The Tibetan book of living and dying.* San Francisco: HarperSanFrancisco.

Teresa of Avila. (1979). *The interior castle.* In K. Kavanaugh & O. Rodriguez (Trans.), *The collected works of St. Teresa of Avila* (Vol. 2). Washington, DC: Institute for Carmelite Studies.

Vaughan, F., & Wittine, B. (1994, October). Psychotherapy as spiritual inquiry. *Revision.*

Walsh, R., & Vaughan, F. (Eds.). (1993). *Paths beyond ego: The transpersonal vision.* Los Angeles: J. P. Tarcher.

Wilber, K. (1980). *No boundary.* Boston: Shambhala.

Wilber, K. (1993). The spectrum of transpersonal development. In R. Walsh & F. Vaughan (Eds.), *Paths beyond ego: The transpersonal vision.* Los Angeles: J. P. Tarcher.

Wittine, B. (1989). Basic postulates for a transpersonal psychotherapy. In R. Valle & S. Halling (Eds.), *Existential-phenomenological perspectives in psychology.* New York: Plenum.

Wittine, B. (1993). *Experiences of the archetypal masculine and feminine in analytical psychotherapy.* Paper presented to the Twenty-Fifth Annual Convocation of the Association for Transpersonal Psychology, Asilomar, CA.

CHAPTER 25

Sustaining the Professional Self: Conversations with Senior Psychotherapists

MARC BERGER, PsyD

After 15 years of practicing psychotherapy full time, I found that I had many important questions, but the question looming largest was how to survive in my chosen profession. At this point in my life, as a man in his late 30s, married, and just beginning a family, I did not see how it was possible to be a full-time psychotherapist while managing, with some grace and vitality, the other responsibilities in my life. Although I was finding some satisfaction and stimulation in my work, on the whole, being a psychotherapist was not feeling worth the price.

It was possible to think of this as solely my difficulty, but my friends and colleagues in the field were expressing similar concerns about the impact of being a psychotherapist on the quality of their lives. Many of us seemed to be experiencing significant stress that was sapping our energy and enthusiasm. As the difficulties with the work continued without clear solutions, serious reservations about our career choice developed. Our growing disillusionment led to serious doubts about whether it was possible to adapt successfully to the "impossible profession" (Freud, 1937/1964).

These questions did not trouble us when we were in our 20s, when there was a freshness to the work and an innocence, naivete, and necessary grandiosity that carried us through. But as my colleagues and I moved through our mid to late 30s, attempting to respond to the demands of this time of life, and with an awareness of approaching middle age, I felt in myself and heard in their voices a quiet panic as we talked of the emotional rigors of practicing psychotherapy. We certainly had young families, which create significant stresses of their own. It was also surely not the best of economic times in which to support families and develop careers. However, what we were feeling seemed to arise more directly from a serious disappointment in our actual work experience and a deep discouragement about finding ways to stay emotionally afloat.

Colleagues used different approaches to address these present difficulties and future worries. Some of them left the profession entirely, pursuing careers in business, law, or medicine. In talking to them regarding their decisions, I realized they felt that, while being a psychotherapist had suited them well at an earlier point in their lives, at present it had lost its meaning. The experience was flat for them and they "had to move on."

Other colleagues chose to deemphasize psychotherapy practice in their work lives, managing the strains of therapeutic work by doing less of it. They shifted the emphasis in their careers toward teaching, research, or organizational or administrative work. Practicing psychotherapy became a minor part of their work lives.

Although I considered making similar changes, I was not ready to give up doing psychotherapy full time. I still found a certain fascination in the process of therapeutic work. Despite the difficulties, I continued to feel that, in ways I did not quite understand, psychotherapy practice expressed the best in me.

In my search for answers to my questions, I initially turned to the professional literature to examine the research completed on the life of the psychotherapist. I was disturbed to find that, in a profession that pays great attention to the issues of development, little had been given to the development of the psychotherapist. The obvious connections between therapist vitality and the quality of treatment seemed of little professional concern. There were early warnings sounded by Freud, Jung, and other prominent psychotherapists about the hazards of the work. Later writers described anecdotally the difficulties they had with one aspect of the work or another, with certain suggested coping strategies. There was, however, no rich discussion of the experience of the psychotherapist over his or her career, with any attention to the impact of practice on therapist functioning.

Only within the past 15 years has the profession begun to seriously investigate the experiences of psychotherapists in practice. The initial findings have been troubling. Studies have identified a broad dissatisfaction by psychotherapists with their work (Kelly, Goldberg, Fiske, & Kilkowski, 1978; Norcross & Prochaska, 1982). Other findings point to significant experiences of emotional depletion and isolation in career therapists (Deutsch, 1984; Hellman, Morrison, & Abramowitz, 1986). Burnout (Freudenberger, 1975) can be a consequence of the emotional toll psychotherapeutic work exacts on the therapist, with the resulting "progressive loss of idealism, energy, purpose and concern" (Edelwich & Brodsky, 1980, p. 14).

Studies have also raised questions about the impact of practicing psychotherapy on the therapist's personal and family life. Deutsch (1985) found a high incidence of depression in the psychotherapists she studied. An increased suicide risk in psychotherapists in comparison with the general population has also been identified (Ross, 1973; Steppacher & Mausner, 1973). The constricted nature of therapeutic work has been shown to have a negative influence on the therapist's family and marital life (Cray & Cray, 1977) and friendships and general social functioning (Cogan, 1977; Farber, 1983).

While reading this research, I was concerned that these findings resonated so closely with my experiences and with those of my colleagues. More disturbing still was an article by Wheelis (1956) on the vocational hazards of psychotherapy practice that identified in detail the midcareer disillusionment and disappointment we were experiencing.

Wheelis described the inevitability of these feelings in the midcareer psychotherapist. He examined the largely unconscious motivations that bring clinicians into the profession, such as the need for emotional connection and intimacy. He saw these needs as inevitably frustrated as the psychotherapist develops a sophisticated understanding of practice. Serious disappointment occurs as the therapist realizes that within the confines of the therapeutic relationship, little attention can be given to deeply felt emotional needs and wishes of the therapist. Wheelis had serious warnings for the psychotherapist who is unaware of the adjustments that have to be made.

The most personally upsetting of Wheelis's observations was his insight that it is only as a midcareer therapist that one can see the profession clearly. Only after many years' experience, after years of schooling, training, and financial and emotional investment, is a therapist able to see realistically what he or she has truly chosen. Wheelis's description of this midcareer experience captured accurately my own sense of awakening from a dream about this profession to a daily reality that felt unrewarding and even dangerous to my physical and psychological well-being. I had a difficult time envisioning myself trapped in the chair in that office for 30 more years.

Although I continued to seek help from my peers and supervisors, I could not escape the feeling that I was caught in an experience I did not understand. I had made a decision in my early 20s that, according to Wheelis, I could not begin to fully understand until this point in my life.

I felt lost, unable to get my bearing in waters that earlier had felt safe and familiar.

THE FOCUS FOR INVESTIGATION

In response to my growing confusion, I decided to talk in depth to the older generation of psychotherapists, to the oldest elephants in the herd. I wanted to understand how these therapists had successfully managed the difficulties inherent in the work and how they had maintained a vital interest and enthusiasm over the course of their careers. I wanted to discover, through these conversations, the factors that contributed to their success. My approach was to be phenomenological, to understand their experience from the inside, in a personal and intimate manner.

I decided to focus our discussions on the broad concept of sustenance, so I began with the general question, "How have you sustained yourself during your career?" I hoped to gather a broad range of information on how these people had maintained and replenished themselves professionally. Whereas I was certainly interested in how these psychotherapists managed the difficulties of their work, I also had a strong desire to understand the satisfactions and rewards of their work that counterbalanced the stresses.

THE PSYCHOTHERAPISTS

I chose to interview senior psychotherapists who, by their own report and the corroborating reports of others, had successfully sustained themselves in their practices. Their success had to result in a continuing interest and enthusiasm for their work as psychotherapists up to the present.

I chose individuals who were recommended to me by colleagues but with whom I had no previous relationship. To participate, these therapists had to be independently licensed practitioners in one of the three major fields of psychology, social work, or psychiatry. They also needed to be psychotherapists who had been practicing psychotherapy at least 20 hours a week during the past 15 years, including at present. I wanted to discuss these questions with therapists who were fully familiar with the daily rigors of therapeutic work.

I interviewed 10 psychotherapists, 5 men and 5 women. Their average age was 59, their average number of years in practice was 29.6. These individuals were all white, middle- to upper-middle-class in income and socioeconomic status. They all lived in a large metropolitan area on the northeast coast of the United States. Five psychotherapists were in full-time private practice, 3 were in part-time practice and worked, in addition, in mental health agencies or hospitals. The final 2 individuals worked exclusively in mental health clinics. Five of the individuals were PhD psychologists, 3 were clinical social workers, and 2 were psychiatrists. All these clinicians had, both in the past and the present, spent the majority of their work time in the practice of psychotherapy.

Our conversations were generally 2 hours in length and took place in each therapist's office or home. The interview was conducted in an unstructured conversational style that focused on our general question. My questions were designed to help clarify and deepen the discussion of their thoughts and feelings.

THE CONVERSATIONS

Our conversations were striking in a number of ways that I will organize and summarize. Uniformly, these psychotherapists emphasized the importance to them of the issues we discussed. They expressed their pleasure in having an opportunity to reflect on and organize their thoughts on the various questions.

As we talked, I became aware that none of these individuals had experienced their careers as a smooth even road of success and satisfaction. They talked about their experiences as uneven, with periods of balance and disequilibrium. They felt at times "on top" of their careers, and at other times tossed about on troubled waters. Their descriptions wove a rich tapestry of their professional and personal lives. A number of factors ultimately emerged that contributed to their professional buoyancy and vitality.

SATISFACTIONS AND REWARDS OF THE WORK

All the therapists I interviewed described a "good fit" between their interests and expectations for psychotherapy work and the opportunities it provided. As Linda, a 52-year-old psychologist reported, "Being a psychotherapist is incredibly ego-syntonic for me. When you get what you're looking for in your work you feel sustained." These psychotherapists generally found what they wanted from their work life and felt satisfied and adequately rewarded. The terms "fun," "excitement," and "fascination" were often used to describe the in-work experiences. Sam, a 61-year-old psychologist, talked of the "incredible blessing" he felt in having discovered the field of psychology. He described his ability over the course of his career to explore all his interests under "one professional umbrella."

As a whole, these people were fascinated by the subject of psychotherapy. They continued to experience, throughout their careers, a sense of intellectual stimulation and challenge from their work. They felt nourished and privileged by the unique view of the human experience that it allowed them. They still actively participated in and led training workshops, seminars, and research projects and were, as Sam said, "still enthusiastically investigating new directions in which I want to see the field moving." They relished the opportunity to have been part of emerging fields of psychotherapy in the 1960s and 1970s, working with populations that, as Margaret, a 59-year-old psychologist said, "no one had any idea how to treat at that time. We were all on our own, creating it as we went along." This excitement was echoed by Gene, a 63-year-old psychiatrist, who described his enthusiasm in learning family therapy in the 1960s when this treatment approach was just being introduced. He was among the pioneers in the city where he was practicing. "The six of us, the members of the training seminar, were probably the only people in the whole area who had even heard of family therapy—it was so exciting and fresh."

One of the most striking aspects of our conversations was the degree to which these therapists emphasized how much they got from the work, rather than what they were giving. While they talked of the "satisfaction in helping people lead richer and fuller lives," their work experience as a whole was for themselves, not others. They felt intrigued by the mystery to be discovered and uncovered in treatment, and enriched by the privilege of accompanying their patients on these personal journeys.

In describing the therapeutic relationship itself, what was striking was the sense of mutuality experienced in these relationships. In contrast to much of the professional literature, which describes the therapist's relationship to his or her patients as involving one-way intimacy, the majority of these individuals appeared to enjoy a real sense of closeness and sharing with their patients. Gene described the pleasure he experiences in his contacts with his patients. "I like talking to my patients and listening to them. You hear very interesting stories, you get to meet nice and interesting people, you get to share in other people's lives."

Many of their descriptions of patient relationships focused on the intimacy and affect shared together. Carol, a 69-year-old clinical social worker, stated, "There are few clients that I did not find a way to like over the 29 years of my practice. They are generally very nice people that I feel close to and attached to." In the majority of these clinicians' descriptions, one is struck by how much personal gratification they receive from their time with patients. Patient relationships are spoken of as important in the therapists' lives. While helping patients resolve problems and improve psychological health was clearly important, they emphasized the satisfaction derived from being in the relationship itself.

It was impossible to ignore, while talking to these senior psychotherapists, that one reason they enjoyed significant rewards and satisfactions from their work derived from their proactive stance. As a whole, this group was actively involved in arranging their professional lives in ways that stimulated and supported them.

For some, this involved a compressed work schedule that gave them more free time. For others, an emphasis was placed on adjusting their patient population; for example, limiting work with a type of patient they found "personally difficult." This proactive stance was reflected in the attention these clinicians gave to doing a variety of work, balancing research, teaching, and practice interests. For example, both Sam and Gene described the pleasures they found in the variety and novelty of professional opportunities open to them. They were not pigeonholed in their work and, as Sam says, "I can do as many things as I like." While emphasizing the opportunities present, these individuals were quite assertive in designing the details of their work lives throughout their careers, addressing their own specific needs, interests, and limitations.

Only two therapists mentioned financial remuneration as an important reward in their work. Only Pauline emphasized the satisfaction of "good pay" as a sustaining factor for her. For Gene, the opportunity to pursue his professional interests was most valued and "you get paid well too." None of the other psychotherapists mentioned money in talking about work satisfactions. Although there may have been a general discomfort in approaching the subject, it was my opinion that it was not discussed because it was not seen as a significant sustaining influence. Given the depth of our discussions, there seemed no reason to leave out this topic unless, compared with other issues, it was relatively unimportant.

SUPPORT SYSTEMS

All 10 therapists used supportive structures to sustain their energy and vitality, and to encourage their professional growth. These therapists concluded that, to meet the daily challenges of their profession, significant support was needed. This support was provided in a number of different formats, both formal and informal, in relationships with teachers, mentors, supervisors, and with their own psychotherapists. Nevertheless their strong reliance on peer support, be it spouse, friends, or colleagues, was emphasized in our discussions.

This emphasis may have been a function of the clinicians' advanced level of professional development. It was my impression, however, that peer support had been critical throughout their careers. It was striking in our discussion of these therapists' support systems, that peer support appeared to blur the boundary between personal and professional life. It seemed that, to the degree the whole person (an integration of the emotional and intellectual sides of an individual) was used in psychotherapy, in turn, the whole person had to be nourished and replenished in these peer support relationships. The terms "friend" and "colleague" were continually intermingled in our discussions.

A blurring of boundaries between the personal self and the professional self was also evident. These support experiences were consistently described as involving an intimate examination of personal and professional issues that impacted work. The birth of a child, the death of a parent, marital tensions, and financial strains all appeared to be open subjects. A number of these individuals described their involvement in ongoing peer support groups that had met for periods of 5 to 15 years. These groups are described as providing a sense of community for these clinicians. Their experience of isolation in the work is countered here and the burdens of professional responsibility shared and lessened.

Len, a 62-year-old psychologist, described his "covision" (as differentiated from "supervision") group, which he has been a member of for many years:

> We do utilization review, peer review, gossip, examine professional issues, and supervise each other's work. It's a support group, a friendship group, and a professional group. We cross-refer, we cover for each other. It's been wonderful. You can tell by the attendance. Nobody has dropped out. There has been a fidelity to the group over the years. It's so important to everyone.

Carol described her work life as "designed around this nurturance." She talked of choosing new staff members at the clinic she directs as much for their ability to be part of the staff support system as for their clinical ability. For Carol, the "sharing and the laughter keeps us going, because if we were not laughing, we'd be crying."

These peer groups are also places for professional validation and appreciation, where encouragement is provided for continued professional and personal growth. Many described the peer groups as providing an important sense of shared journey for their intertwined professional and personal lives. Pauline, a 59-year-old clinical social worker, talked of her peer group in this way:

> One day you had a crisis, and the next day another person had one. There was a quality of experience that was enormously sustaining. It was something about the flexibility of roles, not one person always down and one person always up. You are not as vulnerable to shame. You do not suffer the blame to yourself when you make a mistake. You make the error one day, the other person makes it the next. The next day you pick each other up, bind each other's wounds, then you rejoice when someone has a really good turn of events. You get to know each other very well. There is a trust that sustains you. I will say that this group, from this point of view, was the most important thing in my career.

Pauline's feelings were echoed in the many ways these senior therapists talked about friends, spouses, colleagues, and mentors. Their meetings were consistently described as occurring in an atmosphere of "trust and nonjudgment." Consistent with the literature on gender differences, male therapists tended to rely more on their spouses while the female clinicians relied more on friends and colleagues. The men, however, were also actively involved in a variety of support relationships that they described as essential to their professional development. A number of the male therapists emphasized the importance of relationships with supervisors and personal psychotherapists. These relationships tended to be long-term and were described as taking on a collegial quality after a number of years.

Both male and female therapists were committed to their support systems. They were putting into practice their own beliefs about the correlation between good personal relationships and emotional health. It appeared that they had not shied away from the work they needed to do in order to feel comfortable with the intimacy and healthy vulnerability that they were trying to teach to their patients. Even the most informal and brief contact was seen as important. For example, Pauline described the ways the relationship with a colleague with whom she shares an office suite counters her sense of isolation. "Just having her in the next office is comforting. Just her being there. It's not that we often have time for in-depth consultation. Just seeing her between patients, being able to step out of my role for a moment and knowing that if things get difficult I could have someone to talk to. It's just a lot less lonely."

CHANGES IN ATTITUDE AND APPROACH

As a whole, these therapists described a professional maturing that resulted in a number of changes in their approach to work. These changes in perspective and action developed over a long period and serve to maintain each therapist's vitality and inner strength in approaching his or her work. David, a 50-year-old psychologist, eloquently described how these external resources are internalized and transformed into vigor and self-confidence:

> When I mention my parents, my therapist, my training at the hospital, all of that, it's all inside of me, as it would be in anyone else, and when you talk about sustaining, it's all there. So, as difficult as the work might be, I have some kind of solid foundation on which I am standing most of the time, and as strong as the current may be in the room, with some very difficult people I work with, I'm usually able to tolerate it pretty well. It's a certain strength, it's inside, just a part of me in an unconscious way. It's a level of confidence to help the person sitting in the chair. As long as I can hold them in the room, as long as I can establish some rapport that keeps them returning, then there is something in the relationship that will make a difference. I have this faith in myself and my abilities.

The sense of competence and self-confidence that David spoke of is described by many clinicians as having developed only after numerous years of practice. Both Kevin, a 65-year-old psychologist, and Carol reported that it took 20 years to develop a solid sense of confidence in their abilities. The majority of these clinicians described considerable anxiety and uncertainty during their early and middle years of practice.

These clinicians often talked of straining, in their earlier years of practice, to "get it right," trying to fit what they actually did in psychotherapy into theoretical models. Kevin described how he used to work before he became comfortable with his own style: "It was always first this and then that, always worried about how what I was doing was fitting with theory. I was rigid and self-conscious."

With this comfort in utilizing their individual styles came greater freedom and spontaneity, and a greater peace about psychotherapy practice. As Pauline said, "I no longer need the OK from the team, the supervisor, or even the colleague. I don't need all of that structure. Now, I conference with myself." As Margaret put it, "As a therapist, you now are separating yourself from your teachers. You free yourself. Just as when you grew up and separated from your parents you evolved your own way of living, as a therapist you have to separate and evolve your own way of practice."

The comforts of finding one's own style and of practicing from one's own integration of theory were balanced in these therapists' maturation by a "humbling" understanding of the limits of their abilities and the limitations of psychotherapy itself. These clinicians were now aware of what therapy could and could not accomplish. Through often painful experiences they came to an understanding of their own limitations although this learning process was difficult for people who brought such a deep commitment to their work. Len expressed it most eloquently:

> After a long time, after life beats the shit out of you, you see that there are limitations that you have to respect. For a long time, its just lip service, then your body starts to teach you. It doesn't bounce back as fast. It gives you true messages. "Help, help, I'm suffering. I'm too tired. Rest me. Take me away on vacation." . . . I think it is consonant with advanced age that you are forced to accept these limits. It's been my own challenge to set limits on what I can take on, like the need to be helpful. First this is important, then that is important, then everything is important. So I think I will do everything. I tried to do things I could not do because I didn't know that they were too hard for anyone to do. As I got over the need to be helpful, then I could truly be helpful . . . I know myself. I know who I am and who I am not and there is a comfort to this. But the battering . . . you can't underestimate the battering.

Len's remarks reflected the sobering and somewhat sad feelings that seem to suffuse the therapists' descriptions of coming to terms with the limits of their abilities.

However, this acceptance did allow a greater peacefulness in their work as well as a lessening of pressure, self-criticism, and unrealistic demands. As Margaret said, "When you get older, you take a broader perspective. You are more comfortable and respectful of the complexity and the unknown. You know that uncertainty is a part of life. You tolerate more looseness."

These changes in attitude produced a different emphasis in their views of the treatment process. They had less interest in the idea of "curing" their patients. The effectiveness of psychotherapy was consistently described in more existential terms involving "freedom of choice," the development of "potential," the discovery of "meaning," and the "healing powers" of the therapy "relationship" itself. Gene described this move away from this "technical emphasis":

> Now I approach my patient's problems as if I really do not know the territory because it is someone else's territory and you are a guide on this journey only for a very brief period of time. It is their journey, not yours. You have to be good company with someone you have not met before, and you are going to have to learn some things. It feels very different from what we used to call traditional psychotherapy, where the patient lies down and you do something to them.

Pauline described this shift as a move away from the "pathology" model to a focus on a "search for inner strengths" and the "authentic self."

However, these changes were accompanied by a loss of idealism, from "the times when we felt we could accomplish everything." Linda captured some of this feeling as she talked of how "sometimes doctors lose patients," in describing how she manages her anxiety with acutely suicidal patients. Pauline talked somberly of her attempts to try to help severe chronic pain patients find meaning in their lives. Ann described her disappointment after many years of practice of "really coming to terms with the fact that there were patients I just could not help. This was a very hard realization for me."

Although realistic expectations of themselves and their work replaced some idealistic hopes, it would be a mistake to see these men and women as a discouraged group of professionals. Their interest and enthusiasm for their work was evident in all aspects of our discussions. While tempered by time and experience, they still had a deeply felt, ongoing faith in the process of psychotherapy and its potential benefits for their patients. As Len said, "I don't care what research shows or doesn't show about the benefits of psychotherapy. I know that I am helping my patients lead better lives. No one can shake me from that belief."

This faith in the process of psychotherapy, and this continuing sense of the importance of their professional efforts were strong sustaining factors in their work lives. Their cherished beliefs and deep commitment had been nurtured over years of practice. It formed a fundamental resolve that propelled them into and through many difficult situations. Len seemed to represent the sentiment of the group as a whole when he stated, "Being a psychotherapist has always felt like it is the most useful way I could have spent my life. I have no regrets."

During our conversations, these individuals mentioned many life events and situations that formed the background against which they often struggled to maintain their vitality as people and professionals. In response to my inquiry to each person about what most challenged their professional sustenance, these therapists talked about a variety of circumstances, mostly relating to their own health or the health of immediate family members. Heart attacks, deaths of spouses, loss of jobs, divorce, severe financial pressures, and difficult work settings posed strenuous threats to the therapists' resolve.

When I asked how these circumstances had affected their lives at different points in their careers, the general response could be summarized in a statement by Sam: "You do what you've got to do, you just keep moving on." It was clear from our conversations that the personal support systems were essential during these times of crisis and that, as expected, colleagues and friends formed the basis of the support. There was no real indication that any of these most difficult situations severely challenged their abilities to perform their work adequately. Their resilience and resolve were evident as they described coping with these difficulties.

FAMILY-OF-ORIGIN EXPERIENCES

The practice of psychotherapy provided essential self-expression and a deeply felt sense of purpose for the psychotherapists with whom I talked. As Len said, "Being a psychotherapist has always been deeply woven into the fabric of my life and continues to be so." The beginnings of this fervor and committment for these psychotherapists can be traced back to significant experiences in their families of origin. These experiences provided the raw material that was later shaped through professional maturation into sophisticated skill.

The therapists described these experiences, both positive and negative, as having a profound effect on their interest in psychotherapy practice. They are identified as forming the motivational core for their attraction to the field, for their general psychological mindedness, and for their ongoing passion for the work.

For three of the therapists, the impact of family trauma was central to shaping their interest. The onset of schizophrenia in Len's younger sister during his adolescence created a family crisis that still motivates his work. "I'll never forget the impact on our family. It's no accident that I work with adolescents and their families who are in similar crisis." For Kevin, his mother's subtle insistence that he had to be helpful to his depressed father had "a big impact on my interest in helping others as a psychologist."

Sam reports that his deep feeling for psychotherapy was shaped by the chronic depression of his mother, who was frequently hospitalized, as well as the relationship with a preadolescent first cousin who eventually committed suicide. Sam described this relationship as the one that "got me into this field in the first place." His words capture the intense emotional experiences that fueled these therapists' psychological sensitivity and orientation to caretaking:

> He was a boy, four or five years older than I. He was born deaf, but I was one of the few people that could be with him for sustained periods. He developed . . . a real schizophrenia, and then committed suicide because life was so unbearable. The emotional connection I had with him, to the very end, was very important to me.

These experiences had a profound, lifelong impact on the meaning of helping others with emotional pain. They contributed to the development of psychological sensitivity and compassion.

Five therapists responded to positive experiences in their families of origin that provided deeply ingrained values that have been strong motivators in their careers as psychotherapists. Carol described being "well-nurtured" in a large extended family where she received solid support to develop her independence without sacrificing her strong connection to others. She saw her nurturing of her patients as "coming naturally," as an extension of these positive experiences in her family.

Ann, a 58-year-old psychologist, and Pauline talked of central family values regarding helping and the helping professions. They described a number of close family members who were educators, psychiatrists, social workers, and physicians, and reported their families' clear expectations that they follow similar career paths.

David and Sam described the great faith and confidence that their parents had in their abilities to achieve professionally. Sam talked of the strong sense of optimism that he gained from his father, which carried his family through difficult financial times during the Depression and through his mother's multiple episodes of mental illness. He also noted his father's adventurous nature, which he felt served as a model for him in taking professional and personal risks.

Whether negative or positive, these familial experiences are seen as having equal significance in the development of fundamental attitudes and cherished beliefs regarding psychotherapy. Even experiences of intense trauma are remembered poignantly as shaping important values and defining a career direction that continues to have great meaning. I was repeatedly struck by the inner strength and resolve of the therapists' approach to their work. As Len said, "This is the only thing I can really imagine doing with my life. I feel such a strong sense of purpose in my work. That feeling has not changed."

CONCLUSION

Having tried thus far to summarize and, to some extent, to analyze my conversations with these therapists, I would now like to return to the issues that initially motivated my inquiry—my own struggles with professional sustenance.

I had a number of general reactions to our talks. I appreciated the clinicians' honesty and openness in discussing our topic. I was surprised and impressed by the importance they ascribed to these issues. It was evident early in our conversations that I was not alone in my struggles with the profession. Most all of the therapists commented that these questions had received too little attention within the field.

Emotionally, I had mixed responses as I reflected on our conversations. I was envious of how positive and settled these professionals seemed about their work experience. I felt very far from the sense of peacefulness that they described. I also initially experienced a sense of disappointment about the substance of our conversations, which seemed to contain nothing radically new, nothing that I had not known before. As I sat longer with their words, however, I noticed that, while what they had to say was, in many ways, familiar and not fancy, there was a consistency in their reports of how they sustained themselves that held my attention. I began to reflect on their ways of meeting this challenge and compare them with my own. These comparisons were fruitful for me in a number of ways.

I looked more deeply than I ever previously had into the experiences in my family of origin that shaped my interest and passion for the profession. I certainly had examined these issues before and felt I had understood and worked through the emotions involved, so that they did not interfere with my work. I had known for at least 10 years that my psychological mindedness developed from my efforts to understand complex emotional issues within my family of origin. I was aware that in many ways my training as a psychotherapist had begun quite young, and that I had often functioned as my family's therapist. However, as I began to investigate my present feeling about being a psychotherapist in more depth, I had to face frightening connections between my present sense of being trapped and intense feelings about my family experiences.

Whereas before this time I had viewed my "calling" to be a psychotherapist with pride and dedication, I now was not at all sure I wanted to answer this call. I had a strong feeling that what had felt like a choice at age 22 when I began my training was shaped by powerful forces out of my awareness. As I approached 40 years of age, I saw myself as making my first free choice regarding my occupation.

For the first time in my adult life, I seriously contemplated leaving the profession or significantly deemphasizing practicing psychotherapy. I did some exploratory research into other professions and different activities for psychologists. This process was both frightening and liberating. It felt very difficult to think of leaving the work that had meant so much to me throughout my adult life. In many ways, the practice of psychotherapy was like a partner in my development, a soulmate. Ending the practice of therapy would feel like ending a marriage that had, in many ways, enriched my life but, to my surprise, now seemed to be deadening it.

However, as with all deep long-term relationships, the emotional ties were strong. I found that each time I began to seriously consider a different type of work, I was pulled back by a deep inner part of myself that seemed to say my most meaningful life would be achieved through this work. I rejected and ignored this voice a number of times during this period. I questioned its sincerity and its motivation, but in the end, I had a strong intuitive sense that although I really did not understand its meaning or purpose, I had to follow its direction.

At this point, I found myself returning for help to the words of the psychotherapists I'd interviewed. I searched more seriously for answers to how they had taken control of their professional lives and liberated themselves from family scripts or expectations.

Their descriptions of the influence of their own family-of-origin experiences on their work showed that these experiences still provided passion and meaning to their work life. However, there was no sense that they were still practicing a long-ago assigned family role or working through family-of-origin issues through practice as a psychotherapist. Whatever had fueled their initial interest in the field, they ultimately had successfully made the profession "their own" in a manner that had meaning and fulfillment. They had described a transformation from "neurotic helping" fueled by rescue fantasies to a work experience that was a fair exchange between what was given and received.

Encouraged by this possibility, I decided, after 1½ years of intense ambivalence, to try to make the necessary changes so that the practice of psychotherapy could work for me again. In rechoosing to be a psychotherapist, I knew I had to become much more active in the process and structure of my work life. I vigorously developed short- and long-term professional goals and began including and eliminating work activities in response to my developing needs. I began to use a network of friends and colleagues for support and sustenance more fully than I ever had before.

More fundamentally, I thought about how I wanted to practice psychotherapy. The senior therapists I had talked with had described similar turning points in their work lives after 15 to 20 years of practice, when they began to work from their own integration of theory and experience. Until this point I would not have described myself as an overly orthodox or uncreative therapist, yet I see now that I had not yet made the leap into what my supervisor jokingly describes as "Bergerian therapy."

These changes were both anxiety provoking and surprisingly satisfying and enlivening. While not large in terms of approach or behavior, they seemed to create a fundamental shift in my experience of working. I was practicing now not as expected, according to a theoretical model or mentor's idea, but as I wanted. I worked from my own ideas, experimenting in small but significant ways that increased my involvement and intellectual stimulation. I enjoyed my humor and spontaneity with my patients more, leaving some of the wooden aspects of the therapist's role behind. My relationships with patients became more relaxed, intimate, and mutual. I found that I knew enough about the process of therapy that I could do my work in a much more natural manner that fit my personality and my evolving needs and interests.

While these changes produced more pleasure and satisfaction in practicing psychotherapy, I also developed a new relationship with difficulty and limitation as it relates to the life of the psychotherapist. I accepted that there is a significant price to be paid for being a psychotherapist: It is the price paid for the front-row seat the psychotherapist has on the human condition.

The psychotherapist is offered an uniquely intimate view of the process of living. During a work week, I hear the inside stories of humanity from ages 5 to 75. I am privileged to observe couples, families, children, and adults engaged in their honest struggles with being human. Except for members of the clergy, practitioners of no other occupation get the opportunity to see living so close up. From this vantage point, psychotherapists have a unique opportunity to gain wisdom about the human experience. This is a quest for knowledge and understanding in which I continue to be profoundly interested.

The price of this experience for psychotherapists is the difficulty and strain they must bear as a result of being so close to the action. I have come to accept a certain amount of anxiety, constriction, and emotional suffering as a part of my work experience. I think it is necessary for the therapist to absorb some of the patient's pain for the patient to take in the healing. I also believe that the discipline, concentration and awareness necessary to be good at this work provides continual challenges to physical and psychological health.

To a large degree, I do not believe that this work gets easier the longer you do it. Skill and experience increase, but I do not think the degree of difficulty in a psychological sense really lessens. The psychotherapist is always in a process of adjustment, trying to balance passion and dispassion in practice. His or her position is a volatile and vulnerable one that needs continual adjustment.

I believe that what helps the therapist cope with this difficulty is actually giving up the wish that the experience will become easier. It is also essential to feel that what is gained is worth the dangers involved. For myself, the suffering involved in doing psychotherapy is an important teacher in developing compassion for my patients' suffering. I also see my daily practice as an opportunity to learn to care for myself, to pay attention to my unfolding experience in a manner that no other profession so validates. The importance of being continually involved in this self-care can be reparative for psychotherapists who originally developed their skills in response to inadequate parenting. I also am able to continually investigate the subjects I am most interested in and express myself creatively in the area in which I have most talent.

I believe that it is important to accept that choosing to be a psychotherapist is in many ways a choice to live on the edge, psychologically. There is an inevitable strain in being the holder of emotional truths and secrets that are an active threat to the individual and to society. The pressures of this position are similar to those experienced by the ancient shamans who always lived on the edges of their communities.

It is 4 years now since I talked with these senior psychotherapists and first reflected on what they had to say. Their thoughts gave me important encouragement and direction in resolving my own professional crisis. I do not expect this period to be the last crisis in my professional life. The process of becoming oneself both personally and professionally continues with difficulty over a lifetime. However, I do feel much more able to cope successfully with what arises and to persevere. My conversations with these senior psychotherapists left me with the feeling that, if you want it badly enough, this profession is not impossible, just very difficult.

But, in working with this difficulty, there is the potential for unique satisfactions and rewards that are available nowhere else. What I am receiving now feels worth the price.

My conversations with the older generation of therapists were extremely helpful in the resolution of my professional problems. My hope is that the sharing of their experiences and my own may help others to navigate these difficult waters more easily. Psychotherapeutic work is too difficult on a daily basis for the therapist to ignore his or her own psychological sustenance for even a brief time. This fact has not been clearly enough emphasized in our graduate or ongoing training. I believe these challenges need to be addressed early on in the psychotherapist's professional development. I do not think such exploration will significantly deter those individuals drawn to this work. They will, however, be better prepared to manage the difficulty they face.

This is not to say that professional maturity comes without significant struggle and occasional crisis. You cannot be prepared for all events when you begin a journey. However, you can learn greatly from those who have successfully ventured forth and returned safely. I hope this work serves as a stimulus for the psychotherapeutic community to enter into a richer dialogue among all its generations of practitioners to address these vital questions. The quality of our work and our lives is at stake.

REFERENCES

Cogan, T. (1977). A study of friendship among psycho-therapists. (Doctoral dissertation, Illinois Institute of Technology, 1977). *Dissertation Abstracts International, 78,* 859.

Cray, C., & Cray, M. (1977). Stresses and rewards within the psychiatrist's family. *The American Journal of Psychoanalysis, 37,* 337–341.

Deutsch, C. J. (1984). Self-reported sources of stress among psychotherapists. *Professional Psychology: Research and Practice, 15,* 833–845.

Deutsch, C. J. (1985). A survey of therapists' personal problems and treatment. *Professional Psychology: Research and Practice, 16,* 305–315.

Edelwich, J., & Brodsky, A. (1980). *Burnout: Stages of disillusionment in the helping professions.* New York: Human Services Press.

Farber, B. A. (1983). Dysfunctional aspects of the psycho-therapeutic role. In B. A. Farber (Ed.), *Stress and burnout in the human service professions* (pp. 1–20). New York: Pergamon.

Freud, S. (1964). Analysis terminable and interminable. *Standard Edition, 23,* 209–253. London: Hogarth Press. (Original work published 1937)

Freudenberger, H. J. (1975). The staff burn-out syndrome in alternative institutions. *Psychotherapy: Theory, Research, and Practice, 12,* 73–82.

Guy, J. D. (1987). The personal life of the psychotherapist. New York: John Wiley & Sons.

Hellman, I. D., Morrison, T. L., & Abramowitz, S. I. (1986). The stresses of psychotherapeutic work: A replication and extension. *Journal of Clinical Psychology, 42,* 197–204.

Kelly, E. L., Goldberg, L. R., Fiske, D. W., & Kilkowski, J. M. (1978). Twenty-five years later: A follow-up study of trainees assessed in the VA selection research project. *American Psychologist, 33,* 746–755.

Norcross, J. C., & Prochaska, J. O. (1982). A national survey of clinical psychologists: Views on training, career, and APA. *Clinical Psychology, 35,* 2–6.

Ross, M. (1973). Suicide rates among physicians. *Diseases of the Nervous System, 34,* 145–150.

Steppacher, R. C., & Mausner, J. S. (1973). Suicide in professionals: A study of male and female psychologists. *American Journal of Epidemiology, 98,* 436–445.

Wheelis, A. (1956). The vocational hazards of psycho-analysis. *International Journal of Psycho-Analysis, 37,* 171–184.

Afterword

In choosing to edit this book on the hazards of psychotherapy practice, I initially worried that the topic would prove to be depressing. Indeed, many of the issues addressed in the volume are of a sobering or unsettling nature. What I failed to anticipate, however, was the inspiration I have derived from working on the project. It has been heartening to encounter colleagues who have the courage to tackle such difficult and distressing matters.

In a discussion of the stresses and frustrations inherent in clinical practice, Greben (1975) remarks that the prevention of demoralization is most likely to arise "from our continual insistence upon seeing and describing conditions of our work as they really are" (p. 432). This compilation represents an attempt to do just that. But the process must be ongoing, and for that to happen, we will need to make some changes in our professional culture.

In the current climate, it can be difficult for therapists to discuss problems or to reveal vulnerabilities without fear of negative consequences. Ironically, the honesty and openness that we try so hard to foster in our clients is rarely seen among professionals. This double standard prevents clinicians from acknowledging their distress and from gaining the support and assistance of colleagues and administrators.

The greatest hope for altering attitudes within the profession lies with those students who will be the practitioners of tomorrow. It is imperative that instructors and supervisors devote more attention to preparing trainees to deal with the emotional impact of practicing psychotherapy. They need to model a willingness to discuss in a personal way such issues as motivations for practice, unrealistic professional expectations, countertransference reactions, therapists' fears and doubts, treatment errors and failures, and the warning signs of burnout.

So many questions for the developing clinician are rarely broached in training. What do you do with feelings of love or lust toward clients? How about anger, aversion, or malice? How do you find a balance between vulnerability and self-protection? How do you deal with the emotions that are elicited by positive and negative transferences, treatment impasses, or premature terminations? How do you contend with being unable to assist someone in distress, and how do you handle the anxieties evoked by suicidal patients? How do you manage to mourn and work through the inevitable loss of clients to whom you have become attached?

I am convinced that a seminar focusing on such issues ought to be a required component of every clinical training program. We cannot expect to lower the incidence of burnout and impairment among practitioners if such basic human concerns continue to be treated as taboo. By addressing them with trainees, we are providing a form of early intervention that can reduce the strains of practice and ultimately enhance and prolong careers.

Changing attitudes and training approaches alone will not be sufficient to turn the rising tide of discouragement and pessimism within the field. Broader issues of funding and social policy must also be addressed. As Gumpert and MacNab delineate in Chapter 20, the privatization of Medicaid and of community mental health clinics, the hostile takeover of private practice psychotherapists by corporate mental health, and the growing dominance of managed care organizations are rapidly undercutting our autonomy. Too often, we have passively accepted and adapted to counterproductive measures that have been foisted on us by external agents. Meanwhile, valuable time and resources are squandered on endless turf battles between the mental health disciplines. Unless psychotherapists join together to take decisive, collective action, there will soon be little turf remaining over which to fight. And the ultimate losers will be our clients, who will find it increasingly difficult to obtain satisfactory treatment.

Although this volume surveys a wide range of hazards encountered by psychotherapists, its scope is by no means exhaustive. Perhaps certain topics are simply too personal; I was unable, for instance, to solicit chapters addressing the effects of clinical practice on marriage and personal life, or on the dilemma of falling in love with a client. Some additional subjects that were not covered include codependency, addiction, and depression in clinicians. These topics cry out for further attention, and it is my hope that this book will inspire practitioners to study and write about them.

Few readers who have come this far would contest the assertion that psychotherapists are engaged in a perilous calling. The dangers are real, the obstacles substantial. But perhaps we can take a cue here from the Chinese. Their ideogram for "crisis" connotes a challenge or opportunity as well as a calamity, suggesting that hazardous circumstances can provide occasions for growth. If we continue to grapple with the many dangers we face as therapists, we will certainly never overcome them all; however, we cannot fail to grow and mature as a profession.

REFERENCES

Greben, S. E. (1975). Some difficulties and satisfactions inherent in the practice of psychoanalysis. *International Journal of Psycho-Analysis, 56,* 427–434.

Author Index

Subject Index